# VAGRANT FIGURES

*THE LEWIS WALPOLE SERIES IN EIGHTEENTH-CENTURY CULTURE AND HISTORY*

The Lewis Walpole Series, published by Yale University Press with the aid of the Annie Burr Lewis Fund, is dedicated to the culture and history of the long eighteenth century (from the Glorious Revolution to the accession of Queen Victoria). It welcomes work in a variety of fields, including literature and history, the visual arts, political philosophy, music, legal history, and the history of science. In addition to original scholarly work, the series publishes new editions and translations of writing from the period, as well as reprints of major books that are currently unavailable. Though the majority of books in the series will probably concentrate on Great Britain and the Continent, the range of our geographical interests is as wide as Horace Walpole's.

# VAGRANT FIGURES

## *LAW, LITERATURE, AND THE ORIGINS OF THE POLICE*

Sal Nicolazzo

Yale
UNIVERSITY PRESS
*New Haven & London*

Published with assistance from the Annie Burr Lewis Fund
and the foundation established in memory of Amasa Stone
Mather of the Class of 1907, Yale College.



Yale University Press books may be purchased in
quantity for educational, business, or promotional use.
For information, please e-mail sales.press@yale.edu
(U.S. office) or sales@yaleup.co.uk (U.K. office).

Set in MT Baskerville and Bulmer types by IDS Infotech Ltd.
Printed in the United States of America.

Library of Congress Control Number: 2020936905
ISBN 978-0-300-24131-0 (hardcover : alk. paper)

A catalogue record for this book is available from the
British Library.

This paper meets the requirements of
ANSI/NISO Z39.48-1992 (Permanence of Paper).

10 9 8 7 6 5 4 3 2 1

# *CONTENTS*

# *ACKNOWLEDGMENTS*

The writing of this book has followed me across homes, lives, and networks, both intellectual and intimate.

This project began as a dissertation, and I couldn't have asked for a better mentor than Suvir Kaul, whose rigor, precision, and generosity remain my model in scholarship and teaching. Chi-ming Yang, David Kazanjian, and Michael Gamer enabled this project to flourish with their incisive questions and unflagging support.

A vibrant scholarly community at the University of Pennsylvania shaped me as a scholar, and this project is indebted to wide-ranging conversation and collaboration with the scholars I met there, including David Alff, Marina Bilbija, Toni Bowers, Ashley Cohen, Alyssa Connell, Thomas Dichter, Julius Fleming, Tsitsi Jaji, Travis Chi Wing Lau, Heather Love, Alice McGrath, Don James McLaughlin, Marissa Nicosia, Laura Soderberg, Marie Turner, Sunny Yang, and Mary Zaborskis.

This project has benefited from the generous feedback and support offered by my colleagues at UCSD, including Jody Blanco, Amelia Glaser, Stephanie Jed, Sara Johnson, Lisa Lampert-Weissig, Jin-Kyung Lee,

Margaret Loose, Jacobo Myerston Santana, Sarah Schneewind, Brandon Som, Erin Suzuki, Nicole Tonkovich, Ameeth Vijay, Dan Vitkus, and Kathryn Walkiewicz. My students, meanwhile, consistently give me reason to remember why I wanted to write and teach in the first place, and I am incredibly lucky to know them.

I workshopped portions of this book with a number of groups whose feedback has substantially improved and expanded the work, and I thank them for inviting me: the Columbia University Seminar in Eighteenth-Century European Culture, the Duke University Migrancy Working Group, the USC Race and Empire Faculty Working Group, the UCSB Early Modern Studies Institute, the UCLA Americanist Research Colloquium, and the UCLA/Columbia University Law and Humanities Junior Scholars Workshop.

Throughout my career thus far, I have benefited from the generosity, camaraderie, advice, and intellectual engagement of many scholars I count myself lucky to know, especially Jason Farr, Caroline Gonda, Hsuan Hsu, Carrie Hyde, Emily Kugler, Greta LaFleur, Kathy Lubey, Ramesh Mallipeddi, Micol Seigel, Charlotte Sussman, and Eugenia Zuroski.

The material conditions for the completion of this book were made possible by a Josephine de Karman Dissertation Fellowship and a University of California President's Faculty Research Fellowship in the Humanities; I am deeply grateful to both for granting me the time and space to write. In addition, a UCHRI Book Manuscript Workshop Grant enabled me to workshop a draft of the manuscript, and I am particularly indebted to participants Celeste Langan, Betty Joseph, and Jeannine DeLombard for their careful, insightful, and generous reading and discussion.

I want to thank Jonathan Kramnick for his support of the project, as well as the anonymous readers of the manuscript, whose suggestions have substantially improved the book.

Portions of Chapter 2 were published as "Henry Fielding's *The Female Husband* and the Sexuality of Vagrancy" in *The Eighteenth Century: Theory and Interpretation* 55.4 (2014): 335–353, and portions of Chapter 3 appeared as "Lyric Without Subjects and Law Without Persons: Vagrancy, Police Power, and the *Lyrical Tales*" in *Criticism* 60.2 (2018): 149–170.

Along the way, I have also benefited from the insights of many scholars who have since been unable to continue their academic work due to the scarcity of livable, full-time academic employment. This gesture feels monumentally inadequate, but I hope to at least acknowledge this as the reality of the landscape from which this book emerges.

The writing of this book has been sustained by a much broader life beyond scholarship. My parents, Michael Nicolazzo and Claire Stairiker, deserve many thanks for their foundational support of my curiosity, stubbornness, and intellectual ambitions from the very beginning. Friends both near and far have helped me think through this book and its investments while also reminding me that there's far more to life than writing it, especially Nico Carbellano, Rana Jaleel, Theo Motzenbacker, and Megan Stories. Katherine Aid and Bronwyn Wallace deserve particular gratitude for living with, engaging with, and foundationally shaping this project from its earliest instantiations. For over ten years, all of my trapeze teachers and artistic collaborators—especially Megan Gendell, Caroline Wright, Zoe Irvine, Sable Stewart, Elena Brocade, Lauren Rile Smith, and the women of Tangle Movement Arts—have also taught me how to create, how to learn, and how to persist.

Finally, Kathleen Frederickson came into my life in the middle of this project, and she has made the writing and everything that surrounds it so much sweeter.

# *INTRODUCTION*

# POLICE ARCHIVES BEFORE THE POLICE

In the personal papers of Robert Nailer, a Justice of the Peace (JP) in Surrey during the late seventeenth century, a stack of fragile, miscellaneous scraps testify to the accrued documentary minutiae of a life: lists of reminders, letters received from family members and business partners, notes documenting money owed to acquaintances and neighbors, and even a few pattern poems, copied out in intricate knotwork filling the small pages with intertwined ribbons of text.[1] This collection of otherwise uncategorized and—by most measures—insignificant papers had been wrapped in another piece of unused scrap paper cast off from the realm of minor and everyday legal practice: an unused vagrant pass (Figure 1). Nailer would have used this pass in one of the most routine tasks of a JP of his time. Through the enforcement of vagrancy laws, Nailer was charged with ensuring the welfare and security of the community and the stewardship of its resources, anticipating potential future threat posed by strangers and others deemed suspicious, as well as maintaining geographical, social, and moral boundaries of the parish's responsibility for the subsistence of the poor.[2] All of this, for legal theory and practice throughout the long eighteenth century, fell under the heading of "police."

FIGURE 1: Vagrant pass used to wrap miscellaneous documents (Robert Nailer's Papers, Justices' Papers: Surrey, C 110/3, UK National Archives)

This book is about how minor and miscellaneous forms of writing constitute powerful theories of sovereignty. It is about how this scrap of paper, unexceptional and preserved here only by chance, connects local parish management to global labor markets and new approaches to colonial population. It connects the everyday writing of an ordinary JP to a surprisingly wide array of print and manuscript genres, from the documents of local governance and administration across England and its colonies, to legal and political commentary, to the many forms of imaginative writing circulating in a burgeoning print marketplace. *Vagrant Figures* reveals the narrative, textual, and rhetorical practices that shaped the purview and scope of policing in the Anglo-American legal sphere long before the establishment of the modern metropolitan police force. In the Atlantic world of the long eighteenth century, "police" did not indicate a uniformed, professional law-enforcement agency, but rather the capacious domain of governance dedicated to keeping the peace, preventing disorder, and anticipating future threats to property or security.[3] As the idea of police accrued cultural and political legitimacy—ultimately culminating in late eighteenth-century reformers' calls for the establishment of professional, centralized police forces—ideas about the proper role of police drew on existing legal and administrative practices, as well as on the narrative forms, stock tropes, and modes of writing underpinning these practices. One particularly crucial blueprint that made *the* police thinkable, this book argues, was the capacious category of vagrancy.

Vagrancy offered a legal and tropological model for police as a mode of governance. A juridical category used in England since the fourteenth century to criminalize homelessness, itinerancy, and the perceived refusal to work, vagrancy named a wide variety of marginal populations—including the poor, the unemployed, sex workers, itinerant performers, and strangers—perceived to pose the threat of potential future criminality.[4] A catchall category allowing for the apprehension of a wide variety of petty offenders, vagrancy law granted local authorities discretionary power to punish or expel nearly anyone they perceived as a potential threat or economic burden.[5] As vagrancy laws granted their enforcers powers of summary conviction, these laws provided wide discretion to authorities and located a crucial category of criminality outside the scope of trial by jury. Overseers of the Poor, for instance, routinely used vagrancy law to expel people who threatened to cost the parish too much in poor relief, while magistrates and JPs used it to summarily convict suspected or reputed thieves, sex workers, or unknown persons thought to pose future threat.[6] Neither criminal intent nor the commission of a criminal act is essential to the legal definition of vagrancy in this period.[7] Indeed, as the allowance for summary conviction obviated the need for a trial, vagrancy law concerned itself not with the adjudication of an individual's criminal responsibility, but rather with the anticipatory management of populations and spaces associated with potential future threat.

This places vagrancy squarely in the realm of police offenses. Markus Dubber characterizes vagrancy as the eighteenth-century "police offense par excellence," and William Blackstone prominently features vagrancy in his discussion of "public police and oeconomy," which he defines as "the due regulation and domestic order of the kingdom: whereby the individuals of the state, like members of a well-governed family, are bound to conform their general behaviour to the rules of propriety, good neighbourhood, and good manners; and to be decent, industrious, and inoffensive in their respective stations."[8] As an open-ended category naming neither a fixed social identity nor an easily identifiable criminal act, vagrancy remained flexible and capacious enough to include threats that could not be imagined in advance. Thus, through the capaciousness of this paradigmatic target, police took on the widely discretionary authority to apprehend or expel "suspicious" persons and populations. The capacious and flexible nature of vagrancy law—which relied conceptually on the imagined miscellany and mutability of its targets—made it particularly amenable to local colonial governance; its adaptability made it ideal for the management of new forms of colonial labor, new racialized regimes of sovereignty, and new imperatives of territorial management, especially in the settler and plantation colonies of the Americas.[9] *Vagrant Figures* argues that vagrancy sheds light on the prehistory of the police, as its textualization across a wide array of documents—records of everyday and routine legal practice, political and legal commentary, and literary deployments and redeployments across a number of genres—reveals the often improvisational theorizing of police as a powerful form of sovereignty well suited to the management of population and labor for an emerging racial capitalism.

Vagrancy laws cross the Atlantic, and are almost immediately repurposed and transformed, thus revealing the more general transformability of police in a colonial context. For example, the vagrant passes that Robert Nailer would have used to send paupers to their parishes of legal settlement were adapted during his lifetime by colonial legislators as a technology to control the mobility of the enslaved and thus, they hoped, prevent insurrection.[10] Meanwhile, English vagrancy law also embedded the local maintenance of the peace in the biopolitical management of empire. From the beginning of English colonization in the Americas, political economists, colonial governors, and those with economic interests in colonization promoted the American colonies as a vent for surplus population.[11] Later in the eighteenth century, after the loss of the North American colonies and a reorientation of empire toward an eastward-looking form of free-trade imperialism, increasing calls for more centralized policing of the global metropolis of London hinged on its status as the commercial nexus of empire. Vagrancy remained central to the theories and legal practices that lay the groundwork not only for the Metropolitan Police, but also for the documentary administration of mobility and belonging on a national scale. As I discuss at greater length in Chapter 3, the public debate about London's "Black Poor" (a category that included not only residents of African descent, but also Asian sailors) scaled the longstanding practices of administering belonging and responsibility from the parish to the nation. The Atlantic world is of particular interest in this study because, as Mary Sarah Bilder argues, the Atlantic world was a venue for constant legal negotiation between metropole and colony that forged what she calls a "transatlantic constitution."[12] This negotiation between metropolitan sovereignty and local exigencies of colonial governance continued to shape law and governance in England while also laying the groundwork for early American law after U.S. independence, a legacy I track in Chapter 4 by examining the afterlives of colonial vagrancy law in Charles Brockden Brown's novelistic meditations on the viability of the new republic, as well as in the records of everyday policing in 1790s Philadelphia.

I begin this study in the 1660s, when England's expanding Atlantic colonies institute demands for labor that prompt larger administrative questions about how best to allocate, conceptualize, and manage the rural poor who are migrating to London in unprecedented numbers. I end at the turn of the nineteenth century, amid debates about the abolition of slavery, the reconfiguration of the Atlantic world after U.S. independence, and calls for domestic administrative reforms that would later inspire both the New Poor Law (in Britain) and the establishment of modern metropolitan police forces (on both sides of the Atlantic). This time period sees major transformations in everything from the practices of local governance, to the emergence of Britain as undisputed global hegemon, to new forms of print culture and models of literary value. Across these changes and more, vagrancy statutes remain surprisingly similar, despite many changes in their actual use and interpretation in different locations. Their very capaciousness and adaptability make them resilient, as they absorb new shades of meaning or are easily repurposed to novel uses. The category of vagrancy, as it is explicitly theorized in legal and political debates, repurposed or recirculated in literary texts, and implicitly theorized on the ground by the constables, JPs, and magistrates who use it every day, thus sediments its own history of use and reuse. I approach legal, administrative, and literary texts together as an expanded archive of vagrancy, which offers powerful insights into the prehistory of the police as we know them. Vagrancy reveals the importance of form, trope, and scriptive practices to the theorization of police as a mode of governance.

At the same time, I also reveal hitherto unexamined dimensions of the impress of police upon literary form and aesthetic practice. While the field of literary study has long benefited from several crucial works that reflected the initial reception of Foucault's *Discipline and Punish* in the American academy—most notably John Bender's *Imagining the Penitentiary* and D. A. Miller's *The Novel and the Police*—the definition of "police" that my archive reveals is quite different from the vision of disciplinary authority that Miller and Bender put forth.[13] Most centrally, police operates in this context not to produce disciplined subjects, but rather to produce a flexible, open-ended, discretionary optic for articulating populations' differentiated relationships to labor, resources, and subsistence. Furthermore, while vagrancy statutes themselves convey a sense of wide-ranging surveillance, their long, colorful lists of targets seeming to criminalize nearly every facet of everyday life, the historical record reveals that vagrancy law's actual enforcement was highly irregular and inconsistent; the laws granted local authorities broad powers, but individuals made choices about whether and when to use these powers.[14] Colloquially, and especially metaphorically, we tend to associate policing with a fairly narrow range of affective and aesthetic registers: sternness, seriousness, panoptic omniscience, repressiveness, vigilance. Vagrancy law and the textual records of its enforcement, however, reveal a much broader affective and aesthetic range of the texts that produced and were produced by police, encompassing creativity, boredom, improvisation, outrage, indifference, inconsistency, annoyance, frustration, charity, and more.

Scholars of early modern English literature have long noted vagrancy as a particularly clear point of transfer between law and literature.[15] For instance, the sixteenth-century proliferation of popular print genres like cony-catching pamphlets helped consolidate the figure of the "rogue and vagabond" and portray this figure as a member of a threatening criminal underworld, thus offering both political justification and rhetorical models for vagrancy legislation that followed.[16] Meanwhile, scholars of British Romanticism have revealed how poets—particularly Wordsworth—repurposed the legal category of vagrancy as a key site for the articulation of poetic form, poetic labor, and poetic consciousness.[17] However, while literary scholarship on vagrancy in these periods has yielded much insight into the interplay between law and literature, I diverge from much of the scholarship's prevailing focus on the vagrant as a kind of legal, poetic, or narrative subject, perhaps most clearly epitomized by Patricia Fumerton's claim that the legal and literary archives of seventeenth-century vagrancy offer us insight into early modern "unsettled subjectivity."[18] I argue instead that the category of vagrancy has very little to do with subjectivity or legal personhood, and that we cannot fully understand the significance of vagrancy for the development of policing unless we attend to how its imaginative elaborations often resisted interiority or subjectivity in favor of figurations of opacity, multitude, or inanimacy. Police could remain widely discretionary precisely because "the vagrant" was *not* ever defined as one specific kind of subject. This book reveals how vagrancy's anticipatory charge and resistance to definition were in fact what made the category so legally powerful *and* aesthetically resonant. Vagrancy's adaptability reveals the often uneven and improvisational ways that the people who made up "the state" in its most local instantiations read, wrote, and conceptualized categories of threat and welfare. When authors of literary texts make use of vagrancy toward their own varied aesthetic and political ends, they reveal further facets of how vagrancy resonated as an imaginative category, thus offering insight into the prehistory of the police not only as an institution, but as a mode of perception.

## "Minute Particulars": Improvising the Police

In his *Lectures on Justice, Police, Revenue, and Arms*—the precursor to *The Wealth of Nations*—Adam Smith defines "the objects of police" as "the cheapness of commodities, public security and cleanliness."[19] This broad mandate for "police"—most of which has little or nothing to do with crime prevention—may sound idiosyncratic to contemporary ears, but Smith here reflects some of the most conventional meanings of "police" in the eighteenth century: a diffuse, wide-ranging sense of order, organization, and governance (the latter especially reflected in the common etymologies shared by "police" and "policy"), encompassing not only "security," but also attention to social order, welfare, and subsistence.[20]

Police circulated in eighteenth-century Britain and its colonies as an idea and a set of practices even as the *word* "police" remained a frequent object of both suspicion and confusion. For instance, the famed philanthropist Jonas Hanway comments in 1775 that "the word *police* is not universally intelligible, so little have we attended to it."[21] More than twenty years later, Patrick Colquhoun, author of the magisterial *Treatise on the Police of the Metropolis,* similarly comments that "Police as recently exemplified, may be said to be a new science, not yet perfectly understood."[22] Meanwhile, the early establishment of the police as an institution in France contributed to the popular belief that "police"—especially when centralized—was fundamentally absolutist in nature, and incompatible with English constitutional understandings of personal liberty.[23]

However, continental theories of police were not as foreign to English administrative and legal *practice* as many eighteenth-century English observers held. Montesquieu's characterization of police in *The Spirit of the Laws,* for instance, aptly describes not only the operation of the police forces that existed in eighteenth-century France, but also the more general logic animating flexible legal measures dedicated to preventing threat and securing welfare:

> In the exercise of the police, it is rather the magistrate who punishes, than the law; in the sentence past on crimes, it is rather the law which punishes, than the magistrate. The business of the police consists in affairs which arise every instant, and are commonly of a trifling nature: there is then but little need of formalities. The actions of the police are quick; they are exercised over things which return every day; it would be therefore improper for it to inflict severe punishments. It is continually employed about minute particulars; great examples are therefore not designed for its purpose. It is governed rather by regulations than laws.[24]

Even as Jonas Hanway argued that "police" was definitionally unclear, he nonetheless could also name the poor laws, without hesitation, as "*the foundation of our police,*" and vagrancy law served as a crucial blueprint for the kind of discretionary power and anticipatory orientation toward threat that would later be institutionalized as the purview of the Metropolitan Police.[25] For example, in the 1785 House of Commons debate on Pitt's London and Westminster Police Bill, the Solicitor General attempted to parry accusations that the proposed system would constitute "an arbitrary system of police" that would violate personal liberty.[26] While a petition from the Lord Mayor and Aldermen of London opposed the bill on the grounds that it would create "new officers, invested with extraordinary and dangerous powers," the Solicitor General insisted that "he had no intention of introducing any new punishment, or constituting any new crime, except by extending and enforcing in some degree the vagrant laws."[27]

Meanwhile, this notion of "police" had firmly taken hold in the American colonies as well, and it was central to the evolution of U.S. law in the decades following independence. As William Novak argues, this broad understanding of "police" as the state's responsibility for the people's welfare is the foundation for the emergence of "the police power" in nineteenth-century jurisprudence as the broad constitutional purview of the regulatory state.[28] Local institutions and practices of order-maintenance under the aegis of "police," Novak argues, in fact formed the backbone for a robust regulatory state. At the same time, as Bryan Wagner argues, vagrancy remained conceptually crucial for the continued elaboration of policing as the mitigation of threat—especially when that threat is racialized—noting that his nineteenth- and twentieth-century sources trace their conceptual models of police back to colonial governance.[29]

*Police* relies powerfully on a definitional undefinability—if it is unsuited to "great examples" or "formalities," in Montesquieu's words, that is because it is a domain that is left open to what cannot be anticipated in advance, and thus cannot be limited by too clear a vision of what its future domain of minor, everyday action might be.[30] This undefinability offers a conundrum when it comes to textual interpretation, but vagrancy, I argue, offers a generatively loquacious archive of police. In the archive of vagrancy, we see the making of police *through* the "minute particulars" that Montesquieu asserts are its essence. As it was a paradigmatic target of police, vagrancy also remained crucially resistant to definitional certainty, and yet it had a material, practical life as well—many of its "minute particulars" were elaborated in administrative, theoretical, and literary texts, thus generating an archive of police before "the police" had taken institutional form. Vagrancy was a capacious category, but it was also defined and redefined through practice, legal and textual, and on the bodies of countless individuals who were whipped, confined in bridewells, expelled from a parish or town, compelled into apprenticeship, made vulnerable to re-enslavement, summarily fined for suspected theft, and more—one after another, by thousands of different individuals and institutions, each for a slightly different reason, yet all aggregated under the same broad category naming future threat to property, security, prosperity, and welfare.

By centering vagrancy, a category both conceptually capacious and legally specific, I aim to address the dilemma Micol Seigel names in *Violence Work:* theories of police too often approach the topic in either narrowly institutional terms (the histories of police *forces*) or in expansive Foucauldian accounts of disciplinarity ("police" as a metaphor unmoored from the state).[31] Vagrancy offers us an archive that predates the police force as an object of institutional history, yet keeps our focus trained on police as something more precisely defined than disciplinary power in all its forms. At the same time, however, the very expansiveness of vagrancy also allows us to see just how capacious police is, even as we attend to its specificity; after all, the archive of vagrancy reveals the conceptual scope of police to be far bigger than the narrow ambit of "crime control" popularly perceived to be the central role of both historical and contemporary police forces.

Because this category so crucially relied on its open-endedness for its broad, discretionary scope, I propose that it is most potently theorized in aggregate, on the ground, in everyday and often improvisational legal practice. It is also perceptively theorized in texts that draw on (and thus leave evidence of) the legal common sense animating the idea of vagrancy, but do not themselves directly enact the violence of legal force: poems, pamphlets, novels, treatises, newspapers, and more.[32] These texts, of course, do not simply reflect legal practice; rather, they contribute to a long-established interplay of mutual influence and exchange between genres we now classify as law and literature. Through precise attention to the deceptively small category of vagrancy as it traverses legal theory, legal practice, and print culture, we gain crucial insight into the array of practices, theories, modes and purviews of violence, and habits of perception that coalesced as "police" before the establishment of the modern police force.

## Specters of Political Economy

The etymological link between "police" and "policy" becomes particularly clear when we understand how vagrancy connected local order-keeping to political economy as theorized on a much larger scale. In an era that saw the rise of new forms of charitable institutions and movements for social reform—as well as the gradual end of longstanding systems of parish poor relief—the category of vagrancy embedded criminalization into the fabric of charity.[33] Some of the earliest precursors to what we now think of as the modern prison—a phenomenon often associated with the penitentiary of the late eighteenth century and with the rise of the bureaucratic state—emerge primarily as institutions intended specifically for the incarceration of vagrants.[34] While vagrancy laws had long targeted the supposed dangers of "idleness," idleness also took on new political significance in the eighteenth century.[35] As A. O. Hirschman has influentially argued, economic self-interest was increasingly central to eighteenth-century theories of social and political organization.[36] For these theories, the pursuit of self-interest made for rational actors whose behavior could be predicted.[37] Idleness could therefore index the unknowable, unpredictable threat posed by actors whose behaviors cannot be reliably predicted or harnessed by the market, and thus must be consigned to police. And so while Adam Smith's only explicit mention of vagrancy law in *The Wealth of Nations* is his opposition to such laws as an outmoded form of local protectionism that impedes the formation of a free labor market, he nonetheless relies foundationally on begging as the constitutive outside of otherwise universal human economic behavior; beginning with the "propensity in human nature . . . to truck, barter, and exchange one thing for another," he argues for the universality of self-interest: "Nobody but a beggar chuses to depend chiefly upon the benevolence of his fellow-citizens."[38] Bernard Harcourt argues that the contemporary logic of "neoliberal penality" is foundationally rooted in classical political economy, whose "mode of rationality rendered natural a conception of the penal sphere as lying outside the free market and as being the repository for necessary, legitimate, and competent government intervention."[39] If vagrancy had long signified the supposed refusal to work, it could also signify the realm of human volition that seems unassimilable into the supposedly universal imperative of economically rational activity. This idea also thus accrues to vagrancy as an aesthetic charge for writers engaging with the economically "rational" and its limitations as a theory of human interiority.

In his *Economic and Philosophic Manuscripts,* Marx sought to expose a constitutive exclusion that enables classical political economy to sustain what he would later term the myth of primitive accumulation: "Political economy, therefore, does not recognize the unoccupied worker, the workingman, insofar as he happens to be outside this labor relationship. The cheat-thief, swindler, beggar, and unemployed; the starving, wretched and criminal workingman—these are *figures* [*Gestalten*] who do not exist for *political economy* but only for other eyes, those of the doctor, the judge, the grave digger, and bumbailiff, etc.; such figures are specters [*Gespenster*] outside its domain."[40]

Marx's generative insight here lies not only in his vivid illustration of the dynamic that renders the vagrant a matter not for political economy, but for the police, but also in his metaphor of the specter. Spectrality here makes a vital claim: that what Marx seeks to name here is not a knowable, enumerable population, but rather a collection of *Gestalten*—translated here as "figures," but as *Gestalt* does not name the specifically rhetorical sense of "figure" in English, it might also be rendered here as "shape" or "form." These forms haunt political economy; they limn the "domain" of the properly economic precisely through their indistinct refusal to exist either wholly within or wholly without it. In other words, Marx pushes us to understand "the vagrant" not as a kind of person, but rather as a productively indistinct conceptual category, a spectral form, which constituted the very regimes that claimed only to suppress it. Though the administration of vagrancy law offered a historically crucial blueprint for the bureaucratic forms that would later elaborate personal identity documentation, the legal category of vagrancy was not an identity. In fact, as this book reveals, legal and literary elaborations of vagrancy consistently resisted many of the characteristics we have come to associate with identity: interiority, agency, consistency across time, legal personhood, singularity, subjectivity. And as I will argue, it is crucial not to mistake vagrancy for an identity, as such a misrecognition occludes both the dynamic capaciousness of the category and its foundational role in the evolution of the discretionary power that would later come to be understood as the proper domain of the police. Police authority could remain widely discretionary and adaptable precisely because "the vagrant" was *not* defined as one specific kind of subject.

That said, of course, this does not mean that vagrancy was either empty of particularity or unmoored from social identity; in all its capaciousness and mutability as a legal and imaginative category, its *use* nonetheless frequently enforced and solidified categories of differential social and legal status.[41] I emphasize the linguistic capaciousness of vagrancy not to assert that it incites free play of signification unmoored from materiality, but rather to ask why a legal and imaginative category crucial to the differential distribution of resources, labor-power, and life chances was so much more figuratively capacious than were the material axes of difference along which its force often worked. The archive I work with here is not one that is primarily concerned with elaborating on the lives of those targeted by vagrancy law. Instead, while drawing extensively on the important work social historians have done to this end, I examine how the category of "vagrant" itself circulated as a hermeneutic, a set of legal and interpretive practices, and a theory of governance. This category is best understood not as a population, but as an optic and a relation to police. If we take "vagrant" to name a distinct, knowable population, then we risk reifying this optic and disappearing its foundational role in the establishment of police as a structure of knowledge and a theory of governance.[42]

Thus, the archive I work with largely—though not exclusively—elaborates the theory of vagrancy law and its enforcement from the vantage point of police. At the same time, I also trace how the foundational theories and practices of police took on intellectual and imaginative lives in other kinds of texts, serving divergent aesthetic and political ends. The literary texts I examine offer a wide array of positions vis-à-vis legal practice, ranging from overtly celebratory of police authority to deeply critical. Vagrancy's textual archive reveals the paradoxical *usefulness* to police of capaciousness, play, aesthetic pleasure, indeterminacy, complexity, and multiplicity—precisely the kinds of things literary scholars like to look for in texts, and often imagine constitute fertile ground for resistance. As I trace how the category of vagrancy shaped theories and practices of police, I center this paradox: vagrancy law was able to work as a powerful tool for the consolidation of material differentiation between populations precisely *because* it was so capacious and indeterminate in its imaginative and scriptive elaborations. This, I argue, is at the heart of how police emerges as a powerful theory of governance and regulation in the eighteenth-century British Atlantic world.

## Filling Out Forms

As this book reveals, literary contributions to, reflections on, and resignifications of vagrancy as a legal category have historically both revealed some of the foundational logics underpinning police as a structure of knowledge *and* concealed these same logics by fantasizing "the vagrant" as a kind of person—particularly a lyric subject or a narrative protagonist. As I discuss in more detail in Chapter 4, in which I examine the afterlife of early American literature in a landmark 1972 U.S. Supreme

Court decision striking down vagrancy law, literary texts can obscure legal history when they narrow vagrancy to itinerancy, recast as freedom and valorized transgression—a valence of vagrancy that, I argue, was always more literary than legal. I propose that a careful investigation of literary engagements with vagrancy as a legal category can offer us a fuller understanding of the emergence of the police as a modern institution and cornerstone of governance.

The "police archives" I'm concerned with here are not records kept by a police department, designated "police archives" primarily by the institutional location of their production and storage. I'm interested, instead, in the archive of *police* as an eighteenth-century model of governance, as an attitude toward preventing threat and securing welfare, as a collection of material and scriptive practices that would make *the* police thinkable. What constitutes this archive? I think that literary-critical method can help answer this question, and so I read for what I see as the tropes, forms, categories, and figures that script and theorize police across a series of administrative and literary texts. This means both reading legal and administrative documents with attentiveness to their formal features while also reading nonlegal texts with attentiveness to the material legal practices they draw on and imagine.

Robert Nailer's vagrant pass, for instance, discloses its material uses as well as the formal features of print that articulate its theory of governmentality. This pass, dating from the 1660s, is a document that he would have used routinely in his role in local parish governance and administration: JPs were expected to charge with vagrancy those present in the parish without legal settlement, the "idle and disorderly," and any others deemed to pose a threat to the welfare of the community.[43] A pass like this was intended to enable the transportation of a person charged with vagrancy to their place of legal settlement by mandating that officers of the law in each parish both allow the person to pass through and ensure they continue toward their place of settlement as noted on the pass. This reflects a major aim of vagrancy legislation since the establishment of the Elizabethan poor laws: to preserve parish poor relief funds by keeping outsiders from drawing on them.[44]

The *form* of the pass also reveals much about the underlying logic of vagrancy law and the writing practices through which it was administered.

In what it prints and what it leaves open to be filled in, the pass signals what is flexible and what is fixed (Figure 2). After noting that "[blank] was this [blank] day of [blank] taken at [blank] within this County, as a Rogue and Wandering Beggar . . . ," the pass then mandates that other parish officers facilitate the named person's return.[45] This document is an early form of state identity documentation; indeed, vagrant passes such as this one were among the earliest models for the passports that nation-states would later use to identify their citizens and control movement across their borders.[46] But while contemporary passports link national citizenship to a number of markers thought to confer consistent and unique identity, the vagrant pass prioritizes place of legal settlement above all other information. Instead of the contemporary passport's array of descriptive and biometric information, designed to link an individual body to a unique bureaucratic identity, the pass matches the vagrant's name not to any bodily singularity, but to the generic category of "Rogue and Wandering Beggar"—the only specific information called for here is their place of legal settlement.

The pass thus conceptualizes a geography; it maps a path without mapping anything so specific that it couldn't be used by any JP in any parish, as it authorizes the person here deemed a vagrant "to travel and pass from hence onward, the next and directest way unto [blank] in the County of [blank]," and directs local authorities to "convey the said [blank] from Constable to Constable, through every your Towns, Hamblets, and Liberties, the next directest way to [blank] aforesaid."[47] In carefully enumerating the kinds of jurisdictions through which a vagrant might travel (towns, hamlets, liberties), and by mandating the most direct route, this pass says much more about the terrain through which a vagrant might be compelled to travel than it does about the person here deemed "vagrant."

Today, we commonly think of vagrancy laws as laws against mobility. However, the relation of vagrancy laws to mobility was more complex than this: they sometimes targeted the itinerant, but sometimes compelled movement, and sometimes targeted behaviors and statuses that had no relation to either mobility or immobility. The aim of the administrative practices laid out on this pass is not necessarily to arrest mobility completely, but to map out geographies of responsibility and entitlement: the

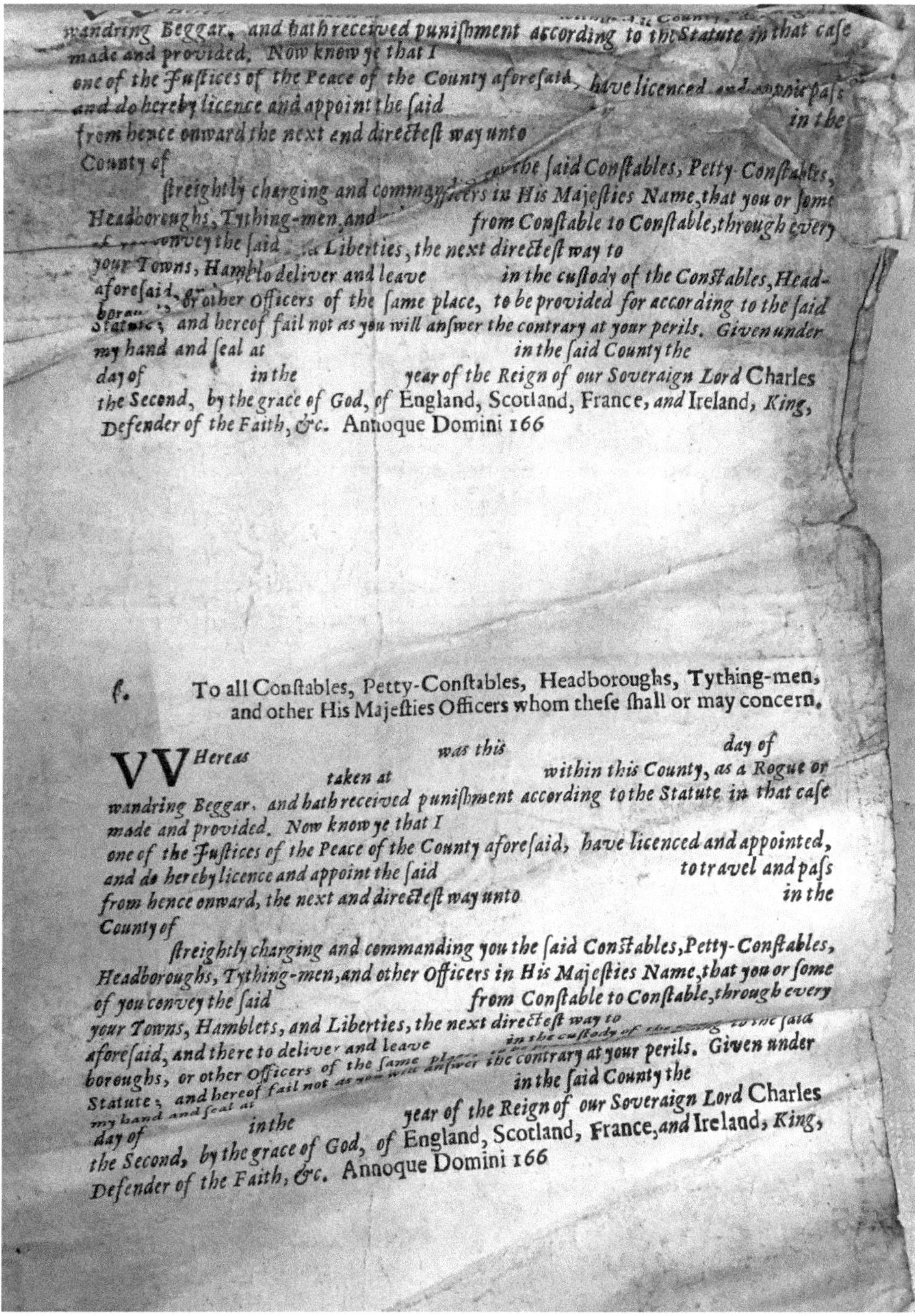

wandring Beggar, and hath received puniſhment according to the Statute in that caſe
made and provided. Now know ye that I
one of the Juſtices of the Peace of the County aforeſaid, have licenced [illegible] paſs
and do hereby licence and appoint the ſaid
from hence onward the next and directeſt way unto in the
County of
the ſaid Conſtables, Petty Conſtables,
ſtreightly charging and comman[illegible]cers in His Majeſties Name, that you or ſome
Headboroughs, Tything-men, and [illegible] from Conſtable to Conſtable, through every
of [illegible]onvey the ſaid [illegible] Liberties, the next directeſt way to
your Towns, Hamb[illegible]to deliver and leave in the cuſtody of the Conſtables, Head-
aforeſaid, [illegible] other Officers of the ſame place, to be provided for according to the ſaid
bor[illegible] Statute; and hereof fail not as you will anſwer the contrary at your perils. Given under
my hand and ſeal at in the ſaid County the
day of in the year of the Reign of our Soveraign Lord Charles
the Second, by the grace of God, of England, Scotland, France, and Ireland, King,
Defender of the Faith, &c. Annoque Domini 166

6. To all Conſtables, Petty-Conſtables, Headboroughs, Tything-men, and other His Majeſties Officers whom theſe ſhall or may concern.

VV Hereas was this day of
taken at within this County, as a Rogue or
wandring Beggar, and hath received puniſhment according to the Statute in that caſe
made and provided. Now know ye that I
one of the Juſtices of the Peace of the County aforeſaid, have licenced and appointed,
and do hereby licence and appoint the ſaid to travel and paſs
from hence onward, the next and directeſt way unto in the
County of
ſtreightly charging and commanding you the ſaid Conſtables, Petty-Conſtables,
Headboroughs, Tything-men, and other Officers in His Majeſties Name, that you or ſome
of you convey the ſaid from Conſtable to Conſtable, through every
your Towns, Hamblets, and Liberties, the next directeſt way to
aforeſaid, and there to deliver and leave in the cuſtody of [illegible] to the ſaid
boroughs, or other Officers of the ſame pl[illegible] anſwer the contrary at your perils. Given under
Statute; and hereof fail not as [illegible] in the ſaid County the
my hand and ſeal at
day of in the year of the Reign of our Soveraign Lord Charles
the Second, by the grace of God, of England, Scotland, France, and Ireland, King,
Defender of the Faith, &c. Annoque Domini 166

FIGURE 2: Vagrant pass (Robert Nailer's Papers, Justices' Papers: Surrey, C 110/3, UK National Archives)

vagrant pass marks its bearer as unentitled to poor relief in the parish in which they were apprehended, and seeks to facilitate (and document the costs associated with) the vagrant's return to the parish that is considered responsible for them. A document like this pass, by marking its bearer as beyond the bounds of a parish's responsibility, also enacts the boundaries—both geographical and moral—of the parish as an administrative unit. By serving as a dividing line between the deserving and the undeserving poor, this category stakes out the borders of a parish's responsibility for the welfare of its people—while also helping define the very nature of "welfare." A vagrant, this pass says, is anyone for whom this place is not responsible. But while its primary function was to serve as a technology to assist a JP in his task of local governance, this pass also helps construct much vaster geographies. The management of resources and population that constituted the purview of police on the scale of the parish also intersected with emerging political-economic conceptions of population as a national resource to be managed across a growing empire, but we would never know this from the pass alone; it stakes out a local geography of contiguous counties and parishes, never naming an administrative unit larger than this subdivision of the nation. Thus, the occlusion of the broader geographies that vagrancy laws implicated is also a formal feature of this print artifact.

Reading for the figurative register of administrative documents reveals how trope and figure helped construct the everyday writing, reading, and speech—as well as the acts of violence—that made up vagrancy law enforcement. For instance, in one routine demand for a certificate of settlement, Henry Norris, a JP in Hackney, recorded on November 29, 1731 that he "Signed a warrant to apprehend Samuel Bodycoate to bring a Cert[ificate] he having Intruded himselfe into the parish to dwell there as a parishoner thereby being likely to bring a burthen & charge upon the said Parish."[48] To say that someone is likely to become chargeable to the parish, for instance, legally allows one to act as if this person *will* become chargeable to the parish.[49] To say that someone is likely to pose a threat allows one to act as if they *will* pose a threat. Thus, vagrancy is proleptic: it attributes its object with future criminality, dependence, or danger as if these things had already happened. It carries the force of a rhetorical figure. Yet it is the actual *use* of vagrancy law that produces this slippage between likely and certain; it is Bodycoate's perceived likelihood of becoming a burden that allows Norris to set in motion the legal procedure to expel him in the interest of preserving the poor relief funds from which he has not yet attempted to draw.

Robert Nailer's vagrant pass also reveals a relationship between vagrancy and the print industry. Such passes were not new in the 1660s—they were used throughout the sixteenth and seventeenth centuries. However, early modern passes tended to be copied by hand from the formulas dictated by statutes and reproduced in popular how-to manuals for JPs.[50] Nailer's pass is printed, with blank spaces left for the justice to fill in by hand. The pass is therefore an artifact of the early history of the now-ubiquitous print genre of the bureaucratic form. This particular genre, with its standardized text reproduced in print and its blank spaces that allow for only the narrowest and most predetermined manuscript insertion of particularities (names, dates, places), is such a commonplace feature of modern life that it can be difficult to appreciate it as remarkable, but during Robert Nailer's lifetime, the production of forms such as this vagrant pass was one facet of an incipient revolution in print that effected the expansion not only of the much-vaunted "republic of letters" mediated through books, periodicals, and newspapers, but also of the humbler print genres on which finance, business, and local governance came to rely: bills of exchange, account books, receipts, certificates, tickets, and legal forms.[51] As Naomi Tadmor argues, the "consolidation of a culture of administrative forms" was profoundly shaped by vagrancy statutes and related laws—particularly the Settlement Act of 1662, which legally defined parish settlement for the first time and contributed to increased demand for certificates of settlement, vagrant passes, and other documents of poor law administration.[52] According to Tadmor, the lapse of the Licensing Act in 1695—long regarded by literary scholars as a decisive event in the rise of eighteenth-century print and literary cultures—also opened space for more printers to fulfill this demand, thus contributing to the increasing (though incomplete) domination of print in this previously scribal form.[53] This was not the only link between the production of printed forms and literary culture; as James Raven documents, the same printers who produced books and periodicals also relied heavily on small-item "jobbing" to offset the risk inherent to bookselling: by printing forms, certificates, and other small items for clients such as local workhouses, hospitals, and businesses, printers could rely on a steady demand for easily produced items that offered more reliable and immediate income than books.[54] In fact, during the Restoration, printing beyond London was largely driven by demand from local government for increasingly standardized administrative forms, and vagrant passes provided a particularly important market for these printers.[55] The production of passes such as this one thus quite literally financed literary production.

Robert Nailer's miscellaneous papers, bound by a piece of minor legal technology, also include some pieces of minor literary (re)production: three pattern poems carefully copied out from Sir John Mennes's *Recreation for Ingenious Headpeeces, or, A Pleasant Grove for their Wits to Walk In.* In one, for instance, Nailer has copied a love-knot poem that forms an infinite loop, and then added his name in an unevenly sketched heart below the poem (Figure 3). This poem, which appears on page Q2r of the 1665 edition of *Ingenious Headpeeces,* is offered as one of many "fancies" including other pattern poems, riddles, rebuses, and texts that can be read forward and backward.[56] This may seem a tenuous place to begin when asserting a link between the kind of linguistic practices we have historically deemed "literary" and the workings of vagrancy law, and in one sense it is—after all, the relationship between these recopied poems and the vagrant pass is one of contiguity to which no meaning or intention can be confidently assigned. They appear next to each other, literally, in the archive, and while the vagrant pass seems to have been wrapped around Nailer's miscellaneous papers for a long time, it is impossible to tell who actually used the vagrant pass in this way. Nailer, as a Justice of the Peace, certainly enforced vagrancy law routinely as part of his duties. And as a consumer of literature, Robert Nailer also copied at least three poems on spare pieces of paper, carefully reproducing the fanciful designs offered for novelty, amusement, and pleasure by the printer of the *Ingenious Headpeeces.*

The scriptive practices that Nailer used to copy out the pattern poem from a printed example resonate broadly with the scriptive practices he would have drawn on to fill in the vagrant pass: manuscript transcription bounded by both literal and imaginative shapes distributed through print. The vagrant pass offers a blank space of a particular size in which to fill

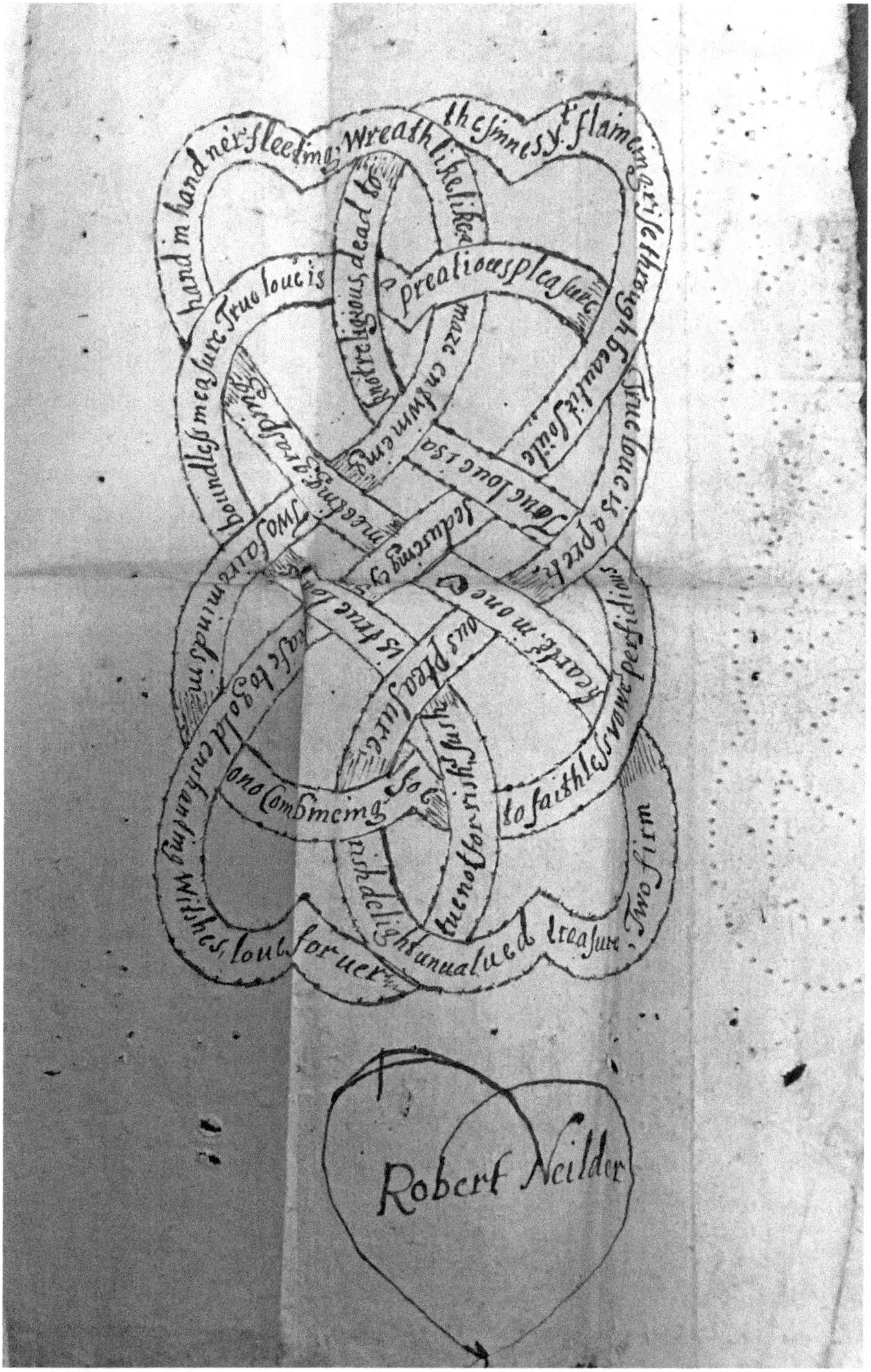


FIGURE 3: Pattern poem (Robert Nailer's Papers, Justices' Papers: Surrey, C 110/3, UK National Archives)

in what he hears when he asks for a name. Meanwhile, the pattern poem printed in the *Ingenious Headpeeces* offers a shape that Nailer has traced onto the scrap of paper; we can see the remnants of tracing in the dotted outlines that are still visible in the line of ink that he subsequently used to draw a smooth outline for the love-knot that contains the poem.

Of course, this connection offers us little in the way of strong explanatory correlation between legal practice and para-literary amusement: after all, many other JPs filled in vagrant passes without necessarily copying poems out of books, and many readers who enjoyed texts like *Ingenious Headpeeces* never once enforced a law. But I do think that the chance contiguity of these documents tells us something important about the archive of vagrancy as this book conceives it: vagrancy moved between law and literature not only as a conceptual category, but as a relation to material practices of writing, reading, manuscript, and print.[57] Policing does not consist only of writing, but the rise of an increasingly administrative state was also intertwined with the rise of mass print culture, increasing literacy, and the growing centrality of writing to a vast array of intertwined forms of authority. The ongoing, active interplay between administrative, legal, and literary reading and writing practices becomes, in turn, an aesthetic resource for literary authors.

For example, by the early nineteenth century, when vagrancy had gained a new measure of poetic currency, George Crabbe's "The Parish Register" (1807) takes the scriptive forms of parish administration as an explicit model for poetry—not only drawing on Crabbe's own practices of administrative writing as poetic inspiration, but also aestheticizing the very process of this transfer. In a poem whose three books—Birth, Marriage, and Death—are structured by the imperative of parish record-keeping, Crabbe dwells on the materiality of the register itself as an aesthetic resource; the legal imperative to write one's name incites a wild variety of handwritten shapes transformed into a botanical landscape that print cannot visually mimic:

> How fair these Names, how much unlike they look
> To all the blurr'd Subscriptions in my Book:
> The Bridegroom's Letters stand in row above,
> Tapering yet stout, like Pine-trees in his Grove;

While free and fine the Bride's appear below,
As light and slender as her Jasmines grow;
Mark now in what confusion stoop or stand,
The crooked Scrawls of many a clownish Hand. (II.284–290)[58]

The very process of asserting "how much unlike" the printed poem is to the manuscript register ends up absorbing the aesthetic power assigned to manuscript into print—while also rendering poetry, rather than administrative writing, the privileged vehicle for aesthetic experience. After all, it's poetry that transforms the handwritten letters into pine and jasmine, even as the poem locates this aesthetic possibility in the capacity of print to gesture to the manuscript it cannot visually reproduce. If the practice of administrative writing—recording names in a parish register, for instance, or filling in a vagrant pass—offers the most obvious construction of vagrancy and settlement through writing, then aesthetic redeployments of vagrancy show how writing without direct legal force played a role that sometimes complemented, sometimes contradicted, and sometimes strayed far beyond vagrancy's legal use, drawing on the imaginative charge of the category toward a variety of ends.

This imaginative charge can reveal surprising links between police and literary form. When Moll Flanders begins her account of her life by cheekily refusing to give her true name, she immediately places the fiction of its existence in the documentary reality of administrative archives: "My True Name is so well known in the Records, or Registers at *Newgate,* and in the *Old-Baily,* and there are some things of such Consequence still depending there, relating to my particular Conduct, that it is not to be expected I should set my Name, or the Account of my Family to this Work."[59] In naming her place of birth (Newgate prison), and in denoting her name's presence in its records, Moll echoes the form of a settlement examination. Because Moll is born in Newgate just before her mother is transported for theft, she is essentially born into vagrancy, both literally and figuratively without settlement anywhere: "As I was born in such an unhappy Place, I had no Parish to have Recourse to for my Nourishment in my Infancy, nor can I give the least Account how I was kept alive" (45). After a hazily recollected early childhood spent wandering with "Gypsies," Moll returns to geographic specificity once again when she encounters parish officers tasked with enforcing vagrancy laws and determining eligibility for poor relief, as she notes that she was "taken up by some of the Parish Officers of *Colchester*" (45). Once again, a specific place invokes her documentary existence in a parish register, justice's notebook, vagrant docket, or other legal record of minor administrative business of the parish.

Defoe carefully lays out how Moll passes from vagrancy to settlement when she leaves the Gypsies in Colchester: "I gave an Account that I came into the Town with the *Gypsies,* but that I would not go any farther with them, and that so they had left me" (45). Her apprehension as a vagrant ultimately ends her brief career of vagrancy: "I was now in a Way to be provided for; for tho' I was not a Parish Charge upon this or that part of the Town by Law, yet as my Case came to be known, and that I was too young to do any Work, being not above three Years old, Compassion mov'd the Magistrates of the Town to order some Care to be taken of me, and I became one of their own, as much as if I had been born in the Place" (45). Moll reframes the end of her time with the Gypsies as her first self-willed act; while she tells the parish officer they had simply abandoned her, the adult Moll proposes another story: "I have a Notion in my Head, that I left them there, (that is, that I hid myself and wou'd not go any farther with them) but I am unable to be particular in that Account" (45).

Moll's childhood vagrancy provides the imaginative gap that she later fills with a radically autonomous subjectivity; the adult Moll narrates her rebirth as the kind of outlaw protagonist that we have long recognized as an important strand in the construction of the bourgeois novelistic subject. But importantly, vagrancy here is not identical to the identities of outlaw, criminal, protagonist, or picara: vagrancy is the blank space in the novel form, the place that Moll later fills in with this "Notion" in her head of her originary disobedience. This disobedience can only be constructed in retrospect, from the subject position of her later criminality, which the adult Moll frames as originating from her legally unsettled childhood; had England developed a state orphanage to house her, she argues, "I had not been left a poor desolate Girl without Friends, without Cloaths, without Help or Helper in the World, as was my Fate . . . nor brought into a scandalous Course of Life" (44). It is the genre of the "scandalous Course of Life"—the genre of criminal biography—that ultimately offers Moll the vantage point of this retrospect; criminal biography, after all, is a genre predicated on the continuous selfhood and interiority presumed by legal concepts like criminal responsibility and *mens rea,* and it is a genre of retrospect: of being turned to account for what one has already done. This is the kind of narrative that lends Moll the legibly autonomous individual selfhood from which she can claim an act of willfulness she cannot remember.

It is the failure of memory here—not the willfulness that Moll imagines or the criminal life that follows—that Defoe most centrally draws from the notion of vagrancy. After all, when Moll says that she is "unable to be particular in that Account," she indicates her absence of memory in the language of vagrancy law: she fails to give a good account of herself to the reader. This is the constitutive illegibility of vagrancy as a legal category; it is the blank space rather than the thing that fills that space. Indeed, if, as Jeannine DeLombard has argued in a different context, criminal responsibility can create a liberal subject when there otherwise would not be one, then it is in fact analytically vital that we not conflate the legal subject capable of criminal responsibility with the target of police, left open for anticipated future threats.[60] The main concerns of vagrancy legislation—threat and welfare—leave individual subjectivity (legal or otherwise) irrelevant; threat can be posed by populations, spaces, wild animals, fire, and other objects of police, just as populations, locales, and itineraries can all be designated as beyond the bounds of responsibility for welfare.

*Moll Flanders* thus reveals the insight as well as the potential challenge of tracing the category of vagrancy through literary archives. Moll's childhood vagrancy is the first incident in a life of continual transgression, and so on one level the novel joins the tradition of the rogue pamphlet in loosely conflating vagrancy with a life of crime. And yet, at the same time, when read with close attention to vagrancy's legal meaning and its association with police, the distinction between vagrancy and criminal responsibility becomes clearer, thus revealing the subtler narrative work that vagrancy does for the novel: Defoe uses vagrancy to clear space for Moll to become a radically self-willed (if also criminal) economic subject—the very opposite of a vagrant. This works because vagrancy has a specific legal and imaginative charge: the name for a kind of threat-placeholder, and for populations and spaces beyond the pale of responsibility. This charge of potentiality is imaginatively powerful. It produces the idea of a figure who might (like "Moll Flanders") go by any name, who might commit any array of future crimes (like the miscellaneous array promised by the title page), and who is nobody's responsibility, and thus can tell "nobody's story."[61]

By leaving the category of vagrancy mutable, miscellaneous, and open to redefinition, vagrancy law figures future threat as protean and unpredictable, and thus authorizes a form of power as open to discretionary revision as the danger it seeks to contain. The reliance of vagrancy law on implication, prediction, and speculation makes it a particularly rich resource for literary texts to take up—and sometimes transform. But the object of my analysis is always both the literary redeployments of vagrancy and the textual records of legal practice, as both, I argue, benefit from the protocols of literary-critical reading. Police develops as both a material and crucially rhetorical practice, and thus our methods as literary scholars can complement the important work of legal and social historians on this topic and offer us powerful insights into what made the police thinkable before their institutional establishment.

## The Color of Dispossession: Primitive Accumulation and Racial Capitalism

Moll Flanders crosses the Atlantic to be remade as a nominally penitent and prosperous economic subject—thus embodying, as Gabriel Cervantes argues, the foundational ideological commitments animating convict transportation.[62] In this frame, the racial triangulation of Moll's vagrancy becomes more visible: Defoe uses her time with "Gypsies" in order to begin her story with a radical contingency that clears the space for her to attain a kind of rogue economic subjectivity—one that allows her to enslave others by the novel's end.[63]

Ironically, Defoe uses vagrancy in order to set up the narrative trajectory that leads Moll from dispossession to accumulation—and to the colonial fulfillment of the promise of a newly consolidating whiteness. At the same time, the transatlantic legal archive of vagrancy offers another view of how administrative geographies of threat and welfare crossed oceans. Early promoters of English colonization in the Americas argued that these colonies could serve as a sink for England's surplus population, where the unemployed, idle, and criminal could be remade into productive laborers. But the American colonies also developed legal mechanisms for managing their own surplus populations, marking some people as suspicious, and instituting police measures to protect property and security. Vagrancy law was repurposed as the backbone of the colonial slave codes that developed in the Caribbean in the 1660s and rapidly spread throughout the Americas, and early colonial vagrancy laws targeted an array of populations deemed dangerous in specifically colonial conditions: fugitives from slavery and indentured servitude, as well as black and indigenous people both enslaved and free.[64] The mutual imbrication of race, labor and colonial governance in the category of vagrancy points to the centrality of race and empire to (both historical and ongoing) primitive accumulation.

Marx conceptualizes primitive accumulation through his account of early modern English vagrancy laws, which he argues were crucial to the reconfiguration of labor, enclosure, and the creation of a landless proletariat.[65] Into the eighteenth century, English vagrancy law, poor relief, and settlement continued to play crucial roles in shaping the social relations of labor that formed the precursors of industrialization. This has been the focus of foundational social history in the tradition of E. P. Thompson as well as classic scholarship on labor, class, and cultural production in the long eighteenth century, such as Raymond Williams's *The Country and the City* and John Barrell's *The Dark Side of the Landscape*.[66] However, the concerns of vagrancy law—labor, population, subsistence, welfare, and the place of local governance in a national body politic—are all crucially caught up in the administration of empire as Britain accumulated commercial and military power over the course of the eighteenth century, and this context for vagrancy—and for primitive accumulation more generally—has been addressed far less extensively in literary scholarship. This book contends that our understanding of vagrancy changes when we see the capitalism to which it is crucial as *racial* capitalism developing in the context of empire. I thus join Jordy Rosenberg and Chi-ming Yang in their project to theorize anew what they term "the dispossessed eighteenth century" and thus "undo a notion of enclosure that is constrained to the English countryside."[67]

Vagrancy offered a remarkably resilient blueprint for adaptable modes of labor regulation, local governance, and theories of sovereignty that emerged differently in different colonial locations, but which also influenced metropolitan governance, offering an optic for understanding population as a rubric linking colony and metropole. In each of the case studies that *Vagrant Figures* spotlights over the course of the long eighteenth century, connections across empire become visible through the category of vagrancy.

I take racial capitalism as a central category of analysis here because my work builds on a long tradition of Marxist social history and literary criticism, but also seeks to incorporate Cedric Robinson's foundational critique of traditional Marxism as insufficiently attentive to race as constitutive of, not epiphenomenal to, the origins of capitalism. In *Black Marxism,* Robinson develops the term "racial capitalism" to name how "the development, organization, and expansion of capitalist society pursued essentially racial directions," and thus "as a material force . . . it could be expected that racialism would inevitably permeate the social structures emergent from capitalism."[68] As Jodi Melamed explains, Robinson's intervention posits that "antinomies of accumulation require loss, disposability, and the unequal differentiation of human value, and racism enshrines the inequalities that capitalism requires. Most obviously, it does this by displacing the uneven life chances that are inescapably part of capitalist social relations onto fictions of differing human capacities, historically race."[69] Such an analysis—whose roots, of course, also include the tradition of Eric Williams, C. L. R. James, and Frantz Fanon, demands a simultaneously material and ideological understanding of race; race works as a fiction for articulating relations to labor, accumulation, and dispossession.

Since foundational interventions such as Laura Brown and Felicity Nussbaum's *The New Eighteenth Century,* Brown's *Ends of Empire,* and Srinivas Aravamudan's *Tropicopolitans,* the field of eighteenth-century British literature has come to rediscover the centrality of empire to eighteenth-century British culture.[70] As a now-established field of scholarship has shown, empire is equally foundational to the development of literary forms, genres, modes of prestige, and print markets throughout the eighteenth century.[71] The textual archive of vagrancy offers us a view of empire's statecraft emerging in everyday practice, through the "minute particulars" that Montesquieu names as the object of police.

For scholars of the eighteenth century, race has come into view as particularly amenable to the work of literary scholarship attentive to its reliance on trope, fiction, form, and genre. Roxann Wheeler's *The Complexion of Race,* for instance, ushered in renewed focus on the historical specificity of the multivalent meanings of "complexion" in the eighteenth century, arguing that eighteenth-century European ideologies of race as changeable, climatically determined, and expressed through religion, dress, civility, and governance gave way—though inconsistently and unevenly—to a nineteenth-century version of race as biological inheritance. Wheeler's central category of analysis is "racial ideology," and she offers a nuanced and detailed account of how this ideology, over the course of the eighteenth century, came to center skin color as the governing trope of hierarchical "human difference."[72] My research into vagrancy as a category, however, leads me to focus less exclusively on the ideological or representational valences of race and more on its material instantiations. I also attend to the racializing work of practices, tropes, categories, and relations to labor that did not necessarily operate through or lead toward racial *classification.* Wheeler's account of how natural-historical schemes of racial classification emerged over the course of the century is an important and persuasive one, but I trace another history of race that unfolded alongside this emergence: the racialization of security, welfare, threat, and sovereignty that relied not on strict classification, but rather on the continued legal enshrinement of open-ended indeterminacy (and also on the bounded circumstances in which such indeterminacy could operate).

Vagrancy, in this time period, was never a racially exclusive or specific category—it's too wide-ranging and diffuse to ever consolidate this way—but it is frequently a *racializing* category. Its very indeterminacy is what makes it such a powerful venue for racialization; it is adaptable to novel situations and structures of power, and it offers a framework for theorizing security and threat that proved crucial for the maintenance of ongoing deprivation, expropriation, vulnerability, and violence that formed (and continue to form) the material articulation of race. Indeed, the adaptability of vagrancy (which helped produce the adaptability of police) is what makes it uncannily similar to race itself; as Ann Stoler argues, "racial formations combine elements of *fixity and fluidity* in ways that make them both resilient and impervious to empirical, experiential counterclaims."[73]

Ambiguity and indeterminacy surrounding racial categories "are not slips in, or obstacles to, racial thinking and practices but the very conditions for their proliferation and possibility."[74] In this context, Stuart Hall's vital theorization of race is worth revisiting; in "Race, Articulation, and Societies Structured in Dominance," Hall argues that historically specific practices of racism work not only to "ascribe the positioning of different social groups in relation to one another," but also to secure "an articulation between different modes of production, structured in some relation of dominance."[75] This discussion of how different modes of production (such as, for instance, slavery and wage labor) can be analytically related to each other, especially in a colonial or postcolonial context, frames Hall's oft-quoted claim that race is "the modality in which class is 'lived,' the medium through which class relations are experienced, the form in which it is appropriated and 'fought through.' "[76] Heeding Hall's call for historical specificity, I want to suggest that vagrancy in the eighteenth-century Atlantic world illuminates how race shapes relations to production, accumulation, subsistence, and dispossession before the solidification of "class" as the category of analysis for naming one's relation to the means of production under capitalism: in other words, race is the modality in which primitive accumulation is lived.

For instance, in the early modern period, when Elizabethan poor laws solidify the link between vagrancy and poor relief, and when vagrancy laws first proliferate, the category of "Egyptian" emerges as a form of vagrancy in both law and literary representation, and in their interplay, new racializing legal categories of persons emerge. The anti-Egyptian statutes of the early sixteenth century, which initially target "Gypsies" or "Egyptians" as foreigners marked for expulsion from the nation, shift by the end of the century to laws that target a much broader array of people as "Egyptians," regardless of national origin.[77] When "Egyptian" begins to be increasingly associated with vagrancy in popular representations such as rogue pamphlets as well as in vagrancy statutes, the category comes to signify mobility, performance, behavioral and sartorial difference from norms of "Englishness," and above all, resistance to wage labor—thus drawing powerfully on the tropes of the rogue pamphlet as well as on the established legal category of "vagrant."[78] However, of course, the category "Egyptian" does not therefore lose its associations with ethnicity, national origin, skin color, or the tropes of emerging categories of race, as John Morgan argues: "Rather than solely persecuting any particular ethnic group, 'Egyptian' laws utilized the flexible foundations of what we now might term ethnicity, cultural practice, and origin to enforce an image of 'Englishness' that was amenable to the needs of government and of agricultural labour."[79] And so when the 1598 Vagrancy Act names "counterfeit Egyptians" as one of its many targeted categories (and this category persists in vagrancy statutes throughout the eighteenth century), it both names a group that exceeds any stable notion of ethnic or racial identity while it simultaneously engages a broader discourse that worked out relations to labor through comparative racial tropes.[80]

For example, in his 1646 natural-philosophical treatise *Pseudodoxia Epidemica,* Thomas Browne repeats the 1598 act's designation of "Egyptians" as inherently "counterfeit" when he claims that the Gypsies' dark skin is the result of masquerade, not a sign of fixed bodily difference: "Artificial *Negroes,* or *Gypsies* acquire their complexion by anointing their bodies with Bacon and fat substances, and so exposing them to the Sun."[81] Browne's claim here, that "Gypsy" is a category defined by its artificiality, both voices a common trope about the Gypsy as artificially dark-skinned and relies conceptually on the category of "Negro" to name indelible and ontological difference in complexion. Indeed, the "natural" blackness of Africans and the "counterfeit" blackness of the Gypsies here constitute each other conceptually. Browne invokes the two groups analogically when he names the national origin of the Gypsies a mystery on a par with the cause of Africans' blackness: "Much wonder is it not we are to seek in the original of *AEthiopians* and natural Negroes, being also at a loss concerning the Original of Gypsies and countrfeit Moors."[82] The first remark about Gypsies' artificial skin color in fact occurs only in the context of a chapter on "the Blackness of Negroes"; Browne invokes Gypsies as an "artificial" counterpoint to the "natural" blackness that he figures as indelible, inherited, and springing from some as yet unknown cause (he argues that the cause of African blackness is neither the influence of the sun nor the biblical curse of Cham, but he reaches no definitive explanation).

The comparison implicit in naming Gypsies "Artificial Negroes" thus relies on the prior racial category of "Negro" as a trope of indelibility.[83] Meanwhile, the construction of the "Negro" is, as Cedric Robinson argues, the erasure of African history, knowledge, and civilization in order to create a fiction of brute labor, available for enslavement—this chapter does this quite neatly, in figuring the "Negro" only as an embodied object of contemplation.[84] Furthermore, Browne's reasoning—his arguments in favor of the indelibility of Africans' blackness—relies materially and conceptually on the slave trade and its place in a broader colonial economy. In refuting heliotropic explanations for blackness, Browne asserts that this complexion is unique to Africa, is not widespread among nations that occupy similar latitudes, and does not change when Africans live elsewhere. He is able to make this argument because of colonial accounts of the indigenous peoples of the Americas and because of the slave trade; of America, he remarks that its indigenous inhabitants are not black, even in the tropics, and that "although in many parts thereof there be at present swarms of *Negroes* serving under the *Spaniard,* yet they were all transported from *Africa,* since the discovery of *Columbus.*"[85] The naturalness of the "natural Negro," for Browne, relies on and solidifies the category of "Negro" as both indelible and removable, a stable commodity that retains its identity, value, and knowability through any imaginable dislocation: "For *Negroes* transplanted, although into cold and flegmatick habitations, continue their hue."[86]

Thus, when we consider the racialization of vagrancy in early modern England through the category of the "counterfeit Egyptian," we see that this designation of fraudulence and disguise is a part of a broader conceptual web of race as it emerges through a global, colonial, early capitalist world system. Just as "Negro" names one relation to labor and value, "Gypsy" names another. Since vagrancy is centrally concerned with labor, it is, of course, intimately bound up in the racialized divisions of labor that emerge and transform over the period I study here, and vagrancy remains adaptable to the evolving definition and management of both of these racial categories, among many others.

When Moll Flanders, then, is propelled from a childhood spent among Gypsies to her transformation of dispossession into economic opportunity, finally ending with her ability to enslave others on her Virginia plantation, Defoe's use of the Gypsy as narrative propulsion here makes use of this intertwined, comparative history of differently racialized relations to labor. If, as I argued above, Defoe uses vagrancy in order to exploit its anticipatory charge as a narrative resource to clear the space for Moll's rebirth as a radically self-willed subject, then I want to emphasize here that the overlay of racialized relations to labor also contributes to the work of vagrancy here. Moll's time as a vagrant is spent specifically among Gypsies, and it is through a retrospective speculation that she must have actively rejected the Gypsies that Moll figures her originary act of will. If we read this episode against the backdrop of anti-Egyptian legislation, then we can also read Moll's rejection of the Gypsies as a gesture of integration into an English body politic; her rejection of a category figured as internally foreign aligns national belonging with her acquisition of the parish settlement to which she is not strictly legally entitled. Paradoxically, this gesture lays the narrative groundwork for her transportation; she can be marked for expulsion from the body politic only because she belonged to it in the first place. If the early modern Gypsy, as a racialized trope of foreignness, fraud, and artificiality, is figured through and against the tropes of indelible blackness, then this, too, resonates with the narrative place of slavery in the novel: the enabling condition of Moll's ascension from bound laborer to propertied subject.

If vagrancy is a conceptual and legal category central to the management of labor, the practice of sovereignty, and the prehistory of the modern administrative state, then race and empire are foundational to this category throughout the long eighteenth century, and demand an analysis centered in racial capitalism. This, in turn, can expand our archive even further for understanding the imbrication of literature and print culture in empire in the long eighteenth century. I also want to complicate the narrative that implies that the rise of nineteenth-century scientific racism, with its emphasis on biological determinism, necessarily constitutes a hardening or consolidation of a racism that is only nascent in earlier models that see racial categories as more fluid. A category like vagrancy is fluid and indeterminate, and its racializing work does not always necessarily proceed along axes of absolute racial differentiation or classification; just as frequently (as in the extremely unstable category of "Egyptian") it works precisely by rendering racializing categories variable and open to interpretation. This, however, does not necessarily constitute a weakness in its ability to foster primitive accumulation through racializing dispossession, vulnerability, and violence.[87]

In the archive of vagrancy, writing relates to the materiality of primitive accumulation in various ways—sometimes it enacts the force of law itself, sometimes it adds to the collection of tropes and perceptual moves that constitute police in its capacity to anticipate threat, and sometimes it critiques or eludes these dynamics. In all of these instances, vagrancy sheds historical light on race in its simultaneously ideological, aesthetic, material, and biopolitical registers.

In the dockets of vagrancy arrests in Philadelphia in the early 1790s, we can see the meaning of vagrancy scripted anew and in accumulation, one arrest after another—and we can also track how these instances offer insight into the category's evolving racialization. These early national records disclose the new republic's inheritance of English legal practice; the vagrancy statutes in force in Philadelphia in the 1790s in fact dated from the colonial period.[88] The dockets show astonishing variety in their particular iterations of vagrancy, thus revealing more about the meaning of vagrancy as the category had been adapted first for a colony and then for the new republic. For instance, some reasons listed for vagrancy arrests include: "being an Idle dissolute and Notorious Prostitute" (Catherine Harbour, 7/29/90), "stroling and beging in the streets contrary to Law" (Jon Hazlehurst, 8/3/90), "being a deserter from the Army" (Daniel Calligham, 6/29/91), "committing a Riot at Night" (Phillis, 7/22/1791), "carrying provisions, to the Convicts" (Mary Callingham, 8/2/91), "attempting to sell Pinchbacks Rings for Gold Rings, and of having no visible way of supporting himself" (Andrew Allen, 8/29/91), "being in Bed with a negro Man, and . . . being an Idle and disorderly woman" (Margaret Simonds, 8/29/91), "being Drunk and fighting and disturbing the Peace" (George Carney, 9/9/91), "Running away from her Master" (Susanna, 9/12/91), "Disobeying the Lawfull Commands of her Mistress" (Mary Mooney, 9/10/91), "being found lurking about the Market and giving Contradictory Accounts of himself" (Joseph Kelly, 6/24/90).[89] If the vagrancy statute, as a form, generates these paratactic lists by elaborating on previous versions of these lists, and by seeking to imagine the wide variety of threat these laws might be called upon to contain, the dockets stretch the temporality of this kind of composition. The clerks recording arrests in the dockets continue to add to the statute's miscellany, arrest by arrest, day by day.

Meanwhile, vagrancy enforcement incorporated not only the manuscript practice of record-keeping epitomized by the dockets, but also popular print—and this, too, adds yet another dimension to the racialization of vagrancy. Though Philadelphia's vagrancy statutes themselves do not explicitly mention the apprehension of escapees from slavery or indentured servitude, the frequency of this explanation for arrest in the dockets confirms that fugitivity was central to the meaning of vagrancy in the American colonies and the early United States.[90] It is through fugitivity that vagrancy laws most obviously intersect with American print culture; some entries in the dockets refer explicitly to runaway advertisements. The city jailors themselves also placed advertisements of their own, hoping to assist in the recapture of people suspected of escaping indentured servitude or slavery, and these translations of the dockets into print also further transform the legal purview and meaning of vagrancy—in this case, by consolidating blackness as the sign of suspected fugitivity and thus the proper target for both popular and official surveillance.[91]

Though the dockets record the arrests of both white and black suspected "runaways," the advertisements explicitly target black fugitives and rarely advertise white indentured servants taken up at the same time. For example, on March 8, 1792, the city jailor, Elijah Weed, published a list of fugitives in custody:

> NED, who says he was the property of James Pearce of Caroline County, in the state of Maryland, who sold him to a person unknown: he is about 28 years of age, 5 feet 4 inches high. JOHN, who says he is the property of William Berry of Talbot County, in the state of Maryland: he is about 26 years of age, 5 feet 4 inches high.
>
> THOMAS SMITH, charged with being a runaway slave: he is about 23 years of age, 5 feet high. PETER, who is charged with being the property of Elisha Price of the township of Chester, Delaware County: he is about 38 years of age, 5 feet 5 inches high.
>
> TOBIAS LEACH, who says he is the property of Elias Smith of Salem county, near Chancery: he is about 21 years of age, 5 feet 7 inches high. CATO, he says he is the property of captain Fostor, who sailed from this port about seven months ago: he is about 60 years of age, 5 feet 6 inches high.

> N.B. the masters of the above Negroes, if any they have, are requested to come prove their property and pay charges, otherwise they will be discharged in the space of thirty days according to law.[92]

All of these men except Thomas Smith appear in the Vagrancy Dockets.[93] None of those with no race listed—and thus most likely white—arrested for vagrancy as suspected fugitives from servitude throughout the fall and winter of 1791/92 appear here, however.[94] For instance, on November 3, 1791, Mark Warren was "charged with not giving a good Account of himself and is supposed to be a Runaway" and Margaret Gillanor was "charged with Running away from her Master Samuel Rowans of New Castle," but neither appears in a newspaper advertisement taken out by the jailor.[95] While white "runaways" do appear with some frequency in the Vagrancy Dockets, they are rarely publicized in these advertisements, which suggests that for popular print culture, the criminalized "runaway" was a disproportionately black figure. The practice of vagrancy arrests as listed in the dockets already incorporated the surveillance of blackness into the legal purview of police—and I discuss this at much greater length in Chapter 5—but the form of publicity through which these arrests enter popular print further hardens this association between blackness, threat, and perceived criminality, thus teaching readers what to imagine when they think of the kinds of threats the state ought to protect its citizens from, thereby materially altering the scope of police as a diffuse, undefined, yet distinct category.

This nexus of legal record-keeping and publicly circulating print culture generated and trafficked in a rich array of descriptive practices and tropes as it constructed, improvisationally and anew with every arrest, the notion of threat against which police is oriented. This, in turn, offered rich resources for literary authors to draw on, sometimes toward radically disparate ends. For example, Charles Brockden Brown's portrayal of Philadelphia intersects with the understanding of the city and its denizens elaborated in the records of these contemporary vagrancy arrests. As I discuss in Chapter 4, his novel *Wieland* (1798) draws on the category of vagrancy and the specific genres in which it circulated when constructing the mysterious white drifter, Carwin, as a bearer of terrifyingly unknowable and unpredictable threat. At the same time, however, Brown also figures these legal and law-adjacent print genres as unstable and themselves suspicious: Carwin later appears as the object of an actual runaway advertisement that claims he is an escaped convict, but the advertisement is ultimately revealed to be a fraud, perpetrated by an enemy of Carwin who is even more mysterious than Carwin himself. The racialization of vagrancy in popular print is also transformed in its novelistic redeployment, as Brown takes up the charge of fugitivity implied by the runaway advertisement, but directs it toward an unsettling meditation on the instability of Carwin's whiteness.

Because vagrancy was a deliberately ill-defined category, left open to wide latitude for discretionary and improvisatory variation in enforcement, understanding it requires looking far beyond the letter of the law. By tracing the broader imaginative life of a legal category that the law insistently refused to define, *Vagrant Figures* offers a model for how literary method can produce new histories of race, empire, law, and sovereignty.

## Outline

Chapter 1, "Atlantic Rogues," argues that in the late seventeenth century, vagrancy statutes are in formal conversation with the picaresque novel as both genres begin to circulate transatlantically. Contextualizing Richard Head's 1665 novel *The English Rogue*—widely regarded to be the first picaresque novel written in English—in the rapid expansion of the Atlantic trade in bound servants, I propose a new way of understanding the genre of the picaresque and its relation to the law. Scholars of early modern picaresque and its affiliated genres have long noted that the literary figure of the "rogue and vagabond" circulated in popular print before it became a legal category. However, as vagrancy law, in the late seventeenth century, became an increasingly important tool for the management of impoverished populations and the distribution of these populations' labor across empire, I read picaresque not for the singular figure of the rogue, but for the way the genre's narrative structure allows for the conceptualization of populations and geographies.

Chapter 2, "The Novel and the Sexuality of Vagrancy," turns to the role of vagrancy law in regulating the affective, sexual, reproductive, and domestic lives of the English poor. In this context, I trace vagrancy's appearance at the margins of both the novel and the marriage plot across a series of texts, including Jane Barker's *Patchwork Screen for the Ladies* (1723), Sarah Scott's *Millenium Hall* (1762), and, most centrally, Henry Fielding's *The Female Husband* (1746). Fielding, as novelist, magistrate, and major eighteenth-century theorist of police, is at the center of this chapter, which reads his figuration of vagrancy as a kind of sexuality that disrupts labor-discipline, marriage, and legitimate inheritance. At the same time, Fielding's text and the archival records of policing that surround it reveal how we might take vagrancy as a category of analysis for transgender history, since the construction of the sexed body as metonym for juridical identity developed through a nexus of policing, surveillance, and transatlantic print culture for which vagrancy was a foundational legal category. Finally, through readings of Scott's *Millenium Hall* and Mary Saxby's posthumously published *Memoirs of a Female Vagrant* (1806), I show that literary histories of sexuality look profoundly different if we center the parish rather than the family as our field of analysis.

Chapter 3, "Lyric Population and the Prospects of Police," pursues a new reading of vagrancy in early Romantic poetry. By reading the poetry of Mary Robinson against the backdrop of police reform and vagrancy law at the end of the eighteenth century, I propose that we turn away from lyric or legal subjectivity in order to see other crucial poetic valences of what Celeste Langan has influentially termed "Romantic vagrancy." Robinson not only pushes us to reconsider a literary-historical narrative that has long been dominated by Wordsworth, but also offers an engagement with vagrancy that theorizes law and lyric as intersecting precisely where legal persons and lyric subjects disappear. Tracing how Robinson's collection brings rural English poverty into the same frame as global war, the scandal of destitute Asian sailors stranded in London by the East India Company, the Sierra Leone colonization project, and the role of police reformers in reshaping dockside labor in London, I argue that poetic vagrancy allows us to understand its most iconic recurring image—the dispossession of the rural English poor—as an optic for invoking vast scales and distant populations. Vagrancy's relation to police, especially as a mode of governmentality that spanned scales from local to global, is in fact crucial to its poetic redeployment; the capacity of the legal category to invoke population and scarcity without necessarily entering the realm of legal subjectivity is precisely what renders it a potent vehicle for Robinson's politicized experiments in lyric.

Chapter 4, "Settler Vagrancy," examines the legal and imaginative specificity of vagrancy law and its relation to land in North America. By reading Charles Brockden Brown's novels *Wieland* (1798) and *Edgar Huntly* (1799)—both long regarded as crucial and ambivalent meditations on the viability of the new American republic—alongside archival records of vagrancy arrests in Philadelphia in the 1790s, I show how the emergent category of nationally distinct American whiteness relied on figures of mobility through the frontier, yet remained uncomfortably difficult to distinguish from the criminalized (and often differently racialized) category of vagrancy. Through a reading of the startling prominence of literary history in the landmark 1972 Supreme Court case *Papachristou v. City of Jacksonville,* which struck down vagrancy laws as unconstitutional, I argue that a particularly potent literary afterlife of the figure of the vagrant rendered this figure a symbol of free, white settler mobility.

Chapter 5, "Surveillance and Black Life in Equiano's Atlantic," argues that Olaudah Equiano's *Interesting Narrative* (1789) critically resignifies some of the crucial narrative and formal tropes of vagrancy in order to articulate blackness as vulnerability to unpredictable violence under the purview of police—while also offering a critique of surveillance that exceeds the terms of the text's dominant investment in juridically recognized personhood as self-possession. Equiano theorizes police and blackness through his own wide-ranging mobility; it is his travel, especially around the Atlantic world, that allows him to aggregate a series of sudden, violent, and unpredictable encounters into something resembling a system. He rhetorically occupies much of the legal position named by "vagrant" except its naming of threat; he does not portray himself as a perpetrator of future unknowable harm, but instead, in his most powerful reversal of vagrancy's optic, places that capacity for threat in the world around him, and especially in the violence of police. Only by reading for vagrancy's narrative and legal forms, for its recurring figures, I argue, can we understand this text as part of vagrancy's legal and cultural archive—and as a crucial critique of the presumed legitimacy of police.

In a brief Coda, I read George L. Kelling and James Q. Wilson's enormously influential article "Broken Windows: The Police and

Neighborhood Safety" (1982) as a remarkably politically successful redeployment of the tropes of eighteenth-century vagrancy. This article, I argue, both draws on and occludes the prehistory of the police; Kelling and Wilson rely significantly on early histories of policing—in particular, the history of vagrancy law—while at the same time, they push their readers insistently away from historical modes of thought. Through my reading of this text, much of whose political influence relies on the persuasive success of its master metaphors, I propose that reading methods of literary history can offer unique critical insights into the deep histories still animating contemporary theorizations of policing.

# *CHAPTER ONE*

# ATLANTIC ROGUES

This seems like how we'd expect to find literary vagrants: early in Richard Head's *The English Rogue* (1665), our picaro Meriton Latroon finds himself without money and tries his hand at begging. He and his temporary begging-companion are "surprized by the Constable, as two sturdy Vagrants; and as *handsail* to my new Trade, we were both soundly whipt out of town."[1] The constable is not the only one to regard them as unwelcome threats: "Travellers observing our garb, countenances, and weapon, which was a battoon, suspecting us, would before they came near us, set spurs to their horses, and ride as if the devil drove them" (38). Their obvious poverty (evident in their "garb" and "countenances") as well as their actions (wandering from their established homes and begging) mark them as vagrants according to both the law and popular representation. Latroon offers himself as proof that poverty must necessarily lead to disorder and criminality: "Necessity is a thing better known by the effects, than its character; and of all things the most insufferable: to prevent which, it puts a man on to venture upon all manner of dishonest and dangerous actions, suggesting strange imaginations, and desperate resolutions, solliciting things infamous, and attempting things impossible;

the product of which is onely disorder, confusion, shame, and in the end ruine" (36).[2] Echoing the established conventions of the early modern cony-catching pamphlet, which, as Craig Dionne and Steve Mentz argue, "reshaped the image of the unfortunate vagabond into a willing and stealthy member of a vast criminal network," Latroon includes this episode in a long career of theft, fraud, assault, and other crimes, as he joins many successive loose confederations of rogues: a band of "Gypsies," an association of female highwaymen, a secret society of thieves.[3]

But one ending to this chapter—included in Henry Marsh's 1665 edition but cut from Francis Kirkman's 1666 edition—complicates any attempt to identify Latroon so easily with the legal category of vagrancy. On the road, they encounter a cart transporting a group of beggars who are counterfeiting disabilities (an accusation ubiquitous in early modern rogue pamphlets), "some predendedly blind, others their leggs tied up in a string."[4] When he asks them where they are going, they answer that they have all been whipped and that they "now enjoy the benefit of a Pass"—that is, they are now being sent to their places of legal settlement, indicated on official passes as mandated by vagrancy legislation of 1662.[5] When an acquaintance of the carter asks *him* where he is headed, he replies he is going to a town called Killum. The "carted crew," hearing the unfamiliar name and thinking they're going to be killed, are terrified. Latroon watches them all start to run away, and invites his reader to join him in laughing at the spectacle: "The blind could see their way down too, the Paralitick could run as swift as a Stag."[6] While Latroon begins this chapter in precisely the same position as the "carted crew"—whipped and expelled from town for vagrancy—and enacts the criminality that was attributed to the itinerant poor to justify their summary punishment, he ends it as the amused observer of the law's operation on others. In drawing amusement from the revelation of false disability, Latroon aligns himself with the authors of rogue pamphlets—which often characterized beggars as uniformly fraudulent and offered their tricks up for the readers' entertainment—and with the authors of the vagrancy laws that enshrined these assumptions as central to both poor relief and crime control.

Meriton Latroon is identified by the book's title as a "rogue," but how much can this figure, and other picaresque figures like him, illuminate about the legal category of vagrancy? The early modern literary and legal histories of the rogue intertwine, but I argue that *The English Rogue* reveals that their relationship was far more contradictory, tentative, and uneven than it appears. In *The London Hanged,* Peter Linebaugh chose the memorable term "picaresque proletarian" to describe the populations most targeted by eighteenth-century criminal justice.[7] Linebaugh goes on to insist on "the contradiction between the individualism of picaresque *presentation* and the collectivism of proletarian *experience,*" and certainly does not take the picaro as a straightforward representation of any historical population.[8] However, the category of analysis remains the picaro, and the question is the degree to which literary and historical rogues match up. More recent literary-critical work on rogue narratives has also taken up this question, revealing that sources like rogue pamphlets are more imaginative than documentary, and thus ought to be approached as sources for literary history but not as documents that illuminate much about the lives of actual people labeled "rogues."[9] What happens, however, when we look beyond the rogue as our central category of analysis? Where else might we see vagrancy in the picaresque novel?

*The English Rogue* is often regarded as the first English picaresque, and it certainly announces itself as such, the title echoing James Mabbe's popular 1622 English translation of Mateo Alemán's *Guzmán de Alfarache* under the title *The Rogue.*[10] The Englishness of *The English Rogue* is emphasized in the preface, which uneasily seeks to defend its status as original and not simply derivative:

> Some may say, That this is but . . . a Collection out of *Guzman, Boscon,* or some others who have writ upon this subject. . . . As if we could not produce an *English Rogue* of our *own,* without being beholding to other *Nations* for him. I will not say that he durst vye with either an *Italian, Spanish,* or *French Rogue;* but having been *steept* for some years in an *Irish Bogg,* that hath added so much to his *Rogueships perfection,* that he out-did them all by outdoing one, and that was a *Scot.* (A4r–v)

The text does in fact lift substantial passages from Alemán and other authors, but as Barbara Fuchs argues, such piracy of Spanish texts was often refigured as virtuous colonial plunder that paradoxically aggrandizes the belatedness of England's entry onto the imperial world stage.[11] Indeed, as the preface insists, it is the rogue's colonial adventures—steeping in an Irish bog—that qualify him to out-rogue his continental predecessors.

Above all, this text and its immense popularity helped transform the longstanding legal and cultural category of "rogue" into a generic marker for the picaresque in English. Picaresque fiction had circulated in England since *Lazarillo de Tormes* was first translated into English in 1576.[12] Mabbe's 1622 translation of *Guzmán de Alfarache* further popularized the genre.[13] Picking up on Mabbe's new title for *Alfarache, The English Rogue* combines the European picaresque with the existing genre of the rogue pamphlet: the very genre from which the legal category of "rogue" had first emerged. As Kathleen Pories has documented, popular pamphlets such as John Awdeley's *Fraternity of Vagabonds* (1561) and Thomas Harman's *Caveat for Common Cursetors* (1567) figure the vagrant poor as a criminal confederation of "rogues," a term that subsequently enters vagrancy law in 1572.[14] The early modern rogue pamphlet consolidates "rogue" as a category of self-evidently undeserving and criminal poor, linked by hidden networks of common cant, counterstructures of governance, and shared repertoires of tricks.[15] This image, as Patricia Fumerton argues, stood in stark contrast to the historical conditions of early modern vagrancy; while authors like Harman imagine a culturally cohesive underworld populated by a distinct class of people, the condition of impoverished itinerancy was in fact one that much of the early modern English population drifted in and out of as their economic fortunes fluctuated.[16]

*The English Rogue,* meanwhile, affixes the rogue to the picaresque—a genre that elaborates on the episodic pleasures of the rogue pamphlet. Leah Orr calls the novel "one of the most reprinted and imitated works of fiction from the late seventeenth century."[17] The publication of *The English Rogue* and its many subsequent continuations and abridgments also inspired a series of imitators that followed the same titling convention: *The French Rogue, The Irish Rogue, The Dutch Rogue.*[18] By 1685, the English title of *Guzmán de Alfarache* had changed from *The Rogue* to *The Spanish Rogue,* falling in line with the titling convention established here.[19] As a text that profoundly shaped the reception of the picaresque in England in the late seventeenth century, *The English Rogue* is thus an ideal text for investigating how the legal category of "rogue" interacted with the literary genre with which the "rogue" was associated.

However, while early modern vagrancy laws rendered "rogue" a criminalized category of social marginality, the afterlife of the literary rogue also invoked forces that were far from marginal. As Srinivas Aravamudan has argued, the imaginative figure of the rogue in the long eighteenth century articulated not only marginality and dispossession, but also the rapacious, expansive mobility of global capitalism: "What we witness in the seventeenth and eighteenth centuries is the rise of something like rogue capitalism, the daily swindling and conniving that takes place in multiple creative ways alongside notions of political domination and subjection through force or fraud."[20]

This tension animates *The English Rogue.* Betty Joseph has recently argued that the novel's rogue protagonist, Meriton Latroon, "mak[es] visible an analogy between masterless men and mercantile exchange," as he ends his circulation through criminal underworlds by establishing himself as an ideal economic subject of empire.[21] As she argues, Latroon's adventures in Asia, together with his appropriation of his Indian wife's economic agency, "produces surplus accumulation for a dispossessed rogue and transforms him into a white, Christian male of property like his historical successor, Robinson Crusoe."[22] Scholarship of the early novel has long built on Lennard Davis's observation that "without the appearance of the whore, the rogue, the cutpurse, the cheat, the thief, or the outsider it would be impossible to imagine the genre of the novel."[23] In *How Novels Think,* Nancy Armstrong argues that the literary outlaw "generate[d] expressions of excessive individualism that simultaneously detached the individual from a restrictive social category and made it possible for him or her to become more fully a citizen-subject, thus the judge and governor of others."[24]

Latroon's story certainly enacts this trajectory from rogue to mercantile adventurer and proto-sovereign. *The English Rogue* follows Meriton Latroon from his birth in Ireland (though he takes pains to note he was conceived in England) and his childhood flight with his mother back to England after an Irish rebellion, to his life as a refractory child, runaway, and increasingly itinerant and disreputable young man. In typical picaresque fashion, he tricks others, sometimes quite cruelly, and is tricked and betrayed in turn; he gains fortunes and loses them; he indulges bodily pleasures and endures pain, starvation, and degradation; he attracts occasional friends, mistresses, and employers but never remains in any one station, profession, relationship, or place for long. After an extended series of increasingly criminal escapades and several stints in Newgate, a sentence of transportation launches him into the wider world; his ship springs a leak en route to Virginia, and he is rescued and brought to the Canary Islands. There, he joins a Spanish crew bound for the East Indies, but is taken by a Turkish galley and sold into slavery, from which he promptly escapes and makes his way to Malabar, where he ends the novel in the nominally penitent prosperity that would be echoed later and more famously by Moll Flanders.

The narrative pull of Latroon's story—which is also the pull of literary history—may be a pull toward the outlaw protagonist and the eighteenth-century novel, but it is also a pull away from the legal regimes that the figure of the "rogue" helped construct, and whose subtler resonances with the picaresque I trace here: the carceral foundations of poor relief, the imbrication of local policing in colonial policy, and the centrality of emerging theories of population to seventeenth-century approaches to vagrancy. And so I read this novel somewhat perversely, as I focus on what exists at the margins of the narrative: the unnamed minor characters who repeatedly disappear, the many women and children Latroon discards as waste, and the rapidly expanding Atlantic market in bound labor from which Latroon is repeatedly spared. By tracing the novel's portrayal of "spiriting"—the illicit, coerced recruitment of indentured laborers for the American colonies—I show how the novel ultimately cannot separate roguery from police. Latroon appears as both a target of spirits and as a spirit himself, placing the "rogue" on both sides of the illicit trade. Meanwhile, spiriting, as an object of both legal and literary concern throughout the Restoration, threatens to blur the lines between roguery and legitimate colonial policy. By reading for population rather than the picaro alone, we can see how this novel engages vagrancy by invoking not only the singular, itinerant rogue, but also the global scope of population management with which late seventeenth-century vagrancy law was increasingly concerned.

## Eating Shit with Meriton Latroon: Waste, Value, Surplus

Perhaps the most obvious connection between vagrancy and the picaresque is physical mobility: the narrative structure of picaresque follows a character through structurally unanticipated and wayward movement, subject to chaotic forces of whim, economic boom and bust, contingent and temporary relationships, and the occasional and unsystematic intervention of the law. Vagrancy law, however, was never about mobility alone. As Anne Middleton reminds us in her analysis of the 1388 Statute of Laborers, vagrancy was "from the outset a highly overdetermined discourse."[25] Middleton's account of medieval vagrancy law identifies its central aim as the imposition of social intelligibility through "documentary fixity and accountability, a project of textualizing and authorizing identity."[26] Meanwhile, the proliferation of sixteenth-century vagrancy legislation that largely laid the groundwork for English poor law until the New Poor Law of 1834 targeted some forms of mobility alongside many other behaviors seen as signals of idleness and disorder.[27] The vagrancy law of 1598, for instance, targets a long list of people including "Seafaring men pretending losses of their ships or goods on the Sea," fortune-tellers, unauthorized performers, "counterfeite Egyptians," and "common Labourers, being persons able in body, using Loytering, and refusing to worke."[28] If early modern vagrancy law can be said to have a central target, that target is not mobility, but the perceived refusal to work. The 1598 act, after all, certainly names "wandering" a number of times, but always in conjunction with some other behavior taken as a sign of the refusal of legitimate labor: begging, unauthorized theatrical performance, imposture, or simple unemployment.

It is for this reason that early modern English vagrancy law is so central to Marx's discussion of primitive accumulation in *Capital,* volume 1. Here, he famously argues that the first early modern wave of enclosures "was of great assistance . . . in 'setting free' the agricultural population as a proletariat for the needs of industry."[29] They were, Marx narrates, "turned in massive quantities into beggars, robbers and vagabonds," and then targeted by vagrancy legislation that "treated them as 'voluntary' criminals, and assumed that it was entirely within their powers to go on working under the old conditions that in fact no longer existed."[30] This discussion of primitive accumulation, of course, offers Marx an opportunity to explain how capitalists historically ended up with the capital necessary to purchase the labor-power of others, and how laborers had no choice but to sell their labor to survive. But it also does something else: it expands his earlier discussion of pauperism, population, and their theorization by political economists of the eighteenth century—particularly

Malthus. In Chapter 25, "The General Law of Capitalist Accumulation," Marx argues that when Malthus figures poverty and premature death as nature's check on population, whose increase must inevitably outstrip the food supply, he obscures and naturalizes the operation of capitalist accumulation, which in fact *produces* surplus population alongside surplus value. Pauperism, for Marx, is not the result of the simple refusal to work, nor is it the pressure of "nature" against the limits of production; instead, it is the direct result of capitalist accumulation, which invests an ever-greater proportion of surplus value in the means of production and an ever-decreasing proportion in labor. He argues, therefore, that surplus population is not a limit case of wage labor, but its enabling condition: "The relative surplus population is therefore the background against which the law of the demand and supply of labour does its work."[31]

Early modern vagrancy law, in this view, is far less concerned with the criminalization of wayward and mobile individuals than with the management of surplus population. These laws often draw on the *story* of the wayward, itinerant rogue to justify their necessity. But what Marx pushes us to do here, especially in his reading of eighteenth-century theories of population, is to understand vagrancy in the context of relative surplus population and its relation to wage labor. Of course, seventeenth-century political economists were not Malthusian in their views of population and labor; generally, they believed the opposite: that population was a national resource whose growth ought to be encouraged in order to ensure national economic expansion and military strength. But those regarded as surplus—those people who did not seem to be contributing their labor to the national interest and who therefore were withholding the benefits that population was supposed to offer the nation—were still regarded as a serious problem.

By the mid-seventeenth century, both vagrancy law and political-economic stances toward vagrancy were shifting significantly. Vagrancy had been a potent political concern since the earliest waves of enclosures in the sixteenth century, but as Ted McCormick argues, the seventeenth century saw "the construction of population as an abstract totality crucial to national wealth and strength," which placed vagrancy squarely in a new realm of thought: "the distribution of the king's subjects as a whole."[32] No longer simply signaling the problem of potential disorder, vagrancy now began to name the misallocation of the nation's laboring population. Political economists debated the significance of the people William Petty referred to as "supernumeraries," asking how these people might be put back into profitable economic circulation. Petty, in his 1662 *Treatise of Taxes and Contributions*, opposed the criminalization of begging and argued instead for the use of state revenue to employ the poor in infrastructural public works, which would in turn assist in the expansion of England's commercial empire, as when he argues that the "employing the Beggars in *England* about mending the High-wayes, and making Rivers Navigable will make the Wool and Cattle of *Ireland* vend the better."[33] Others, meanwhile, favored a more directly punitive avenue to extracting economic value from the unemployed and impoverished, such as John Locke's failed proposal to the Board of Trade in 1697 to overhaul vagrancy laws and employ all male vagrants capable of work either on ships or in English plantations in the Americas.[34]

Read in the context of seventeenth-century political economy, *The English Rogue* offers us an opportunity to rethink vagrancy. We've long thought of picaresque as being fundamentally structured by physical movement, and this novel is no exception: each narrative episode tends to be bound by location and ends when Latroon moves on to the next place and the next adventure. However, I also want to think about this narrative rhythm in other terms: a cycle of extraction in which value is produced and waste is discarded. For many political economists, vagrancy signaled the waste of potential labor-power and the misallocation of surplus populations from whom value might be recouped. The structure of *The English Rogue* yokes the mobility of the picaro to a recurring cycle of accumulation and disposal, in which the political-economic problem of waste, surplus, and value becomes an engine for the production of entertainment—and of a vast population of characters whose only value is their very disposability.

For instance, toward the beginning of the novel, Latroon falls in with a crowd of "Gypsies"—a category criminalized under vagrancy law. He participates in a series of schemes and indulges a variety of pleasures in their company, all of which is presented as a collective endeavor: "For like wilde foul we flie one after another, and though we are scattered like the Quarters of a Traytor, yet like water when cut with a Sword, we easily come together again" (22). However, he quickly wearies of life among the "Gypsies" and both he and the narrative discard them. First, however, he offers the reader a bit of value extracted from them, in the form of a brief canting dictionary: "By this means I grew weary of their practices, and therefore resolved to desert them as soon as the first opportunity should offer it self, which was in a short time; wherefore at the present I shall say no more of them, onely give me leave to give some small account of their Language" (29). The canting dictionary is then presented as an item of value and interest to the reader, extracted from a criminalized population who are then narratively discarded: the chapter ends, and a new episode begins.

The novel's scatological humor draws attention to the interplay between waste and value, as it repeatedly transforms literal excrement into a renewable resource for comedy. As a child, for instance, Latroon wreaks revenge on his schoolmaster for whipping him by means of "a very *shitten trick,* which put him into a *stinking condition;* for having made myself laxative, on purpose squirted into his face upon the first lash given" (15). Sometimes, of course, Latroon is the butt of the same joke, such as when he is surprised by intruders while in bed with one of his mistresses, and is forced to then wear her clothing due to "the stinking condition that the fear had put [him] in" (90). This also serves to advance Latroon to his next adventure and generate more bawdy entertainment for the reader, as he uses this disguise to gain admittance to a boarding school, where he goes on to seduce his bedfellows.

One episode in particular self-consciously highlights the interplay between subsistence, accumulation, extraction, and disposal from which the novel draws much of its narrative motion and charge. After escaping his creditors and running off to Ireland, Latroon finds himself destitute and starving, until he by chance finds a coin. He asks the proprietor of a victualing-house for "any thing which was eatable, as far as a groat would go" (65). After eating, he is about to pay when he drops the coin, and as he sees it precariously perched at the edge of one of the many holes in the floor, the terror of this sight produces its usual effects: "What with hast to recover it, and the fright the danger put me into, I discharged myself of every bit I had eaten" (65). Instead of producing a foul spectacle, however, the waste here is strangely indistinguishable from its previous incarnation:

> There was no body could say, I had fouled my Breeches, or that I stunk; which I made appear to my Landlady by showing her what I had evacuated, but little differing from what I had eaten a quarter of an hour before. The good old woman perswaded me strongly to eat it again; for said she, it cannot be much the worse for just passing through you, and I will frye it if you please. (65)

The landlady here grotesquely reproduces the narrative logic at play here: shit circulates endlessly and yet can produce humor anew each time, and the rogue's body becomes a force that generates value by recirculating waste.

As Emily Cockayne vividly documents, seventeenth- and eighteenth-century Londoners lived amid a sensory cacophony of waste produced by the city's ballooning population and commercial trade. The forms of waste that traversed the everyday—the smell of open sewers, the noise of vendors' cries, the diseases spread by the byproducts of butchers and tanners—were often rhetorically conflated with the impoverished people who also flocked to London from the countryside but who were not enriched by this concentration of commercial activity; beggars and prostitutes encountered in the streets are constantly described as "swarms," or imagined as part and parcel with the filth that surrounded them.[35] As Sophie Gee argues in *Making Waste,* "a glut of waste matter fills the pages of eighteenth-century literature," articulating debates that "engaged with the troublesome relationship of waste to value."[36] The category of "waste," Gee argues, conflated disparate categories of people and things that were regarded as filth, excrement, and obstruction, but that could also generate or signify value. She notes, for instance, that in the *Fable of the Bees,* Mandeville describes both dunghills and beggars as the inevitable byproduct of the growth of trade, and thus they serve ironically as signs of wealth.[37] When the landlady remarks that her food has passed through Meriton so quickly that it could be eaten again, she draws comical and visceral attention to its repulsiveness and to the actual impossibility of reversing the excremental process, while at the same time satirically voicing the political-economic logic that recuperates waste as the source of another kind of value.

Indeed, in *The English Rogue,* waste and value can be disorientingly indistinguishable. When Latroon concludes the novel with his account of penitence, he cheekily apologizes for the bawdiness and immorality that are the novel's most obvious selling points by characterizing the novel itself as bodily waste that produces value for the reader: "If I have in any place transgrest the bounds of modesty by loose expressions, you need not fear to be offended with their unsavoury breath, for I have perfumed it: but if it should chance to stink, it is only to drive you from my former inclination and conversation" (129).

In *The English Rogue,* excremental humor is only the most literal staging of the genre's central paradox: everything and everyone the novel casts off as waste produces precisely the novelty and unpredictability that is its most profitable source of entertainment value. Pulling off a cheat and fleeing the consequences or simply leaving a companion behind: these are the necessary preconditions for a new adventure to begin. Of course, as the picaro, Latroon is never discarded from the narrative. Alex Woloch has argued that in a novel's economy of attention, it is the disparity between the ability of major and minor characters to hold sustained attention that in fact shapes narrative itself.[38] Thus, in his "labor theory of character," minor characters become "*the proletariat of the novel*"; they offer their marginality as a kind of alienated narrative labor in service of the novel's form.[39] The most important thing that minor characters do, for Woloch, is disappear: "What we remember about the character is never detached from how the text, for the most part, makes us forget him."[40] The characters discarded from *The English Rogue* are, to take Woloch's analogy back historically from the nineteenth-century novels that form the basis for his argument, less this novel's proletariat than they are its relative surplus population. By offering themselves up to be tricked, seduced, robbed, or simply left behind when the narrative moves on, they offer Latroon fodder for his roguishness—you can't be a rogue if you have nobody to trick, after all. The nearly uniformly unnamed minor characters of *The English Rogue* aren't even exploited for their narrative labor in keeping the plot going (as in, say, Woloch's reading of Dickens); instead, they exist simply to be discarded, and the text recoups narrative value from their disposal and their disposability.

Indeed, some of those who disappear most spectacularly are simultaneously figured as Latroon's bodily waste: his unwanted children and the women who carry them. Embodying Charles D'Avenant's claim that the American colonies grow from "what was here thought an Excrescence in the Body Politic," Latroon discards a series of women to seventeenth-century

England's most potent imaginative sink for surplus population.[41] The first of these unnamed women prompts Meriton's reflection on reproduction as the generation of waste, as the news of her pregnancy inspires his regret: "Then did I begin to consider what a vast charge, and how many various troubles this momentary lecherous pleasure draws upon a man: how furiously he is upon the outset, and how quickly satisfied, loathing that Object he a little before longed for" (67). Here, the "Object . . . before longed for" (sexual gratification) is transformed through its bodily indulgence into repulsive waste (an expensive child). This is precisely the structure of the victualing-house episode, when Meriton's attempt to stave off hunger results only in the most ephemeral satisfaction and ultimately, the production of waste.

After considering "how to be rid both of Cow and Calf," he devises a plot (67). He tells her that he plans to go to Virginia and asks her to go with him. When she's on the ship, he tells her he's forgotten something on shore, and returns to the docks just as the ship sails. While this trick instigates his momentary remorse—as he remarks, "I was much troubled at what I had done so hardheartedly and cruelly"—he also repeats this trick multiple times, as he reports matter-of-factly:

> In three years that I lived as a Mr. I had nine illegitimates, which I knew, four whereof were begotten by my Maids, which put me to a vast expence. Two of the Mothers would have forced me to have married them, or allowed them competent maintenance (for they were subtil cunning baggages) had I not by a wile got them aboard a Vessel bound for *Virginia,* and never heard of them since. (36)

Meriton's cast-off mistresses and children cannot be used again for the same purpose, but in their transformation into waste, they become that "excrescence in the body politic" whose repurposing as colonial labor is praised by D'Avenant. These scenes constitute a sense of Latroon's body not as waste itself, but as a narrative force that puts waste into profitable circulation.

## Spirited Away

In imagining Virginia as the ideal sink for troublesome surplus population, Latroon voices a common Restoration political-economic sentiment. The fates of these women, as they drop out of the novel and into the

Atlantic labor market, point us toward the importance of vagrancy law and surplus population in both colonial settlement and the overall management of population.

Josiah Child's *The Nature of Plantations, and their Consequences to Great Britain, Seriously Considered* (1669) defends the colonization of the Americas from charges that the colonies depopulate the metropole:

> Virginia *and* Barbadoes *were first peopled by a loose sort of vagrant People,* vicious and destitute of Means to live at Home, (being either unfit for Labour, or such as could find none to employ themselves about, or had so misbehaved themselves by Whoring, Thieving, or other Debauchery, that none would set them on Work), which Merchants, and Masters of Ships by their Agents (or Spirits as they were called), gathered up about the Streets of *London,* and other Places, cloathed and transported, to be employed upon Plantations; and these I say were such, as had there been no *English* Foreign Plantation in the World, could probably never have lived at Home to do Service for their Country, but must have come to be hanged or starved, or died untimely of some of those miserable Diseases that proceed from Want, and Vice. . . .[42]

In other words, the emerging plantation system of the seventeenth century and its insatiable demand for labor did not, as some critics maintained, siphon off a potentially productive English population; instead, Child argues, these colonies are the only place where criminalized surplus populations are likely to survive at all, let alone produce value. While the story Child tells here is rather unsavory—the "spiriting" of people away to the colonies sowed both fear and political controversy in the late seventeenth century—Child nonetheless promotes the American colonies as a vent for surplus population, and the Atlantic labor market as intimately imbricated in the most quotidian local practices of English poor relief, labor regulation, and policing.

The seventeenth-century figuration of population as a national resource necessarily implicated vagrancy in the question of colonial expansion and global trade. As Abigail Swingen argues, domestic labor regulation, vagrancy, and population were all crucial to seventeenth-century colonial expansion in the Atlantic world. Throughout the century, the American colonies were promoted as the ideal destination for the vagrant, poor, and unemployed of England.[43] From the beginning,

English colonies in the Americas imported vagrants and convicts from England to augment their labor forces, though the expansion of the American colonies over the course of the seventeenth century also provoked critique from those who feared that the growing demand for colonial labor would drain England's productive population.[44]

In the late seventeenth century, vagrancy and the Atlantic labor market were intertwined both legally and imaginatively, and vagrancy law firmly linked global markets to local management of migration. Charles II's "Act for the Better Releife of the Poore"—commonly known as the Settlement Act of 1662—reflects this fundamental reorientation of vagrancy around the management of population, migration, and colonial labor sources. It introduced what would be a major feature of vagrancy law until the New Poor Law of 1834: documentary proof of legal settlement, which indicates the parish responsible for its residents' poor relief. The 1662 act was also a response to the massive internal migration to London from the countryside, which taxed London's poor relief system.[45] As Alison Games documents, this migration over the course of the early seventeenth century also fueled the migration of the poor from London to the American colonies, which, she argues, "secured England's precarious Atlantic empire in New England, the Chesapeake, and the Caribbean."[46] Indeed, the Settlement Act also explicitly links internal and colonial migration, noting that "it shall and may be lawfull for the Justices of Peace in any of the Counties of England and Wales in theire Quarter Sessions assembled or the major part of them to transport or cause to be transported such Rogues Vagabonds and Sturdy Beggars as shall be duly convicted and adjudged to be incorrigible to any of the English Plantac[i]ons beyond the Seas."[47] No avenue for funding this transportation is detailed in the act, and until 1718 convict transportation was privately arranged and thus both expensive and complicated.[48] For this reason, while seventeenth-century vagrants—especially orphaned children—were sometimes sent to the colonies, this was not the fate of the vast majority of those arrested for vagrancy at the time.[49]

However, the idea was durable, and it circulated where the idea of vagrancy did. The 1666 edition of Michael Dalton's *Countrey Justice*, a popular manual for JPs, makes sure to note that justices are legally empowered "to transport convicted Rogues, Vagabonds, and sturdy Beggars to

English Plantations beyond the Seas."[50] Colonial governors in Barbados and Jamaica circulated proposals to expand vagrant transportation as they petitioned the Crown for more servants to fill the booming sugar industry's need for labor as well as secure recently acquired colonies like Jamaica against the dual threats of foreign invasion and slave rebellion.[51]

Vagrancy, in the seventeenth century, was embedded in broader mercantile concerns about the proper allocation and employment of the nation's population. In this context, the concept of police could emerge as a legal realm that made global markets and flows of migration a matter for local municipal control. At the same time, the project of putting surplus populations back into profitable circulation could resemble the very roguery that vagrancy laws claimed to target. Nowhere is this more apparent than in the seventeenth-century scandal of "spiriting"—which also offers the backdrop for *The English Rogue*'s most extended meditation on the Atlantic world.

Wandering through London, Latroon is accosted by a man he instantly perceives to be a spirit: someone who profits from tricking the poor into indentured servitude in the Americas. Latroon differentiates himself from the more credulous targets; as the spirit promises to solve his financial woes, Latroon resolves to outfox the spirit and cheat him somehow: "my aim . . . was to understand the drift of this Rogue, and then endeavour to get what I could from him" (4). Pretending to believe the spirit, Latroon thus enters his clutches and offers up the spirit's tricks for entertainment, leading the reader on a tour of an underworld that was the object of scandal, rumor, and occasional prosecutions throughout the Restoration. Throughout the seventeenth century, as the flood of poor and unemployed migrating to London found themselves vulnerable to being sent to the Americas, spiriting circulated as a particularly frightening and scandalous mechanism of colonial relocation. From Head to Defoe, fictional plots hinged on spiriting, and the notion that the servant trade to the Americas relied on kidnapping, made the colonies—especially the Caribbean colonies—an increasingly unattractive destination for poor prospective settlers.[52]

However, as this episode reveals, the line between nominally criminal spiriting and legitimate colonial policy was not always clear. Until the 1718 Transportation Act, for example, convict transportation was carried out not by the state directly, but by private merchants involved in the servant trade.[53] Josiah Child, in praising the expulsion of vagrants to the colonies as good population-management policy, uses the term "spirit" to describe the agents of merchants who accomplished what he lauds as the beneficent task of saving surplus populations from the gallows by repurposing them as useful laborers.

As *The English Rogue* makes vividly clear, those who are discarded from the body politic as and alongside waste are most immediately vulnerable to spiriting. The spirit brings Latroon to a house in Wapping, and ushers him into "a Room where six or seven were all smoaking. They smoak'd out of their mouthes like a Chimney that belongs to a Brewers Stokehole . . ." (2). Here, multiple kinds of filth and waste—smoke, dirt, insects—are narratively crowded into the scene with an unnamed and indistinctly described collection of people discarded from the city's labor market before they ended up here. That night, Latroon doesn't sleep "for the innumerable quantity of *Buggs* (as some call them) that had *invaded* my Body. . . . It might have been a good *Quere,* whether those sheets had ever been washt since their weaving, and continualy since imploy'd by whores and bawds successively, to sweat out their contagious humours, and matter proceeding from their ulcerated Bodies" (5). Here, filth is a byproduct of commercial sexual transaction, and the residue of that transaction then attaches to the body of the rogue as he is warehoused before his own intended circulation as a valuable waste-product: the "excrescence of the body politic" about to be recirculated as colonial labor. The aggregation of humanity and bodily waste here echoes his earlier description of a prison: "Here you may see one Weeping, another Singing; one Sleeping, another Swearing; every one variously imployed; one Eating in a corner, and another Pissing just by him; another Lowsing himself between both" (75).

At the same time, however, spiriting is also portrayed here as a kind of roguery: precisely the kind of fraud that cony-catching pamphlets promise to warn their readers about. When Latroon first sees the spirit, the lines between rogue and spirit are hopelessly blurred:

> I have wondred often why Dogs will bark so incessantly at the sight of a Tinker, Pedlar, Tom-a-Bedlam, nay, any suspitious fellow, till I found it my

> self by experience, that by a natural instinct, they know the scent of a Rogue. And so it appears by smelling out a *Spirit,* who perceiving my idle, loytering motion, accosted me. Well may he be called a *Spirit,* since his nature is like the Devils, to seduce any he meets withal, whom he can perswade with allurements, and deluding falsities to his purpose. (1)

Latroon likens himself to the dogs that bark at the sight of tinkers and peddlers (in other words, vagrants); he and the dogs "know the scent of a Rogue," and he immediately perceives the spirit as such. But the spirit, at the same time, is performing his own appraisal, and he recognizes Latroon's "idle, loytering motion" as an equally clear signal: that Latroon is among the mass of migrant, unemployed, and desperate people who are ideal targets for spiriting. The encounter between Latroon and the spirit is framed as a confrontation between equals; both men are practiced dissemblers, and Latroon willingly engages the spirit in order to stage a kind of battle between rogues: "I could not but smile to my self to hear how this Rascal dissembled; not discovering my thoughts, I willingly went with him to drink, resolving to see what the event would be" (2).

The basic outlines of this episode were familiar, traversing literary and legal accounts. In 1671, King's Bench judge Sir William Morton collected a series of depositions regarding spiriting.[54] These stories follow a familiar plot: the spirit offers friendship or hospitality in ways that readers are expected to immediately mark as suspicious. Thomas Stone, for instance, testifies that William Haverland "came behind him, and touched him on his shoulder, and called him Countryman."[55] Stone signals his immediate suspicion, answering that he did not know Haverland, and the affidavit explicitly positions Haverland's response as fraud; when Stone says he is from Wiltshire, "the said Haverland pretended himselfe to be of the same Country."[56] He invites Stone to drink with him and delivers the drunk man to the captain of a ship. Potential victims, like good readers of cony-catching pamphlets, portray themselves as savvy to the well-known tricks of spirits. Joshua Pretty testifies that three men invited him to drink with them and promised money and tobacco if he'd agree to go to Jamaica. They beat him when he refuses, "apprehending them to bee Spirits."[57] Others testify to the known reputation of spirits, as Griffith Jones describes his encounter with "Marke Collens commonly called a Spirit."[58] Meanwhile, Mark Collens's wife Mary testifies against William Haverland, whom she describes as "generally called a Spirit."[59] In these accounts, the skills to unmask the spirit circulate through rumor, reputation, and the repetition of stories. It is no different in *The English Rogue.* When the spirit claims he can give Latroon a position as a storehouse-keeper in Virginia, Latroon knows this is a lie: "I had heard before, how several had been serv'd in this kinde; so that being fore-warn'd, I was fore-arm'd" (2).

While Latroon here positions himself as the savvy unmasker of a spirit, a potential mark who won't be fooled, the reader already knows that he has, in fact, been a spirit himself. When he discards his first mistress to Virginia, he does so with precisely the same kind of trickery seen as the spirit's stock in trade. He tells her that he intends to go to Virginia and marry her, and he assures her of "the pleasantness of that Continent, and the plenty of every thing, &c." (67). In the face of these enticements, she agrees to board the ship. This is strikingly similar to the spirit's method with Latroon later on, from the promise to accompany him to Virginia to the assurance of familial obligation: "He told me that he would go with me in the same ship, and take as much care of me as he would of his own son, whom I understood afterwards he had to sure, above a year since stoln away, and sold him as a slave" (6–7). Latroon describes the other men who have been lured by the spirit as repeating the same story he had previously told his mistress about the plenty of Virginia: "There was little discourse amongst them, but the pleasantness of the soyl of that Continent (we were design'd for, out of design to make us swallow their guilded Pills of Ruine) and the temperature of the air, the plenty of Fowl and Fish of all sorts . . ." (3).

Like *The English Rogue,* legal and political responses to spiriting cannot maintain tidy distinctions between spirits, their victims, and legitimized means of procuring colonial labor. In 1664, a group of merchants, planters, and masters of ships submitted a petition to the King on the problem of spiriting. The problem, however, is characterized less as the actual practice of spiriting, and more as the general *belief* in spirits and the new forms of fraud such a belief enables:

> Whereas it is generally believed that there is a wicked custome to seduce or Spirit away young people . . . this gives the opportunity to many evill-minded people to list themselves voluntarily to goe the said Voyage; and haveing reserved money, cloathes, dyess and other conveniencies from your

> Petitioners, and comeing to be cleared at Gravesend, or in the Downes, or put into some other Ports, they pretend they were betrayed or caryed away without their consents not only to the scandall, and great vexation of your petitioners and others your Majesty's good Subjects but often-times to the losse of their charge on the said evill persons, and retarding (if not the absolute hindering) of their voyage to the great discouragement of your Petitioners and obstruction of that so important a Trade.[60]

The solution they propose—a registry to document the free consent of all who migrate to the Americas—therefore would serve a dual purpose of preventing spiriting *and* preventing false claims of victimization by spirits. The framing of the problem here further blurs the lines between spirits and their victims, portraying them all as different kinds of rogues and hindrances to legitimate trade.

Spiriting is also only nominally different from the proposals for its replacement by labor recruitment by less roguish means. One 1664 proposal to the Council of Foreign Plantations, for instance, asserts that "people are the Foundacion and Improvement of all plantacions," but decries the ubiquity of spiriting as a method for obtaining this necessary stock.[61] And so, "for the prevention of the many Evills, which doe happen in the forceing tempting and seduceing of Servants and for a more certaine and orderly supply of them," the author proposes an elaborate system of convict transportation to replace spiriting. Under such a system, both felons and "all Sturdy Beggers as Gipsies and other incorrigible Rogues and Wanderes" would be eligible for transportation and indentured servitude. Penal institutions here emerge as a direct replacement for the aggregate of enterprising rogues who make up the spiriting industry. The result is the same—surplus populations are gathered up by force and put back into profitable circulation—but the proposal seeks to redeem the method by legitimizing it as state population management and colonial policy, rather than fraudulent private business. This proposal was not adopted, but its language is representative of how "spiriting" circulated. John Wareing contextualizes the scandal of spiriting in the seventeenth-century servant trade's reliance on a spectrum of coercion, from force to trickery to simple economic necessity.[62] As he argues, spiriting was not commonly prosecuted—likely because its victims were overwhelmingly poor and because this form of coercion is difficult to distinguish from the dubious consent of legitimate bound labor contracts—but it was a ubiquitous object of concern, fascination, fear, and outrage in seventeenth-century print and politics.[63]

"Spiriting" ultimately had no stable definition, but circulated as a trope for the subversion of good colonial population management. For instance, when the Assembly of Barbados passed an "Act to Prevent Spiriting People off this Island" in 1670, they tell the familiar story that "Freemen, whose times of Service have been lately expired, as also other Artificers and small Setlers" have been "inticed, spirited and carried . . . to other Settlements," where they are promised land "but are sold and hurried from Place to Place, and become in no other Quality, or little better than Slaves."[64] However, the motivation for this law was not so much concern for the working conditions or the free consent of these settlers, but rather a desire to stem the tide of settler migration from Barbados to newer, competing colonies like Jamaica.[65] At stake here is the mobilization of populations and their labor. As different interests competed for the power to compel this labor and move these populations, "spiriting" could name nearly any mobilization of laboring population that thwarted the accuser's interest.

Similarly, spiriting becomes a way of staging the scandal of tyranny and distinguishing legitimate state violence from its overreach. The prospect of forcible transportation to the colonies, especially the Caribbean, inspired fear and scandal, especially in cases in which those transported were perceived to occupy a status that ought to exempt them from colonial labor. For instance, the 1659 petition to Parliament of Marcellus Rivers and Oxenbridge Foyle, which was also published as a pamphlet entitled *Englands Slavery, or Barbados Merchandize,* protested their transportation to Barbados as punishment for participation in a Royalist rebellion. They bemoan the lack of deference shown to their social status, as the punishment spared "nor Divines, nor Officers, nor Gentlemen, nor any age or condition of men, but rendered all alike in this most insupportable Captivity."[66] They use the scandal of spiriting to portray the law as another kind of rogue, arguing that "the Maior, Aldermen, and Citizens of London . . . will in time, not be spared by these *West* Indian Spirits," and ask "whether *English,* be Slaves or Freemen."[67] *The English Rogue* repeats this link between spiriting and the specter of slavery; when Latroon surveys the other men in the spirit's house, he reflects that they are doomed to "the slavery they must undergo for five years, among Bruits in forreign parts, little inferior to that which they suffer who are *Gally-slaves*" (3).

While Oxenbridge and Foyle are most concerned with opposing slavery to their status as English *gentlemen,* they do also appeal rhetorically to Englishness in general, and this coincides historically with the increasing racialization of plantation labor in the Americas—most starkly in the Caribbean. While the Americas continued to circulate as an imagined sink for surplus population, late seventeenth-century English planters in the Caribbean relied less on this population for their labor, and relied increasingly on enslaved Africans. At the same time, as Michal Rozbicki argues, proposals to literally enslave the English poor continued to circulate into the eighteenth century.[68] The scandal of spiriting, meanwhile, could also occasionally be rhetorically deployed against the legitimacy of the enslavement of Africans. Aphra Behn's Oroonoko is captured through a trick reminiscent of spiriting, as he and his men are plied with drink and false hospitality, then lured onto a ship bound for the West Indies.[69] To capture a prince with such a trick, Behn implies, reflects the roguishness of Surinam's colonial government, which, she later asserts, "consisted of such notorious villains as Newgate never transported."[70]

For Josiah Child, the beneficial effect of the trade in English bound labor relies on its coexistence with slavery. While Oxenbridge and Foyle raise the specter of enslaved Englishmen, Child is careful to rhetorically insulate the surplus populations of England from slavery, enlisting slaves instead as the supplement that accomplishes the seeming arithmetic impossibility of colonization: that exporting surplus population from England will in fact *increase,* not decrease England's population. He argues that population is driven by employment, and that colonial trade (secured by protectionist policies) will provide employment at home and thus spur population growth:

> The People that evacuate from us to *Barbadoes* and the other *West India* Plantations . . . do commonly work one *English* Man to ten or eight Blacks; and if we keep the Trade of our said Plantations entirely to *England, England* would have no less Inhabitants, but rather an Increase of People by such Evacuation, because that one *English* Man, with the ten Blacks that work with him, accounting what they eat, use, and wear, would make Employment for four Men in *England.* . . .[71]

Child argues that the transportation of Englishmen to Barbados results in no net loss of English population because the transportation of one man creates four jobs—and thus four productive people—at home. However, this is accomplished only because this Englishman labors alongside "ten or eight Blacks," whose transportation to Barbados is counted nowhere in this text as a loss to any nation or people at all. While he maintains the semantic preservation of the "*English* Man" in Barbados, differentiating him from the enslaved "Blacks that work with him," the logic by which expelled English populations create value and growth at home is fully reliant on the enslavement of others.

Slavery remains at the very margins of *The English Rogue,* however, and the Atlantic slave trade goes entirely unmentioned. Latroon eventually escapes the spirit narrowly; he jumps overboard when he's loaded onto the Virginia-bound ship and disappears into the crowd on shore. This prefigures his other dramatic and unlikely escape from another Virginia-bound ship at the novel's end, when he is once again spared the fate of colonial bound labor and is instead propelled to profitable accumulation in the East Indies. He is proximate to the Atlantic economy of bound labor, but ultimately spared from it, and yet it is through this proximity that he achieves his path toward commercial wealth. One can hear the echoes of this in the early life of Defoe's Captain Singleton, whose childhood kidnapping by a spirit launches him into a career as a pirate and then a profitable slave trader. Indeed, Singleton's early life reads as a highly compressed version of *The English Rogue* as well as an eighteenth-century reflection on an earlier moment in colonial expansion; he claims that spiriting "was a Hellish Trade in those Days," then narrates how, in quick succession, he lives with "Gypsies," is expelled and passed through multiple parishes as a vagrant, goes to sea, is captured by the Turks, is captured again by the Portuguese, and finally accompanies a Portuguese captain to Goa—all in the first few pages of the novel.[72] Like Latroon, Bob Singleton is spared initial transportation to the Americas, and is instead propelled east to acquire his wealth; it is only after his voyage across Africa that he enters the Atlantic labor market, not as a laborer but as a merchant of slaves.

In the geography of *The English Rogue,* the English stage for the indefinitely prolonged narrative pleasures of roguery is poised between two possible resolutions. To the west lies the prospect of capture and servitude: roguery arrested through unwilling incorporation into the plantation economy. To the east, however, lies the prospect of accumulation through adventure, trade, and the transformation of the rogue into a new kind of sovereign. As Betty Joseph argues, the novel figures English exclusion from Dutch-controlled spice markets through Latroon's failure to succeed in his usual cheats when he tries them out in the East Indies—one more figuration of Latroon's roguery as another version of "legitimate" trade.[73] Instead, she reveals, he is able to make his fortune only through marriage with an Indian woman, thus transforming him into a rather different kind of economic and novelistic subject: "What was previously unattainable for Latroon—economic mobility through marriage—is now produced through an 'other' woman in a non-European circuit. Now Latroon can enter the sex-gender system with 'natural' capital (his racial and sexual advantages) thus also creating, in foreign space, a subject position he could not attain in England: the middle-class married man of property."[74] *The English Rogue* places different economic fates on opposite ends of the map: surplus population is sent west, economic actors venture east. Our picaro embraces one path and strenuously avoids the other. But both itineraries, understood together, offer insight into the tensions between the literary rogue and the legal vagrant when vagrancy becomes a problem of population management on a global scale. Picaresque is an intensely individualized genre, structured around the singular picaro. Restoration vagrancy law, on the other hand, offered an extremely flexible and open-ended tool to manage population, linking local concerns about parish poor rates and petty crime to political questions about how to mobilize populations globally in the service of a rapidly expanding empire. The logic of vagrancy is everywhere in *The English Rogue,* but you can't always see it by looking at Meriton Latroon.

## Rogue States, Sovereign Protagonists

Famously declaring that "all professions be-rogue one another," John Gay's Mr. Peachum introduces a world in which roguery is indistinguishable from either commerce or the law.[75] Srinivas Aravamudan tracks this paradox through the Enlightenment, arguing that "the project of sovereignty that is the Enlightenment sought doggedly to domesticate and sideline rogues, even while it proved itself to be the biggest rogue of all."[76] The rogue sovereign as laid out here has a distinctly novelistic lineage, echoing the narrative of literary history from the rogue pamphlet, the criminal biography, and the picaresque to Defoe's appropriations of these genres into the novel: "Defoe's pirates, highwaymen, and colonists—whether Robinson Crusoe, Captain Singleton, Jonathan Wild, or Will Atkins—are typical instances of mini-sovereigns, making law through a founding violence."[77] At the same time, the rogue also "reaches through to the grand criminal—in the manner of the self-styled thief-catcher Jonathan Wild."[78]

Aravamudan thus locates, in the eighteenth century, the foundational tropes of sovereignty theorized by Benjamin in his "Critique of Violence" (1921). The grand or "great criminal," for Benjamin, is the figure imagined to threaten the state's monopoly on violence: "In the great criminal this violence confronts the law with the threat of declaring a new law."[79] According to the story of the great criminal, the state, having declared the law through a prior law-making violence, then simply wields law-*preserving* violence in order to sustain the law against those whose violence would remake it. For Benjamin, however, the relegation of this threat to the great criminal occludes the true nature of state violence. The state institution that actually wields the rogue's power to remake the law through violence, he argues, is the police.

For Benjamin, the police are fundamentally defined by discretionary power, and thus the potential to inflict violence that is not subject to the law, as they continually remake the law they claim only to enforce: "In this authority the separation of lawmaking and law-preserving violence is suspended. If the first is required to prove its worth in victory, the second is subject to the restriction that it may not set itself new ends. Police violence is emancipated from both conditions."[80] In the police, the violence to both preserve and remake the law is combined in "a kind of spectral mixture."[81] Benjamin figures this power as ghostly and resistant to fixity, knowledge, or prediction: "Unlike law, which acknowledges in the 'decision' determined by a place and time a metaphysical category that give it a claim to critical evaluation, a consideration of the police institution encounters nothing essential at all. Its power is formless, like its nowhere-tangible, all-pervasive, ghostly presence in the life of civilized states."[82]

The metaphor of the spirit, then, takes on a new dimension here. If the spirit, in *The English Rogue*, is a kind of rogue who acts suspiciously like the law, who captures those already discarded as waste and recirculates them as producers of further value, and who fades from view as quickly as the narrative moves on, then I want to take Benjamin's metaphor of state violence's spectrality seriously. What reading methods can turn our critical attention to the form of sovereignty that constructs vagrancy as a legal category, if that sovereignty is itself elusive, spectral, and constituted through the imaginative category of its much more attention-dominating targets?

While the "vagrant" as defined by law is, I contend, quite different from the picaro, what vagrancy law and picaresque do have in common are elements of their form. The narrative pleasures of the picaresque include digressive, episodic, unpredictable adventures that could be extended seemingly without end. As Kate Loveman argues, this structure not only offers variety and novelty to readers, but also promises advantages for the author, who can elaborate on a profitable formula quickly, easily, and without much planning: "Adopting variety as an important narrative principle . . . meant great freedom for the author: the story would require only loose plotting in advance, with much scope for improvisation and expansion on themes and issues in the writing."[83] Gabriel Cervantes finds in episodic narrative form an analogy to colonial legal practice that is equally open to improvisation, adaptation, and variety.[84] English vagrancy statutes, meanwhile, echo this structure in their own definitions of vagrancy, relying not on any internally coherent definition of the term, but rather on long, miscellaneous, colorful, and paratactic lists of the many different social types targeted for criminalization. The 1597–98 act, for instance, offers this definition of vagrancy:

> That all persons calling themselves Schollers going about begging, all Seafaring men pretending losses of their ships or goods on the Sea, going about the countrey begging, All idle persons going about in any countrey either begging or using any subtile craft, or unlawfull games and playes, or fayning themselves to have knowledge in Physiognomie, Palmestry, or other like crafty science, or pretending that they can tell destanies, fortunes, or such other like fantasticall imaginations: All persons that be, or utter themselves to be Proctors, procurers, patent gatherers, or Collectors

> for gaoles, prisons, or Hospitals. All fencers, Bearewards, common players of Interludes, and Minstrels, wandering abroad (other then players of Interludes belonging to any Baron of this Realme, or any other honourable patronage of greater degree, to bee authorized to play under the hand and Seale of Armes of such Baron or personage) All Juglers, Tinkers, Pedlers, and petie Chapmen wandering abroad All wandering persons and common Labourers, being persons able in body, using Loytering, and refusing to worke for such reasonable wages, as is taxed or commonly given in such parts, where such persons doe, or shall happen to dwell or abide, not having living otherwise to maintaine themselves, All persons delivered out of gaoles that begge for their fees, or otherwise do travaile begging: All such persons as shall wander abroad begging, pretending losses by fire, or otherwise: And all such persons not being felons, wandering and pretending themselves to be Egyptians, or wandering in the habite, forme, or attire of counterfeite Egyptians, shall be taken, adjudged and deemed Rogues, Vagabonds, and sturdy beggers. . . .[85]

This act and its general definition of vagrancy were in force until it was repealed by the Vagrancy Act of 1714, which modified the definition of vagrancy somewhat, but preserved many of the elements of the 1597 act, as well as its miscellaneous, paratactic form:

> That all Persons pretending themselves to be Patent-gatherers, or Collectors for Prisons, Gaols, or Hospitals, and wandring abroad for that purpose; all Fencers, Bear-wards, Common Players of Interludes, Minstrels, Juglers; all Persons pretending to be Gipsies, or wandring in the Habit or Form of counterfeit *Egyptians*, or pretending to have skill in Physiognomy, Palmestry, or like crafty Science, or pretending to tell Fortunes, or using any subtil Craft, or unlawful Games or Plays; all Persons able in Body, who run away, and leave their Wives or Children to the Parish, and not having wherewith otherwise to maintain themselves . . . and refuse to work for the usual and common Wages; and all other idle Persons wandring abroad and begging (except Soldiers, Mariners, or Seafaring Men, licensed by some Testimonial or Writing under the Hand and Seal of some Justice of Peace, setting down the Time and Place of his or their landing, and the Place to which they are to pass, and limiting the Time for such their passage, while they continue in the direct Way to the Place to which they are to pass, and during the time so limited) shall be deemed Rogues and Vagabonds.[86]

While the broader category of vagrancy implies some measure of conceptual unity, the statute's long, colorful catalogue of disparate types does not propose an essential theory of vagrancy, but proliferates the many forms that vagrancy might take while leaving open the possibility that the list could expand to include figures and actions not yet imagined. This effect—not one of hierarchically organized taxonomy, but of endlessly proliferating proximities—is produced through the list's parataxis.

When Marx reproduces this paratactic form to characterize the lumpenproletariat in the Eighteenth Brumaire, he constitutes this category as what Peter Stallybrass describes as a "spectacle of heterogeneity": "Alongside decayed roués with dubious means of subsistence and of dubious origin, alongside ruined and adventurous offshoots of the bourgeoisie, were vagabonds, discharged soldiers, discharged jailbirds, escaped galley slaves, swindlers, mountebanks, lazzaroni, pickpockets, tricksters, gamblers, macquereaus, brothel keepers, porters, literati, organ-grinders, ragpickers, knife grinders, tinkers, beggars—in short, the whole indefinite, disintegrated mass, thrown hither and thither, which the French term la bohème."[87]

After the first two clauses, which enact the very definition of parataxis ("alongside . . . , alongside") the list then echoes vagrancy legislation, journalism, and the many other contemporary deployments of a formal structure that, as Stallybrass notes, "endlessly proliferates categories to encompass the spectacle of the metropolis."[88] In other words, the best way to evoke an "indefinite, disintegrated mass" is not to describe a mass as such, but to list its exemplary members in all their heterogeneity, spectacular juxtaposition, and endless potential for proliferation.

In the context of the Eighteenth Brumaire, this proliferation serves to emphasize the essentially classless and miscellaneous character of the lumpenproletariat. In a vagrancy law, however, it is key for enabling the wide-ranging discretionary power of those who enforce the law; by evoking the vagrant through endless proliferation rather than the theorization of a particular kind of subject, the parataxis at the heart of vagrancy law grants an equally expansive discretionary power to magistrates, JPs, and constables to apprehend figures whose form cannot be known in advance. As Paul Slack notes, the enforcement of vagrancy law was anything but systematic, and this was enabled by the form of the statutes, "which quite intentionally left opportunity for selective enforcement."[89] Indeed, the actual enforcement of these laws was extremely variable and contingent on local resources and concerns, as well as on the decisions of individual constables and other authorities who were required to enforce vagrancy law but rarely wished to bear the costs or inconvenience of doing so with the utmost diligence.[90]

This is the tension between the literary category of picaro and the legal category of vagrant. After all, to be named a vagrant is to be rendered the object of diffuse, proliferative anticipation, not the object of knowledge, narrative, or characterization. If a vagrant is one who, in the words of most vagrancy statutes in the long eighteenth century, can give no good account of themselves, then vagrancy and narrative are not easily aligned. In this sense, I want to offer an alternative here to Patricia Fumerton's account of seventeenth-century vagrancy, as she reads the legal and literary archives of early modern poverty for traces of what she terms an "unsettled subjectivity," a contingent, unpredictable, and serial occupation of multiple places, social roles, professions, and relative depths of poverty.[91]

On the one hand, Fumerton's account certainly resonates formally with the structure of *The English Rogue.* One might, for instance, see in the picaresque structure a fictional enactment of her model of "'low' subjectivity" unbound by specific place or social identity, as Meriton's professions, costumes, social identities, social and familial ties, and places of residence are occupied only as long as they happen to last before they are discarded in favor of whatever might come next.[92] However, Fumerton's focus on subjectivity necessarily keeps our eyes on the individual, as "the vagrant" as a kind of person (or at least a kind of personal experience), and, in the case of this novel, on Meriton Latroon. But where Fumerton sees, in the records of vagrancy arrests, a form of mobile, capacious, and flexible vagrant subjectivity, I see a mobile, capacious, and flexible legal authority, a category of criminalization that is open to improvisatory and expansive use by JPs, constables, and magistrates in their task of managing or expelling surplus populations. One of this book's foundational claims is that the protean mobility of "the vagrant" in textual representation materially enables the expansive mobility of policing.

*The English Rogue*'s complex publication history reveals how claims of rogue identity or subjectivity can sometimes obscure the material workings of vagrancy law. The first installment was published in 1665 by the bookseller Henry Marsh, though it could not be licensed because it was too obscene. In 1666, Marsh died and Francis Kirkman took over the business and reprinted *The English Rogue*.[93] A revised version was licensed that year, and its commercial success prompted Kirkman to author Part 2 in 1668, explaining in the preface that Head had refused to write a continuation, citing concern for his reputation.[94] Head and Kirkman likely collaborated on Parts 3 and 4, which appeared in 1671. A fifth part appeared alongside a 1688 abridgment of the first four parts.[95] In this chapter, I focus primarily on Part 1, which was published as a standalone novel and only expanded by Kirkman when the formula had proven commercially successful. Lisa Maruca argues that Kirkman presents himself, in his autobiography *The Unlucky Citizen* (1673), as a roguish brand of bookseller, while Simonova notes that he also uses the paratexts of the continuations of *The English Rogue* to accuse Head of roguery in refusing to continue authorship of the story.[96] In a move that extratextually replicates a feature of *The English Rogue*'s narrative, the paratextual debates' tendencies to lead us, as readers, to reflect on Head and Kirkman's relative roguishness obscure other unnamed, unrepresented, and largely female members of the book trade who were far more vulnerable to actual criminalization than either authors or printers. While the 1665 edition's lack of license left it more vulnerable to piracy, it did not expose Head or Kirkman to the kind of personal threat of criminalization that their common literary-historical characterization as "rogues" might imply.[97] Meanwhile, as Maruca notes, those most likely to be legally classed as "rogues" were largely women: hawkers and mercuries, who occupied the lowest and most marginal positions in the book trade, were essential in the distribution of politically incendiary material and were also vulnerable to arrest under vagrancy law.[98]

If we resist the economy of attention that draws readers of *The English Rogue* to focus so insistently on its protagonist, we can see new resonances between picaresque fiction and vagrancy law. In particular, we can stop thinking of "the vagrant" as a kind of person or a type of life story, but instead as a relation to the law. As Bryan Wagner argues, "vagrancy has no empirical reference. It is a term that cannot be defined like a word in the dictionary, as it references a category whose members have nothing in common besides their identification as vagrants."[99] The narrative capaciousness, variety, adaptability, and mobility attributed to the picaro more readily characterize vagrancy *law* than they do those labeled vagrants. Indeed, as I will argue in Chapters 4 and 5, vagrancy law proved enormously open to adaptation as it was repurposed to suit the needs of the colonies. But even in England, vagrancy law implicated local poor relief and the management of petty crime and disorder in broad questions of migration, population, and colonial governance—thus proving even more mobile, even more protean, and even more rapacious in the assertion of sovereignty than Meriton Latroon.

## *CHAPTER TWO*

# THE NOVEL AND THE SEXUALITY OF VAGRANCY

To label all this "the police" thus anticipates moving the question of policing out of the streets, as it were, into the closet. . . .
—*D. A. Miller, The Novel and the Police*

In Jane Barker's *Patch-Work Screen for the Ladies* (1723), a story entitled "The Unaccountable Wife" tells of a woman who allows her maid to share her and her husband's bed, then eventually leaves her husband to live with the maid, establishing a topsy-turvy household in which the maid lives in idleness while the wife takes up domestic labor. The wife's family repeatedly fail to understand what motivates her; they can only conclude vaguely "that all proceeded from an Interiour thoroughly degenerated."[1] When the wife and the servant establish a household elsewhere, with no means of supporting themselves, the wife's reasons for choosing such a life utterly confound the narrator: "Now what this unaccountable Creature thought of this kind of Being, is unknown, or what Measures she and her Companion thought to take, or what Schemes they form'd to themselves, is not conceivable."[2]

As the community's response makes clear, however, these questions never need to be answered; instead, the fact of the pair's unaccountability indicates all one needs to know: "But whatever they were, the discreet Neighbourhood put a Period to their Projects; for they got a Warrant to have them before a Justice, in order to prevent a Parish charge."[3] In other words, they invoke vagrancy laws, which allowed Justices of the Peace to expel nonresidents whom they judged likely to require parish poor relief, and which were particularly likely to be used in this way against unmarried mothers.[4] After the wife refuses successive offers from her family—and eventually the Queen—to restore her to her fortune in exchange for leaving her companion, her mysterious and stubborn desires are made apparent in their extremity; she is reduced to begging in the streets to support her household. The Unaccountable Wife is unaccountable not only because her desires defy expectations of gender and kinship, but also because she is economically irrational: offered the choice of leisure and material comfort, she chooses instead to persist as a beggar.

The Unaccountable Wife, by definition, can give no good account of herself. In commonly criminalizing the refusal or inability to give an account of oneself to a magistrate or JP, vagrancy law renders intelligible narrative evidence of one's lawful employment, legal settlement, or legitimate travel. "The Unaccountable Wife," however, revels in the wife's refusal, holding up her opacity for the reader's fascination. In claiming that the wife's thoughts are "not conceivable," the narrator seems to give up in the face of utter opacity and potentially limitless speculation. At the same time, the structure of the phrase refuses closure: we're invited to imagine "what Measures" and "what Schemes" these women might harbor within them, and the narrative, by claiming to have no answers, places no limits on our speculation.

Indeed, while the wife's family bemoans her "Interiour thoroughly degenerated"—in language that seems to prefigure sexological models of desire and invite queer reading on those terms—the residents of the parish who have her family arrested for vagrancy display no interest in her interiority, her desires, or the account she might give of them. Instead, they see two women with small children and no visible means of support, which is an arrangement that poses the threat of dependence on the parish poor rates regardless of the desires that motivated it.

The sexuality and kinship structures of the poor were a constant object of surveillance and regulation by the administrators of parish poor relief, as well as by other authorities tasked with enforcing vagrancy law. In the early eighteenth century, the Societies for the Reformation of Manners (which targeted prostitution, sodomy, and other forms of what they considered sexual deviance) had linked their aims to the concerns about labor that underpinned antivagrancy rhetoric and legislation; such campaigns explicitly hoped to improve the nation's labor force through the regulation of reproduction and the encouragement of sexual virtue.[5] Vagrancy law was the major legal mechanism for criminalizing sex work, which meant that women were routinely confined to bridewells as "idle and disorderly" suspected prostitutes.[6] Officers and magistrates reconstituted households and family structures by mandating some living arrangements and prohibiting others, by alternately preventing marriages and coercing them, and by apprenticing out the children of the poor as a requirement of receiving aid.[7] Furthermore, reproduction among the poor was continually invoked alongside their supposed idleness and disorder; the refusal of labor so central to conceptions of vagrancy was linked to irresponsible sexuality, the production of too many children, and the rearing of these children into habits of idleness—all leading to a drain on the parish coffers in excess poor relief.[8] Meanwhile, gender was a crucial—yet sometimes flexible—element in the legibility of public identity, and thus could also be caught up in concerns about fraud, imposture, and suspicion.[9]

The interplay between the household and the state did not just inform theories of sexuality; it also offered a model for governance. Blackstone's definition of "police," after all, fundamentally relies on the authority of the patriarch over his family: "By public police and oeconomy I mean the due regulation and domestic order of the kingdom: whereby the individuals of the state, like members of a well-governed family, are bound to conform their general behaviour to the rules of propriety, good neighbourhood, and good manners; and to be decent, industrious, and inoffensive in their respective stations."[10] The offenses described in this chapter, under the heading of "Offences against the Public Health, and the Public Police or Oeconomy," all span the tangle of intimacy, property, and privacy, including clandestine marriages, the keeping of bawdy-houses, poaching, and (most prominently) vagrancy. For Markus Dubber, Blackstone's formulation is simply one very canonical expression of a much more wide-ranging notion of police as household governance: "From the perspective of police, the state is the institutional manifestation of a household. The police state, as *paterfamilias,* seeks to maximize the welfare of his—or rather its—household."[11]

If D. A. Miller's foundational reading of the "open secrets" of the nineteenth-century novel brought the police from the streets to the closet, I argue that at the margins of the mid-eighteenth-century novel and its much-debated consolidations of conjugal families, heterosexual desire, and the reproduction of labor in the private household, police lay the groundwork for the closet to be fashioned in the image of the streets.[12] Vagrancy, as a form of both legal and narrative unaccountability, could mark not only the refusal of wage labor, but also the refusal of the reproductive, sexual, or emotional labor that marriage demanded of women. It often, as in "The Unaccountable Wife," linked both sexual and economic deviance under a common rubric. Vagrancy law embedded criminalization in the fabric of poor relief, underpinning the carceral foundations of early modern social welfare, and making the parish, rather than just the family, a crucial site of intimate governance. Tracking vagrancy at the nexus of gender, sexuality, family, and narrative allows us to see another dimension of the novel and the history of sexuality, one that was never confined to the middle-class home to begin with.

"The Unaccountable Wife" portrays its eponymous vagrant as a problem of household management that neatly analogizes the household and the state—or, to be more precise, the household and the legal/administrative unit of the parish. When the husband tries to expel the maidservant, the narrator explains that he is attempting to manage his household's economic and reproductive resources by preventing her from producing more children than he can afford. When the wife takes her children and travels with the maidservant, their collective expulsion from the community takes up the same logic of resource maximization and care for the community's welfare, since they are expelled to prevent them from drawing on the parish's poor relief funds. The problem is not primarily the production of the wife as a deviant subject, whose internal deviance must be uncovered, explained, or accounted for. Rather, the "unaccountability" that resonates so tantalizingly with Miller's "open secret" most insistently names the fact that she is a problem for domestic economy, signaling potential threat to the good management of a family or community's resources.

Thus the long critical tradition investigating the eighteenth-century novel's articulations of emerging models of sexuality as institutionalized in the family can be retold in the context of how gender and sexuality fashioned and were fashioned by parish administration and poor law. If we center the eighteenth-century notion of "police" as the maximization of a community's welfare by managing its economic and reproductive resources, then we arrive at a very different account of the novel and the police than the one we see in Miller's nineteenth century. Through an extended reading of Henry Fielding's *The Female Husband* (1746), I argue that Fielding conceptualizes vagrancy as a kind of sexuality that threatens the good order of the parish. While Fielding uses the same language of interiority and desire to conceptualize both sexual transgression and lower-class criminality, he also ultimately never settles on the interior as a locus of either narrative revelation or governance; instead, the very impossibility of revealing an interior cause for transgression bolsters the broad discretionary scope of policing by refusing to limit its targets to any one kind of person. Furthermore, this text's emphasis on gender-crossing offers us a window into the role of gendered bodily perception in the history of policing, and invites us to pursue a transgender reading that places this text in a long history of surveillance that produces the "visibly" trans body as suspicious. Then, by tracking parish management and gendered dispossession through another text that has been reclaimed as sapphic—Sarah Scott's *Millenium Hall* (1762)—I argue that the sentimental novel's construction of domestic subjects produces queer margins whose queerness lies not exclusively in same-sex eroticism, but also in marginality to the domestic, reproductive economy of the family and the parish. Finally, I show how a rare first-person account of eighteenth-century female vagrancy—Mary Saxby's posthumously published *Memoirs of a Female Vagrant* (1806)—expands our understanding of novelistic narrative by noting its reliance on parish governance, while it also offers space for queer reading that does not necessarily center same-sex desire but nonetheless preserves a genealogical link to the afterlife of queerness as dissidence from familial social reproduction.

## Sexual Vagrancy: Fielding's *The Female Husband*

Henry Fielding had much to say about the dangers of vagrancy, and literary critics have had much to say about the interplay between his legal commentary and literary practice.[13] As Jesper Gulddal notes, Fielding's calls, as a magistrate, for an absolute prohibition of wandering seems strange in light of his novelistic practice:

> Fielding the novelist depended to a considerable extent on wandering as an instigator of narrative—in both *Joseph Andrews* (1742) and *Tom Jones,* the narrative impetus comes from the roving wandering of protagonists repeatedly characterized as 'vagabonds' and 'vagrants,' while individual episodes often focus on 'suspicious' or nomadic characters encountered on the road: highwaymen, beggars, runaway wives, decommissioned soldiers, hermits, thieves, and gypsies. The novelistic dependence on mobility seems to be fundamentally at odds with the political insistence on movement control.[14]

However, he argues, the teleology of the novelistic plot offers an endpoint of all this wandering, and subordinates the characters' waywardness to the structural authority of the narrative itself.[15] Gulddal thus elaborates on John Bender's classic argument that Fielding's development of narrative omniscience enacts the surveillance and discipline of the penitentiary within the world of the novel.[16]

Meanwhile, Scott MacKenzie nuances Bender's claim, focusing less on a generalized sense of discipline and more on the specific legal function of vagrancy, which took the parish, rather than the individual subject or household, as its primary administrative unit.[17] MacKenzie notes that the stock characters and plots of romance resonate quite strongly with the populations and behaviors criminalized by vagrancy law, which therefore "helps define the 'hitherto unattempted' species of writing that Henry Fielding proclaims in his preface to *Joseph Andrews:* he subjects the conventions of romance to the conditions of poor law and poor management."[18] The narrative supervision to which Fielding subjects his wayward characters does not, for MacKenzie, take the form of Bender's universal omniscience, but rather a closer and less anonymous view, akin to that of the magistrate bound to care for the welfare of his own parish.[19] The parish, in this view, is "a closed domain for the confinement, maintenance, and surveillance of the poor that can mediate state power through intimate communal relations," and thus also far more important to the history of domesticity than we might assume.[20]

In this context, *The Female Husband* offers crucial insight into how sexuality, domesticity, the household, the parish, and the state intertwine in Fielding's fiction. Inspired by an actual vagrancy arrest, this novella dwells insistently on the unaccountable opacity of a single vagrant who confounds his vision of intimate governance. At the same time, the narrative surveillance to which Fielding attempts to subject his protagonist does not yield a transparent or disciplined subject, nor does it account for the unaccountability of this protagonist's actions or desires. To restore order, this text implies, one need not account for the unaccountable at all; the fact of unaccountability is all that matters.

In September 1746, a quack doctor by the name of Charles Hamilton was tried at the Somerset quarter-sessions for vagrancy. In the eyes of the law, Hamilton was a woman with the birth name of Mary Hamilton, and it was Hamilton's marriage to a young woman named Mary Price that precipitated the arrest.[21] This was not an ordinary case of vagrancy. "Vagrancy," in the press surrounding this case, alluded to a sensational tale of fraudulent marriage, gender transgression, and sexual deception, a story picked up first by a local newspaper and then by periodicals throughout the country. Hamilton was not simply arrested on the authority of a local Justice of the Peace responding to a complaint of an unknown beggar or suspected thief; instead, in a highly atypical move for a crime like vagrancy, the Corporation of Glastonbury (which included many of the town's wealthiest and most powerful inhabitants) conducted a prosecution on behalf of Mary Price, who likely had neither the financial means nor the social influence required to bring such a prosecution herself.[22]

As newspapers began to reprint accounts of the case, the story caught the attention of Fielding.[23] He took the story presented by the newspapers and spun it into *The Female Husband,* a picaresque criminal biography that expands Hamilton's story to include numerous fictional adventures and sexual intrigues. *The Female Husband* depicts Hamilton as a tireless trickster, driven by both desire and habit to enter into new schemes of impersonation, fraud, and sexual conquest despite repeated failure—a comic evocation of a personality one might imagine illustrating the legal category of "incorrigible rogue." While some of the newspaper reports hint vaguely at rumors that Hamilton had multiple wives, Fielding does much more than hint; he tells Hamilton's story as a rake's progress of repeated seduction and sexual misadventure.

Mary Hamilton, Fielding's story goes, was a virtuous young woman until seduced into both Sapphism and Methodism by an older friend named Anne Johnson. When Anne eventually renounces their relationship in favor of marriage to a man and urges Hamilton to do the same, Hamilton instead runs away, begins dressing as a man, takes the name George (rather than Charles, as in the actual case), and decides to become a Methodist preacher in Ireland. There, upon catching the attention of the wealthy and lustful Widow Rushford, Hamilton decides to seduce and marry her for her fortune. Over the objections of her nephew, who stood to inherit her wealth, the Widow Rushford becomes Hamilton's first wife, and Hamilton's plan to obtain her fortune depends on the use of a dildo (which the text never names but constantly references elliptically) to consummate the marriage. But after a series of comic near-misses, Rushford discovers the dildo and Hamilton is forced to flee. Upon returning to England, Hamilton begins working as a quack doctor and quickly marries a young patient named Miss Ivythorn. Once again, Hamilton's wife discovers the dildo. Rejecting the promise of "all the pleasures of marriage without the inconveniences," Miss Ivythorn declares the marriage invalid and threatens to expose Hamilton as a fraud.[24]

Hamilton then flees to Somerset and courts Mary Price, whom Fielding lampoons as barely literate, comically naive, and questionably virtuous in her eagerness to marry Hamilton despite many hints that Hamilton is not "really" a man (or at least not the right *kind* of man). Price's earnest boasts of her sexual satisfaction with her husband ironically convince her mother that Hamilton is a woman, and it is on those grounds that Price's mother complains to a magistrate and sets Hamilton's prosecution into motion. At this point, Fielding's story realigns with the historical case: Hamilton is tried for vagrancy and sentenced to public whipping and six months' hard labor. The text concludes with a voyeuristic account of Hamilton's whipping and a caution against the consequences of "unnatural affections" in both sexes (51).

In her influential reading, Terry Castle notes that the text's preoccupation with disguise structures both form and content; Fielding's constant euphemisms, she argues, "work to recapitulate on a textual level those 'disguises' which occupy him thematically."[25] The result, according to Castle, is a text whose narrative and syntax are fundamentally structured by the anxiety provoked by destabilized gender epistemology and unfettered sexual deviance. Following Castle, a number of scholars have turned to *The Female Husband,* which was never considered central to Fielding's literary output, as an important source text for gender and sexuality in the eighteenth century.[26] Scholars interested in cultural histories of gender-crossing have situated *The Female Husband* in other generic traditions such as the "passing-woman narratives" tracked by Fraser Easton through the popular press.[27] Such readings have done much to illuminate the complexity and contradiction of Fielding's figurations of gender and desire. Queer readings in particular have carried out an important and ongoing conversation about queer historiographic methodology and its accompanying political investments.

Just as in the historical case, Fielding's Hamilton is finally arrested for vagrancy, and Fielding pauses the narrative to meditate on the applicability of the 1744 Vagrancy Act to this case. What, then, does *The Female Husband* look like when we take vagrancy seriously as a central category of analysis? Vagrancy in this text is inseparable from sexual transgression. Like gender, vagrancy is central to *The Female Husband* as both a thematic and formal concern. The features of the text that appear to be most purely about sexuality—the constant allusions to Hamilton's dildo and the narrative of Hamilton's relationships with many successive women—are simultaneously implicated in concerns about labor, fraud, and imposture. After all, the dildo first enters the story as an instrument of financial fraud, rather than of erotic pleasure; Hamilton first employs a dildo with the Widow Rushford, who Fielding narrates as offering little in the way of sexual attraction: "With this old lady, whose fortune only she was desirous to possess, such views would have afforded very little gratification. After some reflection, therefore, a device entered into her head, as strange and surprizing, as it was wicked and vile; and this was actually to marry the old woman, and to deceive her, by means which decency forbids me even to mention" (37). Not only does this text continually link the sexual and the economic, it also reveals the extent to which these two categories, as Susan Lanser argues, were never separate categories to begin with.[28]

Like the dildo, vagrancy rarely appears explicitly in the text, yet structures the entire narrative. It is cited only once, in the scene (noted above) that occurs after Mary Price's mother has asked a magistrate to investigate Hamilton and evidence is found to support a prosecution. A lawyer named Mr. Gold (a veiled reference to Henry Gould, Fielding's cousin, who did in fact advise the real prosecution) recommends Hamilton's prosecution "on a clause in the vagrant act, *for having by false and deceitful practices endeavoured to impose on some of his Majesty's subjects*" (49).[29] Fielding's citation of the 1744 Vagrancy Act characterizes Hamilton as one particular kind of offender among the many that fall under its purview: a fraudulent impostor. Fielding's characterization of Hamilton insistently echoes vagrancy law, a topic of recurring interest to Fielding in his everyday work as a magistrate and in his writings on law, crime, and social policy.[30]

The Vagrancy Act of 1744 deems "Rogues and Vagabonds" those who engage in a broad array of behaviors that also amount to the refusal to work, as most are construed as fraudulent or otherwise illegitimate means of obtaining money or subsistence:

> . . . all Persons going about as Patent-gatherers, or Gatherers of Alms, under false Pretences of Loss by Fire, or other Casualty; or going about as Collectors for Prisons, Gaols, or Hospitals; all Fencers and Bearwards . . . all Minstrels, Jugglers; all Persons pretending to be Gypsies, or wandering in the Habit or Form of Egyptians, or pretending to have Skill in Physiognomy, Palmistry, or like crafty Science, or pretending to tell Fortunes, or using any subtle Craft to deceive and impose on any of His Majesty's Subjects, or playing or betting at any unlawful Games or Plays; and all Persons who run away and leave their Wives or Children, whereby they become chargeable to any Parish or Place; and all Petty Chapmen and Pedlars wandering abroad, not being duly licensed, or otherwise authorized by Law; and all Persons wandering abroad and lodging in Barns and other Outhouses, not giving a good Account of themselves. . . .[31]

Almost every identifying characteristic of Fielding's Hamilton is a characteristic or practice associated with vagrancy. Hamilton wanders throughout England and Ireland, works in the dubious profession of quack doctor, lives in disguise, and commits acts of financial fraud through imposture. Meanwhile, Hamilton's serial abandonment of wives recalls the act's criminalization of men who abandon their wives and children to reliance on parish relief.

Fielding's Hamilton is, therefore, a composite of many different kinds of vagrant. Fielding ties multiple forms of vagrancy together by narrating their simultaneous display by one person. He then takes this premise further by implying that they are all traceable to one common, interior cause. Fielding gathers Hamilton's many aberrant behaviors under one particular kind of motivation: a repeated impulse that remains stubbornly untraceable to any origin, incites a wide array of unpredictably disparate behaviors, and is rendered most visible through Fielding's expressions of its utter opacity.

Early in the story, after Anne Johnson has ended their relationship, Hamilton "began to consult what course to take, when the strangest thought imaginable suggested itself to her fancy. This was to dress herself in mens cloaths, to embarque for Ireland, and commence Methodist teacher" (33). This decision to dress as a man and enter a disreputable, itinerant profession is described in exactly the same terms as Hamilton's later decision to begin using a dildo with the Widow Rushford: "After some reflection, therefore, a device entered into her head, as strange and surprizing, as it was wicked and vile" (37). These passages, which promise to explain Hamilton's unaccountable behavior, can in fact only reiterate this behavior's resistance to explanation. Hamilton is never the subject of the sentences in which the impulses to vagrancy appear. Instead, these impulses seem to act on their own opaque agency as one thought "suggest[s] itself" and another "enter[s] into her head." This is what resonates most strongly with the idea of sexuality as interior—indeed, as *the* metonym for interiority and subjectivity. And yet, Fielding's preoccupation with the sources of Hamilton's behavior yields no answers: the unaccountable remains unaccountable. I read this persistent opacity as something more than just a failure or incoherence in the text; rather, it is crucial to Fielding's integration of novelistic narrative with the modes of policing he theorizes more explicitly in his writings on crime and poverty. This narrative unaccountability certainly fails to accomplish the revelations promised by the case history, a signal genre of the later sexological models of sexuality that the language of interiority here seems to prefigure. However, it succeeds in constructing a field of vision for police that includes gender and sexuality as legible categories of disorder while resisting limitation of its scope to any specific sexual identities or acts.

In *The Female Husband* and in his commentaries on poverty, law, and crime, Fielding's interest in vagrancy is motivated by the same concerns that we, as contemporary readers, associate with discourses we call sexuality: the theorization of interiority, desire, and the invisible causes that move bodies. Ultimately, the attempt to trace why a laborer refuses to work and the attempt to explain why Hamilton lives and desires the "wrong" genders both concern themselves with the same broad questions. And yet, while Fielding uses the language of interiority and desire to theorize both economic and sexual disorder, he nonetheless never arrives at a coherent theory of interiority or subjectivity. Instead, if we consider his writings on crime and policing alongside *The Female Husband,* we can see how the invocation of unaccountable interiority ironically serves not to reveal what moves bodies from within, but rather to broaden the discretionary power of parish management to anticipate unexpected threats to social order—whether or not these threats can ever be explained, revealed, or systematically categorized.

Hamilton, for Fielding, provides an opportunity to represent a vagrant as a kind of person, and vagrancy as a pattern of behavior that results from a characteristic kind of thought. The narrative's concern with the interior mechanisms of cause and effect is laid out at the very beginning, in a meditation on the nature of "carnal appetites" and their results:

> That propense inclination which is for very wise purposes implanted in the one sex for the other, is not only necessary for the continuance of the human species; but is, when govern'd and directed by virtue and religion, productive not only of corporeal delight, but of the most rational felicity. But if once our carnal appetites are let loose, without those prudent and secure guides, there is no excess and disorder which they are not liable to commit, even while they pursue their natural satisfaction; and, which may seem still more strange, there is nothing monstrous and unnatural, which they are not capable of inventing, nothing so brutal and shocking which they have not actually committed." (29)

The unregulated pursuit of desire's "natural satisfaction" is what leads, paradoxically, to the "monstrous and unnatural" acts that this narrative promises to reveal. If, as Fielding says of those driven by unregulated "carnal appetites," "there is no excess or disorder, which they are not liable to commit," then such appetite is endlessly protean. The capability to commit one kind of "disorder" implies the capability to commit any other disorder that can be imagined.

This logic is not limited to acts that Fielding categorized under the purview of "carnal appetites." In fact, a similar reasoning informs his commentaries on poverty and crime. In his *Proposal for Making an Effectual Provision for the Poor* (1753), Fielding argues that without stricter vagrancy laws, the poor are sanctioned to act on a dangerous, generalized appetite. In a defense of his proposed criminalization of all wandering among the poor, he argues that the impulse to wander can also spur any other kind of social disorder, from robbery to murder:

> I should scarce apprehend, though I am told I may, that some persons should represent the restraint here laid on the lower people as derogatory from their liberty. Such notions are indeed of the enthusiastical kind, and are inconsistent with all order and government. They are the natural parents of that licentiousness . . . which among the many mischiefs introduced by it into every society where it prevails, is sure at last to end in the destruction of liberty itself. But if we must on no account deprive even the lowest people of the liberty of doing what they will, and going where they will, of wandering and drunkenness, why should we deny them that liberty which is but a consequence of this? I mean that of begging and stealing, of robbing or cutting throats at their good pleasure.[32]

"Licentiousness" here acts like the "carnal appetites" invoked in *The Female Husband*, as well as the "strange and surprizing" ideas that animate Hamilton in Fielding's narrative: it is itself unrepresentable because it exceeds the imaginative capacity of law, policy, and narrative. Yet its results can be illustrated by invoking the form of the list: a list of actions (or, in Hamilton's case, the succession of events) reveals the possibility of what "licentiousness" *could* set loose, while the repetition serves as a sinister hint that no list could ever be complete enough to show all that is possible. What Fielding says of "carnal appetites" in *The Female Husband* is equally true of vagrant impulses in his writings on crime and policy: "there is no excess and disorder which they are not liable to commit" (29).

Such "licentiousness," Fielding implies, can be activated by even the most sanctioned and legitimate forms of economic participation. In his *Enquiry into the Causes of the Late Increase of Robbers* (1751), Fielding blames the proliferation of crime on a new structure of desire, attributed to the pleasures of commercial society. With the end of vassalage and the introduction of trade, he argues, the character of the poor was transformed. Instead of force or subjection, money is now both the cause and object of labor. Wages, however, cannot secure the deference or industry of those who work for them, as "none is more rebellious in its Nature, or more difficult to be governed, than that of the Purse or Money."[33]

Fielding's invocation of "licentiousness" as a dangerously protean force that opposes industry and order on all fronts reveals a central contradiction. Hamilton's impulses to vagrancy are characterized as strange and unaccountable thoughts that seem to enter Hamilton's mind from somewhere external and inspire practices as diverse as Methodist preaching and the use of a dildo. But money, in Fielding's own rhetoric, works in exactly the same way for even the most virtuously industrious worker. If, as he argues, the poor are corrupted by their contact with money and its endlessly mutable purchasing power, then wages seem to act like Hamilton's vagrant impulses: as externalized, unaccountable, and ultimately ungovernable forces that enter the mind from somewhere else and animate the body in ways that predictive causality cannot trace. Even as vagrancy is posited as the enemy of wage labor, wage labor itself contains the protean bodily incitement that vagrancy law claims to isolate and contain. By the same logic, sexual virtue and sexual deviance prove difficult to separate in *The Female Husband*; the "propense Inclination" that produces "rational felicity" and reproduction is what also leads to "unnatural" acts as it pursues its "natural ends" (29). Fielding's investigations of property crime, vagrancy, and sexual deviance lead him to the same paradox: that virtuous and unvirtuous behaviors appear to share the same opaque causes. He uses the language of desire and interiority to try to theorize criminality as a recognizable social type, and yet in the cases of both sexual transgression and theft, deviant desires prove deceptively difficult to separate from virtuous ones.

*The Female Husband*'s failure to explain or trace Hamilton's "strange" thoughts actually reinforces the discretionary power underpinning vagrancy law; instead of limiting the scope of vagrancy to a discrete set of thoughts, motivations, or behaviors, the narrative keeps its object relentlessly opaque, undefined, and virtually limitless—and thus in need of an equally limitless punitive response. In the *Enquiry,* he speculates that the ineffectiveness of vagrancy laws lies in the ultimate impossibility of their goal: to identify and detain those who refuse to work. Instead of targeting the many behaviors that signal idleness, he argues, vagrancy laws ought to simply criminalize wandering:

> The Disease seems to be no other than *Idleness,* so here *Wandering* is the Cause of the Mischief, and that alone to which the Remedy should be applied. This, one would imagine, should be the chief, if not sole Intent of all Laws against Vagabonds, which might, in a synonymous Phrase, be called Laws against Wanderers. But as the Word itself hath obtained by vulgar Use a more complex Signification, so have the Laws on this Head had a more general View than to extirpate this Mischief; and by that means, perhaps, have failed of producing such an Effect.[34]

Idleness here is reliably indexed by wandering; if one is idle, one will necessarily wander, and if one is wandering, one is therefore idle. To apprehend the idle, one simply needs to criminalize all wandering and forget the other meanings of vagrancy as encoded in the law.

And yet, the "complex Signification" of vagrancy is still at work in *The Female Husband.* Hamilton is, in fact, arrested for vagrancy not because of wandering, but because of acts interpreted as imposture and fraud—in other words, Hamilton is caught precisely because vagrancy laws criminalize far more than just wandering. Though Fielding argues, in the *Enquiry,* that this far-reaching scope undermines the laws' efficacy, *The Female Husband* seems to imply that it is this very scope that allowed Hamilton to be apprehended at all.

While Fielding attempts, in the *Enquiry,* to impose conceptual totality on vagrancy law by naming its common denominator (idleness), he also recognizes that vagrancy exceeds this supposedly totalizing conception of it. After all, idleness is not itself a behavior or a bodily characteristic that can be directly criminalized, prosecuted, or even seen. Since idleness can manifest itself in relation to many different kinds of conduct, any attempt to apprehend it must then fall back on the long lists of behaviors forming vagrancy's "complex Signification." Idleness can also, as Fielding states, set loose a "licentiousness" that could potentially do *anything.* As such licentiousness exceeds the imaginative capacity of those who might seek to anticipate its effects, it is bound to exceed both these lists *and* the conceptual unity that, in seeking to comprehend vagrancy in its totality, risks delimiting the juridical discretion needed to combat it. Hamilton is ultimately arrested neither for wandering *nor* for a specific behavior listed in the 1744 act; the magistrates must, with some difficulty, interpret the act's proscription of "subtle Craft" as applicable to Hamilton's marriage and sexual practices.

*The Female Husband,* therefore, does more than represent a vagrant. It inhabits, tests, and theorizes the rhetorical structures through which vagrancy is constituted as a category. Fielding's narrative spins out the "complex Signification" of vagrancy by representing one behavioral index of vagrancy after another, yet fails to represent or explain the idleness that Fielding identifies as vagrancy's conceptual basis. This text, framed by its paradoxical inquiry into the nature of "carnal appetites," roots its rhetorical construction of vagrancy in a theory of sexuality, desire, and bodily animation; the sense of opacity that Fielding draws from his theory of desire is crucial to this text's refusal to explain or demarcate the "strange" sources of vagrant behavior, which in turn pushes against the limitation of the scope of vagrancy law or its application. Ironically, it is the *queerness* of vagrancy in this text—its strangeness, its mutability, its origins in somewhere unknown and marginal to normative social existence—that underpins Fielding's call for wide-ranging punitive responses to bodies marked as unaccountable.

## Trans/Atlantic: Gender, Surveillance, and the Vagrancy Archive

In *The Female Husband,* desire seems at first to invoke sexual vagrancy as a kind of identity, but from the vantage point of police, sexual identity turns out to be irrelevant: rather than attempt to locate sexual or economic disorder in the desires of any particular kind of person, vagrancy's open-endedness offers instead a wide-ranging discretionary tool for containing disorder regardless of the desires that motivated it. *Gender* identity, however, remains a more coherent element of the text's theorization of disorder. Indeed, this text, particularly when approached from the vantage point of trans studies, reveals the broader importance of vagrancy to the production of administrative gender as a metonym for trackable, consistent personal identity—as well as the juridical production of "inconsistent" markers of gender as signs of potential criminality, fraud, or threat.

While *The Female Husband* has, since Castle's reading, been revalued for its queer potential, it has far more rarely been critically approached as a transgender narrative, despite the text's own obsessive interest in gender epistemology and the sexing of textual bodies.[35] On the one hand, of course, the text is extraordinarily hostile to experiences of gender that we might today describe as trans; Fielding portrays Hamilton as a deceptive and deviant woman and revels voyeuristically in the punitive bodily exposure that, for Fielding, also constitutes the recapitulation of Hamilton's occluded, "true" womanhood. On the other hand, though, it is generally *contemporary* scholars who have, until quite recently, overwhelmingly used female pronouns to refer to the historical Hamilton, while Fielding's own pronouns shift constantly throughout the text. Fielding, of course, does not shift pronouns out of any attempt to affirm the historical Hamilton's experience of gender, whatever that might have been, but the fact that he does it at all suggests that, as Greta LaFleur argues, the eighteenth century in fact evinced "widespread cultural familiarity with the possibilities for gendered behavior that existed outside a singular, consolidated, and requisite manhood or womanhood."[36]

Narratives of transmasculine gender-crossing in this period, as scholars have long noted, are frequently centrally concerned with labor and class mobility: after all, as men had far greater access to a wider variety of work and earned higher wages, there were clear economic benefits to becoming a man, and representations of this form of gender-crossing in popular print often reflected this.[37] But while economically motivated gender-crossing seems to be at odds with some contemporary popular understandings of transgender identity as a deeply felt interior experience that cannot be reduced to material exigency, eighteenth-century narratives of gender-crossing do not presume these two possibilities as mutually exclusive—thus opening up these narratives about gendered labor to potential trans readings that they have thus far rarely inspired. For example, the anonymously published biography of the famous "female soldier" Hannah Snell describes Snell's motivations for gender-crossing in terms that freely mingle economic necessity with both sexual desire and an interiorized experience of deeply felt masculinity:

> As she was now free from all the Ties arising from Nature and Consanguinity; she thought herself privileged to roam in quest of the Man, who, without Reason, had injured her so much; for there are no Bounds to be set either to Love, Jealousy or Hatred, in the female Mind. That she might execute her Designs with the better Grace, and the more Success, she boldly commenced a Man, at least in her Dress, and no doubt she had a Right to do so, since she had the real Soul of a Man in her Breast.[38]

The author here is, on one level, matter-of-fact about the dire economic circumstances motivating Snell's decision: she has been abandoned by her husband and saddled with his debts, and so her unmooring "from Nature and Consanguinity" has left her destitute. At the same time, the narrator also (as is quite conventional in the genre) cites the power of "Love" over the "female mind" as the most crucial motive for leaving London in male clothing. The narrator then adds a third explanation: "she had the real Soul of a Man in her Breast." Even this statement oscillates between desire and identification; it can be read, after all, as both Snell's possession of a masculine "Soul" *and* as Snell's love for a man that lodges this man's "Soul . . . in her Breast." In this narrative, the language of interiority constructs Snell as both a desiring wife *and* as a masculine spirit; both seem to be taken equally seriously and the narrator never indicates that this is a contradiction to worry about. Was Snell motivated by desperation for an income, love for her absent husband, or a masculine heart? The narrative never asks us to choose. The fact that these can coexist suggests that the language of interiority is doing something other than implying a single, coherent truth that must be exposed and understood.

The anonymously authored *Life and Imaginations of Sally Paul* (1760), which purports to be the autobiography of an actual "female husband," Sarah Paul/Samuel Bundy, narrates an arrest that reveals a similar logic to the one portrayed in *The Female Husband,* as gender-crossing is framed as a form of imposture that signals plebian disorder and the resistance of enclosure:

> I was in the custody of a constable, and by him introduced to the presence of Mr. Justice Clarke, who was not only an acting magistrate in the

> Borough, but, as I suppose, more particularly skillful in the law, and distinction of sexes; and, after a brief hearing by his worship, committed to bridewell, on a presumption, as I take it, that the attempt to alter nature's decree, and deceive under the colour of false apparances, was much the same thing as disguising my face, and thereby bringing myself within the Waltham Black Act.[39]

Reporting on the actual case that inspired this tale, the *London Magazine* noted that Paul/Bundy's marriage was indeed regarded as financial fraud: "She was obliged to depend upon her wife for support, who expended her money and pawned her cloaths for her mate's maintenance; which is the fraud she is charged with."[40] However, when the *Life and Imaginations* takes fictional liberties with this case and likens the role of "female husband" with poaching in violation of the notorious Black Act, the text aligns Paul/Bundy's assumption of maleness with lower-class assertions of customary rights to subsistence in the face of enclosure. As vagrancy laws criminalized many forms of subsistence outside of wage labor, we might here understand vagrancy, as in *The Female Husband,* as criminalizing the unauthorized appropriation of "enclosed" maleness as a kind of subsistence. This, in turn, offers us an avenue for understanding gender-crossing narratives more broadly in the context of vagrancy law's intertwined aims of lower-class labor regulation and the mitigation of threat through the construction of the "suspicious person" as a paradigmatic object of police.

The possibility of pursuing trans reading practices through the textual archive of vagrancy becomes even clearer through a curious archival resonance with Fielding's text from across the Atlantic. Eight years after the publication of *The Female Husband,* another vagrancy arrest echoing the details of the original Hamilton case was recorded in the press. On July 16, 1752, the *Pennsylvania Gazette* published a notice from Chester, Pennsylvania that "a Person, that went by the Name of Charles Hamilton, came here, and offered for Sale at several Houses in Town sundry Medicines for different Disorders; pretending he was brought up to the Business of a Doctor and Surgeon."[41] Like the Hamilton that inspired Fielding's story, this Hamilton's gender presentation attracts the attention of the law: "But it being suspected that the Doctor was a Woman in Mens Cloaths, was taken up, examined, and found to be a Woman; and confessed she had used that Disguise for several Years. She is very bold, and can give no good

Account of herself."[42] Like Fielding, the author of this account uses both male and female pronouns to mark Hamilton's fluctuating perceived gender; when the author describes Hamilton as "pretending he was brought up to the Business of a Doctor," Hamilton's profession, not gender, is emphasized as the fraud here; the article's use of "he" signals that Hamilton was perceived to be a man while selling medicines from door to door. The author then switches to "she" after narrating that Hamilton was "found to be a Woman," thus inviting the reader to adopt the perception of Hamilton's gender imposed by the juridical sexing of Hamilton's body and/or narrative. As was particularly common in the North American colonies, the notice of Hamilton's arrest as a suspicious person was placed in the newspaper as an invitation for readers to match the description to fugitives from bound labor: "She is detained in Prison here, till we see whether any Body appears against her, if not she will be discharged."[43]

In February 1753, a Virginia planter named David Currie placed an advertisement in the *Pennsylvania Gazette,* claiming that he had read the account of Hamilton's arrest and had "reason to believe" that Hamilton was his runaway indentured servant, whom he named as Sarah Knox.[44] Several months earlier, he had placed an advertisement seeking her return, which had evidently proven unsuccessful, as he also reprints his earlier advertisement (dated September 22, 1752) along with his updated advertisement in response to the Hamilton arrest. Interestingly, the previous advertisement also suggested that Knox might take up disguise, but differently gendered:

> Run away from the subscriber, at the Glebe of the said county, on the 4th of May, A convict servant woman, named Sarah Knox (alias Howard, alias Wilson) of a middle size, brown complexion, short nose, talks broad, and said she was born in Yorkshire, had been in t'he army for several years, with the camp in Flanders, and at the battle of Colloden, where she lost her husband. She may pretend to be a dancing mistress; will may a great many courtesies, and is a very deceitful, bold, insinuating woman, and a great liar.[45]

This Hamilton, like the Hamilton who caught Fielding's attention in 1746, disappears from the historical record after this single instance of vagrancy arrest, and David Currie does not appear to have ever recaptured his fugitive servant.[46]

Hamilton's name, profession of quack doctor, and gender presentation all resonate tantalizingly with the case fictionalized by Fielding eight years earlier, raising the question: is this the same person? The few historians who have noticed these similarities reach strikingly different conclusions. Clare Lyons and Jen Manion, for example, posit that this is indeed the same person who had been arrested in Somerset eight years before, while Gwenda Morgan and Peter Rushton believe that this is Sarah Knox, who may have heard Hamilton's story through its notoriety on both sides of the Atlantic and assumed the identity of its protagonist as a disguise while a fugitive from indenture.[47] Both (and other) scenarios are possible—the Hamilton of Fielding's story disappears from definitive historical record after 1746.[48] I am less concerned with determining which is true; seeking a consistent, documented identity from incongruous stories is uncomfortably similar to the objectives of perception that motivated both arrests for vagrancy in the first place. Instead, I want to note how this incident clearly reveals the transatlantic mobility of two things: vagrancy law and the mode of perception through which perceived gender incongruity becomes a sign of imposture, fraud, and potential criminality. Furthermore, I think it is no accident that the transgender resonance of this case comes into particularly sharp focus in this transatlantic frame; the specifically colonial culture of print surveillance of fugitivity makes vagrancy crucial to the tracking of consistent identity through markers of gender, among other features.[49] At the same time, this colonial genre of print surveillance also produces the extensive archive through which we might place vagrancy law and the reading practices that surround it firmly in trans history.

Indeed, besides the shared name and biographical accounts, the other striking resonance between these two arrests is that both are for vagrancy. While the 1746 vagrancy arrest in Somerset, as Claire Derry persuasively argues, was likely motivated by community elites' outrage at both sexual and gender transgression, the reported 1752 arrest in Chester makes no mention of sex; this arrest is instead far more clearly motivated by gender presentation alone.[50] But of course, the flexibility of vagrancy law—which made it amenable both to the Corporation of Glastonbury (as they sought to prosecute a sexual arrangement that did not seem to be technically illegal) and to the local authorities in Chester (as they sought to take up suspicious persons and possible fugitives)—also serves to further unite these cases under a broad, diffuse legal rubric. The notice of Hamilton's arrest in Chester reflects the colonial adaptation of vagrant passes as documentary evidence of legitimate travel and personal identity; Hamilton says "that he embarked on board a Brigantine, at Topsham, in England, last Fall, for Philadelphia, one Robinson Commander, but was cast away the latter End of January on the Coast of North-Carolina; and that he had travelled from thence to Virginia and Maryland, and has a Pass signed by some Magistrates in Virginia and Maryland, and one in Newcastle County."[51] However, in the eyes of local authorities, the incongruity of Hamilton's appearance with expected markers of gender renders the passes suspect as documentary evidence of legitimate mobility. In the North American colonies, marked by broad opportunities for mobility, anonymity, and the assumption of new identities, those charged with the scrutiny of unknown people weighed such documentation against a variety of additional identity markers.[52]

Gender, in *The Female Husband,* becomes a rubric for theorizing interpretation and perception, linking the sexed body to the truth of identity. Miss Ivythorn, for instance, notes details that, to her mind, ought to have rendered her more suspicious in her appraisal of Hamilton's body, thus also teaching the reader precisely how to scrutinize bodies for naturalized signs of sex: "I always thought indeed your shape was something odd, and have often wondred that you had not the least bit of Beard; but I thought you had been a man for all that, or I am sure I would not have been so wicked to marry you for the world" (42). Meanwhile, the Charles Hamilton arrested in 1752 was, according to the *Pennsylvania Gazette,* also scrutinized for consistent markers of gender, "it being suspected that the Doctor was a Woman in Mens Cloaths." Whether or not the arrest in Chester in 1752 concerns the same person, this incident certainly reveals an interplay between gendered literary and legal reading practices, and the embeddedness of both in broader print marketplaces.

David Currie's advertisements exemplify some of the reading practices at the nexus of vagrancy, policing, and print culture. His original advertisement conforms to many of the general conventions that govern runaway advertisements, noting several of the standard characteristics (sex, size, complexion, accent, and any remarkable features or habits) in its description of Sarah Knox.[53] When Currie read the item in the *Pennsylvania Gazette* noting the arrest of Charles Hamilton, he used the same skills as he had earlier used to write his runaway advertisement, scanning the story for personal description that might assist in recognizing a known person, and matching the vagrant's "account" with the habits of self-fashioning he attributed to his servant. He was assisted in this endeavor by the description provided by the newspaper article; in publicizing the arrest of a vagrant, this item echoes the generic conventions of the runaway advertisement, as it participates in the same network of surveillance: "She is very bold, and can give no good Account of herself; says she is about Twenty-eight years of Age, tho' she seems to be about Forty. She wears a blue Camblet Coat, with Silver Twist Buttons, too large for her."[54]

Currie's response to a reprint of this article records traces of his reading practice, as he cites the article and repeats descriptive elements that may have been the most instrumental in leading him to believe that Hamilton was his servant:

> In reading of the Virginia Gazette, No. 87, I find an extract of a letter from Chester, in Pennsylvania, July 13, 1752, mentioning a quack Doctor, by the name of Charles Hamilton, pretending to be brought up under Dr. Green, a noted Mountebank in England, who turns out to be a woman in mens cloaths, and now assumes the name of Charlotte Hamilton, and calls herself about 28 years of age, tho' seems to be about 40: Thus much of the letter, and if she talks broad, I have reason to believe that she is the very servant that belongs to me.[55]

By asking the reader to collate all the features listed in the multiple printed items he has gathered, and to add to this their own observation of the fugitive's speech, he calls on the reader of his advertisement to continue the chain of perception and interpretation, further honing the collective skill of participants in print surveillance. By noting the names of Charles Hamilton, Charlotte Hamilton, and Sarah Knox, and asserting them all to refer to the same person, Currie locates the truth of consistent identity not in a name, but in the (sexed) body rendered in print, made available to the public through description not only of gendered markers, but also of features including age, accented speech, and complexion.

It is this diffuse network of surveillance that I see as particularly resonant as a part of transgender history; whether or not we can or should identify either Charles Hamilton as a transgender individual (or indeed, as the same transgender individual), the use of vagrancy law to understand gender as a marker of embodied, consistent, and trackable personal identity reveals how the rubric of police helps construct gender as metonym for identity—a link that is crucial to the more recent sexological models of gender as well as to the emergence of transgender identity as a relation to this model of gender.[56] Understanding vagrancy law as a nexus for surveillance and print publicity that helped lay the groundwork for this sense of gender as metonym for personal identity allows us to understand not just this particular vagrancy arrest, but vagrancy law in general, as a part of transgender history. In the English Hamilton's deposition from the Somerset Quarter Sessions Rolls, Hamilton's first-person narration has apparently been transcribed, but each instance of "I" has been crossed out and replaced with "she."[57] The juridical production of these "she" pronouns materializes the administrative production of gender in ways that resonate profoundly with contemporary trans experiences of gender administration and bureaucracy.[58] More broadly, the centrality of gender to both of the vagrancy arrests I discuss here allows us to understand the place of vagrancy law in the histories of surveillance and policing that have profoundly shaped modern transgender identity and politics—as well as created much of the surviving archive for early transgender history.

Vagrancy law was, after all, instrumental to the early development of the bureaucratic modes of personal identity documentation that so foundationally structure contemporary transgender experience; vagrant passes formed a blueprint for the modern passport, while the parish register's use as an authoritative confirmation of consistent identity in a settlement examination was an early example of the kind of state identity documentation that would go on to be central to the project of modern nation-states' biopolitical record-keeping.[59] When Toby Beauchamp, then, argues that "the monitoring of transgender and gender-nonconforming populations is inextricable from questions of national security and regulatory practices of the state," the very contemporary modes of surveillance he theorizes are among the afterlives of historical vagrancy law, and thus offer us a way of understanding eighteenth-century vagrancy law as part of this ongoing transgender history.[60] This does not necessarily require us to claim eighteenth-century subjects as themselves transgender. Indeed, Beauchamp's argument, while contemporary, is also not limited to the analysis of individuals who claim transgender identity: "Approaching the relationship between gender-nonconformity and state surveillance in this way means resisting the urge to think about surveillance of gendered bodies as limited only to medical and legal monitoring of specifically transgender-identified individuals. In fact it points to the importance of thinking more broadly about the interactions between regulatory gender norms, racialization processes and ideals of citizenship."[61]

A trans reading of *The Female Husband* and its North American archival echo can offer us powerful insight into the historical relation between vagrancy, police, and what Claire Colebrook characterizes as the "potentialities *to differ*" that articulate "transitivity."[62] Transitivity, for Colebrook, is a conceptual alternative to "trans" as an identity category marked by differentiation from an earlier, stable form of human identity—a stable form that is, she argues, wholly fictive. Building on this notion of transitivity, C. Riley Snorton conceptualizes black and trans theories of history not through the additive confluence of two identities, but through how blackness and transness "overlap in referentiality" and "are brought into the same frame by the various ways they have been constituted as fungible, thingified, and interchangeable, particularly within the logics of transatlantic exchange."[63] For Snorton, archives of nineteenth-century policing, such as records of vagrancy arrests and print surveillance in service of the Fugitive Slave Act, reveal "the transitive relation between fungibility and fugitivity," while the fungibility in question here also highlights the racial histories that enable certain gendered possibilities for transitivity; following Hortense Spillers, he argues that under slavery, "the ungendering of blackness is also the context for imagining gender as subject to rearrangement."[64] This offers us another way to read *The Female Husband* and its North American archival echo as part of an extended and transatlantic archive of vagrancy: in particular, Snorton's work offers a model for how to think through the racial histories of the legibilities and silences that constitute this specific arrangement of documents as potentially legibly "trans" to contemporary readers.

In particular, I want to suggest that whiteness—and specifically, *colonial* whiteness—is part of the matrix that these mid-eighteenth-century texts articulate for forms of crossing that intertwine transmasculinity, economic advancement, and geographical removal. As I argued in Chapter 1, seventeenth-century picaresque fiction makes use of the open-endedness of the "rogue" in order to imagine this social type as ground for spectacular transformation from destitution to sovereignty, often accompanied by colonial dislocation (as exemplified by Meriton Latroon's ascension to wealth in the East Indies, or Moll Flanders's propertied redemption in Virginia). The material and imaginative possibilities accruing to whiteness in a colonial-mercantile world system also shape (in Colebrook's terms) some of the "potentialities" that develop into legible modes of "transitivity." For instance, in *The Widdow Ranter* (1689), Aphra Behn embeds the spectacularization of a freewheeling mode of self-asserting "female masculinity" in its Virginia setting that unsettles a whole host of hierarchical English social relations through the colonial reconfiguration of sovereignty, and the author of Hannah Snell's biography emphasizes her service in the army of the East India Company as enabling her to publicly exemplify both the ideal of feminine chastity and a model of patriotic, adventuresome masculinity.

The description of Charles Hamilton that appears in the *Pennsylvania Gazette* embeds its account of Hamilton's male social existence in an account of colonial mobility: "He embarked on board a Brigantine, at Topsham, in England, last Fall, for Philadelphia, one Robinson Commander, but was cast away the latter End of January on the Coast of North-Carolina; and that he had travelled from thence to Virginia and Maryland."[65] This itinerary—complete with the spectacular reversal of fortune exemplified by the survival of shipwreck—echoes the longstanding place of North America in the English imaginary as the place where people discarded from the metropole might be transformed into valuable subjects of empire, where convicts might be transformed into penitents, where the landless and destitute might transform themselves into expropriators of land. The idea of the American colonies as spaces of both imagined and real possibility for transformation is, of course, a foundational ideological bulwark of settler colonialism. As both Scott Larson and Greta LaFleur have argued, settler colonialism fundamentally shaped the sense of gendered (and gender-transgressive) possibilities for eighteenth-century white North American settlers and their descendents.[66]

At the same time, the technologies of surveillance that caught Hamilton up in the archive of runaway advertisements are also crucial to the genealogy of the surveillance of blackness in particular, as I show in greater detail in Chapter 5. After all, as I discussed in the Introduction, the records of vagrancy arrests in late eighteenth-century Philadelphia show that while both black and white suspected fugitives from bound labor were routinely arrested for vagrancy, the newspaper advertisements that sought to aid in their recapture featured black arrestees far more frequently than white ones; while these techniques of print surveillance were not racially exclusive in their use, they were racializing technologies that played an important role in colonial constructions of blackness as and through fugitivity.

The literary texts most central to consideration in this chapter are largely local, rural, and insularly English in their settings. However, what this transatlantic resonance reveals is that the very construction of English locality as a scale for intimate governance that intertwines the parish with the family and the household relies on its narrative insulation from a largely occluded wider world. For instance, when Fielding invents a career for Hamilton as Methodist preacher in Ireland, he pointedly figures Hamilton as a clearly marked outsider and disruptor of the good order of a rural parish, constructing the locality of the "local" through this window into a disorderly colonial space against which the rural English parish must be defended. As I argued in Chapter 1, vagrancy laws embedded local governance and resource management in broader political-economic questions about the distribution of population across empire. This continues to subtend, however subtly, the political-economic and racial frames for the matrices of gender and sexuality through which these narratives might appear to us today as part of a queer or trans literary/historical archive.

## Settling Down: Dispossession and Domestic Fiction

We have long considered the novel a crucial ideological and affective engine for the consolidation of what would later come to be called "heterosexuality" through the nexus of gendered complementarity, middle-class domesticity, a contract-based model of marriage, the yoking of marital consent to love and desire, and a model of kinship that increasingly privileges the conjugal and the biologically reproductive.[67] The marriage plot, as it increasingly dominated the sentimental fictions that overtook earlier genres such as the picaresque, amatory fiction, and romance, spectacularized women's consent to marriage, thus imposing marriage as inevitable narrative endpoint while also (paradoxically) insisting on consent to marriage as the expression of interiorized female desire.

For good reason, then, scholarship on sexuality and the novel has frequently focused on the marriage plot and its discontents. However, as *The Female Husband* reminds us, the disruption of the marriage plot is not the only threat posed by gender or sexual transgression; Hamilton's sexual transgression disrupts not only the family, but also the good order of the parish. As Scott MacKenzie argues, what we now think of as domesticity was invented first through poor law and parish management, and only later absorbed into the foundational fictions of the middle-class home.[68] As he notes, *Pamela* (as ur-text for sentimental domesticity) draws the analogy between home and parish in particularly vivid terms, reducing the entire world to Mr. B's arena of influence and overlaying his later role as husband onto his existing authority as JP; thus, he argues, "the parish is the primary topos of poverty management, but it might also be called the first topos (and topography) of the English novel."[69] And so if we have come to recognize queerness in, for instance, resistance to the marriage plot as a foundational structure for the conjugal household, then I want to ask: what's queer from the vantage point of the parish?

If we want to understand the emergence of heterosexuality as a class norm, then the history of the parish as a unit for managing social reproduction also helps reveal the importance of poverty management to the history of gender and sexuality in the eighteenth century. Throughout the eighteenth century, parish poor relief played a complex role in the subsistence of the English poor; many—and especially women—who drew on parish poor relief also combined this support with wage labor, gleaning and other forms of commonage, charity, and family support.[70] Poor relief, as it interlocked with kinship networks and other sources of sustenance, is thus implicated in the broader realm of social reproduction.[71] Thus far, in the context of *The Female Husband,* I've been describing gender as a naturalized discourse of trackable identity in the context of policing and surveillance. But the history of vagrancy and poor relief also reveals another simultaneous meaning of gender: a relation to reproduction, subsistence, and material precarity. Poverty in the eighteenth century was extremely gendered, and the category of "woman" was deeply shaped by it. The social meaning of female poverty in particular was also highly sexualized, and the public face of female sexuality took on increasingly economic meanings.[72] For instance, as Laura Rosenthal argues, eighteenth-century attitudes toward sex work marked a departure from earlier models; instead of signifying moral depravity or excessive desire, sex work acquired increasingly economic connotations: it could be either the truth of capitalist logic distilled or the most pitiable symptom of poverty, as midcentury philanthropic attention to "penitent prostitutes" emphasized.[73] Whether portrayed sympathetically or not, the female vagrant was commonly presumed to carry the story of sexual "fall" in her public destitution.[74]

The category of "woman" is thus partly made through the category of vagrancy. To be a woman means that one's dispossession is most likely experienced through or conceptually linked to the realm of kinship, reproduction, or sex. This is precisely the valence of "woman" that is operative and yet gradually effaced in *Pamela,* when Richardson transforms class conflict into a drama of sexual consent and refigures female virtue as transcending class—thus refocusing the category of "woman" on the realm of sex alone. No longer a relation to labor or dispossession as refracted through sex and reproduction, the category is reducible to a sexed body and its mystified interior virtue.

Vagrancy law reveals the conceptualization of the parish as a unit of responsibility for welfare: one that intertwines with and echoes the family, but is also distinct from it. If Foucault's emphasis on the history of sexuality as central to the rise of biopolitics draws our attention to the literal production of life and death as a venue for governmentality, then what I want to emphasize about parish management is that its mandate is not wholly reducible to the realm of biopolitics in these terms.[75] Parish management encompasses governmentality of social reproduction: the social forms, units of affective, material, and social responsibility, webs of at least partial subsistence, and bare minimum levels of material and social welfare that at least partly aim to contain the disruptive byproducts of primitive accumulation.

The complex logic of parish settlement illustrates this. When mid-eighteenth-century magistrates, JPs, and parish officers used vagrancy law, their aim was not to expel *all* impoverished people from the parish, nor did they approach "population" as a unified conceptual problem on a national or global scale (even if, as I argued in the previous chapter, settlement did draw links between the local and the global). Instead, the use of vagrancy law to demarcate who was and was not entitled to relief in the parish helped define the parish as a unit of responsibility, whose limits were complexly articulated around geographical, moral, and social boundaries.[76]

As a unit of responsibility and shared resources, the parish is in some ways analogous to the family. At the same time, those tasked with managing the resources of the parish—especially Justices of the Peace and legal commentators on the role of this office—theorized the family as supplement to the parish but importantly distinct from it. Richard Burn's enormously popular *Justice of the Peace and Parish Officer* (1755) offers some insight into how settlement was intended to work, and Burn's elucidation of extensive court cases to illustrate the nuances of settlement reveal how parish and family intertwine but sometimes diverge. Of course, Burn's instructions do not necessarily straightforwardly reflect actual practice. However, since Burn's text was so widely regarded as authoritative, it offers insight into what circulated as the ideal of settlement, while it also reveals how these ideals—and the different interests that contested them—were disseminated through print.

Burn's explanation of settlement draws foundationally on analogies between parish and household while at the same time elaborating on distinctions between the two. For instance, he introduces the section on settlement with a brief history of the term: "By the common law, a settlement did imply no more, than a man's house and home and habitation; and at the common law a man might gain a settlement any where, and could not be removed, unless in the case of vagrancy."[77] But with the Elizabethan introduction of parish poor relief, he explains, the imperative that parishes provide for the relief of their *own* poor introduced the need for a more complex notion of settlement: one that could determine which parish was responsible for every pauper. Thus Burn's definition of "home"—where a man lives—begins to diverge from legal settlement; settlement is no longer a dwelling place, but a unit of responsibility for one's subsistence, and this could in fact be legally distinct from one's dwelling place in many circumstances.

The life-cycle of family and reproduction, as routed through marriage, provides many of the crucial determinants of settlement: a woman acquires her husband's settlement, legitimate children acquire the settlement of their fathers, and illegitimate children gain settlement in the parish of their birth (though with numerous exceptions).[78] At the same time, settlement can also be acquired through apprenticeship, domestic service, or rent over a minimum yearly amount; settlement thus contains both conjugal and economic arrangements under the same category of local belonging.[79] All of these qualifying events for settlement shaped the forms of life narrative that recurred daily in settlement examinations, as JPs sought to elicit the story that would assign a pauper to their last place of legal settlement and corroborate these stories with the records of birth and marriage in parish registers.

Families, meanwhile, are regarded as supplemental units of responsibility alongside and akin to the parish; in a discussion of assessment of the poor rates, Burn also notes the legal obligation of family members to provide for each other when possible, and notes that parents who abandon their children to rely on parish relief can be arrested as vagrants.[80] In practice, there is evidence to suggest that parish poor relief served, for many, as substitute for family support; Sam Barrett argues that "not having kin (or not having particular sorts of kin) is an important predictor of long-term relationship with the poor law."[81]

However, family and parish don't always operate under identical logics or parameters. For instance, when Burn notes that certificates of settlement are binding, and that a parish is responsible for a person to whom they have granted a certificate until that person gains settlement elsewhere, he uses a legal dispute originating in a case of bigamy to illustrate his point:

> The parish of *Maidstone* gave a certificate to *Hedcron,* acknowledging *Ric. Burden,* and *Mary* his wife, and their four children, to be legally settled at *Maidstone.* Afterwards it appeared, that *Mary* was not his lawful wife, but that he had a former wife then living. Upon which *Maidstone* acknowledged the settlement of the real and true wife, but not of the said *Mary* and their children; and pleaded that it would be hard that they should be

> forced to take two wives, and different children. But by the court, the parish that certifies must take care for whom they certify, and the certificate is conclusive.[82]

Here, the analogy between parish and family breaks down under competing imperatives of legitimacy and responsibility. Richard Burden cannot have two wives, and the parish of Maidstone argues that it ought not to be "forced to take two wives" either. However, since Maidstone has assumed responsibility for Mary Burden upon her presumed marriage, that responsibility (which exempts other parishes from having to assume responsibility for her subsistence) cannot be revoked. So for the purposes of settlement, at least, Richard Burden *does* have two wives, or rather, the parish takes on responsibility for two wives through Richard Burden's extension of settlement to both of them.[83]

Burn's discussion of bastardy and legitimacy underscores the parish's material interest in conceptualizing the family as a primary unit linking reproduction and subsistence: after all, if a family can provide for a child, then the parish won't have to. Generally, illegitimate children gained settlement where they were born, but the many exceptions that Burn lays out here show how illegitimate children were, from the vantage point of settlement law, regarded as a burden that every parish would clearly try to avoid caring for. A parish in which an illegitimate child was born was entitled to track down the child's reputed father and try to extract support from him. Burn's provisos about settlement by birth reveal numerous avenues through which parishes could (and did) try to avoid responsibility whenever possible; for instance, he notes that parish officers sometimes sent pregnant women to another parish only to give birth there, and argues that this amounts to a fraudulent attempt to evade responsibility for the child on the parish officers' parts.[84] However, he explains that if a woman gives birth while traveling through a parish in which she is not settled, and she is deemed a vagrant, the child gains the settlement of the mother, not the settlement of the parish in which it is born. Indeed, in his array of sample vagrant passes, Burn gives a standard "Record to avoid the settlement of a bastard child born in vagrancy," which documents the mother's vagrancy to support the claims of the parish of birth that it is not responsible for the child.[85]

When Burn argues that "there are divers good reasons for requiring certificates with persons coming to settle in any place; namely, that persons residing under them can gain no settlement," he characterizes a settlement certificate as surefire insurance against ever having to be responsible for a newcomer to the parish should they require relief.[86] At least as far as poor relief was concerned, the nation was made up of contiguous and discrete units that managed their own resources and maintained the boundaries of who belonged to them and who did not. The aspect of police that settlement law concerned, then, conceptualized security not as the straightforward *exclusion* of strangers, but rather as the maintenance of boundaries of responsibility for subsistence. To be settled in a parish was, by definition, not to be anyone else's problem.

So what does it mean to be a place's responsibility? What does it mean to be a woman, in this context, and what does it mean to reproduce? From the vantage point of settlement law, the central concern raised by reproduction is not the coherence of filiation, but responsibility for the child's material needs. This is a major distinction between the parish and the family. A bastard, for instance, can be legally unrecognized as a member of any family, but must still have parish settlement somewhere: the child is a mouth to feed and some place must be deemed responsible for its sustenance. Gender and sexuality are thus made and negotiated not only through the family, but also through the overlapping yet distinct realm of parish management and its broad ambit of concern for subsistence, welfare, and local responsibility.

This relationship between parish management and the political economy of domesticity illuminates the scale of Sarah Scott's reconfiguration of the domestic in *Millenium Hall* (1762). This novel has long been acknowledged to offer a feminist and/or sapphic version of domestic fiction that resists the imperatives of both heterosexuality and the marriage plot.[87] *Millenium Hall* imagines a utopia of female homosociality in which the egalitarian bonds of friendship unite "indigent gentlewomen" and other ladies whose marriage plots have failed, while their egalitarianism is enabled by their collective governance of the local poor and disabled.[88] Ann Van Sant has shown that the utopian vision of *Millenium Hall* does not entirely reject the family *tout court,* as feminist and queer readings of the novel have frequently contended; rather, Scott adapts a very traditional version of family—the household family—to be the model for women's community.[89] Based not on conjugality, but rather on co-residence, discipline, and the management of collective resources, the household family, Van Sant argues, "gave Scott a warrant both for her most progressive thinking (through which she achieves liberty of association for women) and her generally conservative social vision (marked by disciplinary relations with those of lower social rank)."[90] Building on Van Sant's important insights, I argue that while the household family was one crucially important model for eighteenth-century understandings of how social reproduction, subsistence, affiliation, and discipline could be coordinated, the parish was another such model—a model that frequently overlapped with both conjugal and household ideas of family. Scott not only adapts the household family as a model for women's affiliations, but also reconfigures gender, sociality, and relation to marriage by granting the ladies many of the powers of parish management.

After all, the ladies of *Millenium Hall* exercise the powers of a local Justice of the Peace combined with those of the Overseers of the Poor. The novel's narrator immediately apprehends the scale of the ladies' influence as reaching beyond the house itself; in the fields surrounding the estate, he notes that the hay-makers display "rural simplicity, without any of those marks of poverty and boorish rusticity, which would have spoilt the pastoral air of the scene around us," and then describes the house as the "Primum Mobile of all we had yet beheld."[91] When wandering the grounds, he observes "the neatest cottages I ever saw," and asks an old woman who is spinning in one of them about them. She credits her happiness to the ladies' beneficent parish management:

> I was almost starved when they put me into this house, and no shame of mine, for so were my neighbours too; perhaps we were not so painstaking as we might have been; but that was not our faults, you know, as we had not things to work with, nor any body to set us to work. . . . Nay, all the parish were so when they came into it, young and old, there was not much to chuse, few of us had rags to cover us, or a morsel of bread to eat, except the two Squires; they indeed grew rich, because they had our work, and paid us not enough to keep life and soul together; they live above a mile off, so perhaps they did not know how poor we were.[92]

In the woman's description, the ladies do not simply improve the parish through acts of charity; they also take up the duties of JPs, clergy, and Overseers of the Poor. For instance, they imitate a common practice of parish poor management—binding out the children of the poor in apprenticeships—when they "take every child after the fifth of every poor person" and send them to the old women "to keep out of harm, and . . . teach them to knit, and to spin."[93] They read prayers and sermons to the residents of the parish every Sunday after church, and they informally mediate quarrels and disputes (as Justices of the Peace also frequently did); the old woman remarks: "We used to quarrel, to be sure, sometimes when we first came to these houses, but the ladies condescended to make it up amongst us."[94] Mrs. Mancel later describes the scope of their influence as precisely the scale of the rural parish—larger than an individual family or household, but smaller than a city or a nation: "We do not set up for reformers, said Mrs. Mancel, we wish to regulate ourselves by the laws laid down to us, and as far as our influence can extend, endeavour to enforce them; beyond that small circle all is foreign to us"[95] Lisa Moore reads this "small circle" as the domestic sphere, but as the old woman in the cottage makes clear, the small circle is not *that* small; instead, it reproduces the administrative and aesthetic scale of the rural parish: a zone of intimate governance that acts through and conceptually invokes the family but whose scope extends farther than a single household.[96]

In the story of Mrs. Morgan and its familiar tropes of parental tyranny colluding with the tyrannical husband, Scott reconfigures this recognizable domestic plot through the crucial material transfiguration of Mr. Morgan's estate into a seat of virtuous, collective, female parish management. The ladies of *Millenium Hall* do not become "female husbands" in the way that Fielding's Hamilton does (taking up the plot of seduction by stepping into the role of the rake); instead, the role they step into is not one fundamentally defined by position within the conjugal family at all. They become the collective paterfamilias of the parish even as they utterly reject the paternal logic of rule among themselves. At the same time, though they claim a resolutely local scope for their philanthropic efforts, their acts of parish management in fact also link the local management of subsistence and reproduction to the management of population across empire, as I have argued that historical vagrancy law also did. For instance, in *The History of Sir George Ellison,* Scott describes the ladies as an inspiration for Ellison's numerous philanthropic projects, which include both "improved" plantation management in Jamaica and poor-relief schemes back in England.[97]

The ladies assume responsibility for the welfare, security, and subsistence of their "small circle"—within its bounds. If being a woman means that your own access to subsistence is routed through the realm of social reproduction, then to be a woman *in power,* Scott proposes, means to govern social reproduction by assuming responsibility for the affective, moral, reproductive, and material resources of a community. While the authors of "female husband" texts propose (whether in horror or admiration, or something in between) that one way to relate to being assigned "woman" as your category of relation to labor and subsistence is to exit it and seek another relation to production and reproduction, Scott proposes an alternative that is nonetheless equally rooted in the relationship of gender to labor. The ladies of *Millenium Hall* do not reject, but rather embrace the tight link between womanhood and social reproduction, offering an avenue for aristocratic female power and autonomy through the management of social reproduction on the scale of the parish.

## Queer Subsistence: Mary Saxby's *Memoirs of a Female Vagrant*

The novel is only one genre among many that linked narrative, biological and social reproduction, subsistence, and consistent identity. Settlement, after all, was determined through narrative. The settlement examination is an imperative to life narrative that is not concerned with interiority, *Bildung,* or the core of the self, but rather combs a life story for pertinent information about whose responsibility a person might be. Burn's sample form for the "Examination of a vagrant" makes the centrality of narrative clear:

> THE examination of A. O. a rogue and vagabond, taken on oath before me ______ one of his majesty's justices of the peace in and for the said county, the ____ day of _____ in the year ____ of the reign of ____
>
> *Who on his oath saith, That he was born at* ____ [and so trace out the history of his life, so far forth as to ascertain his legal place of settlement].[98]

If domestic fiction renders narrative a metonym for the interior, for desire, for sincerity, and for a self, then the settlement examination is an important counterpoint. This routine insistence on narrative sought out a very different sense of the self: the question is *not* "Who are you?" but rather "What place is responsible for your subsistence?" The core of the self is not the mystery of desire, virtue, or consent; the core of the self is the need to eat, and the only real question is who is compelled to feed you. Burn instructs his readers to "trace out the history" of a vagrant's life, but only "so far forth as to ascertain his legal place of settlement"; when the facts of the life narrative match the legal criteria for determining settlement, then the story may end.

In contrast to *Millenium Hall,* in which "lesbian-like" modes of affiliation between women are enabled by the replacement of a novelistic marriage plot with a feminized vision of collective parish management, Mary Saxby's *Memoirs of a Female Vagrant* (1806) renders "lesbian-like" attachments visible as experiences of shared labor and subsistence, which come into view only because the narrator is answering the imperatives of settlement examination by giving a full account of how she supported herself.[99] This text thus offers the unusual opportunity for us to see an author taking up the imperatives of settlement examinations as fodder for narrative from the vantage point of the person deemed "vagrant." As Carolyn Steedman reminds us, this text is not a spontaneous outpouring of autobiographical self-expression, but is foundationally structured by the enforced narratives that poor-law administration had long relied on; while the text does indeed offer the story of one labeled "vagrant" and departs, generically, from the settlement examinations, statutes, and arrest records that more typically make up the administrative archive of vagrancy, the text itself is nonetheless shaped by the institutional and administrative mechanisms that forged "vagrancy" as a legible category.[100] Saxby's redeployment of the structure of settlement reveals not only the formal impress of vagrancy law on an early example of working-class autobiography, but also the role vagrancy and settlement played in the historical construction of heterosexuality—as well as the construction of a repertoire of potentially queer refusals.

The *Memoirs* were edited from Saxby's writings after her death, and as the text's editor, Samuel Greatheed, explains in a prefatory letter to

Joseph Wilson, the project's patron, Saxby's writings also included poems and religious reflections that were ultimately excluded from the memoir, as Greatheed deemed the story of her life most likely to be useful to the poor if published cheaply.[101] Greatheed (sometimes spelled Greathead) was a clergyman and minor literary figure; he was a friend of William Cowper, eventually preaching Cowper's funeral sermon, and he founded a Dissenting literary periodical, the *Eclectic Revew*.[102] In a letter dated June 25, 1802—four years before the publication of *Memoirs of a Female Vagrant*—Greatheed wrote to the Religious Tract Society offering up Mary Saxby as an example of the good works promoted by the society and as "herself a wonderful monument of divine mercy."[103] Noting that Saxby "often endeavoured to settle in business, but could only obtain a livelihood as a hawker," Greatheed credits the rise of cheap evangelical publication with offering Saxby a newly legitimate line of work as a substitute for her earlier, criminalized, and vagrant-identified pursuits of ballad-singing and hawking; he praises her ability, later in life, to earn a living selling Cheap Repository Tracts as well as the publications of the Religious Tract Society and thus become "a zealous, useful, and even a disinterested agent" of Christian conversion.[104]

The collaboration between Greatheed and Wilson—a clergyman and a magistrate—sets up this text as thoroughly embedded in the institutions of poor relief.[105] Greatheed's prefatory letter, as well as his commentary added as footnotes throughout the text, frame Saxby's story as both an opportunity for spiritual education as well as a warning to the nation about the dangers posed by the "wandering classes of the poor"; of these, Greatheed writes that "a ray of light is here thrown on the different shades of their obscure condition; from the vagabond huckster, down to the ballad singer, the beggar, and the gypsy. These outcasts are a reproach to our nation, a pest to the country, and too often a fatal snare to unsteady and unwary youth."[106] At the same time, Greatheed promises that the text will serve as a form of poor relief itself, as the proceeds will be donated to Saxby's daughter Kezia, who "deserves, as well as needs, the assistance that may be derived from it."[107] The text's dual aim—to expose the undeserving as threats and to relieve the deserving—situates it firmly in the use of vagrancy law to govern the parish and distribute its resources.

Saxby begins her story with all the generic trappings of a settlement examination, offering her date and place of birth (easily checked against parish records) and the specific professions and conditions of her parents: "I was born in London, in the year 1738. My mother dying when I was very young, and my father going into the army, I was exposed to distress, even in my infancy."[108] The story of her childhood is a fragmentary recollection of residence and subsistence; she recalls that she "was continually removed from the charge of one relation to that of another," and she details how, after running away from home, she survives on rotten fruit scavenged from markets and food shared with her by beggars, eventually concluding: "Here my memory fails, as to my means of subsistence for some time."[109] In the detailed recollection of her precise modes of subsistence, up to the stated limits of memory, Saxby recalls the narrative imperative of the settlement examination and its demand for a full account of parentage, residence, employment, and sources of subsistence; her life story is, as Steedman argues, "structured by all the other involuntary accounts she had delivered up, over the course of fifty years."[110]

At the same time, Saxby's story—and its theorization of vagrancy as a category—sometimes diverges from Greatheed's editorial framing, with its clear distinction between vagrant and settled. For instance, after Saxby has been abandoned by several partners, she is taken in by an old woman who soon "proved a snare," as the woman's son, she writes, "swore he would kill me, if I did not promise to have him; and I know not how I escaped."[111] Greatheed's footnote attributes this threat of violence to the condition of vagrancy: "A wandering life affords opportunities of eluding the effect of laws, while it tends to eradicate social affections, and to preclude religious instruction. The vagrant classes of the British poor appear to be inferior in civilization to the Bedouin Arabs."[112] However, in Saxby's narrative, violence is most consistently accompanied not by the condition of itinerancy, but by the condition of familial or conjugal relation, whether itinerant or settled. Nor is it identifiable with a stable category of person as implied by Greatheed's racializing metaphor. As a child, for instance, while under the care of her aunt, Saxby is threatened by a knife-wielding man enlisted by her aunt to "intimidate [her] into submission," and her father repeatedly imprisons her in her room—finally chaining her in place by the leg—until she runs away.[113] All of her conjugal arrangements, including her eventual marriage to John Saxby, are marked by constant violence and confinement, and as the second half of the text becomes a tale of Methodist conversion, her husband's abuse fills the narrative role of the trial that tests the newly pious Saxby's religious commitment. In this text, violence is not, as Greatheed argues, the result of vagrancy's degradation of "social affections"; rather, it is precisely the mode through which familial and conjugal "social affections" operate.

Meanwhile, if Saxby theorizes anything within her to be a "vagrant" temperament, it's a consistent distaste for family and its yoking of subsistence and affiliation to obedience; she recalls that as a child, her "perverse temper" led her to resist "the controul of any of [her] friends."[114] After running away from home, she meets a poor woman who serves as a surrogate mother, but it is precisely her similarity to a parent that leads Saxby to resist her: "I might have been very happy; as she was a tender, motherly woman, and would have taught me to get my bread honestly, had I been ruled by her. But here again, my proud, imperious temper, began to shew itself incapable of any restraint."[115] She therefore runs away with one of the woman's daughters, and they become ballad-singers.

The relationships that Saxby repeatedly seeks out are those between her and other women who have no semblance of parental or otherwise familial authority over her. As the only relationships that are not structured by submission to authority, these horizontal relationships with other women recur throughout the story, as the young Saxby repeatedly chooses them over the forms of familial authority she seeks to escape. On one occasion, her association with another woman leads directly to her arrest for vagrancy. She has traveled to Essex, "where they would not suffer any one to travel without a licence, except they could give a very good account of themselves."[116] She sings ballads in the market, where she meets "a middle-aged woman, who looked like a traveller," and they go to sleep in an alehouse, but unbeknownst to Saxby, "she proved to be a common woman."[117] The woman's profession then leads to both of their arrests and confinement in the local bridewell. Her horizontal affiliations with other women are almost always associated with ballad-singing, a profession frequently criminalized as a form of vagrancy and popularly associated with sex work.[118] In Saxby's narrative, it also takes on another implication: only when she sings ballads with other women does she seem to have any kind of relationship with another person that is not predicated on hierarchical authority and an intimate division of labor that intertwines with it.

If we read an undercurrent of the "lesbian-like" in Saxby's text, it's not evidenced through erotic desire for other women—the text doesn't indicate anything like this—but rather through Saxby's own theorization of her youthful vagrancy as resistance of familial governance, and specifically in the portrayal of nonfamilial relationships with women as the only opportunities to escape the violent constitution of "the family" as such—that is, until her conversion to Methodism toward the end of the narrative offers a spiritual escape from domestic violence instead. When she sings ballads with other women, the horizontality of their relationship is predicated on intertwined forms of sameness: they are both women, and they are both performing the exact same kind of labor.

Unlike the Unaccountable Wife, Saxby gives an account of herself, but this account still does not reveal erotic desire as the signal experience of interiority. Instead, like a settlement examination, Saxby's account of herself primarily narrates her relation to subsistence and material responsibility. Meanwhile, as the text itself was intended to both materially benefit Saxby's daughter and spiritually manage the poor readers that Greatheed hoped it would reach, *Memoirs of a Female Vagrant* links life narrative firmly to material subsistence and the management of social reproduction on a broader scale. Even as interiority had ascended as what Deidre Lynch characterizes as the mid-eighteenth-century novel's claim to its "singular distinction" in the print marketplace, this other valence of the narrative account persisted in marginal, ephemeral, and cheap print left behind by the novel's consolidation and "rise."[119] This text, in answering to the settlement examination's demand of an account of subsistence, reveals how the archive of vagrancy can be a rich archive for queer history: the demand to reveal one's means of subsistence may not produce an account of interiorized erotic desire, but it does incite narratives of the attachments, affiliations, and relationships that can emerge from arrangements of subsistence that resist or are excluded from the conjugal family's gendered division of labor, and from the modes of parish management that embedded this division of labor in a broader web of social reproduction.

## Vagrant Figures of Queer History

If vagrancy can function as a nonidentitarian category of deviance, as defined by the intersections of the family, the household, and the state, then its resonance with the anti-identitarian thrust of queer politics becomes clear. At the same time, the queerness of vagrancy in texts such as Fielding's should also remind us that queer narratives or methods are not always as antinormative as we might like to believe. For instance, Foucault's 1977 essay, "Lives of Infamous Men," which was intended as a preface to a collection of fragments encountered in the archives of seventeenth- and eighteenth-century penal regimes, has become something of a touchstone for contemporary theorists of sexuality, history, and temporality.[120] In his attempt to gather the flashes of narrative produced by an encounter with carceral power into "a kind of herbarium," Foucault catalogues lists of figures that are, like the targets of vagrancy law, united only in their opacity and unaccountability: "So I excluded everything in the way of imagination or literature: none of the dark heroes that the latter have invented appeared as intense to me as these cobblers, these army-deserters, these garment-sellers, these scriveners, these vagabond monks, all of them rabid, scandalous, or pitiful."[121] For Carolyn Dinshaw, this miscellany can be read as "the beauty and terror, perhaps, of queer community, constituted by nothing more than the connectedness (even across time) of singular lives that unveil and contest normativity."[122]

But even when vagrancy laws and queer histories take opposing stances toward their objects of scrutiny, they both rely on this feature of anticipatory logic and open-ended, flexible categories of deviance. Indeed, for Foucault, it is precisely the discretionary nature of policing that generates the strange archival juxtapositions that are the stuff of queer history. Of the necessary conditions for the generation of his archival materials, he writes:

> It first required a combination of circumstances that, contrary to all expectations, focused the attention of power and the outburst of its anger on the most obscure individual, on his mediocre life, on his (after all, rather ordinary) faults: a stroke of misfortune that caused the vigilance of officials or of institutions, aimed no doubt at suppressing all disorder, to pick on this person rather than that, this scandalous monk, this beaten woman, this

> inveterate and furious drunkard, this quarrelsome merchant, and not so many others who were making just as much of a ruckus.[123]

The discretionary enforcement of the law is, paradoxically, precisely what generates an archive inviting unknown, erratic, aimless, and nonlinear paths across time: "That is another trait of this dark legend. It has not been transmitted like one that was gilded by some deep necessity, following continuous paths. By nature, it is bereft of any tradition; discontinuities, effacement, oblivion, convergences, reappearances: this is the only way it can reach us. Chance carries it from the beginning."[124]

While for Fielding, the "strange" thoughts of vagrancy are a call to arms, a threat that demands increasingly flexible policing, Foucault evokes this very opacity in order to imagine the police as an unwitting collaborator in the writing of queer history. This collaboration is an ambivalent one. While Dinshaw emphasizes Foucault's intense feeling for his subjects, characterizing it as the creation of a community that exists across time, Heather Love characterizes Foucault's desire as one incited just as much by the violence of the state as by contact with those who suffer under it: "His investment is not so much in these infamous men themselves but rather 'in the darkness in which they could, perhaps should, have remained.' "[125]

More recently, Love has placed queer studies in an intellectual genealogy that, she argues, has long gone unrecognized because it does not neatly align with the antinormative polemical thrust of queer politics: postwar social science carried out under the rubric of deviance studies.[126] This field, with a general interest in the phenomenon of social marginality broader than any given identity category, produce studies whose net was cast as wide as vagrancy law—a net that Love evokes by using the same form of the miscellaneous list of colorful social types that vagrancy law had long relied on: "Through textured, in-depth studies of the social lives of hustlers, con men, prostitutes, alcoholics, and juvenile delinquents, these researchers developed a dynamic, detailed account of the constitution and maintenance of social norms, as well as the consequences of conformity and nonconformity."[127] For Love, returning queer studies to some of its social-scientific roots allows scholars in the field to acknowledge the implication of even the most polemically antinormative scholarship in regimes of "systems of power, management, and control," since the mode of observation behind the theorization of deviance is uncomfortably resonant with the modes of control to which deviance is subjected.[128]

Open-endedness and an anti-identitarian disinterest in the subject have long been considered privileged modes and aesthetics for queer resistance, but the eighteenth-century sexuality of vagrancy offers one example of how open-endedness is not always resistant, and how the subject and its discontents are sometimes beside the point. If Miller and Bender's classic accounts of the novel emphasize omniscience, revelation, and interiority as technologies of discipline, then the traversal of vagrancy across the margins of the eighteenth-century novel and its emerging marriage plot draws our attention to opacity, unaccountability, and deviance as they theorize sex, gender, subsistence, and reproduction—but don't necessarily make deviant *or* disciplined subjects. As Greta LaFleur argues, sexuality before sexology is not necessarily the realm of the subject at all.[129] Eighteenth-century vagrancy law criminalized those who could give no good account of themselves, but it did not ultimately demand its objects' revelations of interior subjectivity, nor did it depend on a mechanism for universal transparency before the law—or before the omniscient narrator. Instead, vagrancy posits a model of deviance that does not depend on identitarian coherence in order to function, and allows us to trace novelistic histories of gender and sexuality outside traditional accounts of the domestic sphere and its subjects.

*CHAPTER THREE*

# LYRIC POPULATION AND THE PROSPECTS OF POLICE

In "Anthropomorphism in Lyric and Law," Barbara Johnson famously writes that "lyric and law might be seen as two very different ways of instating what a 'person' is."[1] Revisiting one of the central questions of her earlier essay "Apostrophe, Animation, and Abortion"—how rhetorical figure simultaneously constructs and undoes legal persons—Johnson argues for the importance of lyric to the rhetorical operations of the law, as both law and lyric insist on the simultaneous urgency and undecidability of the same question: "What is a person?"[2] For Johnson, what lyric and law have in common is that they employ figures (such as anthropomorphism) that seem to rely on the presupposition of the existence of a human subject, yet at the same time continually undo the coherence of this subject by revealing its reciprocal reliance on figure. At stake here is the relationship between two kinds of subject: "the 'first person' (grammatical subject) and the 'constitutional person' (the subject of rights)."[3]

Of course, Johnson relies here on sustaining, or at least not disputing, an identification of lyric with expressive subjectivity sustained through figure. This presumption, however, is precisely what Virginia Jackson seeks to defamiliarize as a creation of twentieth-century critical practice.

Through this practice of "lyricization," she argues, lyric comes to stand in for poetry itself, and the critical practices that collapse poetry into lyric then transform their own protocols of reading into supposed attributes of lyric: expressive subjectivity, unmediated self-presence of the moment of reading, suspension from historical particularity.[4] In a historical process that culminates in New Critical preoccupation with lyric more generally and Romantic lyric in particular, lyric acquires a privileged relation to subjectivity: "Only in lyric poetry is the subject . . . transformed into the sole carrier of meaning, the only true reality."[5] This happens, however, along precisely the "fault line" noted by Johnson: the surprisingly difficult distinction between material human bodies and subjects sustained through figure.[6] In Jackson's account, the New Critical identification of lyric with subjectivity and self-presence ironically effaced historical persons and replaced them with figure, as it "created an abstract personification in place of the historical person, and consequently created an abstract genre accessible to all persons educated to read lyrically."[7]

What is a person? In a sense, this is not actually the difficult legal question. A person—whether a natural person or a fictive juridical person such as a corporation—is a bearer of rights and duties.[8] The difficult question is when legal personhood does and does not attach to human bodies.[9] The central legal text in "Anthropomorphism in Lyric and Law" is a U.S. Supreme Court case, *Rowland v. California Men's Colony, Unit II Men's Advisory Council* (1993), that hinges on the relationship between juridical personhood and human embodiment. When an association of prisoners sought to sue the correctional officers of the prison, they attempted to bring the suit without paying fees, as an indigent person is legally entitled to do. However, courts disagreed as to whether a corporate person such as a prisoners' association could truly prove indigence, or if the state of indigence was limited to natural persons. In her reading of Justice David Souter's ruling that indigence is indeed limited to natural persons, Johnson emphasizes his inability to distinguish natural from artificial personhood without recourse to the very language that sustains artificial personhood before the law: "Souter again turns to Webster's dictionary to find that poverty is a human condition, to be 'wanting in material riches or goods; lacking the comforts of life; needy.' Souter also refers to a previous ruling, which holds that poverty involves being unable to provide for the 'necessities of life.' It is as though only natural persons can have 'life,' and that life is defined as the capacity to lack necessities and comforts. . . . The experience of lack differentiates natural persons from artificial persons."[10] Johnson's legal case study hinges on the question of "indigence": that is, whether the material deprivation and bodily need that characterize poverty can ever attach to a legal person that is not also a human individual. Souter's decision emphasizes the embodied and subjective experience of deprivation—in other words, having a body that can starve or suffer and a mind that can register this suffering—as necessary conditions for the ability to bring a suit *in forma pauperis*. Justice Clarence Thomas's dissent, however, does not concur with a definition of "indigence" that requires a human subject to experience it; he notes that nations can certainly be described as "poor," thus arguing for a notion of legal personhood as capacious as the figurative use of the language that constructs it. As Johnson points out, if we admit corporate personhood, which relies on a figure of personification, then it's hardly an unimaginable leap to allow the anthropomorphism by which a nation or a prisoner's association might be described as indigent.[11]

That Johnson stages the question of lyric subjectivity over the matter of impoverishment and incarceration is, I contend, more significant than it may appear. This particular arena for articulating the boundaries of lyric and legal personhood evokes a longstanding poetic tradition, after all—specifically, the centrality of poverty, indigence, and vagrancy to Romanticism. Romanticism is, of course, at the center of the theoretical lineage that Johnson draws on, and is at the crux of ongoing debates about lyric theory, such as Jackson's periodization of "lyric reading," as she argues that both Romantic poetry itself and its pedagogical afterlife in the New Critical classroom are responsible for the collapse of poetry into lyric.[12]

Scholars have long noted the astonishing ubiquity of vagrancy in early Romantic poetry, and have—particularly in the case of Wordsworth—understood vagrancy as a key site for the articulation of poetic form, poetic labor, and poetic consciousness.[13] In the 1790s, as poets such as Wordsworth, Coleridge, Southey, and Robinson overtly theorized their experiments with and hybridizations of lyric, they also staged encounters between law and lyric through the aestheticization of criminalized poverty.

"Romantic vagrancy," as Celeste Langan defines it, is crucially a *poetic* construction; not to be confused with vagrancy as either a legal status or an economic condition. "Romantic vagrancy" is instead "a representational practice particularly concerned with those aspects of vagrancy susceptible to analogy and subsequent idealization: first, the mobility that appears to guarantee the vagrant a residual economic freedom, despite his or her entire impoverishment; second, the speech-acts that appear to consolidate a residual political identity."[14] Wordsworth, Langan argues, abstracts vagrancy from all specificity into a pure valuelessness that preserves no individual qualities but destitution, thus staging the central premise of liberalism and its reliance on a "logic of equivalence," as "the poet and the vagrant together constitute a society based on the twin principles of freedom of speech and freedom of movement."[15] This articulation of liberalism is echoed in David Simpson's reading of Wordsworth's "poetics of modernity" that stages, without resolving, "the aporias of human interaction in a society of dispersed populations governed by the operation of the commodity form."[16] For Simpson, as with Langan, Wordsworth uses vagrancy not to activate a reparative sympathy, but to stage a capitalist logic of equivalence in stark terms: "What emerges is something darker and more dangerous than any merely democratic brotherhood of man: a solidarity of dispossession and displacement based not on elected but on imposed equalities that we might prefer to live without."[17] Wordsworth's attention to vagrancy in the *Lyrical Ballads* in particular, Thomas Pfau argues, is much more about lyric than it is about vagrancy; the vagrant encounters that Wordsworth repeatedly stages are, for Pfau, "simulated from the very outset" and concerned above all with tutoring the middle-class reader in poetic reading.[18] For Pfau, as for Langan, this version of "Romantic vagrancy" is an avenue for theorizing the relationship between poetry and political representation; in presenting "the lyric as the ultimate aesthetic 'anticommodity,' " he argues, Wordsworth holds up lyric reading as a fount of cultural capital for a middle class whose social and economic ascendancy had not yet found commensurate political representation.[19]

It is, of course, hardly new to claim that Romantic lyric did something other than apotheosize the expressive individual as the paradigmatic lyric subject. As Anne Janowitz and Michael Nicholson have argued, for instance, the Romantic lyric "I" could be collective, expansive, unfixed in time and space—even vagrant.[20] However, in emphasizing the stakes of vagrancy for early Romantic experiments with lyric beyond subjectivity, I seek to defamiliarize what we think we know about "the vagrant" as a poetic figure. In particular, the use of vagrancy by poets like Mary Robinson—the literary focus of this chapter—reveals vagrancy to be a paradoxical vehicle for staging subjectivity in the first place. After all, the *legal* category of vagrancy is not one that presumes, deals with, or sustains legal subjects. Above all, vagrancy law renders its targets' subjectivity, interiority, and power of autonomous action irrelevant: neither criminal intent nor the commission of a criminal act is essential to the legal definition of vagrancy. From the perspective of police, the distinctions so vexed in Johnson's discussion of law and lyric—artificial versus natural persons; rights-bearing legal entities versus vulnerable human bodies or minds capable of intent—are utterly irrelevant.[21]

As I will argue with reference to this chapter's central literary case study, Mary Robinson's *Lyrical Tales* (1800), the legal open-endedness of vagrancy as a category in relation to police renders vagrancy ironically amenable to staging self-conscious poetic experiments in lyric and its limits—experiments that concerned the vexed relationships between lyric, embodiment, life, and death, but did not necessarily resolve in *subjects.* Like the kinds of figure upon which lyric subjectivity relies, vagrancy is so capacious that it could be filled in, theoretically, by anyone. Of course, at the same time, vagrancy was not, in legal practice, empty of social meaning. Vagrancy's availability as a site for lyric experimentation is not embedded solely in the theoretical construction of the legal category; it was also, as scholars of Wordsworth in particular have noted, a site for complexly politicized poetic experimentation because of the precise and increasingly urgent political valences accruing to poverty, scarcity, and population in the 1790s.[22]

Poets in the late eighteenth century made new aesthetic use of the existing charge carried by the figure of the vagrant as invoked by both law and political economy. At the same time, though, the poetic redeployment of this figure, along with its afterlife as a privileged site of lyric reading, sometimes risks obscuring the very histories that lent it such resonance in the 1790s. The most obvious instance of this is the overwhelmingly (though not exclusively) solitary, rural, and English cast of poetic vagrancy in a period in which vagrancy was in fact deeply linked in the public eye to the costs of distant war, scandals of empire, and the politics of population. Vagrancy was also, as I reveal, crucial to major developments in *urban* police reform and, more broadly, the tropes and genres through which reformers and writers sought to render the city legible to readers and legislators. Of course, I do not mean to assert that portrayals of rural vagrancy necessarily simply elide these histories; as I argue of the *Lyrical Tales,* these valences of vagrancy are indeed still present in deployments of "Romantic vagrancy" at its most rural. However, while many scholars have astutely noted how population, empire, and the global resonance of dispossession continue to haunt even the most seemingly solitary poetic vagrant, I take this as a point of departure to ask why such valences of vagrancy are so often relegated to spectrality in the first place, and what this might tell us about the place of race and empire in the development of lyric reading.[23]

In *Lyrical Tales,* her final collection of poetry, Robinson performs astonishing experiments with lyric form in a book dominated by the dispossessed, impoverished, stateless, and fugitive. Robinson not only pushes us to reconsider a literary-historical narrative that has long been dominated by Wordsworth, but also offers an engagement with vagrancy that theorizes law and lyric as intersecting precisely where legal persons and lyric subjects disappear.

## Lyric Hunger: The *Lyrical Ballads* and the Natural Person

Dispossession and scarcity were, of course, already established poetic preoccupations before the appearance of Wordsworth and Coleridge's 1798 *Lyrical Ballads* and its critical interlocutor, Robinson's *Lyrical Tales.* This is well-trodden critical ground for a reason; as Raymond Williams's classic account argues, the melancholy retrospect on rural life as epitomized by poems like Goldsmith's *The Deserted Village* articulate the "structures of feeling" of an age of enclosure while simultaneously providing the tools by which poets theorize poetry itself; for Goldsmith, the depopulation of Auburn is ultimately "an imaginative rather than a social process; it is what the new order does to the poet, not to the land."[24]

But while vagrancy, as a category, is of course deeply intertwined with questions of poverty, enclosure, primitive accumulation, and the central concerns that animated the debates about poor law that intensified toward the end of the eighteenth century, vagrancy is nonetheless not precisely synonymous with poverty writ large.[25] Nor is it precisely synonymous with homelessness or itinerancy, though Romantic poetry in particular can render this distinction difficult to discern. Vagrancy, as I have been arguing, names a relation to police—one that often includes, but is not limited to itinerancy. However, this does not mean that in defining vagrancy as a relation to police, we leave behind the concept's connection to poverty and scarcity. Police, of course, is not only a realm of surveillance and security, but also includes the management and distribution of resources for subsistence; think, for instance, of Adam Smith's assertion that the proper concerns of police were "the cheapness of commodities, public security and cleanliness."[26] Vagrancy emerged as a newly intensive locus of poetic concern in the 1790s, but it was also a long-established legal category that had always presumed the conceptual and material inseparability of subsistence and security.

This leads us to a different approach to Wordsworth—as well as to a more expanded approach to "Romantic vagrancy" that is not limited to Wordsworth alone. Instead of asking how he represents, engages with, makes use of, simulates, or engages readers in ethical relations with people called "vagrants," we might ask instead how police, as a conceptual category, contributes to his theorization of the capacity of poetry to make us feel as if we are reading about people at all. Police here is visible not only in Wordsworth's use of "vagrancy" as a category, but in his very invocation of the *human* as a category, which draws foundationally on the intertwining of subsistence, scarcity, population, and life as increasingly crucial and politically charged concerns of police at the end of the eighteenth century. Here, I offer a brief reading of one of Wordsworth's many critically generative invocations of vagrancy: "The Female Vagrant" as it appeared in the *Lyrical Ballads* of 1798. This, in turn, offers a vantage point from which we can begin to understand the uniqueness of Robinson's contribution to the ongoing poetic conversation of which the *Lyrical Ballads* was a part.

In her reading of *Rowland,* Barbara Johnson is particularly concerned with legal personhood and its reliance on figure, but what I want to emphasize in my reading of "The Female Vagrant" is the Supreme Court's invocation of embodied deprivation as the irreducible marker of a different legal category: the *natural* person. Johnson is interested in how law theorizes the subcategories of "legal person," as divided into "artificial" and "natural," and in this case, the vexed division between artificial and natural hinges on the experience of embodied deprivation. A corporation can file a lawsuit, be held civilly liable, or have rights, but it can't get hungry. Human life is defined by hunger: the embodied experience of coming up against life's limits. This is, in many ways, a deeply Malthusian conception of the human, and thus one that, as Catherine Gallagher and Frances Ferguson have influentially argued, is particularly crucial to Wordsworth's approaches to poetry, consciousness, solitude, and life.[27] Hunger, for Malthus, is not an aberration in the state of human affairs; rather, it is the unavoidably natural result of what humans *do:* reproduce beyond the capacity of subsistence until starvation or other "checks" on population intervene.[28]

Approaching the turn of the nineteenth century, Malthusian debates about population and the broader political problem of food scarcity, food riots, and strained poor relief all contributed to a change in what vagrancy meant: while the category had always had much to do with deprivation, poverty, and the problem of subsistence, the link between vagrancy and hunger was both more pronounced and more politically potent in the 1790s than it had been earlier. As Ferguson notes, the Malthus/Godwin debates are foundationally about "modes of governance" as they relate to freedom and consciousness; meanwhile, as John Bohstedt argues, the wartime conditions of the 1790s meant that the politics of food riots were "nationalized"; the ability of rioters to disrupt military supply lines lent new potency to the food riot as a tactic, while at the same time drawing harsher repression against rioters.[29] Scarcity thus acquires new biopolitical significance.

As Catherine Gallagher and Emily Steinlight have shown, some of the most canonical early Romantic poetry, traditionally read for its emphasis on the solitary lyric subject, is in fact also crucially concerned with the problem of population as it emerged as a touchstone for political economy at the end of the eighteenth century.[30] Meanwhile, Malthus not only characterized the criminalized poor as "redundant," but also used vagrancy as a crucial metaphor for redundancy as a mass of life doomed only to death. In his much-expanded 1803 edition of the *Essay on the Principle of Population,* Malthus elaborates a parable for the pressure of redundant population on the scarcity of resources:

> A man . . . if the society do not want his labour, has no claim of right to the smallest portion of food, and, in fact, has no business to be where he is. At nature's mighty feast there is no vacant cover for him. She tells him to be gone, and will quickly execute her own orders, if he do not work upon the compassion of some of her guests. If these guests get up and make room for him, other intruders immediately appear demanding the same favour. . . . The order and harmony of the feast is disturbed, the plenty that before reigned is changed into scarcity; and the happiness of the guests is destroyed by the spectacle of misery and dependence in every part of the hall, and by the clamorous importunity of those, who are justly enraged at not finding the provision which they had been taught to expect.[31]

As the multitudes who intrude upon the feast and disrupt the guests' pleasure with their "spectacle of misery and dependence" are stand-ins for the "redundant" births that, Malthus argues, result from parish support for the poor, vagrancy here becomes a metaphor for existing-while-redundant. Being born is rendered equivalent to begging, and death is figured as nature's enforcement of vagrancy laws, as she turns away the imagined beggar who "has no business to be where he is."

Vagrancy, as a category that had long named surplus population but now increasingly named surplus *life,* thus became a powerful vehicle for poetic experimentation with the ability of lyric to embody the human. As Maureen McLane argues, Wordsworth's theorization of poetry as "a natural delineation of human passions, human characters, and human incidents" in the *Lyrical Ballads* puts him at the center of a particularly anthropological brand of organicism, as "poets and critics increasingly committed poetry to the discourse of the species, thereby making poetry answerable to the human sciences."[32] And so I read "The Female Vagrant" less exclusively for how vagrancy creates ground for lyric subjectivity and more for how it mediates lyric's relation to two other crucial categories for the *Lyrical Ballads:* "natural" and "human." In Johnson's distinction between legal persons and natural persons, the natural person is just as reliant upon trope as is the legal person, and I propose that the troping of the natural person—not just the lyric or legal subject—is also crucial to why poets like Wordsworth were so preoccupied with vagrancy as a vehicle for lyric experimentation.

"Nature," after all, appears only twice in "The Female Vagrant," and only in the context of human subsistence. After returning from America without really deciding to do so ("as from a trance," waking up on a ship), the Female Vagrant is overcome by the hunger she could not feel until now: "There, pains which nature could no more support, / With blindness linked, did on my vitals fall; / Dizzy my brain, with interruption short / Of hideous sense; I sunk, nor step could crawl" (194–199).[33] "Nature" here is the body reduced to the experience of pure biological need, a need whose impress upon consciousness is most legible in its capacity to override and erase that consciousness. "Nature" is the body that can "support" the pains of hunger, but this body only enters the poem through an articulation of the limits of that endurance. In this sense, hunger is like speech: both require embodiment, and both are simulated poetically as the poem gestures beyond itself.

Simulated speech is, of course, one prominent and longstanding theory of what lyric is; a primary medium through which, as Stephen Burt argues, "lyric poetry disembodies" as it "tries to construct a new, acoustic or verbal, body."[34] Both speech and hunger are invoked here as linked failure. Just before these lines, the Female Vagrant's inability to feel hunger is directly linked to her inability to rhetorically perform her poverty by begging: "At morn my sick heart hunger scarcely stung, / Nor to the beggar's language could I frame my tongue" (188–189). If the *Lyrical Ballads* is composed of a number of experiments in language—including the "beggar's language"—then does the poetic "simulation" (in Langan's and Pfau's terms) of the "beggar's language" also require the poetic "simulation" of life at its limits of sustenance?

On the one hand, the answer seems to be yes: what's more of a spontaneous overflow of powerful feeling than hunger? At the same time, though, hunger as a vehicle for registering "a natural delineation of human passions" is an odd choice—hunger is, of course, not uniquely human.[35] Furthermore, it does not invoke human consciousness here except through its ability to interrupt or override that consciousness; it "fall[s]" on the Female Vagrant, incapacitates her "brain" and robs her of sight, "sense," and the ability for consciously chosen locomotion. The fact that poetry still *happens* here even as she sinks to an experience of animal embodiment that's not at all unique to humanity seems to characterize poetry as the remainder that even the most extreme forms of deprivation can't erase. However, that deprivation must still be simulated poetically in order for this capacity of poetry to be made legible. The poetic simulation of hunger—its ability to make poetry signify as such through gestures of what is irreducibly beyond it—would seem to pick up on the longstanding traditions of poetic death, but while poetic death so often grants the disembodied poetic immortality of the subject, poetic hunger remains stuck in the place of protracted embodiment: an embodiment rendered lyrically sensible precisely because it's so painful in its continuation. Hunger also thus has a far less clear relation to established poetic tradition—elegies and sonnets perform claims to preserve or resurrect the dead all the time, but there's no poetic tradition that claims to feed anyone.

Ironically, this association of vagrancy with life at the limits of subsistence makes room for surplus population to yield lyric solitude; as Janowitz and Ferguson have argued, the communitarian mode of the ballad and the population debates alike all lent Wordsworth the conceptual material out of which to craft solitary lyric subjects.[36] Vagrancy here invokes scarcity as both a political-economic problem *and* potential ground for theorizing the relation between lyric and embodiment. At the same time, however, the poem inhabits the capacity of direct address to conjure a disembodied lyric voice—a figurative capacity placed into even starker focus by the extremity of need that threatens to reduce the Female Vagrant to poetic voice alone through the eroding of the bodily sustenance upon which voices of the nonpoetic variety depend. In other words, her invocation of the "dreadful price of being to resign / All that is dear *in* being" is precisely what draws our attention to the capacity of lyric to produce a sense of this "being" as a presence.[37]

Wordsworth famously invokes the "natural delineation of human passions, human characters, and human incidents" as an alternative definition of poetry that does not rely on "pre-established codes of decision" and the legibility of formally recognizable definitions of poetry.[38] The second and final appearance of "nature" in "The Female Vagrant" further elaborates upon this distinction by staging a contrasting relation between scarcity, embodiment, and *ars poetica.* The Female Vagrant describes her time with the Gypsies as a fantasy of sustenance without scarcity or limits, a fantasy described as rhetorical artifice:

> How kindly did they paint their vagrant ease!
> And their long holiday that feared not grief,
> For all belonged to all, and each was chief.
> No plough their sinews strained; on grating road
> No wain they drove, and yet, the yellow sheaf
> In every vale for their delight was stowed:
> For them, in nature's meads, the milky udder flowed. (219–225)

Their reliance on theft for sustenance is described in centuries-old terms of art: "semblance" and "fancy" (226, 229). Thus, "nature" here hides theft behind figure. It also hides theft behind pastoral; after all, when they claim that "no plough their sinews strained" and focus instead on their ability to find "delight" in "every vale," they could just as easily be conventional pastoral nymphs and swains, depicted not at labor, but at rest. If "vagrant ease" names subsistence that circumvents wage labor and insists on taking the capacity for life back from redundancy, then this capacity to create life when there isn't supposed to be any is uneasily appropriated into highly conventionalized and formally legible capacities of poetry, which can also "paint" seemingly living subjects into existence and turn agricultural labor into leisure. When "nature" names the Female Vagrant's own experience of hunger, it resonates with Wordsworth's definition of poetry, but when it names the Gypsies' *refusal* to starve, it evokes precisely the definition of poetry that he opposes to his privileged relation to the human.

Wordsworth here draws on the centuries-old association of "Gypsy" with disguise—see, for instance, my discussion of seventeenth-century characterizations of "Gypsies" in the Introduction—in order to align that disguise with the empty and unnatural iterability of poetic convention. Here, then, another aspect of what vagrancy offers Wordsworth comes into view: not only a conceptual category for naming the local political and moral status of scarcity, but also a framework for racialized distributions of labor, vulnerability, dispossession, and accumulation. Saree Makdisi characterizes this poem's uneven distribution of lyric subjectivity as emblematic of the *Lyrical Ballads*' broader concern with "the civilization of savagery:" that is, "an attempt to Occidentalize and settle the restless, itinerant, and nomadic in a generic form appropriate to modernity and a new Occidental subject."[39] For Makdisi, the "Occidental" here names a theory of subjectivity that emphasizes (and racializes) individual self-possession—a theory that resonates with the Female Vagrant's ability to coalesce as an individual lyric voice.[40] Through refusing to subsist the way the Gypsies do—through remaining hungry when she could have eaten her fill—the Female Vagrant emerges, at least for a moment, as a coherent subject who can tell us confidently of the difference between herself and others: "But ill it suited me, in journey dark / O'er moor and mountain, midnight theft to hatch" (235–236). Her particular experience of loss and dispossession is held up here as what makes her specific, individual, and innocent: criminal acts, she says, "were not for me, brought up in nothing ill; / Besides, on griefs so fresh my thoughts were brooding still" (242–243). Ultimately, she is capable neither of fraud nor of labor—the spontaneous overflow of powerful feeling prevents both: "Ill was I then for toil or service fit: / With tears whose course no effort could confine" (249–250). If Makdisi emphasizes the poem's uneven racialized distribution of lyric subjectivity, I want to highlight a related, but distinct phenomenon: the poem's racialized distribution of lyric hunger, lyric life, and lyric embodiment. Even as the Female Vagrant emerges as a speaking subject whose subjectivity is most defined in contrast to the collectivity of the Gypsies, she's also the most resolutely *embodied* person in the poem; the Gypsies' poetic artifice seems to allow them to escape embodied need altogether.

In many ways, this is a poem about lyric bodies, not just lyric subjects. And yet, it is still deeply invested in using the embodied limits of life as an avenue for staging disembodying figures of lyric subjectivity. Even as vagrancy names a relation to scarcity, subsistence, and the law that renders subjectivity largely irrelevant, Wordsworth uses this subjectlessness as ground for experimenting with the capacity of lyric embodiment to yield lyric subjects. It is therefore unsurprising that so many readings of Wordsworth have been deeply invested in debating what model of ethical social relations he proposes in his engagements with vagrancy.

Mary Robinson, however, can radically change our understanding of "Romantic vagrancy" because she so frequently turns away from the ethics of intersubjectivity. Readers have interpreted this feature of the *Lyrical Tales* as an element of the text's bleakness—and it does indeed contain its fair share of bleakness—but I propose that Robinson does more than just evacuate the lyric subject as an ethical dead end.[41] Instead, she experiments in lyrics without subjects as another avenue for political critique, and it is vagrancy's relation to police that renders it central to this project. In particular, the subjectlessness of vagrancy—its ability to invoke population and scarcity without necessarily entering the realm of legal or lyric subjectivity—is precisely what renders it a potent vehicle for Robinson's politicized experiments in lyric.

## All/Alone: Mary Robinson's Poetics of Population

In both the title's overt response to the *Lyrical Ballads* and in the collection's overwhelming emphasis on marginality, poverty, and isolation, the *Lyrical Tales* marks Robinson's unique contribution to an intertextual poetic conversation. In so closely identifying her collection with the *Lyrical Ballads,* Robinson draws attention to the distinctiveness of her poetic engagement with dispossession. For Ashley Cross, Robinson's critical, revisionist engagement with the *Lyrical Ballads* draws on the uneasy identification of poet with vagrant that marks Wordsworth's work, but reconfigures it as a comment on gendered authorship; dispossession, Cross argues, is what Robinson portrays as the *female* experience of authorship, which is in turn "displaced onto figures of social otherness" that dominate the collection.[42] In the *Lyrical Tales,* Robinson pushes lyric to its limits; the title announces a hybridization of lyric perhaps more radical than that of the *Lyrical Ballads* (as the "tale" gestures not only beyond lyric, but also beyond poetry itself), while Robinson's metrically and formally experimental poems, as Daniel Robinson argues, "literally perform their artifice in the strangeness of their forms."[43]

The *Lyrical Tales* also begins with vagrancy. With no prefatory material like the "Advertisement" that had graced the 1798 *Lyrical Ballads,* the *Lyrical Tales* opens with a homeless child in a churchyard, disturbing his poet-interlocutor with his insistence on remaining unincorporated into community or narrative—on remaining out of place. The apostrophic opening lines of the first poem, "All Alone," attempt to hail its object into subjectivity that might speak: "Ah! Wherefore by the Church-yard side, / Poor little LORN ONE, dost thou stray?" (1–2).[44] The boy, however, refuses to assent to the speaker's attempt to sketch him as a body capable of sensation and animated to movement. Instead, he begins his response by refusing everything but the stasis of the grave:

> I cannot the green hill ascend,
> I cannot pace the upland mead;
> I cannot in the vale attend,
> To hear the merry-sounding reed:
> For all is still, beneath yon stone,
> Where my poor mother's left alone! (49–54)

He does, with some prodding from the speaker, temporarily occupy precisely the subjectivity asked of him when he tells the story of how he ended up here, but all he can narrate is a catalogue of losses: his parents, their animals, their home. While the speaker claims that this storytelling will incite reparative intersubjectivity—"Thou art not left alone, poor boy, / The Trav'ller stops to hear thy tale" (7–8)—the boy's narrative of his life to the speaker fails to incite any relationship that the boy will recognize, and he ends the poem declaring his only relation to be with the unspoken name of his dead mother:

> No friend shall weep my destiny
> For *friends* are scarce, and *tears* are few;
> None do *I* see, save on this stone
> Where I will stay, and weep alone! (141–144)

In claiming the identity of "Trav'ller" (8) and asking to hear his story, the poet-speaker invites precisely the kind of uneasy identification between vagrant and poet that scholars have long noted in Wordsworth. The poem, however, is dominated by the boy's utter refusal of such an identification with expressive subjectivity. In this sense, Robinson brings vagrancy back to one of its crucial legal valences: it's not a kind of subjectivity, but a placeholder for threat or economic burden. Instead of rendering criminalized destitution the raw material for lyric capacity to make subjects—or, failing that, at least voices and bodies—Robinson dwells on the impossibility of subjectivity within the category of vagrancy and pushes it to the foreground as the poem's most unsettling preoccupation.

The poem's dialogue pointedly echoes Wordsworth's "We Are Seven," but while the girl in "We Are Seven" insists that her dead kin be counted as part of the community of the living, the boy in "All Alone" insists that he be regarded as belonging only to the dead:

> My Father never will return,
> He rests beneath the sea-green wave;
> I have no kindred left to mourn
> When I am hid in yonder grave! (145–148)

In his insistence on being understood as nothing more than a future corpse, the boy in "All Alone" is a striking figure of Malthusian redundancy. "We Are Seven," with its impasse between irreconcilable modes of counting people, also invokes Malthusian logic and policy, but what it most insistently stages is the problem of enumeration: who counts, who doesn't count, and who decides.[45] "All Alone," on the other hand, dwells in the category of the supernumerary. The "all" in the title can paradoxically index both the absoluteness of the boy's solitude *and* the figuration of multitude that haunts the idea of poverty under the Malthusian concept of population.[46] The poem enacts the steady accumulation of death that Malthus warns of as the inevitable result of life's reproduction beyond its means. Redundancy is also the poem's most insistent *formal* concern, as the boy's utter refusal of life takes the form of semantic and sonic repetition. His first words to the speaker are framed by the stubborn anaphora of "I cannot . . . I cannot . . . I cannot" (49–51), and the poem itself adopts his stony recalcitrance: every stanza ends with a couplet repeating the same rhyme, and nearly every one of these couplets contains "stone," "alone," or both.

Even in his painful isolation, the boy's redundancy—his existence beyond the resources available to sustain it—thus also marks him as a figure of anonymous multitude. Ironically, death would grant him a far more stable place in the social order than his current life in the churchyard; after all, as Thomas Laqueur argues, the right to burial in one's parish church was a crucial legal and customary marker of communal belonging.[47] As an anonymous denizen of a churchyard, the boy resembles the village dead more than he does any living person, yet occupies a liminal space between the two. Poetically, he is also positioned between living, speaking subject and featureless dead thing, as he is figured not only as the particular and injured body whose voice produces an address, but also through the recalcitrance he shares with the constantly accruing "stone" that punctuates the poem, recurring equally in his speech and his interlocutor's, piling up with implacable regularity in the couplet ending nearly every stanza no matter what is said before it. It is in his stoniness that the boy exceeds boundaries between subject and object, speaker and spoken-of, person or multitude, living or dead. Across all these divides, he is simply redundant.

In criminalizing populations regarded as redundant, vagrancy law occupies such undecidability between individual and multitude, subject and thing. In legal and political writing of the eighteenth century, "vagrants" were repeatedly figured as vermin, waste, garbage, and debris.[48] The same authorities were tasked with the management of both animate and inanimate disorder. The bridewell, as an early modern carceral institution constructed specifically to combat vagrancy, pioneered the use of incarceration as punishment long before the birth of the penitentiary, marking populations deemed vagrant as the first targets of a prison regime that, as Caleb Smith argues, renders former legal subjects "animate corpse(s)," suspended between (legal) life and (civil) death.[49]

If vagrancy, as a legal category, rests more on anticipated future threat than on criminal responsibility for acts already committed, it has little to do with subjectivity, interiority, or intent. As the boy refuses social belonging and poetic identification, insisting instead on identifying himself only as what he will one day be—a corpse—he enacts this logic at its starkest extremes. He refuses to exist outside the logic of anticipation, while his stasis in living death also echoes this logic's carceral consequences.

The *Lyrical Tales* are densely populated with such strange and solitary figures: people who have disappeared from somewhere else, only to end up here. From "The Alien Boy," who "lives / A melancholy proof that Man may bear / All the rude storms of Fate, and still suspire / By the wide world forgotten" (137–140) to the "Poor, Singing Dame" who dies in prison, and "The Fugitive" or "Poor Marguerite," the *Lyrical Tales* portray countless figures displaced by war, the administration of the law, poverty, slavery, and simple social abandonment. Most of the variously dispossessed figures traversing this collection appear in acute, often painful singularity. At the same time, however, collecting these figures and placing them side by side in a book of poetry draws meaning from their contiguity. The miscellaneous juxtaposition of figures here resonates aesthetically with the form of a vagrancy statute, and the paratactic gathering on the table of contents—The Lascar; The Widow's Home; The Shepherd's Dog; The Fugitive—is reminiscent of the colorful and expansive catalogues that proliferate in vagrancy statutes but constitute no cohesive theory of "the vagrant," constructing instead an expansive, discretionary scope of state violence in the form of police. What comes into focus is ultimately not "the vagrant" as a kind of subject, but rather the spaces in which these figures linger, the itineraries they chart, and the protean legal net that can entrap so many multitudes.

What strands of collectivity, if any, might bind these figures? There's a tenuous web of associative connection across the *Lyrical Tales* that defies narrative or positive enumeration. For instance, "Poor Marguerite" wanders the shore, following visions of her dead lover, Henry. Henry, as an "*alien wand'rer*" (128), "forc'd from his native land" (124) and haunting the edge of the sea, echoes the Henry of "The Alien Boy," the son of a French exile who dies attempting to save a shipwrecked man in a storm. They aren't the same person, precisely—at least, not by the logic of unique identity relied on by a parish register or a census: Marguerite's Henry is a young man, while the Alien Boy is a child, and Marguerite's Henry is dead while the Alien Boy is still alive. And yet the convergence of both names and biographical details is striking. Meanwhile, the eventual fate of the Alien Boy as a seaside hermit and "a maniac wild . . . His garb with sea-weeds fring'd" (128–129) also doubles that of Marguerite herself, who declares in her own solitary madness: "Here will I build a rocky shed, / And here I'll make my sea-weed bed" (99–100). Similarly, the domestic tranquility of "The Widow's Home" resonates unsettlingly with "All Alone." In "The Widow's Home," a soldier's widow (who does not yet know that her husband has died) lives with her son in a cottage "close on the margin of a brawling brook" (1) where "an ozier canopy /

Invites the weary traveller to rest" (4–5). This description reads like a remixing of the boy's story of his family in "All Alone"; after his father "o'er the stormy sea / To distant lands was borne away" (73–74) and later dies, he and his mother become homeless when lightning strikes their cottage. They live on where the boy weaves "the ozier bough" (106), but his mother is killed when a storm causes the "clear brook" to flood (111) and "bore our shatter'd cot away" (110). It's impossible to prove that these are literally the same characters, and yet the details shared between them cast an unsettling pall of precarity over the conclusion of "The Widow's Home," in which the speaker declares the boy "the proud inheritor of Heav'n's best gifts—/ The mind unshackled—and the guiltless Soul!" (109–110)

This subtle patterning weaves together many of the solitary and vagrant figures of the *Lyrical Tales.* It's impossible to say that their stories are definitively interconnected, or that the same characters literally reappear in different poems, but the recurrence and reshuffling of common settings, details, names, and phrases suggest a kind of collectivity: not a collectivity of discrete, knowable individuals who aggregate into a countable population, but one of slippage between individual and multitude. In the *Lyrical Tales,* the faint ghosts of multitude haunt each isolated figure, as the connections between poems remind us that for every Henry or Marguerite, there are countless other possible instantiations of "wageless life"; all surplus in their own way and yet also terribly and endlessly repeatable in nearly the same form.[50]

## "A Vast Aggregate of Floating Wealth": Policing the Metropolis, Seeing the City

Poets took up vagrancy as a crucial and politically volatile trope for thinking through the capacities of lyric to simulate human life. In particular, Robinson makes use of the link between vagrancy and the political charge of scarcity in order to invoke life at its limits. Life at its limits, especially in this Malthusian moment, thus evokes the category of the human as that category was increasingly defined in biological, reproductive terms.[51] At the same time, however, life at its limits also necessarily invokes the uneven distribution of vulnerability, life chances, and relations to subsistence that we can track under the term of "race." This attention to scarcity and subsistence as central to both vagrancy and the theory of police it helped construct can, in turn, help us to push back against the overwhelmingly white and English picture of dispossession we might end up with if we take Romantic poetry—particularly Wordsworth—as our primary image of what "vagrancy" means in this period. Vagrancy, after all, continued to inform ongoing political debates about how space might be secured. In late eighteenth-century police reform, vagrancy is crucially spatial; it is a concept through which advocates of increasingly centralized policing theorized space itself as an object of police, while it simultaneously could index the spatial distribution of scarcity and subsistence—thus disclosing the "truth" of a space through a fuller understanding of the populations it housed. This spatial distribution, I argue, highlighted connections between colony and metropole—and this, I will show, offered Mary Robinson an aesthetic avenue for her experiments in lyric as offering the kind of globally expansive prospects more traditionally seen in the locodescriptive.

When Henry Fielding reflects on the changing geography of London and its supposed propensity to foster crime, he enlists a metaphor that links the city to more distant locales:

> Whoever indeed considers the Cities of *London* and *Westminster,* with the late vast Addition of their Suburbs; the great Irregularity of their Buildings, the immense Number of Lanes, Alleys, Courts and Bye-places; must think, that, had they been intended for the very Purpose of Concealment, they could scarce have been better contrived. Upon such a view, the whole appears as a vast Wood or Forest, in which a Thief may harbour with as great Security, as wild Beasts do in the Desarts of *Africa* or *Arabia.*[52]

By likening the streets of London to the "Desarts of *Africa* or *Arabia,*" Fielding's analogy draws on a familiar colonial geography. Africa and Arabia become metonymic for the as-yet ungoverned, uncivilized criminal underworld, which exists among the English body politic but is not of it, as he characterizes crime as an "Invasion" by "a few of the lowest and vilest among us," which places the nation in the same predicament as "the most enslaved Countries."[53]

This racialized metonymy has a very long afterlife in figurations of English poverty.[54] However, even as this geographical imaginary persisted, another mode of imagining—and policing—London's geography came to prominence toward the end of the eighteenth century, as a new generation of police reformers pushed for the establishment of what has come to be seen as a "modern" penal apparatus: centralized, professional police forces, the penitentiary as default mode of criminal punishment, and a robust and comprehensive theorization of police as a system of crime prevention.

For example, in his influential *Treatise on the Police of the Metropolis* (1796), the prominent police reformer Patrick Colquhoun, like Fielding, places London in a global setting. Here, however, the ties that connect London to distant locales are not analogical, but economic:

> LONDON, from being a great *depot* for all the manufactures of the country, and also the goods of foreign nations as well as colonial produce, is not only the first commercial city that is known at present to exist, but is also one of the greatest and most extensive manufacturing towns, perhaps in the universe; combining in one spot every attribute that can occasion an assemblage of moving property, unparalleled in point of extent, magnitude, and value, in the whole world.[55]

For Fielding, the problem with London's growth is that the city has become savage; the sheer proliferation of streets has expanded beyond the reach of localized surveillance. For Colquhoun, however, what makes London so vulnerable to crime is that it is so *civilized;* its unprecedented commercial expansion brings together so many populations with such a massive "assemblage of moving property," he argues, that there is simply more to be stolen, and more opportunity to steal it.

This status of London as a global "assemblage of moving property," whose wealth, it was increasingly asserted, was generated precisely *through* this movement, was central to the theories and arguments of those advocating for police reform at the end of the eighteenth century. While Fielding's theory of crime largely hinges on a traditionalist critique of luxury—the poor try to emulate the rich and thus are tempted to seek pleasures they cannot afford—Colquhoun follows in the footsteps of classical economic thinkers such as Adam Smith, arguing that the trade in "moving property," including luxuries, is a productive engine of wealth that must be protected from crime.

Vagrancy, as a longstanding concept for elaborating police as a mode of governance, was prominently featured in commentators' proposals to reform and centralize policing in the late eighteenth century. The relationship between vagrancy and police was not limited to the creation of institutional police forces; vagrancy was a flexible model for conceptualizing policing as performed by a wide variety of institutions and individuals. For instance, Thomas Gilbert's *A Plan of Police* (1786) includes a suggested "Inducement to the Inhabitants of Parishes and Places to enforce the Vagrant Laws"—namely, a proposal to fine those who house lodgers later convicted of a crime.[56] This proposal illustrates the broad meaning that vagrancy laws held in relation to police: as a rubric for anticipating future threat, it encompasses a wide array of practices toward a potentially unlimited population. Gilbert does not name any specific type of lodger that innkeepers and others ought to watch out for. Nor does he call upon innkeepers to "enforce the Vagrant Laws" by personally arresting strangers or assessing suspected outsiders' claims to parish settlement (as JPs and Overseers of the Poor would typically do); instead, by proposing that innkeepers and others who board lodgers be held liable for their lodgers' future crimes, Gilbert is using the wide discretionary scope of vagrancy law as a blueprint for dispersed surveillance. If vagrancy names a potential for threat that cannot be anticipated in advance, then the actual practices of surveillance that Gilbert aims to induce are equally in excess of anticipation; he hopes that innkeepers will simply do whatever they think is necessary to prevent the possibility that they may house a future "criminal."

Late eighteenth-century police reformers are increasingly concerned with the surveillance and management of surplus or, in Malthus's influential formulation, "redundant population."[57] Population, as Charlotte Sussman argues, traverses Romantic-period political economy and imaginative writing as a fundamentally *spatial* concept; theories of population were above all "concerned with the mobility of peoples, with ascertaining how and where certain groups might be shifted to better suit the empire's needs."[58] Thus, rather than tracking how "the vagrant" moves through spaces, both poetic and geographical, I am interested in what kinds of spaces and geographies the invocation of "the vagrant" calls into being. How does policing imagine and transform geography? And how might different poetic techniques for imagining scale both aid and critique this project?

The idea of police was deeply concerned with the management of space across multiple scales, from local to global. In 1799, Patrick Colquhoun offered a concise summary of his theory of police as a fundamentally *spatial* enterprise:

> Police as recently exemplified, may be said to be a new science, not yet perfectly understood. . . . Wherever a proper Police attaches, good order and security will prevail; where it does not, confusion, irregularity, outrages, and crimes must be expected; wherever great bodies of aquatic labourers are collected together, risque of danger from turbulent behaviour, will be greater in proportion to the number of depraved characters, who, from being collected in one spot, may hatch mischief, and carry it into effect much easier in Docks than on the River. A Police only can counteract this; and to the same preventive system will the commerce of the Port be indebted for securing both the Docks and the Pool against Conflagration.[59]

Police here responds to a geographical contraction that London's global commerce has instigated: by concentrating so many valuable goods and so many sailors in one place, Colquhoun argues, London creates conditions for crime unprecedented in their scope, and thus requiring an unprecedented response. Just as the causes of crime here are spatial, so is the mechanism of its prevention: the risk here comes from the density of specific populations (both "aquatic laborers" and "depraved characters") drawn into one spot. The river's "vast extent of Floating Property," Colquhoun argues, is what simultaneously elevates and endangers it; as the point of convergence for the empire's military and commercial power, the docks are where London meets the world—and is made vulnerable to it.[60]

The docks—the transnational space where people, goods, and ships converge between journeys that shape the globe in the image of the British Empire—become a metonym for the reach of imperial power, even as (Colquhoun argues) this concentration of goods and people makes it uniquely vulnerable to unrest and disorder. The threat to the city here is not crime alone, but also political unrest and threats to power over dockside and maritime labor. Police, as a system of spatial management oriented toward the prevention of threat to property, security, or global commerce, relies on population-oriented and probabilistic thinking: the best way to secure a space is to have discretionary authority over the riskiest populations that move through or inhabit it.

Vagrancy had long been a legal and imaginative rubric for managing populations and their movements along global flows of capital; in the late seventeenth century, sporadic transportation of vagrants to the Americas funneled the destitute of London into the rapidly expanding plantation economy, and throughout Britain's North American colonies, vagrancy law became a crucial tool in the apprehension of suspected fugitives from slavery and indentured servitude.[61] Meanwhile, vagrancy law was also crucial to the development of modern nation-states' border controls; eighteenth- and nineteenth-century European states drew on the existing model of vagrancy as they legally consolidated what John Torpey terms a "monopoly of the legitimate means of movement."[62] But in the context of late eighteenth-century police reform in London, vagrancy also takes on new, specific relations to space in a rapidly changing city.

In my discussion of Henry Fielding in the previous chapter, I argued that vagrancy offered a legal and imaginative rubric for understanding locality: the scale of intimate governance that includes parish and family in intertwined homology. By the 1790s, however, legal commentators who saw themselves as following in Fielding's footsteps understood London as too big, too chaotic, and too global to be governed in such an intimate, discretionary, and decentralized manner.[63] At the same time, the threats that these authors identified with vagrancy were no longer limited to the localized threats that Fielding identified—namely, the threat of potential crime, especially theft—but rather extended far beyond the immediate and localizable. In the wake of the Gordon Riots, the French Revolution, the food riots that punctuated the 1790s, and the growth of working-class radicalism, "disorderly" poverty could signify not only potential crime or cost to a parish, but also existential threat to the social and political order. Centralization of police was one way to manage scarcity on a vast scale and prevent its eruption into riot or revolution.[64] For instance, when London's police offices were established by the Middlesex Justices Act of 1792, they targeted not only property crime (which had been Fielding's preoccupation), but also political threat by participating in the surveillance of radical organizations like the London Corresponding Society.[65]

If the vagrants of Romantic poetry were so frequently rural, solitary, and English, then Colquhoun's reliance on vagrancy to apprehend the metropolis and propose its more effective policing offers an important urban, global, and collective counterpoint. Vagrancy, for Colquhoun, reveals the truth of the global city: its catchall miscellany allows him to construct a spectacularly comprehensive prospect through which one might survey the city's geographies of risk and unrest, its potentially dangerous populations, and the full complexity of the economic activity that he seeks to protect. It also, on a more practical level, offers a legal model for the role of his proposed centralized police force.

In his *Treatise on the Police of the Metropolis* (1796), Colquhoun repeatedly invites his readers to contemplate prospects that traverse scales from the local to the global, proposing police as the organizing force that can manage these scales and their relation. The model for policing across scale is provided by vagrancy. After asking the reader to contemplate the sheer magnitude of wealth in transit through the city at any given time, he then turns to the potentially criminal types that pose a threat to this property:

> Let the mind pass from the contemplation of this vast aggregate of floating wealth, exposed to depredation in ten thousand different ways, and examine the present state of the morals of the Metropolis by a reference to the various classes of individuals who live idly and support themselves by pursuits that are either criminal, illegal, dissolute, vicious, or depraved; it will then be discovered that acts of delinquency and the corruption of manners, have uniformly kept pace with the increase of the riches of the Capital.[66]

The long, miscellaneous catalogue of people that follows, including categories like "Strangers out of work who have wandered up to London in search of employment," "Strolling Minstrels, Ballad Singers, Show Men, Trumpeters, and Gipsies," "Unfortunate Females of all descriptions, who support themselves chiefly or wholly by prostitution," and "Common Beggars and Vagrants asking alms," reproduces the legal category of vagrancy while claiming to number this population at 115,000 people.[67] This argument combines the longstanding meaning of vagrancy—a flexible category naming potential threat—with a more contemporary concern with *population* as a potential problem for governance.[68] Colquhoun's quantitative tallies of vagrants and disorderly people in the *Treatise* suggest a theory of crime that privileges population management over individual moral reform, despite the emphasis on moral reform expressed by contemporary proponents of the penitentiary. He does not claim to predict which particular vagrants will commit which particular crimes, but rather claims that any city with such a high population of vagrants must necessarily be at risk.

The object of governance here thus seems to be the space more than the people in it. Indeed, when Colquhoun claims success, he tends not to make any claims that these vagrant populations have been reformed or changed in any way; he simply lauds their disappearance from the spaces that concern him: "By means of a Police Guard upon the Quays, which forms a collatoral branch of the General System, *the Scuffle-hunters and Long-apron-men, who were accustomed to prowl about for the purpose of pillage, have in a great measure deserted the quays and landing-places. . . . Not a few of these mischievous members of society have quitted their former residences, and disappeared.*"[69]

Vagrancy, for Colquhoun, is not only a threat to well-governed space; it is also a model for theorizing how urban spaces work. Colquhoun draws on the paratactic miscellany of vagrancy as a category in order to figure physical spaces as disorderly and threatening to the proper course of commerce. For instance, he imaginatively peels away the facade of warehouses near the docks to reveal a prospect of illicit global trade, condensed in one space:

> In their houses, although a beggarly appearance of old iron, old rags, or second-hand clothes, is only exhibited, the back apartments are often filled with the most valuable articles of shipstores, copper bolts and nails, brass and other valuable metals, West-India produce, household goods and wearing apparel; purchased from artificers, labourers in the docks, lumpers, glutmen, menial servants, apprentices, journeymen, porters, chimney-sweepers, itinerant Jews, and others; who, thus encouraged and protected, go on with impunity, and without the least dread of detection, in supplying the numerous imaginary wants which are created in a large capital. . . ."[70]

The list that unites "lumpers," "apprentices" and "itinerant Jews" also places commodities into physical and conceptual proximity; both in the storehouses and in Colquhoun's prose, "copper bolts and nails" brush up against "West-India produce" and "wearing apparel." The stores of stolen goods constitute a shadowy mirror of Britain's global commerce. This resonance happens through form as well as content; the contraction of so many items and people into such a small textual space figures global commerce through paratactic contraction, which echoes the paratactic miscellany of the vagrancy statutes. The "beggarly appearance" that hides secret stores of wealth is also a trope commonly applied to people labeled "vagrants," as vagrancy legislation invoked longstanding anxieties that begging was in fact a form of profitable grift. The house itself, then, is figured in the same terms as vagrancy. Meanwhile, as illicit as this trade is, it is also inseparable from the city's status as global metropolis and hub of empire: the demand for such goods is fed not by exceptional immorality, but by "the numerous imaginary wants which are created in a large capital." The city's concentrations of surplus value also draw surplus population, signified through the rhetorical surplus of *copia* in the long, colorful list.

Vagrancy, then, offers Colquhoun a mode for rendering the city visible and comprehensible. Police, as constructed dialectially through vagrancy, becomes a prospect. The same geographic contraction that allows London to become metonymic for its global commercial reach also renders the city a unique vantage point for comprehending an underworld of crime: "London is not only the grand magazine of the British Empire, but also the general receptacle for the idle and depraved of almost every Country."[71] Just as the vast array of colonial goods circulating through London allows the city's populace to encounter, materially and immediately, the reach of empire, so does the quantified circulation of criminalized bodies allow Colquhoun to imagine policing as a gaze that can comprehend crime as a totality.

In both his writing and his legal practice, Colquhoun drew foundationally on vagrancy law as a practical model for the work of policing. Colquhoun, alongside fellow magistrate John Harriot, was hired by the Committee of West India Planters and Merchants in 1798 to help establish a private police force to patrol the river and docks, with the aim of both preventing theft from ships and instituting tighter control over dockside labor.[72] This same committee was also instrumental in advocating for the construction of the new West India Docks. The West India Docks Company, which administered the docks, instituted uniquely tight controls on the space of the docks, requiring ships to use company laborers for loading and unloading rather than allowing them to hire their own labor, and preventing anyone other than company employees or revenue officers from entering the docks without supervision.[73] This intensive control over a space designated for one specific regional trade was relatively new, but there was precedent for singling out the Thames and its docks as a uniquely vulnerable space requiring uniquely extensive powers of crime prevention. For example, the 1756 Lead and Iron Act (29 Geo. II c. 30) authorized magistrates to demand that those in possession of metals suspected of being stolen from ships or warehouses give an account of how these items came into their possession. Meanwhile, the Bumboat Act of 1762 (2 Geo. III c.28) allowed for the summary conviction of those in possession of cargo suspected to have been stolen from a ship in the Thames.[74]

Colquhoun's published proposal for an officially sanctioned version of this private police force names these acts as the legal prototype for police more generally. After critiquing existing law for being limited to "*penalties* and *legal powers*" rather than preventive policing, he argues for the expansion of "provisions authorizing *slight* penalties, inflictable by summary procedure, on *circumstantial* evidence, aided by the *examination* of the delinquent, as under the *Bumboat* Act, and *Stolen-metal* Act, where, on *regular* proof, it would be *felony;* and for attaching upon the practice of depredation, in such stages of its progress, as are *previous* or *subsequent* to the felonious act."[75] At the same time, Colquhoun's interest in summary conviction was crucial to his spatial understanding of policing: this is the particular legal tool he advocates as the best way to manage spaces and the populations that move through them. The Thames River Police took the exigencies of managing the economically and legally unique space of the London docks as a model for preventive policing more generally.[76]

During the first few months of the Thames River Police's operation, laudatory notices appeared regularly in the newspapers of London. For instance, on August 11, 1798, the *St. James's Chronicle, or, the British Evening Post* published an account that concluded: "Previous to this Institution, numbers of criminal characters were accustomed to ply upon the river after dark, and great dangers were often to be apprehended from river pirates and nightly plunderers, and perhaps too from incendiaries; against whose criminal and treasonable designs the river Thames was never better protected than at the present moment."[77] The River Police made use of existing legal provisions for summary conviction such as the Bumboat Act as well as the practices that had long informed the enforcement of vagrancy law; for instance, in one published instance of summary conviction, the River Police note a man's failure to give a good account of the materials in his possession as evidence for theft: "*Benjamin North* was convicted of a misdemeanor, having in his possession a large quantity of coals, evidently procured unlawfully from some ship or vessel in the River, the account he gave proving very unsatisfactory."[78]

The River Police also played a major role in restructuring labor on the docks. Under the rubric of "theft," Colquhoun targeted customary entitlements that had long supplemented the wages of dockworkers; for instance, he cites traditional entitlements of workers to sweepings (spilled sugar) as a perquisite as constituting "a general license to plunder."[79] Mark Neocleous contextualizes this crackdown in a broader contemporary attack on customary entitlements and a reduction of workers to absolute reliance on wages for subsistence, concluding that "police powers were at the heart of nothing less than the making of the English working class."[80] In reclassifying these entitlements as theft and using the River Police to reorganize the conditions of dockside labor, Colquhoun performed an urban, maritime version of the legal targeting of poaching and gleaning that accompanied rural enclosure—precisely the echoes of enclosure more familiar to us in contemporary literary representations from Godwin's *Caleb Williams* to Wordsworth's "Goody Blake and Harry Gill."

The Thames River Police reveal the foundational place of vagrancy law in the elaboration of urban policing in both theory and practice—as Colquhoun's career combined the two realms. It also reveals that police is theorized on the ground through the apprehension of urban space as a condensation of complex global, imperial geographies. This is particularly clear in the case of the Thames River Police in their initial, private incarnation: their mandate, after all, was to protect the produce of the West Indies from theft, and thus to serve the interests of a company made up of some of the period's most vociferous defenders of slavery.[81] The Committee of West India Merchants and Planters did not only finance the Thames River Police; they were also the major force behind the construction of the new West India Docks on the Isle of Dogs—one of the major infrastructural projects that transformed London's docks at the turn of the nineteenth century in hopes of better accommodating the ever-increasing volume of maritime traffic to and from the city. One of the buildings that constituted the West India Docks—now the Museum of London Docklands—is in fact one of the only physical remnants left of this infrastructure in what is now another kind of global economic nexus: the Canary Wharf financial center. Just as Colquhoun's writings demonstrate the deeply intertwined concerns of police, prison, and poor-law reform, his crucial relationship with the Committee of West India Merchants and Planters also reminds us how embedded these reform efforts were in the ongoing reshaping of London as a commercial nexus of empire.[82] This context offers the backdrop for Mary Robinson's portrayal of vagrancy that entwines country, city, and colony in "The Lascar."

## Country/City/Colony: "The Lascar"

The London docks, as a crucial site for thinking through the politics of scarcity, the meaning of "locality" in an increasingly globalized city, and the theories animating police reform, are a highly visible and charged location for staging vagrancy as a political problem. I want to suggest, then, that it's far more remarkable than we have hitherto presumed that Romantic poets so rarely stage their encounters with vagrancy in such a setting, or indeed in any urban setting at all.[83] However, the London docks do appear at the margins of Robinson's portrayal of vagrancy in another of the poems that make up the *Lyrical Tales.* In "The Lascar," Robinson embeds a highly recognizable version of "Romantic vagrancy"—staged self-consciously in a poeticized English countryside that both evokes the pastoral tradition and pointedly disputes Goldsmith's characterization of rural innocence—in broader geographies that link the country to the city and the colony, thus connecting her ongoing experiments with the politics of lyric to a public scandal that revolved around the docks of London and the colonial world-system that the docks indexed.

Lascars—Asian sailors hired by the East India Company to work on ships returning to England—formed an increasingly visible indigent population in London at the end of the eighteenth century. Hired to replace British sailors lost to death, desertion, or impressment on the way to India, lascars often found themselves stranded in England, unable to secure work on outbound ships due to restrictions in the Navigation Acts limiting how many legally "non-British" sailors could work on British ships.[84] For the East India Company, the visible destitution of lascars in London was an embarrassing political problem.[85] By the early decades of the nineteenth century, however, both public opinion and legal practice were less sympathetic toward lascars, and this population was increasingly treated as a threat to be contained or an unsightly spectacle to be concealed.[86]

Robinson's poem begins by ventriloquizing enforced idleness not as threat or nuisance, but as an excruciating subjective experience:

Another day, Ah! me, a day
Of dreary Sorrow is begun!
And still I loathe the temper'd ray,
And still I hate the sickly Sun! (1–4)

At first, the lascar offers precisely what the boy in "All Alone" refuses to give us: a lyric subject. Indeed, he echoes the stone/alone refrain of "All Alone," but unlike the boy, he does so as he narrates himself as a conscious being who animates his body to move through the world while also registering a subjective experience of bodily pain:

I have no home, no rich array,
No spicy feast, no downy bed!
I, with the dogs am doom'd to eat,
To perish in the peopled street,
To drink the tear of deep despair;
The scoff and scorn of fools to bear!
I sleep upon a bed of stone,
I pace the meadows, wild—alone! (27–34)

However, he ends the poem as a corpse, just as the boy in "All Alone" insists he will end up, and "The Lascar" narrates the steady erosion of its subject's subjectivity. His voice fails him, and his body, so vividly evoked by his litany of suffering and vulnerability, begins to fade from view—"HE was dark, and dark the scene" (223)—until this racialized invisibility proves fatal: he is killed by a fearful traveler who cannot see him in the stormy night.

After leaving London and wandering into the countryside, encountering repeated denials of charity, the starving lascar turns desperately to a traveler for help:

> The LASCAR now with transport ran
> 'Stop! stop!' he cried—with accents bold;
> The Trav'ller was a fearful man—
> And next to life he priz'd his gold!—
> He heard the wand'rer madly cry;
> He heard his footsteps following nigh;
> He nothing saw, while onward prest,
> Black as the sky, the Indian's breast;
> Till his firm grasp he felt, while cold
> Down his pale cheek the big drop roll'd;
> Then, struggling to be free, he gave—
> A deep wound to the LASCAR Slave. (229–240)

Throughout the poem, the lascar attributes Britons' refusals of charity to his racialized invisibility, and here that invisibility becomes tragically literal. To the traveler, he is utterly invisible, and then suddenly, terrifyingly present as the traveler hears the lascar's cries but cannot track them, seeing only "nothing" as the lascar, "black as the sky," cannot be distinguished from the landscape. Everywhere and nowhere at once, unknown and thus carrying potentially unknowable threat, the embodiment of every danger that might befall a propertied traveler on the road: the lascar here is perceived by the traveler as the quintessential vagrant from the vantage point of police. This happens specifically through the ability of a racial metaphor—"black as the sky"—to acquire violent, material force: the racial category that already named his relation to capitalism and empire is precisely what dissolves him perceptually into a landscape to be interpreted as the impersonal bearer of risk and threat. The lascar's disappearance into the landscape is perhaps where the legal logic of vagrancy becomes most apparent. After all, if vagrancy law is centrally concerned with the management of risky spaces, then his seeming transformation into the landscape that so frightens the traveler enacts the figuration of vagrancy as diffuse threat that blurs distinctions between person and place.

Meanwhile, his "transport" here is both, as Miranda Burgess argues, a figure of both affective and geopolitical removal; for Burgess, Romantic "transport" links the material capacities of transport—the ever-increasing mobility of goods, people, and information between colony and metropole, and throughout the globe—to what Adela Pinch terms the "vagrancy of emotions" and the particular anxieties attending the possibility of being emotionally moved against one's will.[87] Before his encounter with the traveler, the lascar constantly voices and incites "transport" in his figurations of vast global geographies condensed palimpsestically into hellish prospects of dislocation.

In conjuring these vagrant prospects, Robinson most insistently engages vagrancy and police when the poem is at its least lyric, and where it flirts instead with the locodescriptive.

After all, if vagrancy law offers an optic to render potential unseen threat perceptible and to transform risky spaces into safe and economically productive ones, then this mode of perception resonates with the locodescriptive prospect and its ability to condense the vast reaches of deep time, state power, and the intangible forces of economic circulation into visible features of a landscape.[88] As Kevis Goodman argues, even as earlier eighteenth-century georgic and locodescriptive modes were eclipsed by variations on the lyric, these modes "could persist in concerns for positioning and sense reception, for the instruments and feelings—the channels of sensation and perception—by which later readers sought to know the world."[89]

The lascar is therefore less a vagrant subject than a vagrant optic. For instance, the lascar's complaint morphs into a prospect view that condenses imperial geographies and traverses vast extremes of scale from world to tomb:

> Shut out the Sun, O! pitying Night!
> Make the wide world my silent tomb!
> O'ershade this northern, sickly light,
> And shroud me, in eternal gloom!
> My Indian plains, now smiling glow,
> There stands my Parent's hovel low,
> And there the tow'ring aloes rise
> And fling their perfumes to the skies!

> There the broad palm Trees covert lend,
> There Sun and Shade delicious blend;
> But here, amid the blunted ray,
> Cold shadows hourly cross my way! (37–48)

The lascar's descriptions here bring metropole and colony into the same frame; he registers both the immediate imaginative presence of his "Indian plains" and their immense distance from where he stands under the "blunted ray" and "cold shadows" of England. These geographies are further mingled later; suffering under the heat of the midday sun in a "sultry waste" (108), he wanders through an English countryside rendered in terms that could equally call to mind colonial figurations of India.

By taking the lascar out of the city and into the country, Robinson reconfigures an existing series of city/country/colony relations that had become conventional by century's end. While the lascar begins the poem as a voice that condenses metropole and colony, he ends it as a silent corpse that obtrudes into the pastoral. In an idyllic village where "the Lark, on flutt'ring wings, / Its early Song, delighted sings" (293–294) and "the Swains their flocks to shelter lead" (296), the lascar takes shelter in a tree, from which he gracelessly falls when he dies of his wounds. Only then attracting the attention of the villagers, he is an object that disrupts the pastoral—a newly inert condensation of the transports and removals of global capitalism. The countryside is not the victim of dispossession here, and the melancholy retrospect that encompasses Goldsmith's Auburn is granted here only to the lascar's unnamed hometown and to the lascar himself. Instead of rural England serving as the most potent index of dispossession—even if the fault of dispossession is imagined to lie in the metropole—the country and its aestheticized "swains" are fully complicit.

## The "Stamp of Sorrow": The "Black Poor" and Vagrancy as Imperial Scandal

The dispossession wrought by enclosure (and memorialized as insularly English in poems like Goldsmith's *The Deserted Village*) was never strictly domestic, as dispossession and dislocation accompanied the creation of new global, colonial divisions of labor.[90] Contemporary commentators, philanthropists, and news reports focused on the presence of lascars as a specifically *urban* problem, embodying the scandalous underbelly of London's privileged position as the commercial hub of the British Empire. By following the lascar from the colony to the city to the country, Robinson reconfigures the public discourse around lascars as a prominent subset of London's "black poor," a category that helped shape the Sierra Leone colonization project as a transnational outgrowth of urban poor relief. By making the lascar a solitary, rural wanderer, Robinson departs from the vast majority of British portrayals of lascars at the end of the eighteenth century, thus offering an alternative to the moral distinction between country and (imperial) city so prevalent in poems like *The Deserted Village*. At the same time, however, her blending of East India Company scandal with the tropes of antislavery poetry also reinscribes the politics of the "black poor" as a category of person marked for putatively charitable national removal. Her portrait of rural dispossession in "The Lascar" takes up vagrancy as a master trope for staging the limits of lyric, but the specific discourse of vagrancy on which she draws here was not a rural, English one; rather, it was a specifically urban crisis that reflected the racialization of primitive accumulation and the racial divisions of labor developing under empire.

In late eighteenth-century Britain, two competing modes of description characterized lascars either as dangerous, vagrant nuisances to be cleared away, or as objects of pity, prompting the condemnation of the East India Company's commercial greed. Either way, lascars were figures that stood in for an entire geography of global dispossession. For example, an anonymous account entitled "The Lascar," which appeared in the *Newcastle Magazine* in 1785, renders an unnamed lascar the occasion for reflections on national charity. As the narrator observes two wealthy passers-by refuse to relieve the lascar's suffering, but then witnesses an impoverished prostitute share her earnings with him, he is moved to reflect on the state of sympathy in a center of imperial wealth.[91]

The lascar's racial difference is transformed here into a spectacle that condenses the narrator's indulgence in sympathetic feeling: "The poor shivering wretch, who occasioned this apostrophe, remained bowing reverently while I spoke; in his expressive countenance—for expression there was, 'even through the veil of black,' and of the strongest kind—there appeared such humility, and so much anguish. . . ." The lascar is the "occasion" for the narrator's oration; instead of using speech, the lascar communicates his suffering with his body. The transmission of feeling here is figured as a powerfully transparent process—the narrator immediately recognizes, beyond a doubt, that the lascar's expression displays "such humility, and so much anguish." And yet the transparency of sympathy here is paradoxically evoked through a metaphor of veiling. The lascar's racial difference, evoked as a "veil of black," surprises the narrator in that it does not block the transmission of feeling or the easy decoding of the man's expression.

Sympathy, therefore, is most potent precisely when it crosses visible markers of national, geographic, or racial difference. In doing so, of course, these portrayals of sympathy must solidify and spectacularize the very boundaries that sympathy purports to cross; the power of sympathy to transmit across bodily difference *requires* the "veil of black" in order to be legible as such. Blocked sympathy becomes the explanation for racial animosity, as the speaker critiques those "on whose hearts squalid wretchedness made no impression" and who cannot feel pity "because Providence had given him a colour different from their own."[92]

These representations mobilize the figure of the lascar as a locus for what Sara Ahmed terms "stranger fetishism": the reduction of the "stranger" to an emblem of knowable, embodied difference.[93] This dynamic is one of reduction and objectification, whether the "stranger" is portrayed as a body to be feared or a body to be embraced; either way, she argues, the body is made to speak a kind of absolute difference that this encounter produces rather than describes. An account of a court case in which lascars sued to receive their wages similarly invokes the image of self-evident helplessness, even as the article's actual subject—a group of lascars who successfully sought legal redress for their mistreatment—contradicts this image of the lascar as abject and isolated sufferer: "On Thursday Sir Watkin Lewes put on his gown, and humanely appeared as counsel on behalf of a Lascar, one of those miserable natives of India, whom we daily see in our streets exposed to every degree of want and distress."[94] In linking the sight of lascars on the streets of London to a vision of sympathy that crosses national borders and imagines a more virtuous mode of global commerce, these accounts enjoin their readers to see the bodies of impoverished people as condensations of geopolitical conflicts that traverse multiple geographic scales.[95] The figure of the lascar was a figure that evoked distant loss even in close proximity. Because lascars were often hired to replace English sailors lost to death, desertion, or impressment on the way to India, the presence of lascars in England signals the absence of these men. For example, the anonymous author of a pamphlet on the coal trade argues that "the East-India trade is so far from a nursery, that it is the grave of our seamen. We see a melancholy proof of this in the number of Lascars and Chinese that are loitering about the streets of this city."[96]

On March 16, 1785, the *Public Advertiser* published a letter signed "Senex," decrying the spectacle of impoverished lascars in London and demanding aid for what he characterizes as victims of national greed:

> I am an old man just arrived from the country, and am shocked at the number of miserable objects, Lascars, that I see shivering and starving in the streets. The little attention hitherto paid to these poor wretches, is a striking instance of the hard-heartedness and insensibility that distinguish the present times. . . . I could wish some persons of sense and worth would take into consideration the wretched situation of these poor strangers, and promote a subscription for their benefit at some of the most eminent bankers in this town, and apply the money thus procured to purchase cloaths and provisions, for a race of human beings, who, though different in religion, and country from ourselves, are still our fellow-creatures, and who have been dragged from their warmer and more hospitable climates by our avarice and ambition.[97]

The author's professed shock upon his arrival from the country emphasizes this spectacle of deprivation as a specifically urban problem.

"Senex" calls on noted philanthropist Jonas Hanway by name, and Hanway did indeed respond by helping found the Committee for the Relief of the Black Poor, which began as a project to relieve lascars, but quickly expanded its scope to include London's growing and largely impoverished Afro-British population, finally becoming the driving force behind the Sierra Leone colonization project.[98] As the poor-relief project took the form of a colonization scheme, the committee drew racial and geographic distinctions in their hierarchies of "deserving" poor; as many of the prospective settlers were Afro-British loyalists from Nova Scotia, the committee emphasized their military service, arguing that the nation owed them gratitude and thus relief.[99]

The Committee for the Relief of the Black Poor and the resulting Sierra Leone colonization project linked the streets of London to multiple distant locales: Nova Scotia, India, Africa. As Ashley Cohen argues, historiography of this project has often emphasized the significance of Sierra Leone's colonization for Afro-British history while downplaying its East Indian roots; thus, "we have largely forgotten the trans-colonial dimensions" of this event.[100] Furthermore, the project coincided with the establishment of Australia as a penal colony, and both places were, as Deirdre Coleman argues, simultaneously proposed by reformers as "sites where slaves and convicts might be re-birthed as free people."[101]

Even as the Sierra Leone project lost exclusive association with lascars, it maintained a clear connection between the spectacle of vagrancy and the colonization plan: it remained a poor-relief scheme. For instance, when a report printed in the *General Evening Post* describes a meeting between Pitt and the chairman of the committee, it ends by noting "our warmest approbation of the conduct of Government and the Committee, jointly, in thus providing for these miserable vagrants, whose appearance in such numbers about the streets of this metropolis, for many months back, have done no credit to our national character, as a humane and generous people."[102] Elsewhere, the committee promoted their efforts to "effectually relieve them, and at the same time render considerable Advantage to the Police of this Country."[103] Meanwhile, when far fewer prospective settlers turned up than expected, an advertisement published by the committee framed this disinterest as a problem of misguided pauper management: "It being apprehended that the Remainder are prevented from embarking by the mistaken, though well-intended Acts of Charity of Individuals, in giving Relief to such of the Black Poor as are still about the Streets, and in the Roads near the Metropolis; the Committee submit to the Consideration of the Public, whether it may not be adviseable to suspend giving Alms to the said Persons, in order to induce them to comply with the Engagement they entered into."[104] The committee threatened to have those who refused to embark taken up as vagrants, but never followed through on their threat, and far fewer settlers than had originally committed to the project ultimately left for

Sierra Leone.[105] Meanwhile, stories about black beggars being deported to Sierra Leone circulated in newspapers—sometimes approvingly and sometimes as critique of the committee and its methods.[106]

In their promises to remove visible poverty from the streets and thus mitigate the risks the visibly poor were assumed to bring, the committee drew on the same logic that had long underpinned the local enforcement of vagrancy law. However, instead of removing the poor to their home parish, the committee planned for removal across the ocean, framing resettlement as "repatriation" despite the fact that many of the "black poor" were not from anywhere in Africa.[107] As Isaac Land notes, the logic of removal and settlement underpinning the project rendered it a kind of referendum on black British national belonging; he therefore argues that the choice of the vast majority of London's black population to remain in England can be understood as a claim to "citizenship from the bottom up."[108] The logic of vagrancy structures the colonization plan thoroughly: as people largely without legal settlement in any parish, the "black poor" are regarded as vagrants not just to the parish, but to the nation, and thus relief and (national) removal are intertwined. Against this backdrop, the choice to reject colonization and remain in England might also be understood as a claim that links local parish settlement to *national* belonging.

The category of "black poor" imagines a particular meaning for vagrancy: it names a category of visible suffering that calls up imperial scandal in the heart of the metropole, and it makes racial difference into a sign of geographic removal and condensed distant geographies. This category persists beyond the Sierra Leone project; in the House of Commons 1814–1815 *Report from the Committee on Lascars and Other Asiatic Seamen,* the committee conceptually classes impoverished Afro-Britons with lascars even as they formally exclude them from the scope of the inquiry: "In the course of the investigations of Your Committee, it has appeared that many *Negroes* and persons of colour are brought into this country, to whose situation the consideration of the House might with propriety be called; but not feeling it expressly within their province on the present occasion, they have abstained from doing it."[109]

What, then, might we make of Robinson's "The Lascar" as an engagement with the category of "black poor"? As Humberto Garcia notes, Robinson employs the language of antislavery in her figurations of sympathy blocked by racial difference, such as when she pointedly echoes the iconic antislavery slogan "Am I not a man and a brother?" in the lascar's lament that he cannot "touch the soul of man, and share / a brother's love, a brother's care" (247–248).[110] In her appropriation of antislavery tropes in "The Lascar," Robinson maintains the conflation of Asian and African asserted by the consolidation of the "black poor" as a category, rendering the lascar's body a condensation of an ever-expanding array of global itineraries. Antislavery was, of course, an established model for the spectacularization of suffering and for imperial scandal—for rendering racialized hypervisibility a conduit for bringing distant violence close to the metropolitan reader. The lascar's dying words juxtapose the representation of lascars as "melancholy objects" whose bodies tell a simple story of East India Company avarice with the possibility of more specific stories of loss and displacement that implicate a much broader net of complicity:

> Here, in this smiling land we find
>    Neglect and mis'ry sting our race;
> And still whate'er the LASCAR's mind,
>    The stamp of sorrow marks his face!'
> He ceas'd to speak; while from his side
> Fast roll'd life's swiftly-ebbing tide. . . . (253–258)

The lascar's statement that "whate'er the LASCAR's mind, / The stamp of sorrow marks his face" explicitly juxtaposes the uniform and narrow signification of the racialized "face" with the possibility that his "mind" holds a much more variable, nontransparent, and complex interiority. Robinson's answer, however, is not for poetry to show his interiority in all its multidimensional complexity; indeed, the negation of this possibility marks the end of the lascar's ability to speak at all, and the poem closes with the villagers' encounter with his dead body. He is, in the end, still reduced to the lifeless body and its signification only as a thing out of place, a "melancholy object." She thus reproduces one of the foundational elements of how the Committee for the Relief of the Black Poor deployed vagrancy: "blackness" out of place is the sign of imperial scandal, a mute demand for sentimental redress.

By portraying the lascar as stranded and wishing nothing more than to return to India, Robinson joins the vast majority of British literary and journalistic portrayals of lascars: the tragedy of the lascar, in these portrayals, is their exile from "home" as exacerbated by cruel East India Company policy.[111] However, historical lascars made a much wider variety of claims to "home" and national belonging; while some laid claim to the status of "native of India" in their efforts to gain passage back to India, others claimed British nationality, which could offer the prospect of increased maritime employment opportunities and higher wages.[112] I've been arguing that vagrancy was crucial to constructing geographies of responsibility on multiple scales, both local and national. In the case of the Sierra Leone colonization project, geographies of responsibility became a medium for the racialization of "Britishness" through the construction of the "black poor" as vagrants who might find relief in their "home parishes"—outside the nation. By rendering the lascar a hypervisible sign of distant removals, Robinson is also participating in a specific, racialized meaning of vagrancy that took up local belonging and its technologies of exclusion as a model for national belonging and citizenship.

As Ashley Cross has argued, "the entanglement of Robinson's texts with those of Wordsworth and Coleridge . . . radically destabilizes the relationship between original and copy, self and other."[113] In showing how attention to Robinson's work forces us to reevaluate analyses of poetic vagrancy that have long taken Wordsworth as their paradigmatic case study, I seek to amplify the longstanding feminist argument that our foundational accounts of literary history change when we center female authors and resist reading them as belated, secondary, or derivative. Such attention reveals that Robinson's poetic attention to empire—her critique of colonial exploitation as well as her use of orientalist tropes and poetics—should be taken not as an unusually exotic variation on a conventionally rural English theme, but rather as a poetic deployment of vagrancy that is actively engaged with longstanding poetic and political treatments of scarcity, dispossession, and population.

After all, Robinson's formal strategies offer a broader insight into the genealogies of Romantic lyric and its relation to vagrancy. As James Mulholland argues, eighteenth-century poetic experiments in "printed voice" looked to marginal and colonized spaces as privileged sources of orality, and the poetic techniques these poets developed to invoke the virtualized voices of Welsh bards and Scottish ballad-singers helped lay the groundwork for Romanticism's apotheosis of voice and lyric personhood.[114] "The Lascar" begins, of course, with the lascar's direct address to the reader, marked as speech by the quotation marks that enclose the first seven stanzas—thus drawing on precisely the typographical and poetic forms by which eighteenth-century poets had sought to "evoke oral voices" in print.[115] The direct speech whose virtuality is also rendered hypervisible through the poetic form that mediates it has, of course, a famous antecedent in Wordsworth's "The Female Vagrant," which begins with a ventriloquized "artless story" that nonetheless takes the form of Spenserian stanzas (2). But Robinson's ventriloquism of the lascar is not only a geographically expanded version of Wordsworth's experiments with the language of common people. The ventriloquism of Indian speakers in particular was, Mulholland argues, already an established practice for poetic engagements—both celebratory and critical—with the East India Company's project of orientalist knowledge production in the era of William Jones and Warren Hastings.[116] These poetic experiments with ventriloquizing orality—an obvious antecedent to Wordsworth and Coleridge's project in the *Lyrical Ballads*—thus shows the global and imperial roots of the very formal features that made "Romantic vagrancy" possible. Its relative Englishness thus becomes all the more remarkable a development. In revisiting the specific form of orientalism that was already an established vehicle for staging political questions about colonial governance, as well as drawing on an analogous tradition of antislavery poetic ventriloquism, Robinson is not a more cosmopolitan imitator of the *Lyrical Ballads*, but rather a participant in poetic traditions that predated and in part enabled it.[117]

## Unsettlement

I conclude with a legal case that illuminates both the conditions of possibility for the "black poor" to cohere as a category as well as the limits of theoretical investigations of law and lyric that center personhood. In 1783, an enslaved young woman named Charlotte Howe apparently emancipated herself: having been purchased in America and brought to England in 1781, she left the home of her enslaver two years later. She traveled to the parish of Thames Ditton, where she had lived upon first being brought to England, where two justices ordered her removed to the parish of St. Luke's, Chelsea, the home parish of the woman who had formerly enslaved her.[118] The justices interpreted Howe as being equivalent to a former domestic servant under the laws of settlement, thus making St. Luke's her parish of legal settlement, and upon arrival there, she was sent to the workhouse. However, St. Luke's appealed to the King's Bench, disputing Howe's settlement, and thus the case of *The King v. Inhabitants of Thames Ditton* reached Lord Mansfield.[119] Mansfield ruled that Howe was not in fact settled in St. Luke's, Chelsea because she had not been *hired* as a servant and thus cannot be considered to be settled there under the poor law. His reasoning and his engagement with slavery thus resonate with his earlier and far more famous ruling in *Somerset v. Stewart* (1772): in *Somerset,* Mansfield had rejected proslavery arguments analogizing slavery to villeinage and other forms of servitude that were recognized under English law. Thus the same legal logic that eroded slavery's perceived legitimacy under English law ended up depriving the formerly enslaved Howe of access to poor relief—thus effectively creating a de facto racialized exclusion from the possibility of parish settlement for her anywhere in England.

If, for Barbara Johnson, *Rowland v. California Men's Colony* illustrates the deep figurative ground of legal personhood as a court attempts to define that personhood through and against incarceration and indigence, then *The King v. Inhabitants of Thames Ditton* offers us a window into how legal personhood can render the sustenance of the natural person irrelevant. For Johnson, lyric's collusion with law in the making of persons rests in how both invoke the subject as if it preexisted the figure that in fact grounds it. In her reading of *Rowland,* the limitation of legal "indigence" to natural persons rested on invoking the material human body through its deprivation, and subjectivity through the subjective capacity to suffer. But in the case of *The King v. Thames Ditton,* indigence does not do legal work analogous to the work it might do for lyric: Charlotte Howe is certainly experiencing a crisis of subsistence and deprivation, yet her subjective experience of deprivation is utterly irrelevant to the case.

Repeating some of the terms of the *Somerset* ruling—which hinged, in part, on a debate as to whether slavery could be considered analogous to villeinage—Mansfield notes in his ruling that while the foundations of the poor law date to an era in which villeinage still existed, "the change of customs and manners has effectually abolished" villeinage, and thus "the statutes do not relate to" bound laborers.[120] By dismissing villeinage completely from consideration, Mansfield invalidates any possible argument that slavery could be recognized in any of the invocations of servitude present in the poor law, rendering the case, in his words, "very plain," since "the statue says there must be a hiring, and here there was no hiring at all."[121] Mansfield's ruling, on the one hand, relies on invoking Howe as a potential legal subject of contract: the counterfactual invocation of an employment contract constructs her as a potential liberal subject who could consent to free labor. However, while Howe is invoked as a free subject through the contract she never had and the consent she never gave, Mansfield's engagement with her legal personhood ends here. Indeed, it is precisely the abolitionist argument that English common law does not recognize the state of slavery that renders Howe's "service" illegible to the poor law—thus excluding *her* from the categories that could grant her settlement under that body of law.

This distinction between slavery and other forms of servitude or bound labor that were present in English law was, of course, a crucial abolitionist legal argument; as I discuss at greater length in Chapter 5, preserving a sharp distinction between slavery and the forms of bound labor that were explicitly present in English law offered abolitionists legal ammunition, not only in their practical aims to diminish the powers of enslavers within England, but also in their broader rhetorical strategies to cast slavery as incompatible with the common law and thus also with the ideal of British liberty. But in the case of Charlotte Howe, the legal refusal to recognize slavery as analogous to servitude ends up producing her as a "free subject" while rendering her material need legally unrecognizable, utterly divorcing the subject of contract from the body that needs subsistence. Born outside of England, unmarried, and with no legally recognized history of employment or apprenticeship that could gain her settlement anywhere in the country, Howe is rendered more *vogelfrei* than most England-born paupers of the time; her legal recognition as a subject of contract renders her access to subsistence utterly dependent on wage labor at a time when many of the poor, especially women, still did not subsist on wage labor alone.[122]

The other thing that lyric and legal subjects have in common comes into stark relief here: neither need to eat. Vagrancy law—especially in its capacity as the punitive obverse of poor relief—was ultimately more concerned with scarcity and subsistence than with subjectivity, legal or otherwise. The late eighteenth-century efflorescence of lyric experimentation that invoked vagrancy as privileged and politicized ground thus stages the capacity of figure to ground both lyric and legal subjects against and through the very materiality of how "natural persons" can be unsettled and undone.

# *CHAPTER FOUR*

# SETTLER VAGRANCY

It is incongruous that this Elizabethan and pre-Elizabethan anti-migratory policy should have been imposed in a country where mobility of population has played a role of such historic and economic importance. . . . The same elements of the population who on one side of the Atlantic were rogues and vagabonds, on the other were frontiersmen.

—*Caleb Foote, "Vagrancy-Type Law and Its Administration,"* 1956

Caleb Foote's critique of vagrancy law, with its valorization of settler mobility, was extremely influential in the twentieth-century American legal battle against vagrancy law and the interpretation of police discretion it advanced.[1] This chapter, in examining the uneasy convergence of vagrancy with white settler mobility, tracks how the "rogues and vagabonds" of English vagrancy law could be imaginatively reclaimed as American "frontiersmen," while also revealing the ambivalent and contradictory nature of this transformation in the early years of the new republic. I locate an early history of this web of associations in the works of Charles Brockden Brown, and I end with its surprising persistence in contemporary U.S. law, as exemplified by the Supreme Court's citation of literary history in its 1972 ruling striking down vagrancy laws as unconstitutional.

As Hsuan Hsu argues, the valorization of white mobility as transgressive freedom, memorably embodied in the nineteenth-century figure of the tramp, both obscures and depends on the actual criminalization of people of color: "As Indian Removal, Emancipation, roundups of Chinese immigrants, and the growth of large-scale agriculture displaced populations from the land they worked on and inhabited, neither status, property ownership, nor means of employment could be counted on to distinguish unemployed whites from other racial groups. Under such conditions, the romanticized figure of the independent white tramp could be sustained only through processes of racialization that selectively precipitated, criminalized, and constrained the mobility of nonwhites."[2] The racial targeting of vagrancy laws was already long established by the nineteenth century.

When vagrancy laws appear in colonial North America, they are based on English law but adapted to local concerns.[3] One of the most significant adaptations of vagrancy law is their enlistment to manage the intensifying racialization of space and labor in the colonies. For example, a 1703 Massachusetts law empowering "all justices of the peace, constables, tythingmen, watchmen, and other her majesty's good subjects" to apprehend "any Indian, negro or molatto servant or slave that shall be found abroad after nine a clock at night, and shall not give a good and satisfactory account of their business, make any disturbance, or otherwise misbehave themselves" is one example of the common association between racially subjugated populations and the potential for future threat or disorder, which, in turn, calls for these populations' preemptive criminalization.[4] In 1790s Philadelphia, as Jen Manion shows, the broad purview of vagrancy law was, in practice, widely used to target suspected fugitives from slavery.[5] At the same time, as Simon P. Newman argues, the labor regulation central to early modern English vagrancy laws formed a crucial legal basis for the development of slave law in the American colonies.[6]

Early promoters of English colonization in the Americas argued that these colonies could serve as a sink for England's surplus population, where the unemployed, idle, and criminal could be remade into productive laborers. But the American colonies also developed legal mechanisms for managing their own surplus populations, marking some people as suspicious, and instituting police measures to protect property and security. Despite the claims of the colonies' promoters, the seemingly endless availability of expropriated land did not mean that North America was free of unemployment or poverty, and the exigencies of establishing a settler colony reliant on both indentured servitude and slavery meant that vagrancy laws were quickly adapted from their English models and retooled to provide for labor regulation, subordination, and settlers' "security."

Against this backdrop, Charles Brockden Brown's *Wieland* (1798) offers a window into an early moment in the formation of the free, wandering vagabond as a literary figure. *Wieland* deploys the imaginative capaciousness of vagrancy as a category that far exceeded the simple portrayal of physical mobility as freedom. Instead, the novel reveals that in the early years of the United States, the idea of vagrancy reconfigured existing associations between labor, dispossession, security, property, and police in the service of a specific, settler-colonial order of differentially racialized mobility. At the same time, *Wieland* uses the mysterious capabilities of a vagrant's body to stage key anxieties about the metaphysically unstable category of whiteness and its role in the early American body politic. The threats posed by the novel's vagrant figure, Carwin, reveal an uncanny inextricability of vagrancy from the social, economic, and physical mobility idealized as the marker of the newly independent white American man.

## Literary Vagrancy: Charles Brockden Brown's *Wieland*

Narrating the terrifying dissolution of one family's pastoral idyll, the plot of *Wieland* registers one of the central concerns animating vagrancy law: that unknown persons out of place might pose unknowable threat to settled citizens. Clara and Theodore Wieland, the children of a religious enthusiast who has died under mysterious circumstances, establish a small, closed community on the family estate, Mettingen. After adopting the mysterious stranger Carwin into their fold, they begin to hear unexplained voices, which sow confusion and conflict among them. Fear and disorientation build until there is a sudden eruption of violence: Theodore kills his wife, children, and a ward of the family, claiming that his actions were ordered by God. When Clara returns to the empty estate, she finds Carwin and accuses him of causing the murders through means she has not yet been able to uncover. Carwin reveals to her that he has extraordinary powers of ventriloquism and is responsible for the mysterious voices heard throughout the novel, but claims (though Clara does not believe him) that he did not produce the divine commands her brother had claimed to hear. Their interview is interrupted when Theodore, escaped from confinement, arrives and attempts to kill his sister. Carwin, who has fled the room, mimics the voice of God and commands Theodore to stop. Upon understanding that he was deluded, Theodore kills himself. Clara settles in France, and Carwin retires to the backcountry of Pennsylvania, determined never to use his gift again.

Carwin has long been approached by scholars as a figure for various threats to republican harmony and security, from those targeted by the Alien and Sedition Acts to the prospect of peasant insurrection or the failure of law to found a stable political collectivity.[7] The nature of Carwin's threat, I argue, remains open to such multiple characterizations because the novel refuses to limit the threat he poses to any one form. Like a vagrancy law, the novel evokes many possible sources and forms of danger but refuses to limit its anticipatory caution to one clearly defined figure. Carwin's imagined vagrancy is as proliferative and multivalent as the legal category. Like legal vagrancy, the imaginative vagrancy at the center of this novel cannot be confined to physical mobility alone.

By the 1790s, Pennsylvania's vagrancy laws already had a long history of adapting existing English legal models to a colonial environment. The Duke of York's Laws (1676), which were in force in what would become Pennsylvania until William Penn's charter of 1681, contained a familiar echo of English vagrancy law in empowering constables to "apprehend without warrant such as are overtaken with Drink, Swearing, Sabbath breaking, Vagrant persons or night walkers provided they be taken in the manner, either by the Sight of the Constable or by present information from others, as to make search for all such Persons."[8] However, this body of law also adapted English models to the specific needs of the colonies. For instance, in 1672, the New York General Court of Assizes ordered that strangers carry passes indicating their place of origin and destination, but while this practice, in England, had generally been intended to slow migration of the poor to London and to prevent parish poor relief from being diverted to nonresidents, its use in New York is cited as a response to "frequent Complaints" about "Servants who runn away from their Masters into other Governments."[9] Three years later, the court adapted the model of the pass yet again, this time to assist in the assertion of settler dominion over land, ordering "That the Indians at Mr. John Pells on Anne Hooks Neck be ordered to remove within a fortnight to their Usuall Winter Quarters within Hell-gate upon this Island during which time Loaden Canooes which shall have Certificates from the Magistrates of the Place from whence they come expressing whether they are goeing shall be permitted quietly to passe along the Shore."[10]

The vagrancy laws that follow continue to maintain the familiar English form—offering wide leeway to apprehend the "idle and disorderly" poor as well as anyone else presumed to pose a threat, while at the same time leaving space for new definitions of "threat" that arise in colonial spaces. The 1718 Pennsylvania "Act for Erecting of Houses of Correction and Work-houses," for instance, notes that houses of correction are "for the keeping, correcting and setting to work of all rogues, vagabonds, or sturdy beggars, and other idle and disorderly persons" as defined "by the laws and usage of Great-Britain, or by the laws of this province."[11]

Throughout the second half of the eighteenth century, vagrancy law was central to the operation of poor relief and the overall regulation of lower-class life and labor in Pennsylvania.[12] By 1795, for example, the majority of prisoners in Philadelphia were imprisoned for vagrancy.[13] The archival records of vagrancy arrests reveal a capaciousness in legal practice that exceeds the already wide letter of the law. For example, the 1767 Pennsylvania "Act to prevent the mischiefs arising from the encrease of vagabonds, and other idle and disorderly persons within this province," whose definition of vagrancy was still in force in 1798, defines as vagrants "all persons who, not having wherewith to maintain themselves and their families, live idly, and without employment, and refuse to work for the usual and common wages," all beggars, and all persons who come to Pennsylvania from elsewhere "and can give no reasonable account of themselves."[14] This already broad scope, however, is even more expansive in the records of actual arrests in the 1790s; for example, vagrancy arrests recorded in the Vagrancy Dockets of Philadelphia's Walnut Street Prison show that vagrancy law was used to target activities including sex work, military desertion, interracial sexual relationships, and escape from servitude or slavery.[15] In addition, magistrates were enlisted to punish enslaved or indentured laborers as vagrants for disobedience, idleness, or suspected "intent to abscond."[16]

Throughout their long, transatlantic history, vagrancy laws had served, above all, to manage and anticipate future threats to public order; these laws, for instance, granted wide leeway to their enforcers to apprehend those whose poverty, reputation, or appearance marked them as likely future thieves, or to expel people perceived as future drains on poor-relief funds.[17] As American colonies adapted English legal practices, vagrancy law also expanded to index threats specific to the colonies, such as the threat of slave rebellion; as Sally Hadden documents, slave patrols enforced vagrancy laws and occupied their general legal purview of targeting unknown, suspicious, or illicitly mobile people as they sought to keep order and prevent insurrection.[18]

Carwin first appears in the novel as a suspicious person: a shabby, unknown wanderer at the edges of the Wieland estate. Clara takes notice of him because his appearance marks him as a person out of place; while men like him "were frequently to be met with on the road and in the harvest-field," they are more unexpected in a place marked out for upper-class leisure: "This lawn was only traversed by men whose views were directed to the pleasures of the walk or the grandeur of the scenery."[19] Clara first sees Carwin from a distance, and is surprised by her own interest in the strange figure:

> His pace was a careless and lingering one, and had none of that gracefulness and ease which distinguish a person with certain advantages of education from a clown. His gait was rustic and awkward. His form was ungainly and disproportioned. Shoulders broad and square, breast sunken, his head drooping, his body of uniform breadth, supported by long and lank legs, were the ingredients of his frame. His garb was not ill adapted to such a figure. A slouched hat, tarnished by the weather, a coat of thick gray cloth, cut and wrought, as it seemed, by a country tailor, blue worsted stockings, and shoes fastened by thongs and deeply discoloured by dust, which brush had never disturbed, constituted his dress.
>
> There was nothing remarkable in these appearances: they were frequently to be met with on the road and in the harvest-field. I cannot tell

> why I gazed upon them, on this occasion, with more than ordinary attention, unless it were that such figures were seldom seen by me except on the road or field. (50)

For one whose appearance is summed up as "nothing remarkable," this is a very detailed physical description indeed. Clara carefully lays out the description in distinct and standard categories for close observation: the speed and manner of his walk, his bodily proportions both in net effect ("ungainly and disproportioned") and in specific details (drooping head, long legs, broad shoulders), and the color, style, materials, and condition of every article of clothing.

Clara's description, in other words, closely follows the format of a runaway advertisement. Fugitivity and vagrancy were closely linked in the eighteenth-century American public sphere, as the high population of enslaved and indentured laborers meant that unknown wanderers were often presumed to be fugitives unless proven otherwise.[20] Runaway advertisements followed a consistent set of genre expectations and conventions of physical description, most commonly noting details such as clothing, size, unusual physical features, gait, and accented speech.[21] Later, when suspicion has fallen upon Carwin for his role in the family's mysterious experiences, Henry reads a newspaper notice advertising the escape of a condemned criminal from a prison in Dublin, and is shocked to recognize the criminal as Carwin. Henry definitively identifies the figure in the newspaper notice by relying on the publication's detailed physical descriptions, which highlight the same features noted by Clara upon Carwin's first appearance: "The descriptions of his person and address were minute. His stature, hair, complexion, the extraordinary position and arrangement of his features, his awkward and disproportionate form, his gesture and gait, corresponded perfectly with those of our mysterious visitant" (129).

The knowledge promised by a supposedly authoritative printed description proves more unstable than initially promised, however, as the newspaper item describing Carwin as an escaped criminal is later revealed to be a forgery. Carwin's capacity for threat begins with mobility but quickly exceeds it, as Clara documents (with increasing terror) evidence of his opacity, social illegibility, unpredictability, and extraordinary bodily capacity. His appearance in the novel as the embodiment of opaque, unknowable threat is as capacious as the concept of vagrancy and its multivalent ability to index threat.

Carwin is quintessentially a stranger; nobody can deduce his origins or his proper social status. When Henry Pleyel (Theodore's friend and Clara's eventual husband) first encounters Carwin, he recognizes him as a traveler he had befriended in Spain several years before: "His garb, aspect, and deportment, were wholly Spanish. A residence of three years in the country, indefatigable attention to the language, and a studious conformity with the customs of the people, had made him indistinguishable from a native, when he chose to assume that character. . . . He had embraced the catholic religion, and adopted a Spanish name instead of his own, which was CARWIN, and devoted himself to the literature and religion of his new country" (67). This recollection is the novel's first revelation of Carwin's name; his true identity is embedded in an aside interrupting a description of an identity he had assumed in the past. Burying Carwin's name within an extended description of his Spanish alter ego, the passage suggests that the true picture of Carwin *is* disguise; that the body attached to the name "Carwin" is most paradigmatically recognizable when swathed in descriptions of another man who, officially, does not exist. Henry's recollection emphasizes Carwin's capacity for mutability and disguise, as his ability to pass as Spanish in dress, language, and even religion anticipates the later revelation that he can mimic the voice of anyone he chooses.

Carwin's "biloquism"—Brown's idiosyncratic term for his character's powers of ventriloquism—literalizes the rhetorical link between vagrancy and spectacular yet unknowable threat. Carwin's voice is endlessly mutable. It can take any form and come from any direction. It allows Carwin to "move" invisibly through space. After discovering and honing his powers of biloquism, Carwin finds that his gift offers an alternative to labor. He uses his power to gain patronage, economic opportunity, and the freedom to travel far from his home on the Pennsylvania frontier. As he explains to Clara near the conclusion of *Wieland:* "For a time the possession of so potent and stupendous an endowment elated me with pride. Unfortified by principle, subjected to poverty, stimulated by headlong passions, I made this powerful engine subservient to the supply of my wants and the gratification of my vanity" (198–199). His gift, he explains, tempts him to follow his insatiable "passion for mystery, and a species of imposture," which, once indulged, becomes increasingly habitual and impossible to resist (201). Carwin's biloquism leads him to an extreme form of "idleness": his action (unlike labor) has no discernible end or product, it generates nothing but fleeting pleasure, and it feeds on habitual impulses that follow no apparent rationale, economic or otherwise, as they lead to actions that even Carwin cannot predict. Carwin's vagrancy is thus as capaciously realized as the legal category. The structure of threat and anticipation invoked by the label of vagrancy might be likened to Clara's reaction when she believes she sees Carwin's face in her home just before the murders: "The intimation was imperfect: it gave no form to my danger, and prescribed no limits to my caution" (148).

Carwin's extraordinary power of biloquism furnishes an extreme example of social unintelligibility. While the textual arms of regulatory institutions, such as runaway advertisements and almshouse records, relied on the bodies, habits, and voices of the poor to fix and disclose consistent and traceable identities, Carwin's body defies such a goal through its ability to transform a feature taken to be so central to consistent identification.

Carwin thus inhabits an impossible identity: he actually brings limitless, unknowable threat to the extent that was invoked rhetorically by vagrancy as a concept and by "vagrants" as a theoretical collectivity, but not necessarily attributed to individuals apprehended under vagrancy law. Indeed, the specific danger he brings to the Wieland family is so bizarre, so unexpected, that it throws into sharp relief the rhetorical function of vagrancy to index future threat utterly exceeding the predictive capacity of the law.

There is, as I have noted, a longstanding scholarly preoccupation with Brown's political stances regarding the viability of the new republic. Here, I am less concerned with deducing Brown's political sympathies and more with understanding how the legal category of vagrancy came to be available to him as a tool, both political and aesthetic. To uncover this, I turn briefly to the treatment of vagrancy, police, and justice in one of Brown's most well known influences: William Godwin's *Caleb Williams* (1794). Carwin's "rustic and awkward" gait, his comparison to a "clown" (50), and his later-revealed facility for imposture all constitute a pointed echo of the first disguise Caleb adopts in his flight from

Falkland's seemingly infinite powers of surveillance: "From my youth I had possessed a considerable facility in the art of imitation; and when I quitted my retreat in the habitation of Mr Raymond, I adopted along with my beggar's attire a peculiar slouching and clownish gait to be used whenever there should appear the least chance of my being observed, together with an Irish brogue which I had had an opportunity of studying in my prison."[22] Caleb's professed talent for imposture is embedded in the description of this particular disguise; the capacity of vagrancy to name a seemingly infinite array of threats or nuisances is here transfigured into a capacity for seemingly infinite self-transformation.

Of course, the problem with this disguise is that it works too well; attempting to sail to Ireland, Caleb is questioned by some "officers of justice" who are not, as he fears at first, carrying out Falkland's will, but who instead mistake him for an Irish thief.[23] They take him before a justice, who sends him to Warwick to be tried: "Perhaps, after all, I should turn out to be the felon in question. But, if I was not that, he had no doubt I was worse; a poacher, or, for what he knew, a murderer."[24] Caleb, when he is first apprehended, fears that his identity has been discovered by Falkland's agents: "Did his power reach through all space, and his eye penetrate every concealment?"[25] However, as the justice makes clear, his apprehension renders his personal identity completely irrelevant; the justice seems untroubled by the mounting evidence that Caleb is not the thief in question and instead simply declares that "it was clear that [he] was a vagabond and a suspicious person."[26] Thus Godwin makes use of vagrancy's legal implication in order to supply Caleb with an extraordinary capacity for self-transformation—a capacity that, by the novel's end, matures into the horror of a consciousness that outlasts the stripping away of Caleb's entire social existence and is perhaps most forcefully articulated in Godwin's original manuscript ending of the novel, concluding with Caleb's declaration that he is now "an obelisk to tell you, HERE LIES WHAT WAS ONCE A MAN!"[27] At the same time, by allowing his protagonist to be *mistaken* for a vagrant, Godwin also stages a terrifying encounter between the narrative subject and a legal category that has nothing to do with subjectivity, thus transforming the everyday operation of justice into one of the "modes of domestic and unrecorded despotism" that is held up as the enemy of the rights of man.[28]

Carwin, of course, displays a far more ambiguous relationship to innocence, justice, and the discourse of the rights of man. The revelation that Carwin is also a man on the run serves only to shore up his aura of menace, not his innocence in the face of persecution, as the history (especially in the *Memoirs*) of his pursuit by the shadowy Ludloe further implicates Carwin in a mysterious transatlantic conspiracy that is never fully explained. Pamela Clemit, in influentially characterizing *Wieland* as a "Godwinian novel," has argued that Brown takes up Godwin's form but in the service of a conservative critique of Godwin's radical vision.[29] Meanwhile, Anthony Galluzzo argues that Brown's participation in a transatlantic "radical Enlightenment" was far more complex than this.[30] For Galluzzo, Brown's target is indeed not identical to Godwin's: "Whereas Godwin works to expose the aristocratic tradition championed by Edmund Burke, Brown attacks the new liberal individualist order that supplants it."[31] However, Carwin's biloquism, Galluzzo argues, amounts to more than a simple repudiation of revolutionary politics, proposing instead its advancement through other means, as he "utilizes powers that encompass fictionality, imagination, and a certain version of the aesthetic enterprise in order to finally upset a familial order that is also social and political."[32] If vagrancy, as I have argued, is a legal category that cannot be reconciled with the liberal subject at the confluence of juridical recognition, economic self-possession, and the capacity for political representation, then Brown's deployment of it in the character of Carwin troubles confidence in a political order grounded in the elevation of such subjectivity to the foundation of sovereignty.

However, as a category for naming anticipation, threat, and opacity, it is also a category well suited to Brown's aesthetic aims, and thus also an engine of readerly fascination and curiosity. In other words, Carwin's voice proves instantly charismatic to Clara, but she's not the only one to be drawn in. Carwin's vagrancy—his capacity to embody any potential future threat and thus exceed prediction—is precisely what allows him to be the engine of the novel's capacity to surprise, terrify, and astound the reader. Like the picaro—the outlaw who also becomes a protagonist, thus linking the "rogue" to new forms of colonial sovereignty—Carwin embodies the emerging archetype of the self-made man, both as a danger and as an ideal. After all, contemporary accounts of counterfeiters and confidence men attracted the fascination of the early American reading public, and while Brown certainly does not valorize Carwin's restlessness and deception, he nonetheless draws on traits that early Americans regarded with both anxiety and fascination, as "a society increasingly organized around the pursuit of wealth" seemed to reward forms of self-fashioning reliant on fictionality and belief: credit, paper money, speculation.[33] At the same time, Carwin's identification—however uneasy and ambivalent—with the revolutionary ideals invested in Caleb Williams also reveals how Carwin's vagrancy lays the groundwork for his literary-historical affinities with later narratives of the "man on the run," as Leslie Fiedler would write in 1960: the valorized transgression that embodies American freedom precisely through a seeming flight from the institutions and laws of American "civilization."[34] Though Brown does not necessarily seek to straightforwardly valorize Carwin's transgression, the possibility of this valorization, I will argue, lies in the entanglement of Carwin's vagrancy with the privileged mobility of whiteness as modes of colonial sovereignty and racial governance are reconfigured in the service of early national expansionism and empire.

## "Infinite Endowments": Vagrancy and Whiteness

Brown's *Memoirs of Carwin the Biloquist* (1803–1805), an unfinished fragment published in installments in his *Literary Magazine*, takes up Carwin's aspiration, in *Wieland*, to retreat to the backwoods and compose a memoir of his life. Most, if not all, of the *Memoirs* were composed in 1798, concurrently with *Wieland*, and the Advertisement to *Wieland* notes the existence of this text, whose future publication (Brown asserts) is conditional on the novel's success.[35] In the *Memoirs*, Brown narrates the story of Carwin's early life and the means through which he acquires his extraordinary powers. Carwin's embrace of the "fleeting and mutable" impulses that spur radical changes in appearance, social identity, and location are ultimately rooted in the refusal of labor and an attraction to pleasures and motivations that, in the language of eighteenth-century vagrancy law, fall under the category of "idleness." Carwin contrasts his character with that of his brother, who is utterly content in his station:

> My eldest brother seemed fitted by nature for the employment for which he was destined. His wishes never led him astray from the hay-stack and the furrow. . . . My character was the reverse of his. My thirst of knowledge was augmented in proportion as it was supplied with gratification. The more I heard or read, the more restless and unconquerable my curiosity became. My senses were perpetually alive to novelty, my fancy teemed with visions of the future, and my attention fastened upon every thing mysterious or unknown. (*Memoirs,* 247)

Carwin's capacity for desire, he explains, renders him unable to tolerate a life of agricultural labor. He is driven by a curiosity that demands constant novelty, is never satisfied, and opposes the repetitive routine dictated by the demands of labor: "I hated manual labour, or any task of which the object was gain. To be guided in my choice of occupations by any motive but the pleasure which the occupation was qualified to produce, was intolerable to my proud, indolent, and restive temper" (*Memoirs,* 262).

While an interior disposition that cannot tolerate labor would mark Carwin, in the language of vagrancy law, as dangerously criminal, a drain on resources, and an obstruction to the life of capitalism, the *Memoirs* also link Carwin's desires to the far more positively valued image of the rugged frontiersman, whose unfettered mobility signals a new and distinctively American form of whiteness. Carwin first acquires his powers in the Pennsylvania backcountry, through the assimilation of American landscapes and people. As he follows a lost cow into the wilderness bordering his family farm, a young Carwin amuses himself with his own vocal capacities: "I uttered the words which chanced to occur to me, and repeated in the shrill tones of a Mohock savage . . . 'Cow! 'Cow! cow! come home! home!' " (*Memoirs,* 250).

David Kazanjian connects this moment, with its invocation of the "Mohock savage," to Brown's larger agenda for American literature as famously articulated in the Advertisement to *Edgar Huntly.*[36] Here, Brown claims the specificity of American representation as a unique feature of his work: "One merit the writer may at least claim; that of calling forth the passions and engaging the sympathy of the reader, by means hitherto unemployed by preceding authors. Puerile superstition and exploded manners; Gothic castles and chimeras, are the materials usually employed for this end. The incidents of Indian hostility, and the perils of the western wilderness, are far more suitable; and for a native of America to overlook those, would admit of no apology."[37] For Kazanjian, this moment is foundational to Brown's own narrative of American literature and his place in it, as he "labors to produce a narrative of the 'natural' emergence of American literature, a narrative that replaces the violent history of white settler colonialism with an aesthetic call to incorporate scenes of 'wild' America into tales of white colonial life."[38] Of course, as Katy Chiles notes, while *Edgar Huntly* begins with this promise of assimilation, the possibility of racial transformation runs both ways; Edgar's increasingly tenuous identification with "civilized" whiteness during his time in the wilderness "draws upon the discourses of transformable race to unsettle rather than articulate an American national identity."[39]

In the *Memoirs,* Carwin's acquisition of extraordinary power through a moment of imagined racial assimilation echoes a widespread articulation of early American whiteness as a privileged site of potential, adaptation, and change. For example, Thomas Jefferson, in his *Notes on the State of Virginia* (1787), famously attempts to refute Buffon's assertion of the diminutive effects of the American climate on plants, animals, and humans by enlisting a rhetorical identification between white and indigenous Americans. Defending the "Indian" against Buffon's claims about the effects of the American climate, Jefferson lays the groundwork for a defense of white Americans against any imputation that the climate might affect them similarly: "I am able to say, in contradiction to this representation, that he is neither more defective in ardor, nor more impotent with his female, than the white reduced to the same diet and exercise: that he is brave, when an enterprize depends on bravery."[40] Here, the potency and valor of the "Indian" signals the potential of America to nurture white manhood.[41]

Meanwhile, in *Wieland,* Carwin tells Clara that he can "mimic exactly the voice of another, and . . . modify the sound so that it shall appear to come from what quarter and be uttered at what distance I please" (225). Carwin's biloquism, once perfected, is detached from the specificities of place and indigeneity that characterized its emergence; he can mimic any voice and thus does not necessarily sound like a "Mohock savage," and his voice can appear to come from anywhere, not just the frontier landscape where he first understood the possibility of this power. Indeed,

*Wieland* registers no trace of his power's racialized origins; this narrative is relegated to the belated, supplementary account of the *Memoirs.* Carwin attains unmarked invisibility through the use of a power whose source is also stripped by the narrative of any specific point of origin.

Eighteenth-century environmental theories of race, in positing the potential contingency and transformability of race, often figured whiteness as a uniquely unmarked state, the default ground upon which transformation might occur. For example, prominent eighteenth-century natural scientist Samuel Stanhope Smith argues in his *Essay on the Causes of the Variety of Complexion and Figure in the Human Species* (1787) that that "the causes of colour are active in their operation, and speedily make a deep impression. White is the ground on which this operation is received. And a white skin is to be preserved only by protecting it from the action of these causes."[42] Just as whiteness here is the empty ground against which human difference is marked, it is also potential, marked by its capacity for variety: "The infinite variety of ideas and emotions in civilized society, will give every class of citizens some distinguishing expression, according to their habits and occupations; and will bestow on each individual some singular and personal traits, according to his genius, education, or pursuits."[43] According to Smith, "savages" do not display such variation, as they all bear the uniform, racializing mark of climate.[44]

This evocation of whiteness thus resonates uncannily with Carwin's voice, which is the result of extraordinary skill and yet is bound by no particularity of physical location, gender, or other marker of identity. Carwin can perform a number of different class positions, literalizing Smith's claim that social stratification is a mark of "civilization" and thus whiteness. While Smith characterizes this class variation as a mark of civilized societies, Carwin manages to display it in his own person, dramatizing the potential of class variation as a capability of the individual white body. His biloquism allows him to occupy a potentially infinite variety of distinct social identities. He convincingly imitates the voices of women; his body transcends markers conventionally understood to be reliable markers of gender. This, once again, elevates him to a kind of universality; he is not just *a* man, but rather a more general embodiment of *man,* the category that includes (while also subsuming) women. Carwin's vagrancy—his resistance to agricultural labor, his physical and social mobility, and his extraordinary powers of self-transformation—is therefore disturbingly difficult to separate from the idealized characteristics of the self-made man, a figure that imaginatively coalesces freedoms granted by American whiteness.[45] In *Wieland*, whiteness implies the transcendence of geographical, biological, economic, and political limitation. And yet the possibility that Carwin's power might be unlimited is the ultimate source of terror for those around him; as Clara remarks: "When I think of all the resources with which nature and education have supplied thee; that thy form is a combination of steely fibres and organs of exquisite ductility and boundless compass, actuated by an intelligence gifted with infinite endowments, and comprehending all knowledge, I perceive that my doom is fixed" (114).

Carwin's propulsion beyond a life of labor by his unknowable and mysterious impulses renders him an unsettling mirror image of the novel's other self-made man: the elder Wieland, whose religious conversion prompts him to abandon his apprenticeship and settle in America. His whiteness underwrites his ability to reinvent himself, both spiritually and materially: he comes to America because he wishes to be a missionary and "the North American Indians naturally presented themselves as the first object for this species of benevolence," and as the novel explains, it is due to the availability of slave labor that he is able to establish the estate on which the novel's events later unfold (17). Carwin's impossible ability to condense the full scope of vagrancy into his own body thus paradoxically evokes another category: what Dana Nelson terms the "impossible identity" of early American white manhood.[46]

Carwin paradoxically unites contradictory meanings of vagrancy: he is both the free white frontiersman *and* a danger to the new republic; both an enterprising economic subject *and* a threat to economic, social, and political stability; both a solitary wanderer *and* a suspicious person. In his unbounded capacity and powers of self-transformation, Carwin poses a threat to social order, and yet also epitomizes many of the characteristics rhetorically assigned to American whiteness. In the convergence of Carwin's vagrancy and his whiteness, we see the conditions of possibility for the later emergence of imaginative vagrancy as a consolidation of white freedom. At the same time, the deep ambivalence with which Brown treats this convergence reveals how Carwin's unfettered mobility cannot be detached from other, less easily valorized meanings of vagrancy: idleness, opacity, and the potential to pose unpredictable future threat to settled citizens.

## Settler Colony, "Vagrant Race"

While Carwin's biloquism attaches firmly to his body, the *Memoirs* place the acquisition of his powers in the landscape. While he appears in *Wieland* as endlessly mobile and rootless, the *Memoirs* intertwine the origins of his power with the landscape of the Pennsylvania backcountry, and this location is significant—even if the most consequential thing to happen here is the acquisition of the power that allows Carwin to leave. The presence of Carwin and his family as backcountry settlers places the acquisition of his extraordinary mobility squarely in the context of Native dispossession, and Brown reveals how white mobility was unevenly, partially, and contradictorily split off from Native "savagery," which was then commonly figured as collective and racial vagrancy.

Toward the end of the Seven Years' War, the Pennsylvania backcountry saw a boom in frontier towns, as young, landless settlers seized opportunities to profit from the prospect of growing demand for commerce between the port cities and settlements pushing farther west.[47] At the war's end, the Proclamation of 1763, which the Crown intended as a curb to settlement past the Appalachians, did not effectively reduce settlement, instead spurring a wave of speculation on land located beyond the boundary.[48] During and after the Revolution, preemption rights to purchase this land became a commodity, traded to land speculators.[49] As Allan Greer argues, even as the Proclamation attempted to declare land west of the boundary as Native property, its very figuration of the land as alienable property in fact laid the groundwork for the forms of land cession by treaty that would predominate throughout British settler colonies.[50] Though the acquisition of preemption rights did not guarantee that the land in question would be sold at all, speculators nevertheless began to treat these preemption rights as fee simple, thus imagining Native peoples as tenants on land that belonged—or would eventually belong—to settlers.[51] As Maureen Konkle argues, the "narrative of savagism and civilization" that underwrote Indian removal first rose to prominence in the eighteenth century as a justification for land acquisition that did not rely on Native people's consent to sell.[52] This narrative of savagery most commonly relied on a dichotomy between "civilized" white settlement and "savage" indigenous itinerancy, mobility, and supposed refusal to cultivate land: qualities that could be, and often were, figured through vagrancy.

For example, during the Seven Years' War, one representative piece in the *American Magazine and Monthly Chronicle for the British Colonies* offers advice, based on "the genius and temper of the Indians," on how to win Native allegiance against the French: "The first thing then is to assist them in making a settlement. This is with good reason mentioned first; for without it none of the other ends can be effectually answered. A vagrant life is unfavourable to instruction; and without settlements and fixed habitations, and that at no great distance from us, we cannot expect, in the present situation of affairs that their friendship will be steady and firm."[53] Using the rhetoric of vagrancy and welfare, the author proposes assimilation into "fixed habitations" as beneficially inducing the very dependency that poor relief, in England, was meant to reduce:

> They will gradually unlearn their natural ferocity; their manners will become more humane and gentle; their wants will be encreased, while on us they must in a manner wholly depend to have them supplied: And thus, being for some time accustomed to live in houses, they will find themselves incapable of encountering the difficulties of an unprovided unsettled life; so that necessity, as well as inclination, nay their own welfare and happiness, which is the strongest cement of national union, will engage them to cultivate our friendship, and attach them to our interest.[54]

This rhetorical transformation of vagrancy from criminalized economic marginality into a marker of racialized, collective lack of civilization recurs throughout colonial and early national writing on America and its indigenous peoples. What is striking here—and quite different from the rhetoric of vagrancy and poor relief in England—is the insistence on dependency as *beneficial;* while Henry Fielding, in the same decade, was decrying what he saw as poor Londoners' tendencies to let their desires outstrip their means, the author here characterizes the link between vagrancy and dependence as beneficial to settlers in compelling both military alliance and dispossession of land.[55] This particular racialization of vagrancy is best viewed through an understanding of settler colonialism's specific and privileged relation to land.

Jodi Byrd argues that settler colonialism cannot be reduced to the racialization of bodies, as "this conflation masks the territoriality of conquest by assigning colonization to the racialized body, which is then policed in its degrees from whiteness."[56] Settler colonialism, as Patrick Wolfe has influentially stated, must be understood first through the acquisition of land: "Territoriality is settler colonialism's specific, irreducible element."[57] And so in this context, what emerges crucially is vagrancy's relationship to land. Early modern English vagrancy laws were particularly targeted at the landless poor at a time of accelerating enclosure.[58] "Vagrant" is thus a term long identified with enclosure by the eighteenth century.[59] When Native people are figured as "vagrants," this figuration reflects on Native land, rendering it ripe for enclosure, or even already imaginatively enclosed. Indeed, the Lockean notion of America as uncultivated waste, which required cultivation, settlement, and improvement, was ubiquitous from the very beginning of English colonization in the Americas, and informed colonists' theories of governance, property, and law. To label a person "vagrant" as a justification for dispossessing them of their land is a powerful prolepsis that reflects the imaginative transformation of preemption rights into fee simple: the transformation of land ripe for the buying into land that has already been sold. The inhabitants of the land, when figured as vagrants, are therefore transformed into trespassers whose continued presence on the land is criminal, illegitimate, and contrary to the security of private property—and thus a threat to civil society itself.

And so when the powers that grant Carwin his unfettered freedom of movement (but also render him a kind of vagrant) are rooted in the imaginative assimilation of Native "savagery" at the edges of a backcountry settlement, Carwin's vagrancy becomes a potent form of "playing Indian."[60] In early America, as Dana Nelson argues, "Indian identity became a resource for national/white manhood in the United States through symbolic as well as literal expropriation and occupation."[61] When applied specifically to vagrancy, we then see Carwin taking up the position of the to-be-dispossessed (the vagrant) and transforming it into the white male capacity to dispossess others, precisely through the very mobility and unsettledness that, when rhetorically assigned to Native peoples, rendered their land expropriatable.

This dual meaning of imaginative vagrancy—both a racialized marker of "savagery" and a quality that assigns enterprising mobility to an indigenized American whiteness—proliferates in literary visions of early national masculinity. For instance, in his post-Revolutionary 1786 revision of *The Rising Glory of America,* Philip Freneau attempts to assimilate the idea of "vagrant" Native mobility into the enterprising, commercial, and free mobility of white Americans while maintaining racial distinctions between the two groups.[62] As three figures engage in a performatively pedagogical discourse about the place of America in the civilizational history of the world, one of the figures, Eugenio, interrupts an account of colonial history with a question:

> But whence arose
> That vagrant race who love the shady vale
> And choose the forest for their dark abode?—
> For long has this perplext the sages skill
> To investigate. (25–29)

The mobility first invoked here by the epithet of "vagrant race" is central to the poem's nationalist project. By assimilating the racialized particularity of an imagined indigenous mobility, Freneau makes an American national claim for a locodescriptive poetic tradition in which, as Julie Ellison argues, "the nation is not fixed in place or time, according to this aesthetic, but is deterritorialized and constructed as a series of nonconsecutive vignettes."[63]

The prospect afforded by contemplation of the "vagrant race" leads to a history of the world as seen from a uniquely American vantage point. Eugenio attempts to answer his own question by speculating that "banish'd Jews, Siberians, Tartars wild" (56) might have come over a land bridge across Greenland, which leads him, in turn, to imagine a history that predates the Atlantic itself:

> . . . Bermuda's isles,
> Cape Verd, Canary, Britain, and the Azores,

With fam'd Hibernia, are but broken parts
Of some prodigious waste, which once sustain'd
Nations and tribes of vanish'd memory,
Forests, and towns, and beasts of every class
Where navies now explore their briny way. (76–82)

This passage names Britain as just one in a series of fragmentary, peripheral islands—in the same class as Ireland and Cape Verde—that persists as a remnant of a vanished supercontinent. Not only does this disrupt climate theories that rely on the assumption that America and Europe are drastically separate places with separate natural histories, it also proposes a form of racial distinction based more on degree of mobility than on geographical location or origin. Indigenous Americans can be classed with Jews, Siberians, and Tartars as members of a geographically nonparticular "vagrant race."

The response of another speaker, Leander, dismisses some of Eugenio's more colorful speculations:

Your sophistry, Eugenio, makes me smile:
The roving mind of man delights to dwell
On hidden things merely because they're hid:
He thinks his knowledge far beyond the all limit,
And boldly fathoms nature's darkest haunts—
But for uncertainties, your broken isles,
Your northern Tartars, and your wandering Jews,
(The flimsy cobwebs of a sophist's brain). . . . (83–90)

Leander places indigenous North Americans back into geographical fixity by asserting that while their exact origin is unknown, they must nonetheless be absolutely rooted in North America:

This indicates they were a different race;
From whom descended 'tis not ours to say—
That power, no doubt, who furnish'd trees, and plants,
And animals, to this vast continent,
Spoke into being man among the rest,
But what a change is here! What arts arise!
What towns and capitals! (130–136)

On the surface, this is a simple repudiation of any possible common ancestry between the civilized, settled Anglo-Americans and the "vagrant race." While Leander dismisses Eugenio's speculations of a primordial Euroamerican continent, he attributes his curiosity about American origins to a basic mark of universal humanity: "The roving mind of man delights to dwell / On hidden things merely because they're hid" (84–85). While civilized (i.e., white) Americans are definitively *not* of the "vagrant race" (after all, their arrival is marked by the transformation of wilderness into "towns and capitals"), they are distinguished by the curiosity of their "roving mind." Their proximity to Native peoples, Leander attempts to insist, does not threaten white Americans with the possibility that they might be or become racially similar. Rather, this proximity offers white Americans a chance to shore up both their American particularity *and* their civilized whiteness through the availability of indigenous objects of contemplation. For Leander, this is a clear and untroubling distinction. But nonetheless, the mobility attributed to the "vagrant race" is still incorporated into the settledness of civilized white Americans, in the form of the metaphorical mobility indexed by Eugenio's "roving mind."

Natural scientist Benjamin Smith Barton elaborates this link between civilizational advancement and the claim to knowledge. For Barton, the contemplation of indigenous history by white Americans offers general reflections on the history of the world and the nature of civilization. To be civilized, he asserts, is to demonstrate the capacity to contemplate the uncivilized: "Natural History, which opens the door to so much precious knowledge concerning mankind, teaches us, that the physical differences between nations are but inconsiderable, and history informs us, that civilization has been constantly preceded by barbarity and rudeness. It teaches us, a mortifying truth, that nations may relapse into rudeness again; all their proud monuments crumbled into dust, and themselves, now savages, subjects of contemplation among civilized nations and philosophers."[64] Thomas Jefferson, to whom Barton dedicates this text, incorporates proximity to Native people and their artifacts into his notion of what comprises an "enlightened" inquiry into their nature (and into human nature more broadly); introducing his refutation of Buffon, he asserts: "This belief is founded on what I have seen of man, white, red, and black, and what has been written of him by authors, enlightened themselves, and writing amidst an enlightened people. The Indian of North America being more within our reach, I can speak of him somewhat from my own knowledge, but more from the information of others better acquainted with him, and on whose truth and judgment I can rely."[65] By contemplating the "vagrant race," Barton and Jefferson assert, one can exercise one's "roving mind," detaching mobility from its racialized associations and transforming it into a feature of civilized whiteness.

In Freneau's narrative of civilizational progress, commercial development is linked to settled whiteness, even as it simultaneously relies on the incorporation of "savage" mobility into that whiteness. For example, Acasto's praise of commerce collapses into an opposition of enterprising mobility and agricultural fixity—one that veers unsettlingly close to Carwin's rejection of agricultural labor as unfulfilling to his desire for novelty and stimulation:

> Such are the visions of the rustic reign—
> But this alone, the fountain of support,
> Would scarce employ the varying mind of man;
> Each seeks employ, and each a different way:
> Strip Commerce of her sail, and men once more
> Would be converted into savages—" (282–287)

Here, the division of labor and the expansion of commerce are the inevitable outcomes of desires that animate the "varying mind of man." While this statement initially positions such a desire as a universal human trait, this capacity for variation and change is, like the "roving mind of man" evoked above, in fact characterized as a property of whiteness. After all, it is the denial of opportunity for commerce, Acasto goes on to state, that causes men to degenerate into "savages."

Enterprising mobility, dissatisfaction with geographically fixed and repetitive agricultural labor, and the desire for endless self-transformation—these characteristics mark, for Freneau, the extraordinary promise of white manhood as it becomes the vehicle for the "rising glory of America." And yet these same characteristics, in *Wieland,* render Carwin a figure not of undisputed national progress and glory, but of uncontainable and unknown threat with the power to destroy the nation from within. This instability, I want to suggest, is made possible by the characterization of early American whiteness as a category that draws its meaning from its supposed capacity for adaptation, change, and privileged relationship to a "savage" landscape. Carwin's "infinite endowments" are the sinister side of the adaptive capacities imagined to be the unique affordance of whiteness.

## *Edgar Huntly*, Hannah Freeman, and Dispossession by Alms

*Edgar Huntly* (1799) is Brown's most sustained novelistic treatment of Native dispossession, white mobility, and the violence of "playing Indian." The novel's treatment of the Lenape has been the topic of much scholarly examination and debate.[66] Edgar's murderous foray into the wilderness is in some sense an intensification of Carwin's paradoxical position as a white vagrant, poised uncomfortably between self-made man and dangerous criminal. Like Carwin, Edgar's physical mobility is linked to a threateningly uncontrollable waywardness and the capacity to wield frightening power. As the story unfolds, Edgar is revealed as increasingly unreliable as a narrator; most pointedly, as he attempts to prove the sleepwalking Clithero guilty of the murder of his friend Waldegrave, he is revealed to be a somnambulist himself. While Carwin, by the end of *Wieland*, is only under suspicion for inspiring the Wieland murders, Edgar's apparently boundless capacity for bloodshed is unquestionable, as he kills two panthers (drinking the blood of one), murders four Lenape men, and fires shots at his friends, mistakenly believing them to be Lenape as well.

As with Carwin, much of what makes Edgar threatening evokes the category of vagrancy. His somnambulism in particular names movement that can be traced to no consciousness or intention, thus evoking vagrancy's association not only with directionless wandering, but also with acts that, more broadly, seem to exceed rational economic activity. His increasing identification with Clithero—an Irish servant who conceals a shadowy, violent past and who descends into madness by the end of the novel—only heightens his association with potential threat. At the same time, Edgar is most unpredictable, violent, and terrifying when he enacts the logic of *police*—when he anticipates and attempts to eliminate future threats to security. For instance, when he awakens after having sleepwalked into a cave, he finds a group of Lenape warriors sleeping near a captured white girl. From the evidence before him, he not only deduces what has already happened—the girl's capture—but also seamlessly slides from the past to the future, as he concludes that this incident may be the beginning of "an implacable and exterminating war."[67] As is characteristic of Edgar's reasoning, the possibility of war progresses from the grammatically conditional to the future tense; he decides he must kill them all preemptively in order to avert the future attack that he believes will certainly come if he doesn't: "I entertained no doubts about the hostile designs of these men. This was sufficiently indicated by their arms, their guise, and the captive who attended them."[68] Here, their dress, their proximate objects, and their presence in this place become proof not only of what they have already done (the presence of the girl proves that they have taken her captive) but also of intent for future action.

Thus Edgar occupies precisely the legal prolepsis I associate not only with vagrancy law (which names people as potential future threats to property, security, or community resources), but with police more generally: the modes of surveillance, summary punishment, and securing of space that rely on reading the world for evidence of what has not yet happened. Edgar justifies the killing of one man in particular in precisely these terms: "He will live only to pursue the same sanguinary trade; to drink the blood and exult in the laments of his unhappy foes, and of my own brethren."[69] Of course, Edgar is the only character actually shown drinking blood in this novel. He shuttles constantly between violent threat and the logic of threat-prevention, as the two become disturbingly difficult to distinguish—a narrative ambivalence made possible by the conceptual reliance of police on its paradigmatic target.

When Edgar claims, of the unnamed man he is about to kill, that "his disfigured limbs, pendants from his ears and nose, and his shorn locks, were indubitable indications of a savage," he enacts a familiar racializing logic that renders indigeneity itself evidence of future threat.[70] At the same time, Edgar's physical mobility is also linked, even more explicitly than Carwin's, to what Dean Itsuji Saranillo terms "settler accumulation by Native dispossession."[71] After all, Edgar's traversal of the Forks of the Delaware reenacts the Walking Purchase of 1737, in which white men's physical mobility literally dispossessed the Lenape of 750,000 acres of land.[72] If constant rhetorical associations between indigeneity and mobility underwrote the logic of Native dispossession, then Edgar's traversals of the Walking Purchase make clear that white mobility is a sovereign exception. The Walking Purchase and its aftershocks permeate the novel; though it is set significantly later, nearly all of the violence in *Edgar Huntly* is traced back to this event.

However, while the novel emphasizes the Walking Purchase as the paradigmatic event of dispossession, Patrick Wolfe reminds us that "invasion is a structure not an event."[73] Indeed, the novel's story of Old Deb reveals modes of dispossession obscured by a singular focus on the fraud of the Walking Purchase (and the spectacle of transgressive white mobility it enlists). Old Deb bears striking resemblance to—and was quite likely directly inspired by—Hannah Freeman, a Lenape woman who spent most of her life in Chester County, Pennsylvania, and who was well known in the area by the 1790s.[74] The historical Hannah has much in common with Brown's figure of Deb: by the 1790s, she was an elderly woman, known by her neighbors for her imposing manner, her independence, and her stubborn claims to her ancestral land, which she refused to vacate even after many of the area's Lenape had long since moved further west.[75] Details of Old Deb's character, like her association with her dogs and her occupation of an isolated wigwam in the dense woods, also appear in early nineteenth-century newspaper accounts of locals' reminiscences of Hannah Freeman.[76] However, the historical Hannah Freeman's *divergence* from the character of Old Deb offers additional insight into Brown's treatment of white mobility and how it resonates with vagrancy and Native dispossession.

Freeman was not, as Old Deb is, regarded as an outcast or an enemy by her white neighbors; she worked for and alongside Anglo-Americans for many years, sometimes caring for their children, and she was financially supported by her Quaker neighbors when she was no longer able to work.[77] When the new Chester County Almshouse opened in 1800, Hannah Freeman, noted by the clerk as "Indian Hannah," was the first inmate to be listed in its entry book.[78] She died there in 1802 and was buried in the almshouse potters' field. Her place in the historical record, and much of what we know about the details of her life, was set down in her 1797 examination by a Justice of the Peace looking to determine her place of settlement and eligibility for county poor relief.[79]

As Dawn Marsh painstakingly documents, Freeman's incorporation into local networks of charity and poor relief, both informal and formal, in fact seal the fate of her and her nation's dispossession: the very documents that establish her eligibility for relief also insistently (and falsely) name her as the last Lenape in the region. This claim thus underwrites settlers' claims to the land by perpetuating the fiction that the Lenape had entirely abandoned it.[80] Meanwhile, her need for charity in the first place was also a direct result of dispossession; if her kin network had remained in the Brandywine Valley with her, they would have customarily supported her as a respected elder. Instead, she ended her life in the county almshouse, which had been built on the very land to which she continued to maintain ancestral claims.[81]

As I argued in Chapter 2, the settlement examination is a genre of life-narrative—grounded in vagrancy law and the structures of poor relief—whose aims diverge radically from those of the novel; at the center of a settlement examination is subsistence, not interiority. The settlement examination of Hannah Freeman is no exception; Moses Marshall, the county's Justice of the Peace, conducted and recorded this examination to determine proof of her legal settlement in Chester County, and thus her eligibility for poor relief.[82] The narrative that resulted from this examination, however, also tells a story that exceeds the scope of a singular life-narrative. Furthermore, Hannah Freeman's settlement examination offers us an alternative to *Edgar Huntly*'s novelistic theorization of mobility, property, and dispossession—even as a highly mediated legal document, the examination shows us glimpses of what the story of Old Deb alludes to but does not fully admit.

Sydney Krause has influentially argued for the centrality of the Walking Purchase to *Edgar Huntly*, and Chad Luck has argued more recently that Brown uses the Walking Purchase as a case study for elaborating a philosophical fiction interrogating the phenomenological grounds of property.[83] Luck is right to emphasize the link between physical mobility and dispossession as equally central to the Walking Purchase and to the novel itself, but more attention to Old Deb's historical resonance allows us to see the novel's more expansive links to vagrancy: not just to vagrancy's association with mobility, but also with dispossession, poor relief, and the administrative structure of charity. Edgar Huntly's spectacular mobility, like

Carwin's, contributes to a mode of literary vagrancy that links locomotion to ambivalently valorizable transgression, but minimizes vagrancy's other crucial legal meanings—especially its importance for the administrative structure of poor relief. However, Old Deb's historical links to Hannah Freeman allow us to track poor relief and legal settlement as equally central to how the novel draws on vagrancy to dramatize the intimate relations of mobility, writing, and dispossession.

While Brown makes it clear that he is indeed drawing on local legend and reputation in his construction of Old Deb as a character, little evidence exists to confirm the accuracy of stories he alludes to; the reminiscences of Hannah Freeman that resemble Old Deb's characterization only began to appear in newspapers as local history in the 1820s. As Marshall Becker argues, many of these reminiscences cannot be corroborated with any contemporary written records, and ought to be looked at with at least some skepticism; some of their claims, for instance, are demonstrably false, and many others line up suspiciously with common nineteenth-century tropes of Native representation.[84] At the same time, Andrew Newman argues that the appearance of some of the characteristics later attributed to Freeman, such as her association with her dogs and her imposing manner, in the character of Old Deb, can serve to at least suggest some truth to some of the reminiscences published in the 1820s; Brown had an uncle in Chester County and thus would certainly have had access to local, intimate knowledge of its inhabitants, and his introduction to the excerpts of the novel that appeared in the *Monthly Magazine and American Review* states that Old Deb "is a portrait faithfully drawn from nature."[85] And so while a number of readings have helpfully illuminated the novel's engagement with Pennsylvania's local histories of settler-colonial dispossession and violence, I am interested in what we might learn from an expanded sense of this novel's participation in a broader web of documents, tropes, and formal strategies that were woven through Hannah Freeman's life, from texts she at least partially shaped (like the settlement examination) to texts that would fix her posthumous reputation in ways that only perpetuated her dispossession.

What the story of Old Deb and the settlement examination of Hannah Freeman have in common is that both are about the relationship between writing, land, and dispossession. Freeman's settlement examination takes a familiar form: Moses Marshall shapes Freeman's narrative of her life into a sequence of events that emphasizes her geographic, economic, and social embeddedness in legal networks of responsibility for subsistence, beginning with her place of birth and ending with her current sources of subsistence: "Since this time she has been moving about from place to place making baskets &c and staying longest where best used but never was hired or rec'd wages except for baskets &c but at Centre amongst the Chandlers."[86] However, this form (which I discuss at greater length in an English context in Chapter 2) takes on new meanings in a settler colony, and so I also read this examination for its inclusion of competing models of how subsistence, land, mobility, and belonging can be theorized, narrated, and recorded. Lisa Brooks describes eighteenth- and early nineteenth-century Native writing not as a Native adoption of a European practice, but rather as the incorporation of a particular set of European writing practices into an existing and much broader Native "spatialized system" of thought, memory, communication, and relationality: "Transformations occurred when the European system entered Native space. Birchbark messages became letters and petitions, wampum records became treaties, and journey pictographs became written 'journals' that contained similar geographic and relational markers, while histories recorded on birchbark and wampum became written communal narratives. All of these forms were prolific in the northeast long before Indian people began writing poetry and fiction."[87] Though the locations and itineraries in Hannah Freeman's narrative held specific, narrow legal meanings for Moses Marshall—her place of birth, for instance, or the households from whom she received wages—we might also read Freeman's narrative for spatial knowledge, practice, and experience that exceed the imperatives of poor relief and offer us a glimpse, however mediated, into an instance of Native writing that articulates relations to land that settlers deemed "vagrancy."

As Brooks argues, settlers' reliance on deeds and treaties as authoritative claims of absolute land ownership came into conflict with more expansive Native understandings of both documentation (which included "oral communication and material exchange in council" in addition to written deeds) and land use; purchases, she argued, were frequently negotiated between settlers who believed they were buying absolute and exclusive rights to land and Native people who believed they were negotiating use and access to land that would continue to be held in common.[88] Moses Marshall's settlement examination uses Freeman's narrative of her life in order to reinforce one particular relation between biographical narrative and spatial belonging: entitlement to local poor relief based on her social, legal, and economic belonging to the locality, which is imagined as a network of settlers bound together by their continuous, fixed habitation in parcels of land that form contiguous pieces of private property. For example, he writes that "she was born in a Cabin at Webb's place in the Winter and in the Summer moved to Newlin to Plant Corn."[89] Even as Marshall reports Freeman's own narrative of her "mode of living," which continued many features of established Lenape land use and mobility despite the impact of colonization, he most consistently records her mobility with reference to fixed habitations rooted in either private property or colonial settlement: "Christianna, New Castle County," "a Cabin on Swithin Chandler's place," "Kennett," "Newlin."[90] However, at the same time, Freeman's narrative also asserts relations to land, subsistence, kinship, and sovereignty that are not legible to the logic of settlement-based poor relief; for instance, when Marshall notes that "the Country becoming more settled the Indians were not allowed to Plant Corn any longer her father went to Shamokin and never returned," Freeman can be seen providing an alternative story of dispossession that explains her need for relief not as the "natural" result of her age or illness, but rather as the continuation of a much broader process of what Leanne Betasamosake Simpson terms "*expansive dispossession*": not only the loss of land, but rather "a gendered removal of our bodies and minds from our nation and place-based grounded normativities."[91] In other words, the impact of colonial settlement—whose logic depends on an assertion that land can be parceled out and sold to individuals who are entitled to assert absolute and exclusive rights to that bounded tract—ripples outward far beyond the boundaries asserted by property lines. Settlers' farms and dams interfered with Lenape access to hunting and fishing grounds as well as to their cornfields, while undermining their systems of cooperative land use by imposing the foreign notion of private land ownership.[92]

This "expansive dispossession"—loss of modes of affiliation, kin networks, and ways of subsisting in and thus theorizing the world—is registered here largely through its narrative absence; the examination generally declines to even describe Freeman's mode of subsistence when it is not mediated through colonial settlement and its local economies. When Freeman's female kin are still alive, for instance, Marshall describes their geographical movements but not their sources of subsistence; he narrates that they "continued living in their Cabins sometimes in Kennett and sometimes at Centre" and then that they "lived with the Jersey Indians for about Seven Years" after the Paxton Boys massacre drives them from Pennsylvania.[93] Here, he notes *where* they live, but not how; their modes of subsistence are either illegible or irrelevant to his determination of Freeman's entitlement to poor relief in Chester County. However, after her grandmother, aunt, and mother die, Marshall narrates Freeman's affiliations with local settlers and describes these relations in terms of how she literally survives: whether she receives wages or not, and what she receives in lieu of wages, such as room and board, or occasional money in exchange for the baskets she sells. The narrative, especially in Marshall's linear rendering of it as Freeman's progressive incorporation into settler society, thus increasingly decouples subsistence from land except as mediated through wages, private property, and colonial constructions of space and locality.

Similarly, for the authors of "Kindness Extended"—an agreement drawn up by a number of Freeman's neighbors, formalizing their informal charitable support of her before her eventual admission to the almshouse—Hannah Freeman's story embedded her in one specific relation to place: she is a local pauper for whom the community is responsible. Her familiarity, social relationships, and itineraries are all cited as evidence for her existence within the ambit (both moral and geographical) of local settlement and thus local responsibility for subsistence: "Hannah Freeman Commonly Called Indian Hannah an ancient Woman of the Delaware Tribe and the only Person of that Description left amongst us," the document states, is "afflicted with Rheumatism and unable to support herself accustomed to Travel from house to House . . . it is thought her situation Claims the Sympathy of the humane in order that she may be more Regularly and Permanently Provided for in a manner suited to her Usual way of living."[94] Of course, at the same time, her description as embedded within local social life is precisely what dispossesses her of any claims to land or Lenape kinship; as Marsh notes, the statement that she is the only remaining Lenape "left amongst us" effectively undermined any remaining Lenape land claims; by claiming that the land had been "abandoned" by the Lenape, the local Quaker settlers made a case for the legal and moral legitimacy of their claims to absolute and exclusive property rights in that land.[95]

In transforming Hannah Freeman into Old Deb, Brown also relocates her from Chester County to the Forks of the Delaware, thus removing her historical experience of dispossession from the actual places and social relations in which it was rooted and enfolding it into the singular event of the Walking Purchase. In *Edgar Huntly,* Old Deb's murderous grievances are all traced to the Walking Purchase, which Brown makes use of as a particularly pointed crisis of legitimacy that endangered the popular narrative of William Penn's "peaceable kingdom." However, what emerges from the documents that both narrated and materially contributed to Hannah Freeman's dispossession is a much broader picture of how that dispossession unfolded, not in a singular instance of fraud, perpetrated with the assistance of spectacularly mobile white men, but rather through much more everyday, unspectacular exercises of colonial settlement and its forms of legal, economic, and moral belonging: the naming of a tract of land as someone's farm, the extension of charity, the paying of wages, the construction of a local legend as a posthumous figure of curiosity. Scholars have noted how both of the novel's mobile white men—Edgar and Clithero—are indigenized in Brown's portrayal, but through Hannah Freeman's narrative transformation into Old Deb, we can see what is left out of the novel's incorporations of indigeneity into vagrant whiteness.[96] If Edgar embodies both the logic of police and a kind of transgressive mobility frequently imagined as police's paradigmatic target, then the picture of vagrancy that he ultimately concretizes is one that highlights physical mobility as a hypervisible marker of both dispossession and the ability to dispossess others. Hannah Freeman's settlement examination, however, registers her physical mobility not as a definitive sign of vagrancy, but rather as a sign of multiple kinds of belonging that play out against a backdrop of ongoing settler-colonial dispossession reshaping the entire landscape through which she can move. Above all, the settlement examination reminds us that a focus on the singular, spectacularly transgressive, mobile individual as the paradigmatic image of "the vagrant" obscures how both vagrancy law and the linked administration of charity relied on foundational spatial logics underpinning settler-colonial dispossession. This image of the white male vagrant as embodying—and sometimes ambivalently valorizing—the violence of the frontier has persisted in both literary and legal afterlives that, as this chapter's conclusion will show, continue to shape the everyday regulation of American public space.

## "Unwritten Amenities": White Mobility, Literary History, and Vagrancy's End

In 1972, the U. S. Supreme Court's ruling in *Papachristou v. City of Jacksonville* struck down vagrancy law as unconstitutional. The plaintiffs in this case had been arrested for vagrancy under an ordinance that criminalized a wide array of social categories, the familiarity of which testifies to the long afterlife of early modern and eighteenth-century vagrancy laws: "rogues and vagabonds," "persons who use juggling or unlawful games or plays," "common railers and brawlers," "habitual loafers," "disorderly persons," "common drunkards," and "persons wandering or strolling around from place to place without any lawful purpose or object."[97] The case of Margaret Papachristou, who had been arrested along with three friends traveling in one car with her, encapsulates the logic of anticipatory threat-prevention at the heart of vagrancy law, as well as the racial governance that these laws had long enabled. As the Court's opinion recounts, the police officers claimed that they had arrested the group "because the defendants had stopped near a used-car lot which had been broken into several times."[98] No break-in had occurred that night, but this is precisely the kind of fact that had long been irrelevant to the enforcement of vagrancy law; while an arrest or prosecution for theft would logically require a theft to have already taken place, vagrancy law allowed for the arrest of those considered suspicious because of what police officers believed they might do in the future. Though the police officers in this case denied that race played any role in the arrests, Justice William O. Douglas noted that the defendants were a group of two black men and two white women traveling together, and given the extremely widespread use of vagrancy law to criminalize civil-rights protestors, interracial couples, and others regarded as challenging racial hierarchies in the decades before this decision, this case also illustrates the leeway that vagrancy law granted for police officers to wield their discretionary power to enforce racial subordination and segregation.[99]

As Risa Goluboff argues, this case was the culmination of many decades of legal challenges to vagrancy law, which had been intertwined with both the Warren Court's "due process revolution" and many of the civil-rights struggles of the 1960s.[100] Fundamentally at stake here was police power and the right to due process, and the Court recognized this in its conclusion that the vagueness of the ordinance encouraged arbitrary arrests in its potential to criminalize nearly anyone. However, in his majority opinion, Justice Douglas also sought to reclaim vagrancy itself as a uniquely American virtue, and it is American literary history that offers some of his most compelling evidence.

Douglas ruled that vagrancy laws were unconstitutional, not only because their vagueness placed "almost unfettered discretion in the hands of the police," but also because their restrictions on social and physical mobility impinged on freedoms essential to what he evoked as the American character.[101] The freedoms signified by mobility, according to Douglas, comprise a distinctly American way of feeling, acting, and being in the world:

> The difficulty is that these activities are historically part of the amenities of life as we have known them. They are not mentioned in the Constitution or in the Bill of Rights. These unwritten amenities have been in part responsible for giving our people the feeling of independence and self-confidence, the feeling of creativity. These amenities have dignified the right of dissent and have honored the right to be nonconformists and the right to defy submissiveness. They have encouraged lives of high spirits rather than hushed, suffocating silence. They are embedded in Walt Whitman's writings, especially in his "Song of the Open Road." They are reflected, too, in the spirit of Vachel Lindsay's "I Want to Go Wandering," and by Henry D. Thoreau."[102]

When Douglas seeks to reclaim vagrancy as an "unwritten amenity" of American freedom, he turns to literary history as a supplement to the Constitution. Literature, it seems, offers Douglas an opportunity to valorize vagrancy where the Constitution does not. However, the turn to the literary also directs the force of the ruling away from a critique of unfettered police discretion and toward a much more limited reclamation of vagrancy as free mobility. In the logic of this passage, the legal definition of "vagrant" remains open-ended; the category grants the police "almost unfettered discretion" because the definition is so vague that nearly anyone could potentially be deemed a "vagrant" by the police at any moment. However, its *literary* invocation is much more narrowly specific, defining vagrancy as physical mobility that indexes free will and the potential for some particularly American capacity for creativity and dissent.

As U.S. vagrancy laws came under increasing constitutional scrutiny during the mid-twentieth century, literary history was a surprisingly common resource for legal argumentation.[103] On the one hand, literary comparisons could help reinforce the critical claim that vagrancy laws were un-American because they were both outdated and essentially English. For example, in *United States v. Kilgen* (1970), a judge comments on a vagrancy law "which, we think appellant aptly, although somewhat colorfully, characterizes in the following terms, 'a college English major might read it as a casting advertisement in an Elizabethan newspaper for the street scene in a drama of that era.' "[104] Meanwhile, in a 1960 article, which Douglas cites in the *Papachristou* decision, Arthur Sherry begins with an epigraph from *Much Ado About Nothing*. Here, Sherry uses Dogberry's invocation of "vagrom men" as an example of the category's essential anachronism:

> The archaic pattern of Dogberry's speech by which he commissioned the constable of the watch is an inseparable part of the charm and interest so characteristic of the writing of Shakespeare. Transposed to the contemporary American scene, however, and cherished on the pages of what we are pleased to call a modern statutory system, its anachronistic character is ill-suited to the objectives of the administration of justice in a modern world. It has been so transposed, nonetheless, to the vagrancy statutes of virtually every jurisdiction in the United States.[105]

Mid-twentieth-century critics of vagrancy law consistently emphasize the laws' origins in medieval and early modern England in order to argue for their temporal and national incompatibility with American freedom. The appeal to Elizabethan drama here recasts the proper place of vagrancy law as the foreign and fictive past.

On the other hand, the literary could also be the source for another definition of vagrancy, one whose supposed American cultural value served to protest the stigma of criminalization. In his 1960 article "Vagrancy and Arrest on Suspicion," which anticipates many of his arguments in the *Papachristou* decision twelve years later, Douglas claims that those currently arrested en masse for vagrancy "are wanderers, men of the 'open road'; persons whose only crime in many cases is being jobless and homeless, the same people who have been the heroes of much of our great literature."[106] John Muir, he argues, "was certainly a vagrant in the pure sense of the word," and of a federal court that struck down a Hawaii vagrancy ordinance, he writes approvingly that the judge "wrote in the spirit of Carl Sandburg and Robert Louis Stevenson."[107]

In turning to American literature in the *Papachristou* decision for clues about an essential American character, Douglas participates in a powerful exceptionalist narrative that animated American literary history in the mid-twentieth century. Douglas's argument, for example, proceeds in the vein of F. O. Matthiessen's canonization of the same mid-nineteenth-century authors by lauding "their devotion to the possibilities of democracy."[108] The identification of mobility in particular with a sense of transgressive freedom, as expressed most overtly in American literature, is as crucial for Douglas's legal argument as it is for the literary-historical claims of Leslie Fiedler, who writes influentially in 1960 that "the typical male protagonist of our fiction has been a man on the run, harried into the forest and out to sea, down the river or into combat—anywhere to avoid 'civilization.' "[109] For Douglas, law and literature offer complementary, but entirely separate, critiques of the Jacksonville vagrancy ordinance. When his argument focuses on the limits of police discretion, legal precedent is sufficient; literary history has nothing to do with his ruling that the ordinance is void for vagueness. It is when he turns his attention to the figure of "the vagrant" that Douglas relies on literary history to supply the "unwritten amenities" missing from the Constitution.

Douglas's dual argument—that the problem with vagrancy law is both the leeway it grants the police *and* its criminalization of physical mobility—relies on the simultaneous deployment of two distinct meanings of vagrancy. On the one hand, the "vagrant" is anyone the police might choose to target, for nearly any reason. In this sense, the "vagrant" is not a kind of person, but rather the name for a particular relation to the law: an endlessly fungible target of police power.[110] But on the other hand, when Douglas valorizes mobility as "part of the amenities of life as we have known them," the "vagrant" is no longer just anyone targeted by the police, but a particular *kind* of person: a solitary wanderer whose transgressions are celebrated as the consolidation of free American subjectivity into physical movement. In *Wieland,* the affordances of free white mobility and the threats posed by vagrancy are coalesced into one ambivalent figure. However, the version of literary history that appears in the *Papachristou* ruling is much less ambiguous: the free, male vagabond is celebrated for his mobility, creativity, and enterprise, while other meanings of vagrancy—those less associated with whiteness or physical mobility—are occluded and left unreclaimed as positive rights.

This historically racialized understanding of freedom persists as a powerful influence on the *Papachristou* ruling—even as Douglas's overt intent was to curtail the racist deployment of police discretion. His claim for wandering as an "unwritten amenity" of American citizenship is footnoted by an extensive quote from early in Thoreau's essay "Walking," in which Thoreau figures mobility as a kind of errand into the wilderness:

> I have met with but one or two persons in the course of my life who understood the art of Walking, that is, of taking walks,—who had a genius, so to speak, for *sauntering:* which word is beautifully derived from "idle people who roved about the country, in the Middle Ages, and asked charity, under pretence of going *à la Sainte Terrer,*" a Saunterer, a Holy-Lander. They who never go to the Holy Land in their walks, as they pretend, are indeed mere idlers and vagabonds; but they who do go there are saunterers in the good sense, such as I mean. Some, however, would derive the word from *sans terre,* without land or a home, which, therefore, in the good sense, will mean, having no particular home, but equally at home everywhere. For this is the secret of successful sauntering. He who sits still in a house all the time may be the greatest vagrant of all; but the saunterer, in the good sense, is no more vagrant than the meandering river, which is all the while sedulously seeking the shortest course to the sea. But I prefer the first, which, indeed, is the most probable derivation. For every walk is a sort of crusade, preached by some Peter the Hermit in us, to go forth and reconquer this Holy Land from the hands of the Infidels.[111]

Here, Thoreau begins by telling a story about vagrancy criminalized as a form of fraud—that is, collecting alms based on false claims of intending to undertake a pilgrimage. But by refiguring *all* mobility as a kind of pilgrimage, he renders these fraudulent claims retroactively truthful. Thus an expansive legal meaning of vagrancy, which indeed commonly included fraudulent imposture and begging for alms under false pretenses, is dismissed in favor of an imaginative definition of vagrancy as *mobility*, which can then be reclaimed from criminalization as the "art of Walking."

Throughout this essay, Thoreau reads his own tendency to walk west as indicative of a broader racial imperative of westward expansion: "I must walk toward Oregon, and not toward Europe. And that way the nation is moving, and I may say that mankind progress from east to west."[112] In describing his own walks, Thoreau locates his westward movement not in conscious choice, but in embodied feeling—something akin to what Douglas, just before his citation of Thoreau, calls "the feeling of independence and self-confidence."[113] The directionality of his movement is deduced from felt experience: "Eastward I go only by force; but westward I go free."[114] He goes on to locate this feeling as a collective racial instinct: "I know not how significant it is, or how far it is an evidence of singularity, that an individual should thus consent in his pettiest walk with the general movement of the race; but I know that something akin to the migratory instinct in birds and quadrupeds . . . affects both nations and individuals, either perennially or from time to time."[115]

Certainly, Thoreau opposed the aggressively expansionist policies justified by the doctrine of manifest destiny, as well as many of the deadliest racialized legal restrictions on mobility, such as the Fugitive Slave Law, which he explicitly references later in this essay.[116] However, the availability of the "migratory instinct" as a metaphor for human mobility and ease with which that mobility coalesces into economic and political freedom are nonetheless made possible by new racial logics that made race increasingly determinative of civic belonging in nineteenth-century America. Peter Coviello names a similar dynamic when he discusses the rise of what he terms "anti-state nationalism."[117] This sense of felt allegiance (like participation in a collective "migratory instinct") becomes available in the nineteenth century, he argues, as race emerges as "a language of affiliation" that "gives even those who revile the state a way to believe in a unified, incarnate America, one whose substance is not the government and its institutions but the specifically affective ties that knit its citizens, its *white* citizens, into lived cohesion."[118] This dynamic persists in Douglas's argument when he claims dissenting "lives of high spirits" as distinctly American rights despite their lack of explicit guarantee in the Constitution. In the section of "Walking" that Douglas footnotes, Thoreau follows a similar form of reasoning: transgression of the letter of the law (vagrancy as a form of fraud on the part of false pilgrims) is reclaimed as the expression of a valorized collective character that transcends the state but still coheres the nation (the collective free mobility of men walking westward).

The stakes of this transformation in racial thinking are particularly apparent in the changed relation between race and mobility. Physical mobility through an American landscape is easier to reclaim as a valorized property of whiteness once race is no longer considered to be climatically determined. Under an earlier, environmental model of race, mobility had the potential to transform the raced body, as climate and geography were regarded as the major historical determinants of racial difference. At the same time, one's mode of living—including whether one was nomadic or lived a settled existence—was also thought to have the potential to transform the raced characteristics of one's body and interior disposition. For example, Samuel Stanhope Smith argues that "colour and figure may be styled habits of the body."[119] Movement from one climate to another is a primary cause of racial transformation for Smith, as he argues in his invocation of Europeans who emigrate to America and "have already suffered a visible change" in skin color.[120] The effects of climate are modulated, for Smith, by behavior, habit, and mode of living; of the poor, who "are always first and most deeply affected by the influence of climate," he argues: "If they were thrown, like the native Indians, into a savage state, they would be perfectly marked, in time, with the same colour."[121] And so for Smith, relocation to America causes some form of racial transformation among Europeans, and it is only the avoidance of a "savage state" of living that mitigates the effects of climate and prevents wholesale conversion from one race to another, as "the effect of climate is augmented by a savage state of society and corrected by a state of civilization."[122]

Meanwhile, in the early decades of the nineteenth century, racial science generally argued the precise opposite in its appraisal of whiteness, climate, and "civilization." When Thoreau employs the language of instinct and feeling, he characterizes race in terms that proliferated in early nineteenth-century natural science, law, and political rhetoric alike. Dominant American racial ideologies underwent a radical transformation in the early decades of the nineteenth century, between the historical moments of Brown and Thoreau.[123] Eighteenth-century theories of race imagined racial categories as subject to change over time, especially under the influence of climate and other environmental factors, while the new orthodoxy that emerged in the early nineteenth century posited racial categories as heritable, immutable, and reflective of fundamental truths about human interiors.[124] While, as Katy Chiles argues, race in early America was primarily "an exterior bodily trait," race by the 1840s had become an interior phenomenon, increasingly linked, legally, to the body's unseen history of descent, and thought to signify essentially divergent capacities for thought, feeling, and civic belonging.[125] Above all, if whiteness is interior, then mobility can *express* whiteness rather than threaten or transform it. Indeed, as Ezra Tawil argues, mobility not only lost the ability to threaten whiteness, but was, by the early nineteenth century, newly regarded as an essentially white racial characteristic, which allowed the mobility and physical dislocation inherent to westward expansion to be figured as the expression of an immutable racial instinct for movement.[126]

By using Thoreau's "Walking" to illustrate the centrality of free mobility to American national character, Douglas enshrines a narrow range of valorized transgressions as particularly worthy of protection from criminalization: nonconformity, physical mobility, purposeful social or political dissent. As the *Papachristou* ruling reveals, literary history is not entirely isolated from the fields of discursive struggle in which the law intervenes. Douglas both cited and contributed to literary history, as his reading of Thoreau resonated deeply with the readings that animated the study of American literature in the middle of the twentieth century. The foundations of this reading, I have argued, are already present at the very beginning of what this tradition of literary history would name as "the American novel."

Carwin paradoxically unites contradictory meanings of vagrancy: he is both the suspicious bearer of threat and the epitome of the freely mobile self-made man. In *Wieland,* whiteness is inseparable from both images of vagrancy. But the paradox expressed by this novel also contains the seeds of the racialized split that Thoreau evokes in "Walking," and which finds its way into the *Papachristou* ruling, as whiteness comes to constitute the kind of valorized transgression that is to be enshrined as a right, while other, differently racialized markers of "criminality" remain unreclaimed and unvalorized. The availability of free mobility for rhetorical reclamation thus relies on what Lisa Marie Cacho terms "the violence of value"; as the most easily valorized meanings of vagrancy are reclaimed from criminalization through their identification with American whiteness, then the meanings of vagrancy left unreclaimed serve to deepen existing rhetorical associations between "criminality" and populations of color.[127] If Cheryl Harris has influentially described how, in the early republic, "whiteness became a shield from slavery, a highly volatile and unstable form of property," the long legal and imaginative histories of vagrancy—and their surprising persistence into the legal landscape of the present—suggest how whiteness could become a shield from policing as well.[128]

# *CHAPTER FIVE*

# SURVEILLANCE AND BLACK LIFE IN EQUIANO'S ATLANTIC

When Olaudah Equiano arrives in Savannah, he summarizes his entire experience of the city in two disturbing encounters with white public authority, both legal and extralegal. First, while he is in the home of his friend Mosa, they are accosted by "the watch or patrole," who inform Equiano that "all negroes, who had a light in their houses after nine o'clock were to be taken into custody, and either pay some dollars, or be flogged."[1] He disputes the patrol's logic of threat-assessment, marshaling the qualities he hopes will render him unthreatening to the patrol: "I told them that I was a free man . . . that we were not making any noise, and that I was not a stranger in that place, but was very well known there" (158). However, his status as a free man does not protect him, but rather renders him more vulnerable: "As the man of the house was not free, and had his master to protect him, they did not take the same liberty with him they did with me" (158). When Equiano asks the patrol "if there was no law for free men," and exclaims that "if there was I would have it put in force against them," the futility of this protest serves as his answer (159). They bring him to the watch-house, where he is only spared a flogging through the intercession first of one patrolman, "more humane than the rest," and then of a white doctor "known to be an honest and worthy man" (159). By protesting that there is "no law for free men" here, Equiano rhetorically stages this incident as an encounter between police and law: if law constitutes the fantasized counterfactual of knowable formal procedure that respects and guarantees the freedom of "free men," then police emerges here as its opposite: the unpredictable and unsystematic show of force that defies narrative logic and empties "freedom" of meaning.

Equiano links this encounter with the patrol to another "disagreeable incident" that immediately follows: outside Savannah, he is "beset by two white men, who meant to play their usual tricks with me in the way of kidnapping" (159). One says to the other that Equiano "is the very fellow we are looking for, that you lost," but when Equiano tells them that he "had seen those tricks played upon other free blacks," the men are deterred by his resistance and perhaps also by the "revengeful stick" he carries, remarking that he "talked too good English" for their purposes (159). Unlike the patrol, these men are not officially sanctioned or paid to keep public order, and Equiano uses the language of criminality to position their assumption of authority as illegitimate, referring to their attempt at "kidnapping" and calling them "rogues" (159).

At the same time, their authority is on a continuum with that of the patrol. Equiano draws attention to this through the proximity and structural similarity of these two encounters. Most prominent, of course, is the racialized structure of these encounters; Equiano is careful to note that these two incidents are absolutely predicated on his blackness. The account of the patrol begins with his statement that he "went to a friend's house to lodge, whose name was Mosa, a black man," and it becomes clear that this fact is material in drawing the attention of the patrol (158). Similarly, he begins his narrative of the second encounter by noting the whiteness of the two men before any other detail, and framing their kidnapping attempt not as an aberration, but as the systematic "usual tricks" (159) of white men. While the first group treats him as a potential threat because he's black, the second group sees his blackness as rendering him uniquely vulnerable and unprotected by the law, an easy mark for profitable violence. Of course, slavery underwrites both of these things, as it converts people into fungible commodities and only acknowledges the agency of the enslaved in the context of criminality or threat.[2] While only the first group of men acts in an official legal capacity, the second uses many of the techniques of the first: looking for and apprehending black people in public space, and exercising whiteness as the power to wield legitimated violence. While Equiano seeks to use the language of legality to cast both groups' actions as illegitimate, the material precarity of his rhetorical appeals reveals the opposite to be true: even if the second group is not necessarily "honestly" apprehending a "real" fugitive, their expectation that they can easily capture Equiano and sell him into slavery is enabled by the legal mechanisms and practices underpinning the actions of the official, paid patrol.

Slave patrols, such as the men Equiano encounters in Savannah, were a ubiquitous feature of life in the plantation colonies of the Atlantic world. The institution emerged in the Caribbean in the seventeenth century, and quickly spread to the southern colonies of North America alongside many of the other legal and social institutions that emerged to support these colonies' transitions to increasing reliance on slave labor.[3] Slave patrols were concerned with more than just the apprehension of fugitives; they were tasked with regular surveillance and discipline in hopes of preventing rebellion and maintaining the social fabric of racial domination upon which these societies depended. Especially in cities (such as Savannah), slave patrols were tasked with many of the functions that fell under the heading of "police" as it was understood in the eighteenth century: the prevention of perceived threat through wide-ranging regulation of social order.[4] Thus, patrols interrogated people they found suspicious, examined enslaved people's passes authorizing their movement, and enforced the many far-reaching restrictions on black life and assembly dictated by local slave codes, such as the regulation cited by Equiano that prohibited lighting a house after nine o'clock.[5] Slave patrols did not simply serve as extensions of individual enslavers' authority over those they enslaved; rather, they operated under the more broad-reaching imperative of regulating *all* black people, whether enslaved or free. Indeed, as Equiano notes, free black people could be rendered even more vulnerable to the patrols' capacity for violence than those whose enslavers might be occasionally economically motivated to intercede.[6] Even in colonies that did not institute distinct slave patrols, "police" in any slaveholding colony in the British Atlantic world encompassed elaborate codes of racialized governance that specifically subjected black life to constant surveillance with the aim of preventing insurrection and apprehending fugitives.[7] More broadly, vagrancy and its relation to police helped construct the very category of the "runaway"—a category that assigns a trajectory to perceived mobility, privileging a point of origin in capture over any sense of a destination. After all, to apprehend someone as a "runaway" is to foreclose the possibility that "away" can become any specific, reachable destination, even as it collapses the apprehended person's mobility into a trackable status that sticks to the body wherever that body might be. Equiano, however, renders his mobility not a trackable property of his body, but rather a formal feature of his text, whose meanderings are not only geographical, but also generic, narrative, rhetorical, and affective. Taking up picaresque form as the grounds for political speech, he resists the category of "runaway" in formal terms that exceed his claims to legal self-possession. In counterpoint to the criminalization of "runaway" mobility as vagrancy, Equiano incites narrative mobility as a source of knowledge—following Fred Moten, a form of fugitive "black study."[8]

Equiano repeatedly juxtaposes the hoped-for consistency of law against a terrifying and unpredictable violence to which his blackness renders him constantly vulnerable. This violence, I argue, is what this book has been tracking under the name of "police." Encounters such as these events in Savannah repeat themselves throughout the *Interesting Narrative:* Equiano has the law on his side—whether in the form of his rhetorical recourse to what Edlie Wong terms "lawful liberty" or of his manumission papers, reproduced word for word in the text—but finds himself subject to constant surveillance, violence, theft, kidnapping, and other forms of unconstrained racial tyranny.[9] One of his most consistent refrains is a protest that he has been subject to maltreatment without trial, such as when he is kidnapped by a ship's captain off the Mosquito Coast and narrowly escapes being sold back into slavery: "Thus I hung, without any crime committed, and without judge or jury, merely because I was a freeman, and could not by the law get any redress from a white person in those parts of the world" (212). Through his narrative staging of what it means to live largely outside the law's protection, but never far from both state and extralegal surveillance, Equiano theorizes blackness as a relation to police, and is in fact deeply engaged with definitions of "police" that circulated throughout the eighteenth-century Atlantic world and were crucial to underpinning the legal architecture of slavery in the century preceding the emergence of the modern municipal police force. Equiano makes police most visible as a violent and capricious counterpoint to an imagined world of formal legal procedure—a world that, he demonstrates, is constantly beyond his reach. By invoking formal legal procedure—especially trial by jury—as metonym for fully realized freedom, Equiano draws strategically on existing ideological links between the ideal of British liberty, the rights of the subject under the English common law, and the invocation of the "ancient constitution" as guarantor of individual freedom.[10]

The *Interesting Narrative* is a text deeply concerned with legal personhood, written from legal personhood's precarious margins. Between his manumission and his final arrival in London, Equiano narrates his travels throughout the world from the vantage point of partial freedom: he is no longer enslaved, but his wished-for status as free British subject is invoked as counterfactual. This absence is most pointedly invoked as he narrates his encounters with the colonial logic of police as constructed vis-à-vis the surveillance of blackness. He does this, I argue, by critically inhabiting a narrative position created at least in part through the colonial adaptation of vagrancy law as a crucial tool for policing slave colonies. Of all the literary texts I read in this book, the *Interesting Narrative* is the least explicitly concerned with vagrancy; it is not a word that Equiano ever uses, for instance. However, as I will argue, this text's enactment of mobility becomes a vantage point from which to critique the criminalization of black mobility that vagrancy laws in slave colonies often accomplished. Furthermore, Equiano simultaneously inhabits the dynamic of threat and anticipation that characterized police as a mode of governance. However, just as he recasts his mobility as lawful and economically rational—the opposite of vagrancy—he also recasts threat as that which is posed by the world around him, not anything he brings to the many places where he is subjected to the violence of the police law of slavery.

By pairing these two encounters in Savannah, for instance, Equiano reflects on the nature of "threat." The men of the patrol apprehend him because their mandate of risk management casts any form of black mobility, sociability, and life beyond the regime of the plantation as a potential threat. But as Equiano makes clear, *he* is the one rendered repeatedly vulnerable to violence; in a powerful reversal of vagrancy's optic, he inhabits the space marked as "threat" and reveals police to be the true threat here. If, as I have been arguing, vagrancy comes to name the potential for future threat that defies prediction and can take any possible form, then the patrol is what erupts into threat with no narrative warning. After the men knock on the door of Mosa's house and drink some of the punch the men have been sharing, Equiano makes clear that their intentions to imprison him exceed his anticipation: "They told me I must go to the watch-house with them; this surprised me a good deal after our kindness to them; and I asked them, Why so?" (158).

While black mobility in the Atlantic world was (as I will argue below) increasingly criminalized as vagrancy, Equiano theorizes police and blackness through his own wide-ranging mobility; it is his travel, especially around the Atlantic world, that allows him to aggregate a series of sudden, violent, and unpredictable encounters into something resembling a system. His mobility renders him vulnerable to white legal and extralegal violence in a number of locales, and resonates particularly with the use of vagrancy law to criminalize black mobility in the eighteenth century. But while vagrancy laws were particularly crucial to constructing a regime of what Simone Browne terms "racializing surveillance" as an apparatus of slavery, Equiano critically inhabits the mobility that renders him a target of surveillance and instead transforms this mobility into a vantage point.[11] He is being watched, but through the medium of autobiography, he watches back. Indeed, his mobility is what grants him a comparative and critical vision that connects each instance of racialized vulnerability and implies a system that links the West Indies to London, even as abolitionist arguments frequently hinged on the fantasized preservation of the purity of English law, people, and land from the contamination of West Indian slavery.[12] After all, the threats he faces and witnesses are not confined to the Caribbean, but occur throughout the Atlantic world—including London, where he is unable to stop the kidnapping of a free black man back into slavery even post-*Somerset*. He also deploys his own global mobility as a critical stance; when he is kidnapped off the

Mosquito Coast, he remarks, both to the captain and to his readers: "I said I had been twice amongst the Turks, yet had never seen any such usage with them" (211).

The *Interesting Narrative* is hardly a straightforwardly radical text, nor is it a text that is easy to understand as critical of the law: indeed, Equiano is deeply invested in the rhetorical capacity of the English common law to offer a vision for universal human rights that far exceeds its actual geographic scope. However, this appeal to juridical recognition is accompanied by a critique of police that exceeds the terms of legal personhood. Alongside the legal subjectivity he attempts to claim, he also keeps police itself firmly in view, as he reconfigures the racialized invocation of "threat" that animated vagrancy law in the Americas into a portrayal of white men as the true source of unpredictable threat and sudden outbursts of violence. He mobilizes this as theory by critically inhabiting the *form* of vagrancy—the unpredictable and unsystematic aggregation of (racialized) sovereignty through its everyday enactment—to conceptualize blackness as a relation to police that far exceeds the bounds of the nation, and is instead as mobile and wide-ranging as the narrative itself.

## Mobility and Capture: Slavery, Vagrancy, Police

In her massively influential book *The New Jim Crow,* Michelle Alexander contextualizes contemporary practices such as "stop-and-frisk" as the inheritance of the vagrancy laws used in the United States during Reconstruction to perpetuate the system of plantation labor and its regime of racial terror.[13] These vagrancy laws did indeed proliferate anew during Reconstruction as part of a larger attempt to reconsolidate racial domination after slavery, and as Sally Hadden documents, the institution of the slave patrol persisted in its simultaneous legal and extralegal iterations as the police and the Ku Klux Klan.[14] While emancipation in the United States and in British colonies differed in many crucial ways, the use of vagrancy law to subject newly free black people to what Saidiya Hartman terms "an elaborate micropenality of everyday life" was common to both places, and as Demetrius Eudell argues, the centrality of vagrancy for Black Codes in the United States closely echoed the appearance of similar vagrancy laws in the Caribbean thirty years earlier.[15]

This use of vagrancy law, however, was not strictly a postemancipation phenomenon. Vagrancy law had already acquired meaning and use for slave societies long before the rise of abolitionist politics. The link between vagrancy and slavery, in fact, goes back to the earliest establishment of colonial slave law. Early modern English vagrancy legislation, after all, was primarily concerned with compelling the labor of the poor (while at the same time targeting the threat and disorder imagined to stem from itinerancy and so-called idleness). One infamous sixteenth-century English statute even proposed enslavement as a formal punishment for vagrancy; while this statute was never enforced and was repealed two years later, proposals to enslave vagrants continued to circulate in England into the seventeenth and eighteenth centuries.[16] The bridewell, as an institution dedicated primarily to the punishment of vagrants and prostitutes (who were also arrested under vagrancy law until the nineteenth century), differed strikingly from earlier prisons in that it used imprisonment as the punishment itself, rather than as a means to confine a person awaiting corporal punishment, and employed forced labor as its primary avenue toward "reform."[17] This existing model of penal compulsion to labor and its attendant system of restrictions on mobility formed the legal foundation for slave laws in English colonies in the Caribbean and North America, as pass systems, provisions for summary conviction, and other elements of the "police law of slavery" were drawn directly from English vagrancy laws.[18]

But while early modern English vagrancy law provided a crucial model for colonial slave codes, colonies also developed new, racialized redeployments of existing legal practices as they grew increasingly dependent on slave labor. When the Barbados Assembly passed its 1661 "Act for the Better Ordering and Governing of Negroes," it both codified existing practices that planters had devised to maintain control over an increasing enslaved population and formed a model for slave codes that would later be exported to other English colonies as planters left Barbados for Jamaica, Carolina, Virginia, and other locations, bringing their legal practices with them.[19] The 1661 Barbados law, therefore, would be extremely influential, offering a foundation for slave laws throughout the empire. The act signals the Barbados Assembly's recognition that existing English models of police (such as vagrancy law) were not adequate to the task of keeping the growing majority of the island's population under the absolute power of the island's white minority.[20] This legislation, as Susan Dwyer Amussen argues, "created an entirely new judicial system," declaring that the enslaved would be governed by special summary courts rather than trial by jury, and instituting a vast array of harsh corporal punishments specifically for slaves.[21] Designating the enslaved as ineligible for trial by jury was crucial to hardening the racialization of slave status; removing the right of trial by jury, "which had long been fundamental to English justice," she concludes, "was central to the process of defining slaves—and ultimately all people of African descent—as entirely different from white people."[22]

At the same time, however, while the 1661 act enacts fundamental divergence from English common law, and thus constitutes a colonial innovation that goes far beyond the importation of English vagrancy law, it might be better understood as a massive *expansion* of vagrancy law and the orientation toward threat prevention that constitutes the purview of police. It is, as Richard S. Dunn argues, "a policing measure," and the preamble justifies the new regulations by racializing the anticipatory language of threat: as "Negroes" are "an heathenish, brutish and an uncertaine, dangerous kinde of people," the Assembly argues, these regulations constitute necessary measures for preventing insurrection and ensuring ongoing subjection of a population that was rapidly outnumbering the planters.[23] In codifying the slave as a distinct legal category, the 1661 act contributes to what Cedric Robinson characterizes as the early modern invention of the "Negro" as a relation to labor, while at the same time also codifies this category as a distinct relation to *police*—after all, in the 1661 act, "Negro" means threat: "an uncertaine, dangerous kinde of people."[24] Ironically, the planters who enacted such legislation conceptualized their divergence from English law as their prerogative as free English subjects; by claiming their right to govern the colony according to its local conditions and exigencies, they positioned their rejection of common-law criminal procedure as the exercise of their own liberties as English subjects.[25] Thus this expansion of vagrancy law not only racializes blackness as threat, it also helps constitute colonial *whiteness* as the prerogative to enact police measures in anticipation of this threat.

Vagrancy law offered a whole repertoire of punishments, surveillance tactics, and conceptual frameworks for slavery's police law, even as this body of law also substantially transformed the English antecedents it was built on. For instance, as Diana Paton argues, planters in Jamaica adopted the workhouse as a primary mechanism of plantation discipline; as a public institution for the incarceration of the "idle and disorderly," planters made widespread use of workhouses to assist in the private punishment of those they enslaved.[26] In addition, the network of workhouses across the island assisted in the apprehension of escapees by providing centralized locations where suspected fugitives could be imprisoned.[27] This use of the workhouse was not confined to the plantation colonies of the Caribbean; for instance, keepers of jails and workhouses throughout colonial North America frequently advertised the descriptions of those arrested for vagrancy as suspected fugitives from slavery and other forms of bound labor.[28] I've been arguing throughout this book that vagrancy is more than just the wandering or mobility with which it is frequently colloquially associated. However, in the context of slavery, vagrancy law *is* deeply concerned with mobility, because in the eyes of enslavers and the legislative bodies they populated, black mobility alone could signify fugitivity, insurrection, and other threats to the system of slavery. As vagrancy law had long been used in American colonies to target and apprehend suspected fugitives from slavery, it had the broader effect of de facto criminalizing black mobility, even for the free.[29]

Such an optic of threat anticipation extended beyond the law itself; it structured whiteness as both an entitlement to move through space and a perceptual stance toward how that space was to be encountered, described, and narrated. For instance, in his 1791 natural-historical account of his travels throughout the South, the botanist William Bartram narrates an encounter on the road outside Charleston:

> OBSERVED a number of persons coming up a head which I soon perceived to be a party of Negroes: I had every reason to dread the consequence; for this being a desolate place, and I was by this time several miles from any house or plantation, and had reason to apprehend this to be a predatory band of Negroes: people being frequently attacked, robbed, and sometimes murdered by them at this place; I was unarmed, alone, and my horse tired; thus situated every way in their power, I had no alternative but to be resigned and prepare to meet them, as soon as I saw them distinctly a mile or two off, I immediately alighted to rest, and give breath to my horse, intending to attempt my safety by slight, if upon near approach they

> should betray hostile designs, thus prepared, when we drew near to each other, I mounted and rode briskly up, and though armed with clubs, axes and hoes, they opened to right and left, and let me pass peaceably, their chief informed me whom they belonged to, and said they were going to man a new quarter at the West end of the bay, I however kept a sharp eye about me, apprehending that this might possibly have been an advanced division, and their intentions were to ambuscade and surround me, but they kept on quietly and I was no more alarmed by them.[30]

This encounter is a non-event: Bartram passes through the group without incident and both go their separate ways. However, Bartram's narrative of the encounter is a drama of anticipated threat that maintains its stance toward future menace even after the "chief" defuses the supposed threat by giving an account of their authorized movement. To see a "party of Negroes," in this account, is by definition to apprehend threat, and Bartram emphasizes his vulnerability by noting that he is unarmed and alone. However, what he does not narrate is precisely what Equiano would emphasize in his accounts of such encounters on the road: when the "chief" tells Bartram "whom they belonged to" and explains, unprompted, the reasons for their travel, he is most likely acting on a calculus of threat anticipation of his own. If, for Bartram, these roads are dangerous sites of potential robbery, then for the enslaved, such roads are dangerous because they are precisely where slave patrols demand such explanations of "authorized" movement and threaten violent reprisal even when such explanations were forthcoming.[31] As a white man on the road, Bartram thinks of himself as vulnerable, but being a white man on the road also is what makes him a bearer of potential threat for the people he so viscerally fears; slave patrols incorporated white men of all classes and thus both drew on and reinforced a sense that racial terror was the prerogative and duty of whiteness itself.[32]

By the end of the eighteenth century, the legal architecture of slavery had long incorporated both the practical technologies of vagrancy law enforcement—such as passes and summary conviction—as well as the conceptual basis of police as an anticipatory stance toward potential future threat that might take any imaginable form. Given this embeddedness of vagrancy in slave law, as well as the longstanding use of vagrancy law in both England and its colonies as a widespread tool of labor regulation, it is no surprise that references to vagrancy were ubiquitous in debates about slavery as abolitionism rose to increasing political power. Since vagrancy could index the refusal of a free person to choose legitimate labor, vagrancy was an imaginative resource for defining free labor, questioning how free labor might be ensured, and reconciling the ideal of freedom with economic rationality.[33] At the same time, as an index of future threat, vagrancy could also invoke marronage and rebellion, as evidenced by the conceptualization of slave patrols' regulation of seemingly minor offenses as part of a broader aim of preventing insurrection. Vagrancy was a resonant concept for authors on all sides of slavery debates as they sought to advance competing visions of the future of colonial labor. For both supporters and opponents of slavery, vagrancy could index a disparate array of dispositions, behaviors, and political stances that exceeded or refused the order of "free labor" that might follow. At the same time, as vagrancy law was a long-established mechanism for the control of lower-class labor in Britain, it haunted the invocation of these histories as they were invoked in debates about slavery, such as the attempts of abolitionists to cast slavery as utterly unlike villeinage and other forms of bound labor historically legitimized by English law, or the arguments by planters that the enslaved were in fact better provided for than the English poor.

In his influential *History of Jamaica,* proslavery planter Edward Long ranks vagrancy and idleness alongside murder and rebellion as serious threats to plantation authority: "The severest punishments ought, in justice and policy, to fall on rebels, murderers, conspirers against the public tranquility, incendiaries, and rioters; runaways, found carrying unlawful weapons; and such as stubbornly and wilfully refuse to labour; for it is in consistent with the general welfare, that any should be rebellious, guilty of outrage and violence, idle, or vagrant."[34] Long's description of slave law in Jamaica repeats the history of English labor regulation—most centrally, vagrancy laws—as the precursor for the legal reinforcements for slave labor: "The Negroe code of this island appears originally to have been copied from the model in use at Barbados; and the legislature of this latter island, which was the first planted by the English, resorted to the English *villeinage* laws, from whence they undoubtedly transfused all that severity which characterizes them, and shews the abject slavery which the common people of England formerly laboured under."[35] Just as he compares historical English vagrants to enslaved Africans, he also asserts that the enslaved are literal vagrants. Of the slave trade's supposed benefits to the rulers of African states, he claims: "They have gained by this means a constant vent for all their rogues and vagabonds."[36] Long repeatedly asserts an equivalence between slavery and criminal transportation, justifying the slave trade by drawing on a longstanding economic rationale for colonization as a method for expelling vagrants and other "surplus" populations from the metropole. Long understands vagrancy law as a precursor for slavery's legal apparatus. Both, for him, are fundamentally about compelling and managing the labor of populations that cannot govern themselves. He uses the existing logic of vagrancy law—that labor must be compelled among the idle, disorderly, and criminal—in order to characterize *all* enslaved Africans as idle and disorderly. By equating the slave trade with the transportation of convicts, he renders the state of slavery evidence of prior (or potential) criminality.[37]

Long thus figures blackness as a permanent, intractable sign of vagrancy. In a sense, he draws on the legal logic underpinning colonial slave codes since the 1660s in order to fantasize a racial solution for a problem that had long plagued commentators on vagrancy, idleness, and labor in England. If English critiques of the poor-law system bewailed the difficulty of parsing those who could not work from those who would not work, the deserving poor from the undeserving, the innocent from the idle, Long's characterization of blackness as a visible index of the "idle and disorderly" implies that the regimes of surveillance enforced by institutions like the slave patrol obviate any need to speculate about the unknowable interiors of those who might pose the threat of crime or fraud. He relocates potential threat to the skin and concretizes threat along the lines of the plantation's racial logic. If the first generations of English West Indian planters had drawn on English models of bound labor and its regulation, but then transformed them to suit the needs of governing a slave colony, then Long's reappropriation of this history allows him to speak to a potentially skeptical metropolitan audience in terms that would be deeply familiar to them in their own practices of local governance.

For Long, vagrancy law also offers a model for delimiting black freedom both materially and imaginatively. For example, he praises vagrancy law as a way of mitigating the effects of occasional manumission: "In a publick view, it is better that a Negroe should continue an honest and industrious slave, than to be turned into an idle and profligate freeman. All however that is meant is, that, in imitation of the Antigua law, all those freed-men, who have neither lands to cultivate, nor trade to follow, should be obliged to enrol themselves in some white family, as domesticks; a list should annually be taken, and registered, of all the classes, and their occupations annexed to their names."[38] Long here draws on the language of vagrancy in naming as threat the "idle and profligate freeman" and praising the imposition of labor—either through slavery or through vagrancy law—as producing the "honest and industrious" laborer. His discussion of laws governing slaves ends with a vision of partial emancipation—a form of emancipation, however, calculated to *reinforce* racial subordination and planters' access to labor and obedience:

> If the native slaves in our colony can with safety be brought under an enlarged degree of protection, and secured by rational provisions from violence and barbarity; or be permitted to redeem themselves from perpetuity of servitude, with the fair and honest earnings of their private industry; it seems highly just, human, and politic, to favour them; that their allegiance to the country and white inhabitants, may be more firmly engaged; after obtaining their freedom, it still remains by legal regulations to enforce their employing themselves in some honest course of livelihood.[39]

Under this plan, the limited possibility of emancipation for some is a tool to incite both "industry" and "allegiance" to the planters, and this freedom, once achieved, is further regulated by vagrancy law that compels the formerly enslaved into "some honest course of employment." This vision of freedom imagines emancipation as another medium for coercion.

Long and other proslavery authors take up the idea of vagrancy, which turns nonlabor into unknowable threat, in order to imagine an entire population as de facto vagrant when not under direct control and compulsion to labor. While opponents of emancipation evoked vagrancy as the threat of uncontrollable refusal of economic order, many advocates of emancipation sought to reassure the British public that colonial free labor could still be regulated.[40] The full title of Britain's 1833 Abolition Act reveals the influence of such longstanding concerns about work-discipline on antislavery politics and legislation: "A Bill Intituled An Act for the

Abolition of Slavery throughout the *British* Colonies, for promoting the Industry of the manumitted Slaves, and for compensating the Persons hitherto entitled to the Services of such Slaves."[41] The act goes on to detail the necessity of laws ensuring order and discipline under the transitional apprenticeship system, including laws

> for the Prevention and Punishment of Indolence, or the Neglect or improper Performance of Work by any such apprenticed Labourer, and for enforcing the due Performance by any such apprenticed Labourer of any Contract into which he or she may voluntarily enter for any hired Service during the Time in which he or she may not be bound to labour for his or her Employer, and for the Prevention and Punishment of Insolence and Insubordination on the Part of any such apprenticed Labourers towards their Employers, and for the Prevention or Punishment of Vagrancy or of any Conduct on the Part of any such apprenticed Labourers injuring or tending to the Injury of the Property of any such Employer, and for the Suppression and Punishment of any Riot or combined Resistance of the Laws on the Part of any such apprenticed Labourers, and for preventing the Escape of any such apprenticed Labourers . . . .[42]

Many decades before legal emancipation became politically viable, administrators, regulators, and defenders of slavery used the rhetoric of vagrancy in their attempts to delimit in advance what black freedom might look like.

Long's vision of occasional and exceptional manumission for those who can purchase themselves with the "earnings of their private industry" echoes Equiano's very situation. However, in his narrative of his postemancipation commercial ventures, Equiano decouples the idea of industrious freedom from Long's vision of continued subordination, domestic labor, and submission to racialized restrictions on mobility and employment. Equiano also decouples his industry from "allegiance to the country and white inhabitants." His stated allegiance is to Britain and not any of its colonies; he displays little deference to the white inhabitants of the colonies and speaks of these spaces—especially the West Indies—in consistently critical terms.

Furthermore, he portrays his maritime labor as compelled not by paternalist legal compulsion, but by his own desire for profit and mobility, such as when he obtains employment as a hairdresser on a ship bound for

Turkey: "I thought it best, therefore, to try the sea again in quest of more money, as I had been bred to it, and had hitherto found the profession of it successful. I had also a very great desire to see Turkey, and I now determined to gratify it" (166). Here, Equiano frames his movement as almost entirely self-willed; he is driven by his desire to see Turkey and make money, and he displays his choice as the conclusion of unassailable reasoning: he has gone to sea before, found it profitable, and thus reasons that he can expect similar returns.

Equiano thus contests this racialized deployment of vagrancy by resignifying black mobility as vagrancy's opposite: the achievement of rational economic, national, and rhetorical subjectivity. As Srinivas Aravamudan notes, "Equiano turned the opposition of British master and African slave into its dialectical synthesis of manumitted black British entrepreneur."[43] However, while the antislavery proposal that ends the text is thoroughly commercial and imperial, it is also curiously silent on the question of what model of labor might succeed slavery in the Americas. Equiano makes no proposals to salvage the sugar industry, nor does he envision continued agricultural or domestic "free" labor for those currently enslaved. Instead, he turns his eye to Africa, which he describes as a model trading partner, and a future market for British goods: "If a system of commerce was established in Africa, the demand for manufactures would most rapidly augment, as the native inhabitants would insensibly adopt the British fashions, manners, customs, &c. In proportion to the civilization, so will be the consumption of British manufactures" (233). If anything, he is most explicitly concerned with providing employment for *British* laborers: "The manufacturers of this country must and will, in the nature and reason of things, have a full and constant employ, by supplying the African markets" (234). By concerning himself with the employment of British laborers, Equiano places himself in the long tradition of political economists and poor-law reformers who thought of the colonies primarily in terms of their utility as markets for British manufactures. He speaks not as someone whose own future capacity for labor is up for debate, but rather as one with the knowledge and expertise to promote the employment of laborers in Britain.

David Kazanjian reads Equiano's assumption of economic subjectivity through trade as his primary rhetorical defense against his own commodification.[44] By positioning himself as an entrepreneurial and mobile self-made man, Equiano posits an alternative not only to his commodification as a slave, but also to his subjection as a nominally free laborer under the ideals of postemancipation regimes that took the racialized compulsion to labor as their foundational premise. This is, of course, an alternative rooted deeply in Equiano's demand to be recognized as a legal and economic subject, one whose liberty rests on the protection of his person and property rights under the law.

In the remarkable geographical mobility of his narrative, as well as his insistent characterization of himself as an entrepreneur (and thus not as the kind of subordinate laborer that vagrancy law aimed to create and keep docile), Equiano's narrative offers a contrapuntal engagement with the racialization of mobility enforced by vagrancy law in the Atlantic world. For instance, Equiano's encounters with white discretionary authority tend to end by positioning mobility as his deliverance: he's only safe when he gets out of town. And more broadly, as a text that includes the travel narrative in its many generic influences, mobility provides the frame for every event, even when those events are seemingly quite unconnected with the fact of where they occur. His evangelical conversion experience, which is necessarily an experience that transcends the worldly specificity of place, is nonetheless bookended by his arrival and departure from Cadiz: "The place is strong, commands a fine prospect, and is very rich. The Spanish galleons frequent that port, and some arrived whilst we were there. I had many opportunities of reading the Scriptures" (189). A long account of his spiritual awakening follows, including an account of spiritual transport that utterly exceeds his physical location: "I saw clearly, with the eye of faith, the crucified Saviour bleeding on the cross on Mount Calvary: the Scriptures became an unsealed book" (190). Nonetheless, the episode concludes with a return to the worldly form of transport: "During this period we remained at Cadiz until our ship got laden. We sailed about the 4th of November, and having a good passage, we arrived in London the month following" (192). This episode is the spiritual climax of the text, but it's also thoroughly embedded in the specificity of place and global economic circulation.

Equiano's mobility is both a literal fact of his "extremely chequered" life and a defining formal feature of his narrative (236). Gretchen Holbrook Gerzina contextualizes this dual sense of mobility in the established genre of the travel narrative and its redeployment by black authors in the Atlantic world: "The spatial freedom of moving across landscapes becomes coupled in the narratives of black people in the eighteenth and early nineteenth centuries with the more formal conventions of digression and the sense of movement itself, all played out against a highly racialized geographical and psychological terrain."[45] Saidiya Hartman reads the physical mobility of the formerly enslaved as the defiance of a regime dictating that "the free(d) individual was nothing if not burdened, responsible, and obligated," as she notes: "As itinerancy, nomadism, migration, roving, or simply walking, moving about occurred below the threshold of formal equality and rights and articulated the limits of emancipation and the constrained terms of agency."[46] Meanwhile, as Sarah Jane Cervenak argues, the surveillance regime of the plantation relied on the criminalization of "wandering," which was not limited to physical movement alone.[47] Just as slavery relied on the racialization of perceived capacities for self-governance and "self-direction," it also rendered the conceptualization and surveillance of movement a vector of racialization: "The unpredictable kinesis engendered by the secret impulse became permissible and unpunishable for bodies otherwise presumed to be innately self-determined. For bodies and ontologies said to lack such capacity, any unrestrained movement, or wandering, was paradoxically figured as at once impossible, injurious, and criminal."[48]

In many ways, Equiano's most overt argument echoes what Cervenak characterizes as a fairly conventional abolitionist argument that did not necessarily contest these terms, as he renders "self-direction and self-mobilization" foundational to his contribution to "antislavery consolidations of humanness."[49] However, the role of mobility in shaping the narrative structure of his text also participates in what she terms "an aesthetics of diversion," and what Katherine McKittrick describes as "a black sense of place" that actively resists the governing logics of plantation geographies.[50] Equiano's travels do not just consolidate him as a liberal economic subject or as an expert qualified to propose commercial projects to Parliament—though these claims are indeed central to Equiano's rhetorical project. His travels also render him an aggregator of painful, terrifying, and dangerous experiences repeated throughout multiple national, colonial, and maritime spaces, thus transforming his racialized vulnerability into a roving optic that can theorize blackness as a diasporic condition and relation to the law that crosses national borders and legal jurisdictions. By accumulating experiences of vulnerability that are never resolved through any sort of legal redress, Equiano speaks from a geographical itinerary associated with fugitivity, but recasts the world around him—and particularly the discretionary authority of white men—as the true bearer of unpredictable and terrifying threat.

## Without Judge or Jury

Cathy Davidson has characterized the dominant formal feature of the *Interesting Narrative* as the "existential rug-pull," a narrative rhythm that renders any experience of freedom or safety deeply precarious.[51] One of the more common forms taken by this "rug-pull" is a legal one: Equiano expects some protection from the law, but finds it suddenly and dangerously absent or meaningless. For instance, when his seemingly beneficent enslaver sells him, Equiano protests that the sale is illegitimate: "I have been baptized, and by the laws of the land no man has a right to sell me: and I added, that I had heard a lawyer, and others at different times, tell my master so" (93–94). His new enslaver's response does not even entertain the possibility of a debate on these terms; he exits the realm of law altogether and responds in terms that will be echoed later by the white men in Savannah: "Captain Doran said I talked too much English; and if I did not behave myself well, and be quiet, he had a method on board to make me" (94). Much later, when he is free and on a trading voyage in Grenada, he and a fellow sailor sell some goods to a white man who refuses to pay him, but his complaints to the local Justice of the Peace are fruitless: "being negroes, although free, we could not get any remedy" (170). This anecdote ends more happily than expected, but only due to the chance opportunity to circumvent law altogether. Since the man also turned out to owe money to three white sailors, Equiano joins the white men as they extract their money through force and intimidation, only managing to collect after they threaten to cut the man's ears off (171).

One strikingly recurring form of this legal "rug-pull" is Equiano's repeated protest that he has been confined or threatened without trial, thus invoking the procedural workings of criminal law as metonym for recognized legal personhood more generally. For instance, immediately following his account of his emancipation, Equiano uses this procedural counterfactual to illustrate the fragility of his manumission papers and the limits of their protective power. Now employed as a sailor, he is staying in Savannah when an enslaved man insults and strikes him. He knows that he has little recourse, as he reflects that "there was little or no law for a free negro here," but when his entreaties with the man fail, he "beat[s] him soundly" (139). The man's enslaver, a Mr. Reed, approaches Equiano's captain on board the ship the next day "that he might have me flogged all round the town, for beating his negro slave" (139). It is immediately clear to Equiano that he is still subject to the nearly unlimited authority of white men regardless of his legal status: "I was astonished and frightened at this, and thought I had better keep where I was, than go ashore and be flogged round the town, without judge or jury" (139). Read leaves the ship, threatening to "bring all the constables in the town," which in turn prompts Equiano to recall another story that he takes as emblematic of his likely treatment: "There was a free black man, a carpenter, that I knew, who for asking a gentleman that he had worked for, for the money he had earned, was put into gaol; and afterwards this oppressed man was sent from Georgia, with false accusations, of an intention to set the gentleman's house on fire, and run away with his slaves" (139).

When he remarks that there is "little to no law for a free negro here," what he means is his unlimited vulnerability to unpredictable violence that is not meted out through standardized or predictable legal procedure, as he emphasizes that he fears he will be flogged "without judge or jury." The anecdote of the carpenter evokes total legal and existential precarity; the act of asking for money he has earned leads not to the fulfillment of the terms of social contract but to a punitive response that feels like a procedural non sequitur: the accusation of intended arson. It's also a narrative non sequitur: as readers, we are given no tools that could possibly lead us to expect the accusation of arson as a predictable result of a demand for payment. This nonsystematicity shapes Equiano's world, and is a foundational structure for the text. John Bugg emphasizes the importance of narrative discontinuity to Equiano's project, as he traces what he terms "Equiano's trifling counterplot" as the accrued critical force of numerous "textual disruptions" that challenge the reader to decipher what, if anything, connects seemingly unrelated events that succeed each other in close proximity.[52] For Bugg, this "counterplot" ultimately amounts to a critique of the limits of the law to grant true freedom—thus, an undercurrent that complicates some of the text's more overt investments in Enlightenment universalisms as potential guarantors of human rights.[53]

Of course, as the narrative makes clear, Equiano's vulnerability is not entirely unpredictable, since there is in fact an extremely predictable rule underlying it: blackness can always render you vulnerable, especially when you attempt to move through the world as if free, expecting to be paid for your labor or allowed to pass through a port unmolested. However, as Equiano narrates it, you never know when this vulnerability will subject you to violence and when you will find yourself spared. Equiano never knows when a white man will pay him for his merchandise and when he will rob him or attempt to have him jailed, and there is no description that can offer his readers a clue as to which white men pose a threat and which ones don't. He never knows if demanding payment will lead to him being accused of arson or theft, or to being captured as a suspected runaway, or to simply being paid without incident.

This happens over and over, throughout the American and Caribbean colonies, and even at sea. After leaving his stint as an overseer on a plantation on the Mosquito Coast, Equiano attempts to purchase passage to Jamaica. The owner of the ship then tries to hire him to work on another of his ships as a sailor, but when Equiano declines the offer, the owner resorts to force, holding him captive and threatening to sell him into slavery in Cartagena if he does not comply. He orders Equiano tied to the ship, and Equiano invokes the utter absence of formal legal procedure to illustrate the nature of his predicament: "Thus I hung, without any crime committed, and without judge or jury, merely because I was a freeman, and could not by the law get any redress from a white person in those parts of the world" (212). The repeated invocation of the "judge or jury" that he never actually faces invokes the same formal legal procedure throughout the Atlantic world, thus imposing a counterfactual legal uniformity—at least, as a wished-for ideal—on spaces that were in fact sites of legal contestation, pluralism, and uneven application of metropolitan law.[54]

The appeal to judge and jury in particular casts the slights, attacks, and threats that Equiano experiences as the many faces of one specific and politically charged impingement on the rights of the subject as understood by eighteenth-century theorists of English common law: unlawful imprisonment. Equiano's invocation of unlawful imprisonment renders his narrative a rhetorical stand-in for a writ of habeas corpus, the legal mechanism through which one might challenge unlawful imprisonment by invoking the sovereign's right to obtain an account of why one of his subjects is confined. By invoking habeas corpus, Equiano is deploying a politically powerful concept at the center of debates over liberty, legally recognized personhood, and the Englishness of the English common law.

The seventeenth-century reconfiguration of habeas corpus as a foundational right of the subject rendered unlawful imprisonment a powerful metonym for "slavery" as it then circulated in English political theory—that is, tyranny. As Edward Jenks famously asserts, "the writ Habeas Corpus was originally intended not to get people out of prison, but to put them in it."[55] However, seventeenth-century invocations of the writ took up habeas corpus to reconfigure sovereignty, transforming what had been conceptualized as the king's prerogative to hear an account of why his subject was imprisoned into the emblem of the *subject's* right to appeal an unlawful exercise of power.[56] The 1679 Habeas Corpus Act—in many ways the legislative culmination of this reconfiguration of sovereignty—is framed explicitly as a defense of the liberty of the subject, and its popular perception as the central legislative guarantor of this liberty persisted throughout the eighteenth century, perhaps most famously in Blackstone's formulation of the act as a "second *magna carta*."[57]

Of course, the invocation of habeas corpus as the emblem of the subject's liberty also renders law the exclusive avenue for recognizable personhood; as Nasser Hussain observes, "whether used to intern or to free, habeas corpus is a mode of binding subjects to the law and to its economies of power."[58] In a colonial context, the rhetoric of the liberty of the subject coexisted uneasily with the exigencies of colonial rule, producing racialized exclusions from the kind of legal subjectivity that habeas corpus names.[59] For instance, as discussed above, the Barbados Assembly enacted a code of law that fundamentally violated the principles of the "ancient constitution" as invoked by the Habeas Corpus Act and its enabling discourse of the rights of the subject. However, by enshrining slavery as a status exempt from due process and other foundational legal attributes of the free subject, members of the Assembly argued that they were exercising *their own* fundamental rights as free Englishmen: they were governing themselves as they saw fit, and their ability to "self-govern" relied on the legal production of "the slave" as recognizable only as property of—or threat to—the king's subjects. At the same time, colonial governors repeatedly argued in court (sometimes with success) that colonial rule demanded a more relaxed conception of the rights of the subject than the Habeas Corpus Act asserted, thus rendering habeas corpus a flashpoint for debates about the extent to which colonies ought to be considered distinct legal spaces with regard to English common law and whether colonial subjects were subjects of the king—and thus subjects of the law.[60]

As an emblem of what Edlie Wong terms "lawful liberty," and as venue for debating the applicability of the common law in the colonies, habeas corpus is unsurprisingly crucial to abolitionism, both in rhetoric and in practical legal strategy.[61] Granville Sharp—who made frequent use of writs of habeas corpus in his antislavery legal advocacy—also invoked habeas corpus as a central pillar in his political writing. Citing the 1679 Habeas Corpus Act, Sharp argues that "every man who presumes to detain any person whatsoever as a Slave, other wise than by virtue of a written contract, acts manifestly without '*due process of the law.*'"[62] The act, Sharp argues, extends as far as does the king's sovereignty; all in the realm are subject to the king's laws and thus also to the protection of these laws. And it is precisely the sovereignty of these laws that becomes the guarantor of humanity; of the legal treatment of a person as property, Sharp writes: "The Negro must be divested of his humanity, and rendered incapable of the King's protection, before such an action can lawfully take place."[63] Here, "humanity" is rendered equivalent to "the King's protection," which also goes by the name of subject of the realm or subject of the laws—thus routing humanity through law and neatly illustrating Alexander Weheliye's claim that habeas corpus indexes the reduction of personhood to a "juridical acknowledgement" that relies on an unacknowledged presumption of "the tabula rasa of whiteness . . . as the prerequisite for the law's magical transubstantiation of a thing to be possessed into a property-owning subject."[64]

Writs of habeas corpus, of course, were also one of Sharp's practical legal tools in his efforts against slavery—most famously in *Somerset v. Stewart* (1772). In this case, a writ of habeas corpus interrupted the attempt of Charles Stewart to recapture James Somerset and have him sent to Jamaica against his will. Because Lord Mansfield ruled that the laws of England did not grant enslavers the ability to force those they enslaved to leave the country with them, the case was popularly (though inaccurately) interpreted as declaring slavery illegal in England.[65] In this widely publicized case, habeas corpus was a highly visible bulwark against slavery, recasting some of the basic powers that the institution of slavery granted to enslavers as a form of unlawful imprisonment that violated the rights of the subject as recognized by the common law. At the same time, however, the abolitionist redeployment of this ruling as unequivocal legal victory also yoked "freedom" ever more tightly to the recognition of legal personhood and to specifically national belonging; as Edlie Wong argues, the redeployment of this case in transatlantic abolitionist print culture rendered the debate about slavery a foundational debate about "the meaning of British freedom."[66]

The *Somerset* case also did not resolve the question of habeas corpus in the colonies; instead, Mansfield's ruling hinged on the distinction between English and colonial law and thus could not extend beyond England. As Daniel Hulsebosch argues, the rhetorical reach of the ruling's invocation of liberty was able to extend farther, geographically, than the actual ruling could, since the King's Bench jurisdiction did not include the colonies, and colonial charters had long legitimized legal divergence of colonial law from the English common law: "In this sense, the case contributed to the abstraction of English liberty into a human right. Still, it remained a liberty available to people *in England* rather than everywhere, including the royal territories of Virginia and Jamaica. The empire's legal pluralism allowed Mansfield to rationalize the brutality of slavery while locating it offshore, thus facilitating the coexistence of slavery and freedom."[67]

Meanwhile, as Dana Rabin argues, the ruling also solidified another overlapping version of national distinction that limited freedom to the rights of Englishmen. To counter proslavery arguments that slavery was a form of villeinage (and thus did exist in English law), Somerset's lawyers argued instead that villeinage was "a specifically English status" passed down by descent, tied to (English) land, and inapplicable to Africans.[68] By racializing villeinage, these arguments also racialized the distinctions between colonial and metropolitan law that were so central to this case, ironically linking whiteness to Englishness and to the liberty that was the inheritance of the ancient constitution.[69] This case thus affirmed habeas corpus as a viable practical tool for contesting the legitimacy of slavery as well as an emblem of an ideal of liberty to which abolitionist authors like Equiano could morally appeal, but it also relied foundationally on explicit distinctions between England and its colonies as legal spaces, as well as implicit distinctions between English and non-English people as potential legal subjects. The claim that slavery was repugnant to *English* common law in particular, after all, could (and did) easily shade into rhetoric aiming to preserve England from the racialized contamination of colonial slavery—and also, by extension, of blackness.[70]

When Equiano invokes habeas corpus as an absent ideal of liberty preserved by the rule of law, he not only, as Wong argues, questions the ability of English law to offer redress; he also fundamentally reconfigures some of the national and racial logic operative in *Somerset*.[71] By imagining, however counterfactually, habeas corpus in the colonies, or even at sea, he proposes a universalism for *Somerset* that the ruling itself necessarily excluded. He appeals to its notion of the rights of the subject, but invokes it wherever he happens to be, thus transforming his own mobility into a force that could insinuate an imaginative extension of the king's sovereignty far more powerfully than the law itself ever could.

Of course, another legal avenue for imprisonment without judge or jury—one for which habeas corpus offered no clear remedy because it was perfectly lawful—was the summary imprisonment allowed for by vagrancy laws. Vagrancy law, and more broadly the embeddedness of police in the legal architecture of slavery, is also a proslavery answer to habeas corpus. After all, vagrancy law had long allowed for summary imprisonment without judge or jury, and this lends a legal legitimacy to such wide-ranging discretionary force that Edward Long makes full rhetorical use of in his pamphlet opposing the *Somerset* decision. Long argues that the enslaved are "perhaps, vested, by the spirit of our common and statute law, with a right to his *Habeas Corpus cum causa*, yet neither bailable nor deliverable, if the cause returned should be, *his refusal to serve his Planter-master,* in any lawful employment."[72] With this argument, Long hopes to militate against the use of habeas corpus that the *Somerset* decision enables: namely, the recasting of forcible transportation out of England as a form of unlawful imprisonment. Long characterizes the absolute power of the enslaver to confine and transport his "property" as a form of *lawful* imprisonment by drawing on the language of vagrancy law, which had long granted wide leeway to imprison the "idle and disorderly" for their perceived refusal to work.

Equiano, in invoking legal procedure as the remedy for unexpected eruptions of violence and tyranny, thus casts colonial modes of police sovereignty as unlawful. Analogously, he also claims legal personhood—the capacity to be tried by a jury—as an alternative to being seen as what the Barbados slave code would make him: not a legal subject, but a threat. Bryan Wagner, in his reading of the colonial slave codes that proliferated from the Barbadian prototype, notes that their form enables precisely the wide discretionary leeway that vagrancy laws do (and indeed, for Wagner, this is no coincidence, as both are foundational for police):

> These codes employ neither principle nor example to organize their long lists of heterogeneous threats to the public peace. Statutes governing clothing, trade, domicile, outlawry, miscegenation, baptism, permits to travel, custody of firearms, hiring out, false petitions to indenture, flight, literacy, inveigling, insurrection, lurking, keeping livestock, and religious observance are enumerated, without subordination or any indication as to how their entries are supposed to be combined or connected to each other. Neither do the codes profess anything like comprehensive coverage. The entries are presented merely as consecutive illustrations. They say nothing about the limit to the law's breadth. It is always possible to attach new entries to the list, and it is always conceivable that some threat may arise that is wholly unanticipated in the existing law, to which the law's authority nonetheless immediately applies.[73]

Thus, Wagner argues, "from the standpoint of police power, blackness is imperceptible except for the presumed danger it poses to public welfare."[74] To be recognized as something other than a threat, Equiano inhabits the paradox that Jeannine DeLombard notes when she emphasizes criminal responsibility as an avenue, however attenuated, to recognized legal personhood: he proclaims himself innocent in an imagined trial before a judge and jury.[75]

When Equiano transforms himself into a legal subject—one whose imprisonment could be challenged as unlawful, and one who could stand trial before a jury—he reconfigures the optic of police, portraying the white men around him to be the true source of unpredictable threat. While he is still enslaved, Equiano tries to do some business in Charleston, where he encounters treatment similar to what he will encounter again and again after his manumission. He sells rum to a man who refuses to pay him: "Although I used the interest of my friendly captain, I could not obtain any thing for it; for, being a negro man, I could not oblige him to pay me" (128). When he eventually obtains the money, he objects that some of the coins are worthless, but once again, his racialized vulnerability puts him in no position to negotiate: "He took advantage of my being a negro man, and obliged me to put up with those or none, although I objected to them. Immediately after, as I was trying to pass them in the market amongst other white men, I was abused for offering to pass bad coin; and though I shewed them the man I had got them from, I was within one minute of being tied up and flogged without either judge or jury" (129). This incident ends, as so many do, with the threat of unlawful imprisonment and the counterfactual invocation of the absent "judge or jury"; the violence that Equiano narrowly escapes here comes not in the form of routinized legal procedure, but in the form of unpredictable threat that could emerge from any interaction between him and a white man. In other words, as long as his status as "a negro man" is operative and meaningful in the legal context of an Atlantic world structured by a slave economy, actions like selling rum or spending coins in a marketplace take on extreme risk, and as the narrative recounts, an attempted commercial transaction can erupt into sudden violence within the space of a sentence.

This is a powerful redeployment of the temporality of threat and anticipation that the police law of slavery invoked so foundationally in the Barbados slave code: for the Barbados Assembly, invoking "Negroes" as an "uncertaine, dangerous kinde of people" set in place a racialization of threat with a long afterlife, one that concretizes blackness as a kind of being that could erupt into threat at any moment, thus also constructing whiteness, through a claim of vulnerability, as a form of sovereignty that links the rights of the free subject to the prerogative to wield, as Nikhil Pal Singh argues, "rigorous and ongoing applications of 'legitimate' violence along a potentially limitless vector."[76] Equiano reveals the operations of this logic by reversing it rhetorically and narratively; repeating his status as "a negro man," he reveals that he speaks from a position of vulnerability, and the broad powers that accrue as whiteness are what threaten to erupt into violence or transform everyday commercial activity into spectacles of terror and tyranny. His position as narrator, after all, renders his actions more predictable to us than the actions of any other; he tells us what he intends to do and we see his actions unfold accordingly. The people he encounters, however, are frequently opaque and unknowable to him and, by extension, to us. Equiano draws us into this disorienting temporality when he moves from a scene of commercial dispute to the sudden escalation of violence: he is "within one minute of being tied up and flogged" before we, as readers, see any specific embodied action that might signal this as the intentions of the men in the market. While the police laws of the slave colonies—built foundationally upon adaptations of vagrancy law—theorize blackness as potential threat and cast black mobility as criminal, Equiano reconfigures this optic: he theorizes blackness as vulnerability to threat, and portrays his own mobility as a source of knowledge that can aggregate experiences into such a theory, as well as a potential vector for the imaginative universalization of "liberty" that the English common law might rhetorically invoke but in practice could not accomplish.

Is formal legal procedure, then, Equiano's ideal bulwark against police? His invocations of the absent judge and jury seem to suggest that it is. However, in the *Interesting Narrative,* legal procedure is most predictable, stable, and just when it appears as a counterfactual. Equiano's account of the instance in which he actually makes use of habeas corpus casts some doubt on the promise that law seems to hold when it is absent. In 1774, Equiano finds himself in London and is hoping to find employment on a ship bound for Turkey. Also employed on the ship is a man named John Annis, who had previously been enslaved by William Kirkpatrick, but from whom he had "parted by consent" (179). Kirkpatrick, Equiano narrates, boarded their ship with six other men and kidnapped Annis to bring him back to St. Kitt's—an action that is, post-*Somerset,* clearly illegal. Equiano attempts to rescue him by obtaining a writ of habeas corpus and enlisting the assistance of Granville Sharp, but Kirkpatrick evades the order and carries Annis off to St. Kitt's, where, Equiano later hears, he dies soon after.

In this episode, formal legal procedure and extralegal force mingle, and the writ of habeas corpus fails to produce the free legal personhood it rhetorically invokes. For instance, one newspaper report of the case notes that Kirkpatrick seems to have simply ignored the demand that he produce Annis and bring him before a judge; he pleaded that he did not have Annis and left the country shortly thereafter.[77] Equiano notes Kirkpatrick's plea "that he had not the body in custody," but he also adds another detail, blaming the result not only on Kirkpatrick's lie but also on his own attorney's failure: "But alas! my attorney proved unfaithful; he took my money, lost me many months employ, and did not the least good in the cause; and when the poor man arrived at St. Kitt's, he was, according to custom, staked to the ground with four pins through a cord, two on his wrists, and two on his ancles, was cut and flogged most unmercifully, and afterwards loaded cruelly with irons about his neck" (180, 181). Here, the rule of law disappoints Equiano by turning out to be the rule of men after all; the whims and desires of white men hold sway over what legal procedure seems to guarantee. Equiano narrates the will of these individual men, not the law, as sovereign: not only does Kirkpatrick defy the law simply by lying to a judge and leaving the country, but Equiano's lawyer, as he narrates it, also contributes to this failure by being "unfaithful," which makes the operations of law rest not on evidence or procedure, but on an individual white man's feeling toward him. The structure of this sentence, which begins with a complaint about inadequate legal representation and ends in torture, also recapitulates Equiano's narrative configuration of threat. The failure of the law—and in particular, Equiano's accusation that he has been cheated out of his money—erupts suddenly and spectacularly from the register of the commercial transaction into one of brutal violence. This is the threat that was there all along, and his constant tonal shifts force the reader to see the world as far more uncertain and unpredictably violent than would be implied by a confident belief in the constitutional guarantee of liberty of the subject.

At the same time, the moment in this story when Equiano is most successful is a moment in which both he and Kirkpatrick both circumvent formal legal procedure altogether. Kirkpatrick, knowing that Equiano has obtained the writ and hoping to avoid being served with it at all, sets a watchman in front of his house to try to prevent Equiano from coming near it. Equiano, however, evades the watchman with an overdetermined disguise: "I whitened my face, that they might not know me, and this had the desired effect" (180). The entire incident reads like a parody of policing and the threat against which it is invoked: Kirkpatrick's private watchman patrols in order to prevent the law from actually being enforced, while Equiano engages in "suspicious" behavior—disguising his identity—that ironically renders him far more free to pass without suspicion. Even his overdetermined deployment of whiteness is not an attempt to access legal recognition as a free Englishman once and for all, but rather assists him in carrying out a deception that is necessary for the exercise of the rights he supposedly already had.

Legal procedure, for Equiano, is thus somewhat akin to his deployment of literacy in Srinivas Aravamudan's account of the *Interesting Narrative.* As an alternative to readings that would too easily understand literacy as an uncomplicated avenue for agency and thus reinscribe "the evolutionary narrative so dear to early abolitionists, that of humanizing the African," Aravamudan argues instead that "in the manner of catachresis, the book is a concept-metaphor without an adequate referent. It stands for the workings of culture, the ultimately secreted and untraceable origin of change. The more readily the 'factitious universal' of the book makes itself available to Equiano, the more it represents a utopian escape from subjection through the acquisition of literacy."[78] Law becomes another such "factitious universal"; Equiano's invocations of the "judge or jury" he never faces take on the aura of William Blackstone's ideal of legal formalism; after all, Blackstone's most general and introductory definition of "law," which traverses laws of the physical world, as well as all forms of divine, natural, statutory, canon, and common law, is a "rule of action," a consistent and predictable force that dictates in advance what may and may not happen, and what consequences may be expected to follow actions.[79] Against this ideal, however, we see both the actual workings of legal procedure—epitomized in the failure of habeas corpus in the John Annis incident—and the extreme unpredictability of the world around Equiano as embedded in the form of the narrative itself. Neither vagrancy nor threat, as theorized from the vantage point of police, is constituted as a subject position or identity from which to speak, but in narratively fashioning his "life and fortune" as "extremely chequered" (236), Equiano redeploys the picaresque as critique. If, as I argued in my reading of *The English Rogue* in Chapter 1, the picaresque offers formal structure for vagrancy legislation to characterize potential future threat as limitlessly unpredictable and in need of equally unbounded legal authority to counter it, Equiano uses the charge of unpredictability to return the accusation of unlimited threat and violence to the very forms of sovereignty that the idea of vagrancy underwrote.

## On Being a Threat

I return, once more, to Equiano's encounter with the patrol in Savannah. When Equiano is in Mosa's house, the patrol knocks on the door and shares their punch before telling them that they must all go to the watch-house. Like Equiano, the reader is left unprepared for this particular legal "rug-pull"; he remarks that "this surprised me a good deal after our kindness to them," and it is only after he questions them that both he and the reader learn that they have violated a local regulation by keeping their light on past nine o'clock (158). With the patrol already in the house, posing a threat of capture and violence, the previously innocuous details of the carefree scene belatedly take on an air of danger, as Equiano had narrated it before the patrol's arrival: "We were very happy at meeting each other; and, after supper, we had a light till between nine and ten o'clock at night" (158). The effect of the passage is deeply disorienting; the action that draws the attention of the patrol is indistinguishable in tone or importance from the other activities that precede it here: being happy, eating supper, meeting a friend. This is precisely Equiano's point: to be black is to be potentially targeted for any number of supposed infractions or for no stated reason at all (as in the case of the men who simply want to kidnap him); it is to be existentially precarious and utterly unable to use the law as a guide to predict what might draw violence upon you and what might protect you from violence, both legal and extralegal.

But is that all it is? Scholars such as Saidiya Hartman, Marisa Fuentes, Christina Sharpe, and Katherine McKittrick have insisted on the ethical imperative to grapple with an archive that reduces blackness to the reinscription of violence without simply reproducing this epistemic violence as unmarked historiographic ground.[80] In this vein, Simone Browne's important recentering of blackness in the long history of modern surveillance offers us another way to understand the scene here in Savannah, one that does not just reduce the narrative to one of wholly successful apprehension and capture. Arguing for the centrality of slavery to the early development of personal identity documentation, spatial regimes of visuality, and biometric identification, Browne traces a long history of "surveillance in and of black life as a fact of blackness."[81] Just as crucial to this history, however, is a counterhistory of what she calls "dark sousveillance": a mode of both eluding notice *and* looking back, thus creating "an imaginative place from which to mobilize a critique of racializing surveillance."[82]

Equiano, of course, by narrating the actions of the patrol, places himself in a position to offer their actions up to the gaze of the reader. Because the men of the patrol see the interior of Mosa's house as being within the ambit of their potential surveillance, they intrude into the social scene and drink the men's punch—but unbeknownst to them, this very intrusion renders the patrol visible to the future author of an autobiography, opening their behavior to the view of countless strangers in Equiano's reading public. The regulation forbidding Mosa from lighting his house after nine o'clock also indexes the inextricability of illuminated visibility—so frequently enlisted as a technology of surveillance—from the forms of sociability, affiliation, and contact that could exceed and elude the surveillance regime of slavery.[83] In other words, the light allows Equiano and Mosa to see and speak to each other, and it is precisely this kind of social contact that the patrol interprets as threat; after all, slave patrols understood any social affiliation or gathering as the potential seed of an insurrection.[84] The light in Mosa's house is, in this case, a technology not of surveillance, but of sociability. They "were very happy," Equiano tells us, but he doesn't tell us more; we don't hear what they said to each other, just as we don't know how he and Mosa knew each other in the first place. By contrast, the men of the patrol are quoted directly, and the social scene is far more closely observed when they arrive: "Discerning a light in the house, they knocked at the door; we opened it, and they came in and sat down, and drank some punch with us; they also begged some limes of me, as they understood I had some, which I readily gave them. A little after this, they told me I must go to the watch-house with them" (158). The ensuing conversation is the only one that evening documented in any detail; he exposes the patrol to the reader's observation but keeps his conversation with Mosa private. This privacy is political; as Sarah Cervenak reminds us, "in the context of racial slavery, black privacy figured as dangerous, a highly pursued philosophical scene of potential insurrection and unreadable desire."[85]

Equiano thus also preserves a realm of black sociability as outside the possibility of surveilling apprehension or anticipation. It is by *not* representing or recounting their conversation that he keeps the encounter beyond the reach of police. In noting what Equiano preserves as private, I attempt here to heed Christina Sharpe's call for method that can "attend to physical, social, and figurative death and also to the largeness that is Black life, Black life insisted from death."[86] Life, as Katherine McKittrick writes, is what exceeds the archive of death, and emerges in "black absented presences: the unspeakable, the unwritten, the unbearable and unutterable, the unseeable and the invisible, the uncountable and unindexed, outside the scourge, that which cannot be seen or heard or read but is always there."[87] In the "happy" reunion of which we hear nothing, what might have been narratively illuminated remains unremarked upon, and Equiano thus figures intimacy not through exposure, but through silence.

Equiano's argument, of course, quite frequently proceeds through silence. What Bugg terms Equiano's "counterplot" happens through juxtaposition, irresolution, and nonlinearity—the absence of a transition or conclusion to an episode. This is, as Bugg argues, one counterweight to the text's prevailing appeals to humanitarian universalisms, allowing Equiano to cast doubt on the foundational modes of apprehending personhood upon which abolitionist argument depended, while at the same time still making a legible abolitionist argument.[88] In the context of police and surveillance, the formal structure of the "counterplot" is also a mode of narrative that inhabits the unanticipated and the unpredictable. Equiano takes up the very experience of unpredictability he encounters—he never knows whether a new acquaintance will attempt to kidnap him, do business with him without incident, or simply let him pass by—and fashions this into the very medium of his narrative.

In the formal structure of his narrative, and in the invocations of life and sociability that exceed and elude surveillance, Equiano thus positions himself as more than just an object of police, and he posits redress in terms that at least occasionally exceed the terms of legal personhood in which he is also deeply invested. If, as I have been arguing, police is an orientation toward potential threat that renders personhood (legal, political, subjective) irrelevant, then "the threat" can become a position from which to speak critically without assuming personhood as self-possession.[89] This is a narrative that is foundationally formally structured by fugitivity. Equiano is not a literal fugitive, as he takes pains to show us, but that also doesn't matter; he knows, from his encounters in Savannah to his witnessing of the kidnapping of John Annis, that he can be regarded as "fugitive"—that is, either dispatchable as threat or available for profitable recapture—regardless of what his manumission papers say. At the same time, however, this is also a text whose aims are frequently far from radical: the extension of national belonging, the making of a self-possessing subject, and the transfiguration of diasporic blackness into a privileged position from which to propose and direct the British colonization of Africa.

This tension within the text—between demands to be recognized as a self-possessing legal subject and the narrative unraveling of the terms through which this recognition is made possible—registers the inadequacy of straightforward appeals to formal legal procedure as a bulwark against the racialized discretionary license of police. It also reveals the potential for another avenue of critique that does not rely on claiming legal subjectivity as the opposite of the "threat" against which this subjectivity is defined. In short, it shows how Equiano's narrative form—its reliance on discontinuity, variety, mobility, and juxtaposition—can reconfigure the foundational logic of police by strategically inhabiting it, redeploying it, and reversing its terms. This, in turn, offers us an opportunity to expand our sense of the formal and aesthetic properties of surveillance. Equiano's strategic silences and juxtapositions, his ability to make narrative exceed our anticipation or prediction, his mobility—all of these features, I argue, constitute a critique of policing, but they do not necessarily do this by opposing the static and panoptic gaze of surveillance to the text's improvisational elusiveness. Police, as an eighteenth-century mode of governmentality, was frequently improvisational, irregular, and flexible; it relied foundationally on the imagined resistance of its targets to prediction or definition because this, in turn, lent police a reciprocal resistance to limitations on its scope or targets. Thus, the most mobile, elusive, discontinuous, and improvisational features of the text can critique police because they so often mimic its narrative and perceptual forms so well.

This becomes legible only in light of an expanded understanding of vagrancy's archive—including its imaginative and literary redeployments—as crucial to the history of police. Sixteenth-century English vagrancy statutes took the legal category of "rogue" from popular print genres that helped justify these laws' existence, and authors of seventeenth-century picaresque fiction made use of the imaginative charge of these laws and the powers they authorized in their redeployment of the laws' formal structure in service of their own aesthetic and commercial aims. Over the course of the eighteenth century, literary authors took up vagrancy toward various political and aesthetic ends: sometimes, as in the case of Henry Fielding, making use of the open-endedness of the conceptual category to demand more wide-ranging juridical powers to contain disorder, and sometimes, as in the case of Mary Robinson or Charles Brockden Brown, using the uneasy aporia between vagrancy and legal subjectivity to dramatize troubling failures of juridical recognition, as well as to theorize the capacities of their literary genres to call up or unravel personhood in terms that exceed the strictly legal. Equiano, in using picaresque as a mode of explicitly legal critique, takes the literary redeployment of vagrancy back to the legal categories and practices that lent it such aesthetic charge in the first place. Even as the universalist promise of the law repeatedly fails him, the narrative forms that register this failure also allow Equiano to demand that his readers imagine, however tenuously and elusively, the possibility of black life that does not depend for its legibility either on racializing surveillance or on the recognition of legal personhood such surveillance constitutes as its obverse.

## *CODA*

# TOWARD AN ABOLITIONIST LITERARY HISTORY OF THE POLICE

Police, as a theory and practice of governance, was slowly constructed, tested out, and sometimes challenged in realms that were never limited to the strictly "legal" or "governmental"—including the aesthetic and the affective. One of the major claims of this book has been that police and aesthetics have a long history of mutual influence, but that police does not necessarily take any one particular aesthetic form. In particular, it can take forms we may not expect: even as we can certainly fruitfully trace connections between policing and aesthetic or formal gestures of closure, omniscience, limitation, clarity, or certainty, we miss potential insights when we assume that police always carries these aesthetic qualities. As the archive of vagrancy across the eighteenth-century British Atlantic world shows, the aesthetic history of the police is in fact a history of very different qualities, including improvisation, creativity, narrative idiosyncrasy, loquaciousness, humor, terror, and more. This matters because we so frequently colloquially collapse a wide array of everyday and nonstate activities into "policing" if they fit the former aesthetic—such as, for instance, the possibility that my stern critique of another scholar's choice of words might be called "language policing"—but we are much less likely to spot the material connections that exist between the literal activity of policing and everyday modes of aesthetic and emotional life that don't necessarily fit this set of formal expectations. Throughout this book, I have used the category of vagrancy to track an expanded aesthetic and literary archive of police, while at the same time resisting the common tendency to lose the specificity of police by conflating it with all forms of disciplinary power.[1] In this Coda, I reflect more broadly on how literary history, as a method, can help us theorize, critique, and unravel the foundational legitimacy of police as a theory of governance.

Literary history, as I argued in Chapter 4, appears as a jurisprudential method in William O. Douglas's majority opinion in *Papachristou v. City of Jacksonville* (1972). Taking up a romanticized figure of the vagabond as a noble dissenter who embodies the affordances of American freedom, Douglas invokes a literary history that drew on the actual legal category of vagrancy, yet also obscured the legal history of this term by characterizing "the vagrant" as a free, white man exercising liberty through mobility rather than, for instance, a fugitive from slavery or bound labor, a gender-nonconforming person, a sex worker, a suspected thief, a person whose lack of employment is perceived (rightly or not) as the refusal to work, or any of the other countless and varied reasons given for vagrancy arrests in the archives of both theory and practice during the centuries of these laws' persistence on both sides of the Atlantic. At the same time, however, I have argued that literature does not always merely obscure, distort, or fictionalize the legal histories and concepts with which it is in conversation; indeed, literary redeployments of legal categories, even as they take factual, ideological, or formal license with these categories, offer us a rich archive of how legal ideas circulated through the publics we now identify with literary reading and print marketplaces—often transforming as they did so.

Literary history and "historicist" modes of criticism have also recently come under fire from a number of critical positions. Perhaps most prominently, "postcritique" methods such as Stephen Best and Sharon Marcus's "surface reading" or Rita Felski and Heather Love's invocations of social-science methodologies posit alternatives to "depth hermeneutics" that privilege the exegetical mastery of the critic as a self-evident ethical good.[2]

Such interventions register a dissatisfaction with the historicist methods that have been, in recent decades, so thoroughly assimilated into literary study as to hardly register any longer as "methods," which, for critics of historicism, renders these textual approaches ripe for rote repetition without the self-reflexivity or abstraction we tend to associate with "theory." Rita Felski, for instance, notes a tendency for historicist work to produce remarkably similar metanarratives of power and resistance: "While suspicion can manifest itself in multiple ways, in the current intellectual climate it often pivots on a fealty to the clarifying power of historical context. What the literary text does not see, in this line of thought, are the larger circumstances that shape and sustain it and that are drawn into the light by the corrective force of the critic's own vigilant gaze."[3] At stake here is also what registers as "political"; Felski also characterizes such faith in the clarifying power of context as working hand in hand with a consistent suspicion that "the texts we study are permanently engaged in coercing, mystifying, and hoodwinking their readers" and that the critic, by contrast, is on the right side of history in exposing this deception.[4] At the same time, if "postcritique" characterizes historicism as a gesture toward the "political" that misrecognizes interpretation as political action and valorizes critique as more politically useful than it actually is, the V21 Collective's manifesto argues, by contrast, that historicism is not "political" enough: "One outcome of post-historicist interpretation may be a new openness to *presentism:* an awareness that our interest in the period is motivated by certain features of our own moment. In finance, resource mining, globalization, imperialism, liberalism, and many other vectors, we are Victorian, inhabiting, advancing, and resisting the world they made."[5] Here, "presentism" is aligned with avowed political commitment, while "historicism" is aligned most prominently with the manifesto's opening critique of "positivist historicism" as "a mode of inquiry that aims to do little more than exhaustively describe, preserve, and display the past. At its worst, positivist historicism devolves into show-and-tell epistemologies and bland antiquarianism. Its primary affective mode is the amused chuckle."[6] What is implied here, but what has, to my mind, been more powerfully and precisely articulated in fields like queer studies, ethnic studies, and critical race theory, is that the stylistic and affective registers of scholarship—like the amused chuckle—are deeply politically and epistemologically consequential: think, for instance, of Patricia Williams's classic theorization of "the ideology of style" in legal scholarship.[7]

As others have already noted, this anxiety about "the way we read now," for all its rejection of subtext, seems to be symptomatic in its own right of the current institutional context of literary study, especially demands for austerity, instrumental knowledge, and "relevance."[8] Meanwhile, analogous but distinct debates within queer studies have tackled the political valences of "historicist" versus "presentist" work, while also offering competing definitions of these central terms.[9] What queer scholarship has most fruitfully added, I want to suggest, is the insight that this debate is not just about the politics of history, but rather about the politics of *time*. Thus, I draw from this work a focus on temporality both as a malleable effect of text, figure, and performance and as an epistemology, and I take up Elizabeth Freeman's notion of "temporal drag" as "an excess . . . of the signifier 'history' " that draws on "all the associations that the word 'drag' has with retrogression, delay, and the pull of the past on the present."[10] For Freeman, what "temporal drag" offers us as a method is "the interesting threat that the genuine *past*-ness of the past—its opacity and illegibility, its stonewalling in the face of our most cherished theoretical paradigms—sometimes makes to the political present."[11]

I therefore end this book with a foray into anachronism that is, I will argue, also a kind of perverse historicism, arguing for the vitality of avowedly political literary historicism as a self-reflexive method, even as I also share many of the sympathies animating contemporary critiques of historicism. If such a method seems old-fashioned, I want to suggest (following Freeman's interest in the sometimes surprising political and theoretical effects of the dowdy, the unfashionable, and the apparently retrograde) that in at least some political and intellectual contexts, this is precisely its strength. In what follows, I read a crucial text from the early 1980s both in the "historical context" of its own moment as well as from the vantage point of the eighteenth century, in order to show these moments (and more) coalescing as an ongoing history of the present. I don't claim that this is of universal intellectual or political utility, or that political and intellectual utility always coincide with each other. But I do want to suggest that in the very specific context of policing and police violence in the contemporary United States, our legal, political, interpretive, and narrative horizons are frequently radically limited to the present and the immediate future—think, for instance, of the legal standards for "reasonable" force on the part of a police officer as established in *Graham v. Connor* (1989): "The 'reasonableness' of a particular use of force must be judged from the perspective of a reasonable officer on the scene, rather than with the 20/20 vision of hindsight."[12] This "reasonableness" is explicitly limited to a decontextualized instant in time, radically limited to the perspective of a police officer: "The calculus of reasonableness must embody allowance for the fact that police officers are often forced to make split-second judgments—in circumstances that are tense, uncertain, and rapidly evolving—about the amount of force that is necessary in a particular situation."[13] Police invokes a realm of anticipation and futurity, and in this case, that speculative futurity is what legally legitimates violence. In the face of futurity's potential limitlessness, the past—its alterity, its accessibility only through incomplete mediation, its limitation to what was rather than the limitlessness of what might be (even as "what was" can never be known completely)—can be a source of resistance, a "drag" on the present, a refusal to make "split-second judgments" of what seems necessary.

In 1982, George L. Kelling and James Q. Wilson published an article in the *Atlantic Monthly* whose profound consequences for policing and incarceration continue to reverberate today. In "Broken Windows: The Police and Neighborhood Safety," Kelling and Wilson advocated a retrenchment against what they saw as a prevailing trend of restrictions on discretionary police power in the name of civil liberties. Their advocacy of what they term "order-maintenance" policing, underpinned by what would come to be known (following their most vivid metaphor) as "broken-windows theory," proved enormously influential for police practice and the politics of law enforcement for decades to come.[14] At its simplest, Kelling and Wilson's vision is one of anticipatory, preventive policing, in which police presence tends the social, moral, and physical order of the community by attempting to prevent the smallest signs of disorder, whether those signs are vandalism or the mere presence of the homeless. The actual policies that emerged from this—most famously in New York under Mayor Rudolph Giuliani, who had campaigned on a law-and-order platform explicitly inspired by "Broken Windows"—translated this injunction against the appearance of disorder to intensifying arrests for small infractions, policies such as "stop-and-frisk," and an overall massive intensification of policing, especially of people of color.[15]

The literature on "broken-windows" policing is vast. What I seek to add to this existing conversation is modest but distinct: I read this essay as a literary critic, with particular focus on the essay's narrative temporality. "Broken Windows," after all, was immensely rhetorically successful: it proved remarkably persuasive as a narrative, as a collection of tropes, and particularly as the vehicle for the deployment of an extremely powerful master metaphor, the broken window. I therefore ask what the reading methods of literary criticism can help us understand about how this piece of writing both draws on and occludes colonial history, how the essay enlists its readers into the narrative temporality of policing, and what we might gain by thinking through historicism alongside a text that is ultimately deeply hostile to historical thinking.

Kelling and Wilson's basic theory of causality is this: visible disorder in a neighborhood will cause law-abiding citizens to feel afraid in public, which will make them more reluctant to call the police or use any other mechanism of enforcing social order. Meanwhile, visible disorder will cause potential criminals to feel *less* fear; the visible markers of disorder signal a lack of social or police surveillance, and thus imply to criminals that they are more likely to get away with a crime in such disorderly surroundings.[16] Disorder is signaled, for them, by both physical markers and the presence of disorderly people: "We tend to overlook another source of fear—the fear of being bothered by disorderly people. Not violent people, nor, necessarily, criminals, but disreputable or obstreperous or unpredictable people: panhandlers, drunks, addicts, rowdy teenagers, prostitutes, loiterers, the mentally disturbed."[17] The list Kelling and Wilson reproduce ought to be familiar by now: this is the form and content of centuries of vagrancy law, the kind of legal category and formal structure that allows for the apprehension of a wide array of people for extremely flexible reasons and thus endows the police with the power to act as they see fit to forestall future threat.

Kelling and Wilson use narrative vignettes to construct imaginative links between disorder and threat. The "broken window" is metonymic for a vast array of signifiers of urban disorder, and this metonymy flattens distinctions between the physical environment and the "disorderly" people encountered by those who move through this environment. For example, their narrative of a community's "breakdown" describes physical changes in the landscape (the growth of weeds, the existence of broken windows) and human behavior (teenagers gathering, people drinking in public) in the same register:

> We suggest that "untended" behavior also leads to the breakdown of community controls. A stable neighborhood of families who care for their homes, mind each other's children, and confidently frown on unwanted intruders can change, in a few years or even a few months, to an inhospitable and frightening jungle. A piece of property is abandoned, weeds grow up, a window is smashed. Adults stop scolding rowdy children; the children, emboldened, become more rowdy. Families move out, unattached adults move in. Teenagers gather in front of the corner store. The merchant asks them to move; they refuse. Fights occur. Litter accumulates. People start drinking in front of the grocery; in time, an inebriate slumps to the sidewalk and is allowed to sleep it off. Pedestrians are approached by panhandlers.[18]

This narrative is emblematic of the essay's rhetorical work as well as of the content of the argument: the claims take the form of broad statements of transhistorical, immutable sequences of events that transcend the particularity of time and place (after all, this is not any specific neighborhood in any specific historical moment). These narrative sequences accrue predictive force: signs of disorder, Kelling and Wilson argue, make threat more likely, and thus those signs of disorder ought to be eradicated in order to ensure the prevention of this future threat. This is the narrative temporality of vagrancy law, packaged in an argument *about* vagrancy: the final sign that a neighborhood has become a "jungle," after all, is the presence of "panhandlers."

Syntactically and stylistically, human behavior here is flattened into the landscape: "Fights occur. Litter accumulates." The formal repetition of syntactic parallelism ("weeds grow up," "families move out") implies an unspoken commonality and thus a theory of disorder: whether it's the appearance of people whose relational arrangements don't register as "family" or the markers of infrastructural neglect, all of these things signify equally as "disorder," and all work together to formulate a diffuse target for discretionary policing. When the imagined threat (and thus appropriate target for policing) encompasses an entire space, then the implicit demand is for policing unrestrained and flexible enough to secure all elements of this space—indeed, this, too, is a familiar claim, reminiscent of Patrick Colquhoun's late eighteenth-century assertions that intensive surveillance of the London docks would secure the wealth, resources, and relations of labor that held together an entire empire.

Here, as in early modern and eighteenth-century vagrancy laws, parataxis does crucial ideological work. What, after all, is the connection between any two adjacent sentences in this narrative? These signs of disorder follow each other, but their relationship is often nonsequential: "A piece of property is abandoned, weeds grow up, a window is smashed. Adults stop scolding rowdy children; the children, emboldened, become more rowdy." Within each sentence is an implication of causality (the weeds grow *because* the property is abandoned, the children are rowdy *because* they are not scolded), but what is the relation between the window and the children? And why does the paragraph leave this relation implicit, one of adjacency and not explanation? I want to suggest that this has to do with narrative temporality: it's an insistent present with an anticipatory stance toward a future, but not such a clear narrative progression that we see the future definitely unfold as the effects produced by causes that preexisted it. Instead, the future here inhabits the realm of close anticipation: it is what we watch for, what we imagine, and what we speculate, but it is not so concrete as to be tied down into taking any one form or bearing any clear causal explanation. We anticipate that abandoned property might appear, and then rowdy children, but instead of asserting any specific chain of events that might definitively name the rowdy children as an effect of the abandoned property, the text refuses any possibility of material explanation and instead keeps both the abandoned property and the abandoned children in the realm of the anticipated, the feared, the not-yet-happening and yet imminently threatening: in other words, the proper realm of police. This narrative form thus echoes the contemporary ideological commitments of what Bernard Harcourt terms "neoliberal penality": the evacuation of the political legitimacy of state power from all realms except the penal.[19] If welfare and subsistence are no longer regarded as legitimate venues for state intervention, then it makes sense to tell a story that doesn't ask *why* the "panhandlers" here have no other means of subsistence and what material link, if any, this predicament might have to the abandoned property—after all, these questions occupy the realm of welfare, not security. Instead, the story simply invokes all of these problems as forms of threat and disorder that can be relegated to the police alone.

Narrative temporality is crucial to the rhetorical success of the argument. The form of this description, for instance, occludes any avenue for thinking historically—even on the smallest time-scales—about the events described here. "Property is abandoned." By whom? Why? Is the property in question a speculative investment, left vacant on purpose by absent owners? Or is the property a home whose owners can no longer afford it? Why can't they afford to stay? The passive voice and the present tense, combined with the piece's curious mix of vivid description and vague generality, present the story as a parable: an infinitely portable illustration of deep, transhistorical truths. The avowedly race-neutral narrative—a neutrality that Kelling and Wilson defend later in the article, when they invoke the "hope" that police "do not become the agents of neighborhood bigotry" but admit that they "can offer no wholly satisfactory answer to this important question"—relegates the role of race to "neighborhood bigotry," thus obscuring the long racialized history of the very categories of "disorder" and "criminality" themselves.[20]

Of course, to present this story of urban decline as ahistorical in 1982 was almost comically overdetermined in its disavowal of its own deep historicity. This account of decline begins with abandoned property and ends with "panhandlers," and yet while this trajectory ought to ask us to consider the fairly obvious material connection between, say, housing and homelessness, Kelling and Wilson consider this a narrative of "the breakdown of community controls"—an explanation that refuses any historicity to what was in fact regarded *at the time* as a historically unprecedented "homelessness crisis."[21] What is remarkable about "Broken Windows" is the insistently ahistorical description of a set of phenomena that they link narratively, yet refuse to name as a historical moment of "urban crisis" more broadly—even as precisely this combination of phenomena registered as historical "crisis" at the time.[22] Of course, the argument—that signs of urban "disorder" are caused by the breakdown of "community controls"—depends on keeping the focus of cause and effect insistently on the scale of the "community," and not on larger political or economic forces that may be in evidence here, such as the economic crises that offered such fertile ground for neoliberal critiques of Keynesianism to flourish, or indeed mass incarceration itself, which, as Heather Ann Thompson argues, was already starting to impact American cities and thus worsen the crises that it was purported to combat.[23] It enlists its readers to inhabit a temporality as close and constricted as its spatial scale: a present shot through with frightening glimpses of an anticipated and imminent future—clear enough to justify immediate action, but inchoate enough to keep the targets of that action not yet fully determined.

The narrative form of the passage illustrating neighborhood decline seems to beg for precisely the move of "ideology critique" that Felski suggests we ought to be done with, and indeed, my reading here can certainly sound like a replication of a Jamesonian template so extreme as to totter at the edge of self-parody: in essence, the narrative here is persuasive fiction that represses the historical real, which nonetheless reappears within the text as symptom. But while I'm sympathetic to the critical desire for something other than paranoid reading as routinized procedure—after all, this conclusion *does* seem fairly obvious to a literary critic, and I do, in other contexts, want to resist a reduction of "historicity" to positivist empiricism that fights fiction with facts—I also want to note the degree to which Kelling and Wilson's narrative was wholeheartedly embraced by readers *as fact* for decades, and I want to make the case that we still sometimes need to marshal historical interpretation and explanation in order to, as Emily Hodgson Anderson argues, model the forms of reading that we hope to teach.[24] Critique of the premises of "Broken Windows" has only been visible in mainstream political discourse for the past decade or so, thanks mostly to the tireless work of prison-abolitionist organizing and thought that was regarded, until quite recently, as utterly relegated to the fringe of political discourse.[25] At the same time, of course, Best and Marcus aren't entirely wrong when they ask whether the unmasking of ideology alone is really all that useful. There are, by now, plenty of empirical critiques of "Broken Windows." Literary critics are less well equipped than scholars in other disciplines to debunk this theory on an empirical level, but we are well trained to explicate why this piece of writing was so persuasive in the first place; as Carrie Hyde argues, literary method is well attuned to help explain "the concrete historical impact that words so often have—even when their literal claims are misleading or manifestly untrue."[26]

The timelessness of the "problems" that Kelling and Wilson present are, ironically, rhetorically bolstered by their rare foray into historical thinking—and this happens through their nostalgia for vagrancy laws and the model of police they authorized. Kelling and Wilson call for a return to an earlier model of policing that emphasizes anticipatory prevention of threat rather than the investigation of crimes already committed; as they state approvingly: "From the earliest days of the nation, the police function was seen primarily as that of a night watchman: to maintain order against the chief threats to order—fire, wild animals, and disreputable behavior."[27] For Kelling and Wilson, the ideal vehicle for such discretion is the revival of vagrancy law. It's no coincidence that vagrancy is everywhere in this essay, from the assertion that "the unchecked panhandler is, in effect, the first broken window" to their description of disorderly people: "panhandlers, drunks, addicts, rowdy teenagers, prostitutes, loiterers, the mentally disturbed."[28] Vagrancy law offers them a model for policing more generally: "Until quite recently in many states, and even today in some places, the police made arrests on such charges as 'suspicious person' or 'vagrancy' or 'public drunkenness'—charges with scarcely any legal meaning. These charges exist not because society wants judges to punish vagrants or drunks but because it wants an officer to have the legal tools to remove undesirable persons from a neighborhood when informal efforts to preserve order in the streets have failed."[29] In this sense, their historical interpretation of vagrancy law is correct: it did indeed develop as a catchall category that was ultimately more useful in allowing wide discretionary leeway for policing than it was in naming or constraining any one specific population or type of behavior. And as Risa Goluboff argues, the legal challenges to vagrancy law that arose in the twentieth century—culminating in *Papachristou*—were indeed challenges to police authority more broadly.[30]

Kelling and Wilson's invocation of policing as it existed "from the earliest days of the nation" casts police itself as a timeless force, attempting to regain equilibrium in its fight against the equally timeless forces of "disorder." From the vantage point of the eighteenth century, however, this reciprocal construction of police and disorder is anything but timeless;

instead, from the perspective of this past, we can see how the presumed legitimacy of police as a mode of governance was built, debated, bolstered, and challenged with explicit reference to the forces that shaped it: capitalism, empire, slavery, settler colonialism. The legitimacy of police had to be constructed and defended—politically, legally, affectively, and in the everyday practice that rendered it habit for those countless individuals who played a part in its legal development. The police were never inevitable. And yet policing here, as in so many other places, takes on an air of unquestioned necessity. This happens not only in the content of the argument, but also in the aesthetic choices of the writers, and this is something that literary history equips us to see: after all, what I've argued throughout this book is that literary, imaginative, and aesthetic texts played crucial roles in both constructing and challenging the legitimacy of police in the century before the establishment of the modern metropolitan police force. At the same time, "Broken Windows" both drew on this long history and also worked as a powerful agent in its own specific historical moment; what Kelling and Wilson actively helped construct was not just a steady continuation of legal practices stretching back to "the earliest days of the nation," but rather a form of mass incarceration unprecedented in its scale and scope.[31]

From vagrancy statutes to the stories that make up "Broken Windows," expansive discretionary power is granted through implication, through what is not narrated or specified, through rhetorical adjacency that implies causality but shies away from pinning down causality in any material way. The future tense is enormously productive for police; designating people or populations as the sources of potential future threat calls for discretionary power equally resistant to limitation.[32] As Ravit Reichman argues, the *Graham* standard for reasonable force, in invoking the legal fiction of the "reasonable person," makes use of "reasonableness" not as a knowable mental state, but as an affect encoded in formal properties of language: "Reasonableness . . . has a tense; its story may be told retrospectively, but its tense is always the present."[33] The eighteenth-century texts I have assembled in this book may not be able to tell us in any great detail about the alternate futures foreclosed by the narrative form of immediate, imminent threat and the mode of governance it authorizes. However, what they *can* tell us is something of value: the vast scope of affective, conceptual, and material reinvention needed in order to make something else thinkable.

If that sounds pessimistic, I don't mean it to be. Instead, I join Crystal Bartolovich in calling for humanists "to pay attention—as did Milton, who never shied away from big questions—to *scale,* one of the keywords conjured up by the current crisis of the humanities as we are enjoined to 'scale back.' "[34] If Best and Marcus entertain doubts about the political efficacy of interpretive work and call instead for a renewed humility in the face of the text, then Bartolovich argues that such a stance "mistakes the constraints that produce the effect of apparent insignificance of political modes of reading for constraints of thought—of theory and method—when such constraints actually derive from the intransigence of material social structures, which bring us back to the issue of scale."[35] Rather than scale back, she argues, we ought instead to be "asserting the importance of humanistic inquiry to the most pressing problems facing our planet."[36] If, for Love or Felski, such a stance constitutes a self-congratulatory, even embarrassing elevation of the critic to the status of hero, I would argue that it need not—and that indeed, the best work enacting the past's "drag" on the present takes a very different view of both textual and critical agency than the caricature of heroism implies.

In other words, we don't need a heroic critic to enact the past's "temporal drag" on police's futurities; instead, as I hope I have shown, this friction is already there in the historical archive. In her own engagement with another, related archive of vagrancy, Saidiya Hartman demonstrates just how much this archive can bend time and space if we only turn our attention to what's already in it. For Hartman, the records generated by the use of vagrancy laws in early twentieth-century Harlem yield not only an account of ongoing racial histories of police, but also a "speculative history of the wayward" in her "critical fabulation" of the life and everyday revolution of a woman named Esther Brown:

> This speculative history of the wayward is an effort to narrate the open rebellion and beautiful experiment produced by young women in the emergent ghetto, a form of racial enclosure that succeeded the plantation. . . . State violence, surveillance, and detention produce the archival traces and institutional records that inform the reconstruction of these lives; but desire and the want of something better decide the contours of the telling.

> The narrative emulates the errant path of the wayward and moves from one story to another by way of encounter, chance meeting, proximity, and the sociality created by enclosure.[37]

As Hartman reveals in her account of the deep historical sedimentation of twentieth-century vagrancy laws and their racialized deployment, the legal regimes that constructed the archives of Esther Brown's encounters with the state reach forward and back in time: "Not quite two centuries after the conspiracy to burn down New York was hatched at a black-and-tan dive called Hughson's Tavern, black assembly and the threat of tumult still made New York's ruling elite quake in fear. The state was as intent on preventing the dangers and consequences posed by *Negroes assembled in a riotous manner.*"[38] But Hartman's determination to narrate "the forms of life" archived as crime also opens space to imagine affiliations across time that exceed this archive's governing logics. In opening up the past as a place of speculation, desire, and affective attachment, she takes an archive built upon an insistence that there is one imminent future—one that must be prevented—and she forces this archive to say something else instead. Thus, in allowing "the want and the desire for something better" to structure her narrative, she is not proposing the aesthetic as the savior that might redeem us all from the law; rather, she reveals the legal archive itself to be engaged in aesthetic and affective projects of its own, and calls for a critical method that can engage with it and transform it within that terrain.

The long history of vagrancy law, for Hartman, is both its own moral undoing—that is, it is the historical link that renders Esther Brown's arrest most clearly apprehensible as the afterlife of slavery—as well as an opening that creates "wayward," revolutionary, and "beautiful" collectivities across time, reminiscent of Carolyn Dinshaw's invocation of the "touch across time" as a mode of affectively charged and avowedly political queer historiography.[39] The very historical persistence of this category, after all, is also what might open up a throughline from Esther Brown back in time to others about whom the legal archive discloses even less: for instance, the four black women named Catharine Davers, Mary Brown, Ann Duffield, and Rebecca Nailor who were arrested for vagrancy in Philadelphia on February 24, 1791, and charged with "riotously

Assembling at the House of Pompey Carpenter and disturbing the Neighbourhood."[40] Hartman calls on us to want better for them, too, than what the archive gives us, and to understand this vast and "wayward" archive as a renewable incitement of "aspiration and longing" for futures other than what these pasts seem to—but do not—render inevitable.

I do not seek to posit literature, or aesthetic experience more broadly, as the ethical conscience that can redeem the law; this is not, after all, a role that "literature" has consistently played in the history I have narrated here.[41] But I do want to emphasize that legal practices, categories, institutions, and modes of common sense are forged in systems of interaction that include trope, figure, narrative, genre, and the historical evolution of interlocking publics and counterpublics enacted through the circulation of writing. Texts like Henry Fielding's *The Female Husband,* for instance, helped teach readers what security ought to feel like and what counts as a community's welfare, while texts like Equiano's *Interesting Narrative* or Mary Saxby's *Memoirs of a Female Vagrant* staged a more uneasy aporia between ethical claims to subsistence or safety and the failures of legal personhood to guarantee either. Legal and literary utterances do indeed, as Robert Cover has influentially stated, have radically different powers to enact material force in the world.[42] But as Carrie Hyde argues, the intertwined histories of legal and literary epistemologies also reveal "the power of the subjunctive to emplot and concretize possible histories—possibilities that reflect and transform cultural assumptions even if they are only imagined."[43] Texts and practices we currently know how to study as "literary" helped make the police as we know them thinkable—while at the same time producing a vast archive through and along with which we might make a future without them both more possible and more urgent to imagine.

# *NOTES*

## Introduction

1. Robert Nailer's Papers, Justices' Papers, Surrey, UK National Archives C 110/3.

2. Norma Landau, *The Justices of the Peace, 1679–1760* (Berkeley: University of California Press, 1984), 20–24; Joanna Innes, "Prisons for the Poor: English Bridewells, 1555–1800," in Francis Snyder and Douglas Hay (eds.), *Labour, Law, and Crime: An Historical Perspective* (London: Tavistock, 1987), 102–107; Lynn Hollen Lees, *The Solidarities of Strangers: The English Poor Laws and the People, 1700–1948* (Cambridge: Cambridge University Press, 1998), 46–50.

3. F. M. Dodsworth, "The Idea of Police in Eighteenth-Century England: Discipline, Reformation, Superintendence, c. 1780–1800," *Journal of the History of Ideas* 69.4 (2008): 586–587; J. M. Beattie, *Policing and Punishment in London, 1660–1750: Crime and the Limits of Terror* (Oxford: Oxford University Press, 2001), 77–82; Christopher Tomlins, *Law, Labor, and Ideology in the Early American Republic* (Cambridge: Cambridge University Press, 1993), 35–39.

4. The classic historical overview of early modern vagrancy law is A. L. Beier, *Masterless Men: The Vagrancy Problem in England, 1560–1640* (London: Methuen, 1985); for medieval predecessors of this legislation, see Anne Middleton, "Acts of Vagrancy: The C Version 'Autobiography' and the Statute of 1388," in *Written Work: Langland, Labor, and Authorship*, ed. Steven Justice and Kathryn Kerby-Fulton (Philadelphia: University of Pennsylvania Press, 1997), 208–318.

5. Lees, *The Solidarities of Strangers,* 46–51; Steve Hindle, *On the Parish? The Micro-Politics of Poor Relief in Rural England, c. 1550–1750* (Oxford: Clarendon Press, 2004); Landau, *The Justices of the Peace,* 24–25.

6. Nicholas Rogers, "Policing the Poor in Eighteenth-Century London: The Vagrancy Laws and their Administration," *Histoire Sociale / Social History* 24 (1991): 127–147; Rogers, "Vagrancy, Impressment and the Regulation of Labour in Eighteenth-Century Britain," in Paul Lovejoy and Nicholas Rogers (eds.), *Unfree Labour in the Development of the British Atlantic World* (Ilford, Essex: Frank Cass, 1994), 102–113.

7. Beier, *Masterless Men,* xxii; for the long afterlife of this feature of vagrancy law in the United States, see also Risa Goluboff, *Vagrant Nation: Police Power, Constitutional Change, and the Making of the 1960s* (New York: Oxford University Press, 2016), 27.

8. Markus Dirk Dubber, *The Police Power: Patriarchy and the Foundations of American Government* (New York: Columbia University Press, 2005), 62; William Blackstone, *Commentaries on the Laws of England* [1765–1769], 4 vols. (Chicago: University of Chicago Press, 1974), 4:162.

9. Legal historians have long noted the importance of police in laying the colonial foundations for early American law; see, for instance, William J. Novak, *The People's Welfare: Law & Regulation in Nineteenth-Century America* (Berkeley: University of California Press, 1996); and Christopher Tomlins, *Law, Labor, and Ideology in the Early American Republic* (Cambridge: Cambridge University Press, 1993), 35–59.

10. Sally Hadden, *Slave Patrols: Law and Violence in Virginia and the Carolinas* (Cambridge: Harvard University Press, 2001), 58–59; Bradley J. Nicholson, "Legal Borrowing and the Origins of Slave Law in the British Colonies," *American Journal of Legal History* 38.1 (1994): 38–54.

11. See, for instance, Abigail Swingen, *Competing Visions of Empire: Labor, Slavery, and the Origins of the British Atlantic Empire* (New Haven: Yale University Press, 2015); Mark Netzloff, *England's Internal Colonies: Class, Capital, and the Literature of Early Modern English Colonialism* (Basingstoke: Palgrave Macmillan, 2003).

12. Mary Sarah Bilder, *The Transatlantic Constitution: Colonial Legal Culture and the Empire* (Cambridge: Harvard University Press, 2008).

13. Michel Foucault, *Discipline and Punish: The Birth of the Prison* [1975], tr. Alan Sheridan (New York: Pantheon Books, 1977); John Bender, *Imagining the Penitentiary: Fiction and the Architecture of Mind in Eighteenth-Century England* (Chicago: University of Chicago Press, 1987); D. A. Miller, *The Novel and the Police* (Berkeley: University of California Press, 1988).

14. Lees, *The Solidarities of Strangers,* 48; see also Walter J. King, "Vagrancy and Local Law Enforcement: Why Be a Constable in Stuart Lancashire?" *The Historian* 42.2 (1980): 264–283.

15. Middleton, "Acts of Vagrancy"; Linda Woodbridge, *Vagrancy, Homelessness, and English Renaissance Literature* (Champaign: University of Illinois Press, 2001); and Patricia Fumerton, *Unsettled: The Culture of Mobility and the Working Poor in Early Modern England* (Chicago: University of Chicago Press, 2006).

16. Woodbridge, *Vagrancy, Homelessness, and English Renaissance Literature*, 3–10; Kathleen Pories, "The Intersection of Poor Laws and Literature in the Sixteenth Century: Fictional and Factual Categories," in Constance C. Relihan (ed.), *Framing Elizabethan Fictions: Contemporary Approaches to Early Modern Narrative Prose* (Kent, OH: The Kent State University Press, 1996), 17–40.

17. Gary Lee Harrison, *Wordsworth's Vagrant Muse: Poetry Poverty, and Power* (Detroit: Wayne State University Press, 1994); Celeste Langan, *Romantic Vagrancy: Wordsworth and the Simulation of Freedom* (Cambridge: Cambridge University Press, 1995); Toby Benis, *Romanticism on the Road: The Marginal Gains of Wordsworth's Homeless* (Basingstoke: Macmillan, 2000); and Quentin Bailey, *Wordsworth's Vagrants: Police, Prisons, and Poetry in the 1790s* (Farnham: Ashgate, 2011).

18. Fumerton, *Unsettled*, xx.

19. Adam Smith, *Lectures on Justice, Police, Revenue, and Arms*, ed. Edwin Cannan (Oxford: Clarendon Press, 1896), 3.

20. For both etymology and a sense of the broad meanings of "police," see "police, n." *Oxford English Dictionary Online* (accessed August 2018).

21. Jonas Hanway, *The Defects of Police the Cause of Immorality* (London: J. Dodsley, 1775), xx.

22. Patrick Colquhoun, *A General View of the Depredations Committed on the West-India and Other Property in the Port of London* (London: H. Baldwin, 1799), 5.

23. David G. Barrie, "Policing Before the Police in the Eighteenth Century: British Perspectives in a European Context," in Paul Knepper and Anja Johanson (eds.), *The Oxford Handbook of the History of Crime and Criminal Justice* (Oxford: Oxford University Press, 2016), 435–455.

24. Charles de Secondat, Baron de Montesquieu, *The Spirit of the Laws*, trans. Thomas Nugent (London: Crowder, Ware, and Payne, 1777), 2:172–173.

25. Hanway, *Defects of Police*, 7; David Taylor, *The New Police in Nineteenth-Century England: Crime, Conflict, and Control* (Manchester: Manchester University Press, 1997), 16–17; F. M. Dodsworth, "Introduction," *The Making of the Modern Police, 1780–1914*, vol. 1 (London: Pickering & Chatto, 2014), xxv–xxxiv.

26. William Cobbett, *Parliamentary History of England*, vol. 25 (London: Longman, 1815), 910.

27. Cobbett, *Parliamentary History of England*, 900, 889.

28. Novak, *The People's Welfare*, 13.

29. Bryan Wagner, *Disturbing the Peace: Black Culture and the Police Power After Slavery* (Cambridge: Harvard University Press, 2009), 3–21.

30. For more on the foundational undefinability of police, see Wagner, *Disturbing the Peace*, 7–20; Markus Dubber and Marina Valverde, "Introduction: Perspectives on the Power and Science of Police," in Dubber and Valverde (eds.), *The New Police Science: The Police Power in Domestic and International Governance* (Stanford: Stanford University Press, 2006), 1–16; and Gregoire Chamayou, "Fichte's Passport: A Philosophy of the Police," trans. Kieran Aarons, *Theory & Event* 16.2 (2013): n.p.

31. Micol Seigel, *Violence Work: State Power and the Limits of Police* (Durham: Duke University Press, 2018), 6.

32. For the distinction between texts that enact legal force and those that do not, and the stakes of this distinction for literary study, see Robert Cover, "Violence and the Word," *Yale Law Journal* 95 (1986): 1601–1629.

33. Donna T. Andrew, *Philanthropy and Police: London Charity in the Eighteenth Century* (Princeton: Princeton University Press, 1989). See also Steve Hindle, *On the Parish? The Micropolitics of Poor Relief in Rural England, c. 1550–1750* (Oxford: Oxford University Press, 2004).

34. Joanna Innes, "Prisons for the Poor," 42. See also J. M. Beattie, *Crime and the Courts in England 1660–1800* (Princeton: Princeton University Press, 1986), 18.

35. For the multivalence of "idleness" in eighteenth-century Britain and its colonies, see Sarah Jordan, *The Anxieties of Idleness: Idleness in Eighteenth-Century British Literature and Culture* (Lewisburg: Bucknell University Press, 2003).

36. A. O. Hirschman, *The Passions and the Interests: Political Arguments for Capitalism Before Its Triumph* (Princeton: Princeton University Press, 1977).

37. Hirschman, *The Passions and the Interests*, 52–54.

38. Adam Smith, *The Wealth of Nations* [1776], ed. Edwin Cannan (New York: Modern Library, 2000), 14, 15. See pp. 156–163 for the discussion of vagrancy law.

39. Bernard Harcourt, *The Illusion of Free Markets: Punishment and the Myth of Natural Order* (Cambridge: Harvard University Press, 2011), 48–49.

40. Karl Marx, *Economic and Philosophic Manuscripts of 1844*, ed. Dirk Struik (New York: International Publishers, 1980), 120–121; emphasis original. The original German reads: "Die Nationalökonomie kennt daher nicht den unbeschäftigten Arbeiter, den Arbeitsmenschen, soweit er sich außer diesem Arbeitsverhältnis befindet. Der Spitzbube, Gauner, Bettler, der unbeschäftigte, der verhungernde, der elende und verbrecherische Arbeitsmensch sind *Gestalten*, die nicht *für sie*, sondern nur für andre Augen, für die des Arztes, des Richters, des Totengräbers und Bettelvogts etc. existieren, Gespenster außerhalb ihres Reichs" (Karl Marx and Friedrich Engels, *Werke*, vol. 40 [Berlin: Dietz Verlag, 1968], 523–524).

41. Social historians have long understood the importance of vagrancy law for the maintenance of hierarchies of status and race in the early modern and eighteenth-century Atlantic world; recent work includes Peter Linebaugh and Markus Rediker, *The Many-Headed Hydra: Sailors, Slaves, and Commoners and the Hidden History of the Revolutionary Atlantic* (Boston: Beacon Press, 2000); David Hitchcock, *Vagrancy in English Culture and Society, 1650–1750* (London: Bloomsbury, 2016); Jen Manion, *Liberty's Prisoners: Carceral Culture in Early America* (Philadelphia: University of Pennsylvania Press, 2015); Kristin O'Brassill-Kulfan, "'Vagabonds and Paupers': Race and Illicit Mobility in the Early Republic," *Pennsylvania History: A Journal of Mid-Atlantic Studies* 83.4 (2016): 443–469.

42. Here, I am particularly influenced by Bryan Wagner's trenchant discussion of vagrancy and the police power in *Disturbing the Peace*, 39–42.

43. Beattie, *Crime and the Courts,* 18; Lees, *The Solidarities of Strangers,* 19–24, 48–58; Innes, "Prisons for the Poor," 100–102.

44. Paul Slack, *Poverty and Policy in Tudor and Stuart England* (London: Longman, 1988), 92, 127–128.

45. Vagrant pass, Robert Nailer's Papers, C 110/3, UK National Archives.

46. John Torpey, *The Invention of the Passport: Surveillance, Citizenship, and the State* (Cambridge: Cambridge University Press, 2000), 18.

47. Vagrant pass, Robert Nailer's Papers, TNA C 110/3.

48. Ruth Paley (ed.), *Justice in Eighteenth-Century Hackney: The Justicing Notebook of Henry Norris and the Hackney Petty Sessions Book* (London: London Record Society, 1991), 413, British History Online (accessed August 3, 2018).

49. See Lees, *The Solidarities of Strangers,* 46–58, for more on the specific procedures through which magistrates could expel those found likely to become chargeable.

50. Naomi Tadmor, "The Settlement of the Poor and the Rise of the Form in England, c. 1662–1780," *Past and Present* 236 (2017): 53–54.

51. James Raven, *Publishing Business in Eighteenth-Century England* (Woodbridge, Suffolk: Boydell and Brewer, 2014), 5.

52. Tadmor, "Settlement," 48.

53. Tadmor, "Settlement," 95.

54. Raven, *Publishing Business,* 48.

55. Raven, *Publishing Business,* 76–78.

56. John Mennes, *Recreation for Ingenious Headpeeces, or a Pleasant Grove for their Wits to Walk In* (London: John Stafford, 1665), Q2r. The poems were tracked with assistance from Dick Higgins, *Pattern Poetry: Guide to an Unknown Literature* (Albany: SUNY Press, 1987), 99–100.

57. In *Police Aesthetics,* Cristina Vatulescu theorizes an analogous interplay between practices of policing and aesthetic forms; while many of the specific practices and forms at issue in her study of Eastern European surveillance regimes during the Cold War are necessarily quite different from those I investigate here, I nonetheless draw on her powerful methodological insight that policing and literary aesthetics can meet in the realm of form as well as in the realm of content (Vatulescu, *Police Aesthetics: Literature, Film, and the Secret Police in Soviet Times* [Stanford: Stanford University Press, 2010]).

58. George Crabbe, "The Parish Register" (1807), in Crabbe, *The Complete Poetical Works,* vol. 1, ed. Norma Dalrymple-Champneys and Arthur Pollard (Oxford: Clarendon Press, 1988).

59. Daniel Defoe, *The Fortunes and Misfortunes of the Famous Moll Flanders* [1722], ed. David Blewett (New York: Penguin Classics: 1989), 43. Hereafter cited parenthetically.

60. Jeannine DeLombard, *In the Shadow of the Gallows: Race, Crime, and American Civic Identity* (Philadelphia: University of Pennsylvania Press, 2012), 1–11.

61. Catherine Gallagher, *Nobody's Story: The Vanishing Acts of Women Writers in the Marketplace, 1670–1820* (Berkeley: University of California Press, 1994).

62. Gabriel Cervantes, "Convict Transportation and Penitence in *Moll Flanders*," *ELH* 78.2 (2011): 315–336.

63. For more on the dynamic of the rogue protagonist who becomes an entrepreneurial subject of empire, see Srinivas Aravamudan, "Subjects/Sovereigns/Rogues," *Eighteenth-Century Studies* 40.3 (2007): 457–465; Betty Joseph, "The Political Economy of the English Rogue," *The Eighteenth Century: Theory and Interpretation* 55.2–3 (2014): 175–191; as well as my own reading of Richard Head's *The English Rogue* in Chapter 1.

64. I discuss these uses of vagrancy law in much greater detail in Chapters 4 and 5.

65. Karl Marx, *Capital*, vol. 1, trans. Ben Fowkes (New York: Penguin, 1990), 885–896.

66. E. P. Thompson, *The Making of the English Working Class* (New York: Pantheon, 1963); Raymond Williams, *The Country and the City* (New York: Oxford University Press, 1973); John Barrell, *The Dark Side of the Landscape: the Rural Poor in English Painting, 1730–1840* (Cambridge: Cambridge University Press, 1980). The social history of poverty in eighteenth-century England by now constitutes a vast field of scholarship; major works include, for instance, K. D. M. Snell, *Annals of the Labouring Poor: Social Change and Agrarian England, 1660–1900* (Cambridge: Cambridge University Press, 1985); Beier, *Masterless Men;* and Deborah Valenze, *The First Industrial Woman* (Oxford: Oxford University Press, 1995).

67. Chi-ming Yang and Jordana [Jordy] Rosenberg, "Introduction: The Dispossessed Eighteenth Century," *The Eighteenth Century: Theory and Interpretation* 55.2–3 (2014): 138.

68. Cedric Robinson, *Black Marxism: The Making of the Black Radical Tradition* [1983] (Chapel Hill: University of North Carolina Press, 2000), 2.

69. Jodi Melamed, "Racial Capitalism," *Critical Ethnic Studies* 1.1 (2015): 77. See also Geraldine Heng's important critique of theories of race that identify racism as *only* a product of (capitalist) modernity (Heng, "The Invention of Race in the European Middle Ages I: Race Studies, Modernity, and the Middle Ages," *Literature Compass* 8.5 [2011]: 315–331).

70. Felicity Nussbaum and Laura Brown (eds.), *The New Eighteenth Century: Theory, Politics, English Literature* (London: Methuen, 1987); Brown, *Ends of Empire: Women and Ideology in Early Eighteenth-Century English Literature* (Ithaca: Cornell University Press, 1993); Srinivas Aravamudan, *Tropicopolitans: Colonialism and Agency, 1688–1804* (Durham: Duke University Press, 1999).

71. See, for instance, Suvir Kaul, *Poems of Nation, Anthems of Empire: English Verse in the Long Eighteenth Century* (Charlottesville: University of Virginia Press, 2001); Simon Gikandi, *Slavery and the Culture of Taste* (Princeton: Princeton University Press, 2011); Lynn Festa, *Sentimental Figures of Empire in Eighteenth-Century Britain and France* (Baltimore: Johns Hopkins University Press, 2006); Bridget Orr, *Empire on the English Stage, 1660–1714* (Cambridge: Cambridge University Press, 2001).

72. Roxann Wheeler, *The Complexion of Race: Categories of Difference in Eighteenth-Century British Culture* (Philadelphia: University of Pennsylvania Press, 2000), 5–6. See Also Katy Chiles, *Transformable Race: Surprising Metamorphoses in the Literatures of Early America* (Oxford: Oxford University Press, 2014).

73. Ann Laura Stoler, *Duress: Imperial Durabilities in Our Times* (Durham: Duke University Press, 2016), 239.

74. Stoler, *Duress,* 245.

75. Stuart Hall, "Race, Articulation and Societies Structured in Dominance" in UNESCO (ed.), *Sociological Theories: Race and Colonialism* (Paris: UNESCO, 1980), 338, 320.

76. Hall, "Race, Articulation and Societies Structured in Dominance," 341.

77. Sujata Iyengar, *Shades of Difference: Mythologies of Skin Color in Early Modern England* (Philadelphia: University of Pennsylvania Press, 2005), 174–176; John Morgan, "'Counterfeit Egyptians': The Construction and Implementation of a Criminal Identity in Early Modern England," *Romani Studies* 26.2 (2016): 105–128.

78. Iyengar, *Shades of Difference,* 176.

79. Morgan, "'Counterfeit Egyptians,' " 123.

80. 9 Eliz c 4, "An Act for Punishment of Rogues, Vagabonds, and Sturdie Beggers," (London: deputies of C. Barker, 1598), 1. For an overview of changes in vagrancy law before 1714, see Audrey Eccles, *Vagrancy in Law and Practice Under the Old Poor Law* (Abingdon: Ashgate, 2012), 1–5. The 1714 Vagrancy Act, which fully repealed the 1598 act, nonetheless preserved most of its definition of vagrancy, which remained fairly consistent until English vagrancy law was entirely overhauled in 1824 as part of the broader array of reform measures leading up to the New Poor Law of 1834. I use the terms "Gypsy" and "Egyptian" to name the ethnicized legal and imaginative category that appears in seventeenth- and eighteenth-century texts; vagrancy laws criminalizing "counterfeit Egyptians" targeted not only people who might today identify as Romani, but also a much wider array of people that exceeded any one actual or perceived ethnic identification or national origin.

81. Thomas Browne, *Pseudodoxia Epidemica, or, Enquiries into Very many Received Tenets and commonly presumed Truths,* 3rd ed. (London: for Nath[aniel] Ekins, 1658), 276. Sujata Iyengar contextualizes Browne's assertion here in the longstanding tropes of rogue literature, which associate Gypsies with disguise, fraud, and theatricality (173–174).

82. Browne, *Pseudodoxia Epidemica,* 284.

83. See Srinivas Aravamudan, *Tropicopolitans,* for the early modern and eighteenth-century ubiquity of this trope (1–4).

84. Robinson, *Black Marxism,* 3–4.

85. Browne, *Pseudodoxia Epidemica,* 274.

86. Browne, *Pseudodoxia Epidemica,* 273.

87. As Nikhil Pal Singh argues, the long afterlife of this open-endedness continues to enable the racialization of policing in the United States (Singh, "The Whiteness of Police," *American Quarterly* 66.4 [2014]: 1096).

88. *Compilation of the Laws of the State of Pennsylvania Relative to the Poor* (Philadelphia: Zachariah Poulson, 1796), 55–56.

89. Philadelphia Prison System, Vagrancy Dockets (Record Group 38.44), Philadelphia City Archives.

90. Jen Manion, *Liberty's Prisoners: Carceral Culture in Early America* (Philadelphia: University of Pennsylvania Press, 2015), 24–25; Kristin O'Brassill-Kulfan, "Vagabonds and Paupers: Race and Illicit Mobility in the Early Republic," *Pennsylvania History: A Journal of Mid-Atlantic Studies* 83.4 (2016): 444–469.

91. For the long afterlives of this structure of surveillance, see Simone Browne, *Dark Matters: On the Surveillance of Blackness* (Durham: Duke University Press, 2015), as well as my own more extended discussion of Browne's work in Chapter 5.

92. *Claypoole's Daily Advertiser,* March 8, 1792.

93. "Ned," 12/23/1791; "John," 12/23/1791; "Peter," 11/22/1791; "Tobias Leach," 1/27/1792; "Cato," 10/11/1791, Vagrancy Dockets, Philadelphia City Archives.

94. For more on the recording of racial classification in the records of criminal justice in Philadelphia, see Manion, *Liberty's Prisoners,* 132–133.

95. "Mark Warren," 11/3/1791; "Margaret Gillanor," 11/3/1791, Vagrancy Dockets, Philadelphia City Archives.

## Chapter 1. Atlantic Rogues

1. Richard Head, *The English Rogue Described, in the Life of Meriton Latroon, A Witty Extravagant* (London: Francis Kirkman, 1666), 38. Hereafter cited parenthetically. Note that the page numbering in this edition begins again from p. 1 twice throughout the book; it was most likely printed to be bound in three volumes but was bound instead as one.

2. This passage is lifted from Mateo Alemán's *Guzmán de Alfarache,* whose influence will be discussed at greater length below. The passage in James Mabbe's 1622 translation reads: "This was the first time, that I look't that Hereticke Necessity in the face: I knew him then by his Character, but afterwards I did better consider him by his effects. How many dishonest actions doth it venture on? what cruell imaginations doth it represent unto thee? what infamous things doth it sollicite? what disorders doth it drive thee into? and what impossibilities doth it not attempt?" (Alemán, *The Rogue, or the Life of Guzmán de Alfarache*, trans. James Mabbe [London: Constable and Co., 1924], 235).

3. Craig Dionne and Steve Mentz, "Introduction" to Dionne and Mentz (eds.), *Rogues and Early Modern English Culture* (Ann Arbor: University of Michigan Press, 2004), 7–8.

4. Richard Head, *The English Rogue* [1665], vol. 1 (London: Chatto, 1874), 59.

5. Paul Slack, *Poverty and Policy in Tudor and Stuart England* (London: Longman, 1988), 194. As Slack notes, sending vagrants to their place of settlement was already a common practice in the sixteenth and seventeenth centuries, but it was not formally codified in law until 1662.

6. Head, *The English Rogue* (1665), 60.

7. Peter Linebaugh, *The London Hanged: Crime and Civil Society in the Eighteenth Century* (Cambridge: Cambridge University Press, 1991), 119.

8. Linebaugh, *The London Hanged,* 122.

9. Linda Woodbridge, *Vagrancy, Homelessness, and English Renaissance Literature* (Urbana-Champagne: University of Illinois Press, 2001).

10. For the place of *The English Rogue* in the history of the picaresque and its adaptation into English, see Paul Salzman, *English Prose Fiction, 1558–1700: A Critical History* (Oxford: Oxford University Press, 1986), 205–207; and J. A. Garrido Ardila, "Origins and Definition of the Picaresque" and "The Picaresque Novel and the Rise of the English Novel," in Garrido Ardila (ed.), *The Picaresque Novel in Western Literature: From the Sixteenth Century to the Neopicaresque* (Cambridge: Cambridge University Press, 2015).

11. Barbara Fuchs, *The Poetics of Piracy: Emulating Spain in English Literature* (Philadelphia: University of Pennsylvania Press, 2013), 5–8.

12. Salzman, *English Prose Fiction*, 207.

13. Fuchs, *The Poetics of Piracy*, 32.

14. Kathleen Pories, "The Intersection of Poor Laws and Literature in the Sixteenth Century: Fictional and Factual Categories," in Constance Relihan (ed.), *Framing Elizabethan Fictions: Contemporary Approaches to Early Modern Narrative Prose* (Kent, OH: The Kent State University Press, 1996), 38. See also Woodbridge, *Vagrancy*, 4.

15. Woodbridge, *Vagrancy*, 4.

16. Patricia Fumerton, *Unsettled: The Culture of Mobility and the Working Poor in Early Modern England* (Chicago: University of Chicago Press, 2006), 33–36.

17. Leah Orr, "*The English Rogue:* Afterlives and Imitations, 1665–1741," *Journal for Eighteenth-Century Studies* 38.3 (2015): 361.

18. *The Irish Rogue: or, the Comical History of the Life and Actions of Teague O Divelley* (London: for George Conyers, [1690]); *The Dutch Rogue or, Guzman of Amsterdam* (London: A. M. for Gregory Hill, 1683); *The French Rogue* (London: by T. N. for Samuel Lowndes, 1672).

19. *The Spanish Rogue, or, The Life of Guzman de Alfarache* (London: for Andrew Thorncomb, 1685).

20. Srinivas Aravamudan, "Sovereigns/Subjects/Rogues," *Eighteenth-Century Studies* 40.3 (2007): 460.

21. Betty Joseph, "The Political Economy of the English Rogue," *The Eighteenth Century: Theory and Interpretation* 55.2–3 (2014): 178–79.

22. Joseph, "The Political Economy of the English Rogue," 186, 189.

23. Lennard Davis, *Factual Fictions: The Origins of the English Novel* (New York: Columbia University Press, 1983), 125.

24. Nancy Armstrong, *How Novels Think: The Limits of Individualism from 1719–1900* (New York: Columbia University Press, 2006), 48.

25. Anne Middleton, "Acts of Vagrancy: The C Version 'Autobiography' and the Statute of 1388," in *Written Work: Langland, Labor, and Authorship,* ed. Steven Justice and Kathryn Kerby-Fulton (Philadelphia: University of Pennsylvania Press, 1997), 243.

26. Middleton, "Acts of Vagrancy," 222.

27. For an overview of how early modern vagrancy legislation underpinned poor law throughout the eighteenth century, see Paul Slack, *Poverty and Policy in Tudor and Stuart England* (London: Longman, 1988), 127–128, 194.

28. 9 Eliz c 4, "An Act for Punishment of Rogues, Vagabonds, and Sturdie Beggers," [London: deputies of C. Barker, 1598], 1.

29. Karl Marx, *Capital: A Critique of Political Economy*, vol. 1, trans. Ben Fowkes (New York: Penguin, 1990), 885–886.

30. Marx, *Capital,* vol. 1, 896.

31. Marx, *Capital,* vol. 1, 792.

32. Ted McCormick, "Population: Modes of Seventeenth-Century Demographic Thought," in Philip J. Stern and Carl Wennerlind (eds.), *Mercantilism Reimagined: Political Economy in Early Modern Britain and Its Empire* (Oxford: Oxford University Press, 2014), 40, 33.

33. William Petty, *Treatise of Taxes and Contributions* [1662], in *The Economic Writings of Sir William Petty*, ed. Charles Henry Hull (Cambridge: Cambridge University Press, 1899), 7.

34. "Draft of a Response containing [a] scheme of methods for the Imployment of the Poor, 26 Oct 1697, proposed by Mr. Locke," National Archives CO 388/5, 232.

35. Emily Cockayne, *Hubbub: Filth, Noise, and Stench in England, 1660–1770* (New Haven: Yale University Press, 2007), 232–233.

36. Sophie Gee, *Making Waste: Leftovers and the Eighteenth-Century Imagination* (Princeton: Princeton University Press, 2010), 2, 43.

37. Gee, *Making Waste*, 2.

38. Alex Woloch, *The One vs. the Many: Minor Characters and the Space of the Protagonist in the Novel* (Princeton: Princeton University Press, 2003), 17.

39. Woloch, *The One vs. the Many*, 26–27; emphasis original.

40. Woloch, *The One vs. the Many*, 38.

41. Charles D'Avenant, *On the Plantation Trade* [1698], in *Select Dissertations on Colonies and Plantations* (London: W. Hay, 1775), 29. For the long history of figuring colonial "vents" for surplus population in the language of excrement from the body politic, see Mark Netzloff, *England's Internal Colonies: Class, Capital, and the Literature of Early Modern English Colonialism* (Basingstoke, Hampshire: Palgrave, 2003), 92–93.

42. Josiah Child, *The Nature of Plantations, and their Consequences to Great Britain, Seriously Considered* [1669], in *Select Dissertations on Colonies and Plantations,* 4.

43. Abigail Swingen, *Competing Visions of Empire: Labor, Slavery, and the Origins of the British Atlantic Empire* (New Haven: Yale University Press, 2015), 12.

44. Swingen, *Competing Visions of Empire,* 1, 14–15.

45. Alison Games, *Migration and the Origins of the English Atlantic World* (Cambridge: Harvard University Press, 2001), 15–17.

46. Games, *Migration,* 4.

47. "An Act for the better Releife of the Poore of this Kingdom," in *Statutes of the Realm,* vol. 5: *1628–80,* ed. John Raithby (London, 1819).

48. Swingen, *Competing Visions of Empire,* 25.

49. For more on the transportation of vagrants to the Americas, see Games, *Migration,* 15–16; and Susan Dwyer Amussen, *Caribbean Exchanges: Slavery and the Transformation of English Society, 1640–1700* (Chapel Hill: University of North Carolina Press, 2007), 26.

50. Michael Dalton, *The Countrey Justice: Containing the Practice of the Justice of the Peace as well in as out of their Sessions* (London: John Streater et al., 1666), 158.

51. See, for instance, "Certaine Propositions for the better accommodating the Forreigne Plantations with Servants reposted from the Committee to the Councill of Forreigne Plantations" [1664] (National Archives CO 324/1, 275–283), which called for the consistent transportation of "Sturdy Beggars as Gipsies and other incorrigible Rogues" as well as "poore and idle debauched persons" (278–279) in order to help populate Jamaica and other Caribbean colonies, "It being Universally agreed that people are the Foundacion and Improvement of all plantacions and that people are increased principally by sending of Servants thither" (275).

52. Simon P. Newman, "In Great Slavery and Bondage: White Labor and the Development of Plantation Slavery in British America," in Ignacio Gallup-Diaz, Andrew Shankman, and David J. Silverman (eds.), *Anglicizing America: Empire, Revolution, Republic* (Philadelphia: University of Pennsylvania Press, 2015), 68–70; Amussen, *Caribbean Exchanges,* 69.

53. Swingen, *Competing Visions of Empire,* 25.

54. For an overview of these depositions, see John Wareing, " 'Violently Taken Away or Cheatingly Duckoyed': The Illicit Recruitment in London of Indentured Servants for the American Colonies, 1645–1718," *The London Journal* 26.2 (2001): 7.

55. "Affidavits Against Spirits," National Archives CO 389/2, 14.

56. "Affidavits Against Spirits," 14.

57. "Affidavits Against Spirits," 17.

58. "Affidavits Against Spirits," 16.

59. "Affidavits Against Spirits," 13.

60. "Petition of Divers Merchants Planters and Masters of Shipps," July 13, 1664, National Archives CO 1/15 no. 31, 16.

61. "Certaine Propositions for the better accommodating the Forreigne Plantations with Servants reposted from the Committee to the Councill of Forreigne Plantations" [1664], National Archives CO 324/1, 275.

62. Wareing, " 'Violently Taken Away or Cheatingly Duckoyed,' " 1–22.

63. Wareing, " 'Violently Taken Away or Cheatingly Duckoyed,' " 9–10.

64. William Rawlin, *The Laws of Barbados, Collected in One Volume* (London: for William Rawlin, 1699), 93.

65. Justin Roberts, "Surrendering Surinam: The Barbadian Diaspora and the Expansion of the English Sugar Frontier, 1650–75," *William and Mary Quarterly* 73.2 (2016): 244. See also Swingen, *Competing Visions of Empire* for the broader context of competition between colonies.

66. Marcellus Rivers and Oxenbridge Foyle, *Englands Slavery, or Barbados Merchandize* [1659], in Carla Gardina Pestana and Sharon Salinger (eds.), *The Early English Caribbean, 1570–1700,* vol. 3 (London: Pichering & Chatto, 2014), 108.

67. Rivers and Foyle, *Englands Slavery,* 110.

68. Michal J. Rozbicki, "To Save Them from Themselves: Proposals to Enslave the British Poor, 1698–1755," *Slavery & Abolition* 22.2 (2001): 29–50.

69. Aphra Behn, *Oroonoko* [1688], ed. Janet Todd (New York: Penguin, 2003), 37.

70. Behn, *Oroonoko,* 69.

71. Child, *The Nature of Plantations,* 22.

72. Daniel Defoe, *Captain Singleton* [1720], ed. Shiv Kumar (Oxford: Oxford World's Classics, 1990), 1, 2–4.

73. Joseph, "The Political Economy of the English Rogue," 187.

74. Joseph, "The Political Economy of the English Rogue," 187.

75. John Gay, *The Beggar's Opera* [1728], ed. Bryan Loughrey and T. O. Treadwell (New York: Penguin Classics, 1986), 43.

76. Aravamudan, "Sovereigns/Subjects/Rogues," 458.

77. Aravamudan, "Sovereigns/Subjects/Rogues," 461.

78. Aravamudan, "Sovereigns/Subjects/Rogues," 460.

79. Walter Benjamin, "Critique of Violence," in *Walter Benjamin: Selected Writings,* vol. 1: *1913–1926,* ed. Marcus Bullock and Michael W. Jennings (Cambridge: Belknap Press of Harvard University Press, 1996), 241.

80. Benjamin, "Critique of Violence," 243.

81. Benjamin, "Critique of Violence," 242.

82. Benjamin, "Critique of Violence," 243.

83. Kate Loveman, "'A Life of Continu'd Variety': Crime, Readers, and the Structure of Defoe's *Moll Flanders,*" *Eighteenth-Century Fiction* 26.1 (2013): 9.

84. Gabriel Cervantes, "Episodic or Novelistic? Law in the Atlantic and the Form of Daniel Defoe's *Colonel Jack,*" *Eighteenth-Century Fiction* 24.2 (2011–2012): 247–277.

85. 9 Eliz c 4, "An Act for Punishment of Rogues, Vagabonds, and Sturdie Beggers," [London: deputies of C. Barker, 1598], 1.

86. Vagrancy Act 1714 (12 Ann. c. 23). For an overview of changes in vagrancy law before 1714, see Audrey Eccles, *Vagrancy in Law and Practice Under the Old Poor Law* (Abingdon: Ashgate, 2012), 1–5.

87. Peter Stallybrass, "Marx and Heterogeneity: Thinking the Lumpenproletariat," *Representations* 31 (1990): 70; Karl Marx, *The Eighteenth Brumaire of Louis Bonaparte,* ed. C. P. Dutt (New York: International Publishers, 1975), 75.

88. Stallybrass, "Marx and Heterogeneity," 72.

89. Slack, *Poverty and Policy,* 92.

90. Walter King, "Vagrancy and Local Law Enforcement: Why Be a Constable in Stuart Lancashire?," *The Historian* 42.2 (1980): 264–283.

91. Fumerton, *Unsettled,* xx.

92. Fumerton, *Unsettled,* 3.

93. Natasha Simonova, "Owning *The English Rogue:* Commerce and Reputation in Restoration Authorship," *Restoration* 40.1 (2016): 68–69.

94. Leah Orr, "*The English Rogue:* Afterlives and Imitations, 1665–1741," *Journal for Eighteenth-Century Studies* 38.3 (2015): 362.

95. Orr, "*The English Rogue*," 362.

96. Lisa Maruca, *The Work of Print: Authorship and the English Text Trades, 1660–1760* (Seattle: University of Washington Press, 2007), 67–68; Simonova, "Owning *The English Rogue*," 72.

97. Simonova, "Owning *The English Rogue*," 76–77.

98. Maruca, *The Work of Print,* 109–113.

99. Bryan Wagner, *Disturbing the Peace: Black Culture and the Police Power After Slavery* (Cambridge: Harvard University Press, 2009), 40.

## Chapter 2. The Novel and the Sexuality of Vagrancy

1. Jane Barker, *A Patch-Work Screen for the Ladies; or, Love and Virtue Recommended* (London: E. Curll, 1723), 100.

2. Barker, *A Patch-Work Screen for the Ladies,* 103.

3. Barker, *A Patch-Work Screen for the Ladies,* 103.

4. For a detailed account of such uses of vagrancy laws, see Lynn Hollen Lees, *The Solidarities of Strangers: The English Poor Laws and the People, 1700–1948* (Cambridge: Cambridge University Press, 1998), 51–57.

5. Donna T. Andrew, *Philanthropy and Police: London Charity in the Eighteenth Century* (Princeton: Princeton University Press, 1989), 25.

6. Robert Shoemaker, "Reforming the City: The Reformation of Manners Campaign in London, 1690–1738," in Lee Davidson, Tim Hitchcock, and Tim Keirn (eds.), *Stilling the Grumbling Hive: The Response to Social and Economic Problems in England, 1689–1750* (New York: St. Martin's Press, 1992), 106–108.

7. Steve Hindle, *On the Parish? The Micro-Politics of Poor Relief in Rural England, 1550–1750* (Oxford: Oxford University Press, 2006), 57; Lees, *The Solidarities of Strangers,* 57–58.

8. Hindle, *On the Parish?,* 225.

9. Dror Wahrman, *The Making of the Modern Self: Identity and Culture in Eighteenth-Century England* (New Haven: Yale University Press, 2004), 45–82.

10. William Blackstone, *Commentaries on the Laws of England* [1765–1769], 4 vols. (Chicago: University of Chicago Press, 1979), 4:162.

11. Markus Dirk Dubber, *The Police Power: Patriarchy and the Foundations of American Government* (New York: Columbia University Press, 2005), 3.

12. D. A. Miller, *The Novel and the Police* (Berkeley: University of California Press, 1988), 205.

13. For a thorough analysis of Fielding's intertwined legal and literary careers, see Lance Bertelsen, *Henry Fielding at Work: Magistrate, Businessman, Writer* (Basingstoke, Hampshire: Palgrave, 2000).

14. Jesper Gulddal, "Henry Fielding's Proposals for an Internal British Passport System," *ANQ* 27.4 (2014): 156.

15. Gulddal, "Henry Fielding's Proposals," 157.

16. John Bender, *Imagining the Penitentiary: Fiction and the Architecture of Mind in Eighteenth-Century* England (Chicago: University of Chicago Press, 1987), 166.

17. Scott MacKenzie, "'Stock the Parish with Beauties': Henry Fielding's Parochial Vision," *PMLA* 125.3 (2010): 606–621.

18. MacKenzie, "'Stock the Parish with Beauties,' " 607.

19. MacKenzie, "'Stock the Parish with Beauties,' " 611.

20. MacKenzie, "'Stock the Parish with Beauties,' " 618.

21. Until very recently, scholarship has been nearly unanimous in referring to Hamilton with female pronouns. In recent years, important new work in transgender studies has led to renewed historiographic reflection on gendered pronouns in scholarship. For a trans analysis of the category of "female husband," including reflection on pronoun usage by scholars, see in particular Jen Manion, *Female Husbands: A Trans History* (Cambridge: Cambridge University Press, 2020). In this chapter, I have chosen not to use gendered pronouns to refer to the historical Hamilton; my focus is ultimately on the process through which Hamilton's gender and sexuality were fictionalized, and I wish to leave multiple possibilities open for our understanding of the historical Hamilton's social and experiential gender.

22. Caroline Derry, "Sexuality and Locality in the Trial of Mary Hamilton, 'Female Husband,' " *King's Law Journal* 19.3 (2008): 600.

23. See Sheridan Baker, "Henry Fielding's *The Female Husband:* Fact and Fiction," *PMLA* 74.3 (1959): 213–224, for a detailed account of the text's sources as well as the history of its attribution to Fielding.

24. Henry Fielding, *The Female Husband* [1746], ed. Claude Jones (Liverpool: Liverpool University Press, 1960), 42. Hereafter cited parenthetically.

25. Terry Castle, "Matters Not Fit to Be Mentioned: Fielding's *The Female Husband,*" *ELH* 49.3 (1982): 610.

26. See, for instance, Emma Donoghue, *Passions Between Women: British Lesbian Culture, 1668–1801* (New York: Harper Perennial, 1996), 73–80; [Jack] Halberstam, *Female Masculinity* (Durham: Duke University Press, 1998), 50–53, 67; and Jill Campbell, *Natural Masques: Gender and Identity in Fielding's Plays and Novels* (Stanford: Stanford University Press, 1995), 55–60.

27. Fraser Easton, "Covering Sexual Disguise: Passing Women and Generic Constraint," *Studies in Eighteenth Century Culture* 35 (2006): 98. See also Lynn Friedli, "'Passing Women'—A Study of Gender Boundaries in the Eighteenth Century," in G. S. Rousseau and Roy Porter (eds.), *Sexual Underworlds of the Enlightenment* (Manchester: Manchester University Press, 1987), 234–260; and Theresa Braunschneider, "Acting the Lover: Gender and Desire in Narratives of Passing Women," *The Eighteenth Century: Theory and Interpretation* 45.3 (2004): 211–230.

28. Susan S. Lanser, *The Sexuality of History: Modernity and the Sapphic, 1565–1850* (Chicago: University of Chicago Press, 2014), 110–145.

29. On Henry Gould's involvement in the case see Derry, "Sexuality and Locality," 595–598, 614–616; and Baker, "Henry Fielding's *The Female Husband,*" 220.

30. Lance Bertelsen notes, for example, that vagrancy was the crime Fielding dealt with more than any other in his tenure as magistrate for Westminster and Middlesex (*Henry Fielding at Work,* 16).

31. Vagrancy Act, 1744, 17 Geo. II c. 5.

32. Henry Fielding, *Proposal for Making an Effectual Provision for the Poor* [1753], in *The Complete Works of Henry Fielding,* vol. 13, ed. William Ernest Henley (New York: Croscup & Sterling, 1902), 181.

33. Henry Fielding, *Enquiry into the Causes of the Late Increase of Robbers* (London: A. Millar, 1751), xiii.

34. Fielding, *Enquiry,* 85–86.

35. For an early discussion of the text's transgender potential, see Halberstam, *Female Masculinity,* 68–72. Jen Manion's *Female Husbands* offers the most comprehensive trans analysis to date of Hamilton's life and Fielding's fictionalization of it (17–33).

36. Greta LaFleur, "Sex and 'Unsex': Histories of Gender Trouble in Eighteenth-Century North America," *Early American Studies* 12.3 (2014): 478.

37. Fraser Easton, "Gender's Two Bodies: Women Warriors, Female Husbands, and Plebian Life," *Past and Present* 180 (2003): 131–174; Caroline Derry, "'Female Husbands,' Community and Courts in the Eighteenth Century," *The Journal of Legal History* 38.1 (2017): 54–79.

38. *The Female Soldier, or, The Surprising Life and Adventures of Hannah Snell* (London: for R. Walker, 1750), 7.

39. *The Life and Imaginations of Sally Paul* (London: for S. Hooper, 1760), 145. I am indebted to Susan Lanser for her attention to this text, which exists in only one known copy and has been very rarely studied; for more, see Lanser, *The Sexuality of History,* 163–166. For more on the Black Act and its place in the history of enclosure, customary rights, and class conflict, the classic account is E. P. Thompson, *Whigs and Hunters: The Origins of the Black Act* (New York: Pantheon Books), 1975.

40. "Adventures of a Female Husband," *London Magazine, or, Gentleman's Monthly Intelligencer,* vol. 29 (London: for R. Baldwin, 1760), 160.

41. "Extract of a Letter from Chester," *Pennsylvania Gazette,* July 16, 1752.

42. "Extract of a Letter from Chester."

43. "Extract of a Letter from Chester." I examine the connections between vagrancy and fugitivity at much greater length in Chapters 4 and 5.

44. Advertisement, *Pennsylvania Gazette,* February 27, 1753.

45. Advertisement, *Pennsylvania Gazette,* February 27, 1753.

46. Gwenda Morgan and Peter Rushton, "Fraud and Freedom: Gender, Identity, and Narratives of Deception Among the Female Convicts in Colonial America," *Journal for Eighteenth-Century Studies* 34.3 (2011): 347.

47. Clare A. Lyons, "Mapping an Atlantic Sexual Culture: Homoeroticism in Eighteenth-Century Philadelphia," *William and Mary Quarterly* 60.1 (2006): 119; Jen Manion, "The Queer History of Passing as a Man in Early Pennsylvania," *Pennsylvania Legacies* 16.1 (2016): 6–11; Morgan and Rushton, "Fraud and Freedom," 347–349.

48. Allyson May, "Hamilton, Mary [Charles]," *Oxford Dictionary of National Biography Online* (September 2004).

49. Sharon Block, "Making Meaningful Bodies: Physical Appearance in Colonial Writings," *Early American Studies* 12.3 (2014): 524–547; David Waldstreicher, "Reading the Runaways: Self-Fashioning, Print Culture, and Confidence in Slavery in the Eighteenth-Century Mid-Atlantic," *The William and Mary Quarterly* 56.2 (1999): 243–272.

50. Derry, "Sexuality and Locality," 601–603. Vagrancy, as a catchall category for disorder, offered a viable avenue for targeting sex between women; since English sodomy laws, of course, only applied to men, there was no obvious legal sanction against sex between women in this period.

51. "Extract of a Letter from Chester."

52. Morgan Rushton, "Fraud and Freedom," 338.

53. See Waldstreicher, "Reading the Runaways," for more on the generic conventions of the runaway advertisement.

54. "Extract of a Letter from Chester," *Pennsylvania Gazette*, July 16, 1752.

55. Advertisement, *Pennsylvania Gazette*, February 27, 1753.

56. Major historical accounts of transgender identity and its historical relation to gender, identity, and narrative include, for instance, Joanne Meyerowitz, *How Sex Changed: A History of Transsexuality in the United States* (Cambridge: Harvard University Press, 2002) and David Valentine, *Imagining Transgender: An Ethnography of a Category* (Durham: Duke University Press, 2007).

57. Sheridan Baker reprints a transcription of the deposition in "Henry Fielding's *The Female Husband:* Fact and Fiction," 219.

58. See, for instance, Dean Spade, "Administrating Gender" in *Normal Life: Administrative Violence, Critical Trans Politics, and the Limits of Law* (Brooklyn: South End Press, 2011), 137–169.

59. For the place of vagrancy law in the history of the passport, for instance, see John Torpey, *The Invention of the Passport: Surveillance, Citizenship, and the State* (Cambridge: Cambridge University Press, 2000), 18.

60. Toby Beauchamp, "Artful Concealment and Strategic Visibility: Transgender Bodies and U.S. State Surveillance After 9/11," *Surveillance and Society* 6.4 (2009): 356.

61. Beauchamp, 365.

62. Claire Colebrook, "What Is It Like to Be a Human?" *TSQ: Transgender Studies Quarterly* 2.2 (2015): 229.

63. C. Riley Snorton, *Black on Both Sides: A Racial History of Trans Identity* (Minneapolis: University of Minnesota Press, 2017), 5–6.

64. Snorton, 64; 57. I discuss the place of vagrancy law in longer histories of racial surveillance in the Americas in greater detail in Chapter 5.

65. Extract of a Letter from Chester," *Pennsylvania Gazette*, July 16, 1752.

66. Scott Larson, "'Indescribable Being:' Theological Performances of Genderlessness in the Society of the Publick Universal Friend, 1776–1819," *Early American Studies* 12.3 (2014): 600; Greta LaFleur, *The Natural History of Sexuality in Early America* (Baltimore: Johns Hopkins University Press, 2018), 140.

67. The literature on heterosexuality and the novel is vast. Particularly crucial accounts of the place of the novel in the history of heterosexuality include Nancy Armstrong, *Desire and Domestic Fiction: A Political History of the Novel* (Oxford: Oxford University Press, 1987) and Ruth Perry, *Novel Relations: The Transformation of Kinship in English Literature and Culture, 1748–1818* (Cambridge: Cambridge University Press, 2004).

68. Scott MacKenzie, *Be It Ever So Humble: Poverty, Fiction, and the Invention of the Middle-Class Home* (Charlottesville: University of Virginia Press, 2013).

69. MacKenzie, *Be It Ever So Humble,* 78.

70. Jane Humphries, "Enclosures, Common Rights, and Women: The Proletarianization of Families in the Late Eighteenth and Early Nineteenth Centuries," *The Journal of Economic History* 50.1 (1990): 37; Steven King, "'Meer Pennies for my Baskitt will be Enough:' Women, Work, and Welfare, 1770–1830," in Penelope Lane, Neil Raven, and K.D.M. Snell (eds), *Women, Work and Wages in England, 1600–1850* (Woodbridge, Suffolk: Boydell & Brewer, 2004), 140.

71. For theoretical discussions of gender, labor, and social reproduction, see Barbara Laslett and Johanna Brenner, "Gender and Social Reproduction: Historical Perspectives" *Annual Review of Sociology* 15 (1989): 381–404; Silvia Federici, *Caliban and the Witch: Women, the Body, and Primitive Accumulation* (New York: Autonomedia, 2004); and Kathi Weeks, *The Problem With Work: Feminism, Marxism, Antiwork Politics, and Postwork Imaginaries* (Durham: Duke University Press, 2011); and Tithi Bhattacharya (ed), *Social Reproduction Theory: Remapping Class, Recentering* Oppression (London: Pluto Press, 2017).

72. David Hitchcock, *Vagrancy in English Culture and Society, 1650–1750* (London: Bloomsbury, 2016), 130; for configurations of female sexuality, labor, and poverty through representations of domestic service in particular, see Kristina Straub, *Domestic Affairs: Intimacy, Eroticism, and Violence between Servants and Masters in Eighteenth-Century Britain* (Baltimore: Johns Hopkins University Press, 2009), 47–82.

73. Laura Rosenthal, *Infamous Commerce: Prostitution in Eighteenth-Century British Literature and Culture* (Ithaca: Cornell University Press, 2006).

74. Hitchcock, *Vagrancy,* 127.

75. Michel Foucault, *The History of Sexuality,* vol. 1 [1978], trans. Robert Hurley (New York: Vintage Books, 1990), 135–159.

76. For more detail on the local contexts that influenced how individual enforcers of vagrancy laws drew and understood the boundaries of their communities, see Jeremy Boulton, "Double Deterrence: Settlement and Practice in London's West End, 1725–1824," in Steven King and Anne Winter (eds.), *Migration, Settlement and Belonging in Europe, 1500–1930s: Comparative Perspectives* (Oxford: Berghahn Books, 2013), 54–80; and Norma Landau, "Who Was Subject to the Laws of Settlement? Procedure Under the Settlement Laws in Eighteenth-Century England," *Agricultural History Review* 43.2 (1995): 139–159.

77. Richard Burn, *The Justice of the Peace, and Parish Officer,* 3rd ed. (London: Henry Lintot for A. Millar, 1756), 507.

78. Burn, *The Justice of the Peace,* 510–512.

79. Burn, *The Justice of the Peace,* 508–530; see also Landau, "Who Was Subject to the Laws of Settlement?"

80. Burn, *The Justice of the Peace,* 561–563.

81. Sam Barrett, "Kinship, Poor Relief, and the Welfare Process in Early Modern England," in Steven King and Alannah Tomkins (eds.), *The Poor in England, 1700–1850: An Economy of Makeshifts* (Manchester: Manchester University Press, 2003), 219.

82. Burn, *The Justice of the Peace,* 510.

83. At the same time, this form of bigamy—leaving one living spouse to take another—was in fact a common informal method of divorce among the English poor in the eighteenth century, and so while the extension of settlement to Richard Burden's second wife departs from the strict legal understanding of legitimate marriage, it does, in another sense, follow existing customary and informal practices of marriage and divorce (Boulton, "Double Deterrence," 74).

84. Burn, *The Justice of the Peace,* 510.

85. Burn, *The Justice of the Peace,* 723.

86. Burn, *The Justice of the Peace,* 530. This logic was also the logic underpinning the distinctive "warning out" system adopted by colonial Boston; as Cornelia Dayton and Sharon Salinger argue, the practice of warning out was not an attempt to exclude all strangers from the city, but rather a formal announcement that if stranger chose to remain in Boston, they did so with the understanding that they were not entitled to local poor relief (Dayton and Salinger, *Robert Love's Warnings: Searching for Strangers in Colonial Boston* [Philadelphia: University of Pennsylvania Press, 2014]).

87. See, for instance, George Haggerty, "'Romantic Friendship' and Patriarchal Narrative in Sarah Scott's *Millenium Hall,*" *Genders* 13 (1992): 108–122; Lisa Moore, *Dangerous Intimacies: Toward a Sapphic History of the British Novel* (Durham: Duke University Press: 1997), 22–48; and Sally O'Driscoll, "Lesbian Criticism and Feminist Criticism: The Case of *Millenium Hall,*" *Tulsa Studies in Women's Literature* 22.1 (2003): 57–80.

88. Sarah Scott, *A Description of Millenium Hall* [1762], ed. Gary Kelly (Peterborough: Broadview, 1994), 115.

89. Ann Van Sant, "Historicizing Domestic Relations: Sarah Scott's Use of the 'Household Family,' " *Eighteenth-Century Fiction* 17.3 (2005): 373–390.

90. Van Sant, "Historicizing Domestic Relations," 376.

91. Scott, *Millenium Hall,* 57, 58.

92. Scott, *Millenium Hall,* 65.

93. Scott, *Millenium Hall,* 67.

94. Scott, *Millenium Hall,* 67.

95. Scott, *Millenium Hall,* 166.

96. Moore, *Dangerous Intimacies,* 28.

97. Sarah Scott, *The History of Sir George Ellison* [1766], ed. Betty Rizzo (Lexington: University Press of Kentucky, 1996); see also David Oakleaf, "At the Margins of Utopia:

Jamaica in Sarah Scott's *Millenium Hall*," *Eighteenth-Century Fiction* 28.1 (2015): 109–137; and Moore, *Dangerous Intimacies*, 25–27.

98. Burn, *The Justice of the Peace*, 720.

99. Judith Bennett theorizes "lesbian-like" as a term for premodern affiliations between women that do not necessarily center on erotic desire or align completely with contemporary lesbian identity, yet offer potential lesbian identification through a recognition of common exclusion from historiography and genealogical lineage (Bennet, "'Lesbian-Like' and the Social History of Lesbianisms," *Journal of the History of Sexuality* 9.1–2 [2000]: 1–24).

100. Carolyn Steedman, *Dust* (Manchester: Manchester University Press, 2001), 54–55.

101. [Mary Saxby], *Memoirs of a Female Vagrant, Written by Herself* (London: J. Burdett, 1806), viii.

102. *Memoirs of the Life and Writings of William Cowper, Esq.* (London: for T. Williams, 1803), 27; Samuel Greatheed, *A Practical Improvement of the Divine Counsel and Conduct, Attempted in a Sermon, Occasioned by the Death of William Cowper, Esq.*, 2nd ed. (Newport-Pagnel: J. Wakefield, 1801); John Morison, "Memoir of the Late Rev. Samuel Greatheed, F.A.S., of Newport-Pagnell," *The Fathers and Founders of the London Missionary Society* (London: Fisher, Son, & Co., 1844), 396.

103. Religious Tract Society, "Extracts of Letters, &c. Relating to the Beneficial Effects of the Society's Publications," in *Proceedings of the First Twenty Years of the Religious Tract Society* (London: Benjamin Bensley, 1820), 44.

104. Religious Tract Society, "Extracts," 44; on ballad-singing and hawking as disreputable and feminized forms of labor criminalized as vagrancy, see Tim Fulford, "Fallen Ladies and Cruel Mothers: Ballad Singers and Ballad Heroines in the Eighteenth Century," *The Eighteenth Century: Theory and Interpretation* 47.2–3 (2006): 309–329.

105. For Wilson's life and legal career, see "Obituary—Joseph Wilson, Esq.," *The Gentleman's Magazine*, vol. 35 (London: John Bowyer Nichols and Son, 1851), 669.

106. Saxby, *Memoirs of a Female Vagrant*, vi.

107. Saxby, *Memoirs of a Female Vagrant*, v.

108. Saxby, *Memoirs of a Female Vagrant*, 1.

109. Saxby, *Memoirs of a Female Vagrant*, 1, 7.

110. Steedman, *Dust*, 54–55.

111. Saxby, *Memoirs of a Female Vagrant*, 19.

112. Saxby, *Memoirs of a Female Vagrant*, 19. See Saree Makdisi, *Making England Western: Occidentalism, Race, and Imperial Culture* (Chicago: University of Chicago Press, 2013) for an extended analysis of such racialization of poverty at the turn of the nineteenth century.

113. Saxby, *Memoirs of a Female Vagrant*, 3.

114. Saxby, *Memoirs of a Female Vagrant*, 1–2.

115. Saxby, *Memoirs of a Female Vagrant*, 8.

116. Saxby, *Memoirs of a Female Vagrant*, 15.

117. Saxby, *Memoirs of a Female Vagrant*, 15.

118. Fulford, "Fallen Ladies."

119. Deidre Lynch, *The Economy of Character: Novels, Market Culture, and the Business of Inner Meaning* (Chicago: University of Chicago Press, 1998), 28.

120. See, for instance, Carolyn Dinshaw, *Getting Medieval: Sexualities and Communities, Pre- and Postmodern* (Durham: Duke University Press, 1999), 100–142; Heather Love, *Feeling Backward: Loss and the Politics of Queer History* (Cambridge: Harvard University Press, 2007), 31–52.

121. Michel Foucault, "The Lives of Infamous Men," in *Power,* ed. James D. Faubion, trans. Robert Hurley et al. (New York: The New Press, 2000), 157, 160.

122. Dinshaw, *Getting Medieval,* 138.

123. Foucault, "Lives," 163.

124. Foucault, "Lives," 163.

125. Love, *Feeling Backward,* 48.

126. Love, "Doing Being Deviant: Deviance Studies, Description, and the Queer Ordinary," *differences* 28.1 (2015): 75.

127. Love, "Doing Being Deviant," 75. Indeed, in the mid-twentieth century, U.S. vagrancy laws frequently targeted queer and trans people as well as the groups Love lists here; the possibility that they might be arrested for vagrancy is perhaps the clearest point of commonality uniting all these figures (Goluboff, *Vagrant Nation,* 147–185).

128. Love, "Doing Being Deviant," 90.

129. LaFleur, *Natural History of Sexuality.*

## Chapter 3. Lyric Population and the Prospects of Police

1. Barbara Johnson, *Persons and Things* (Cambridge: Harvard University Press, 2008), 188.

2. Johnson, "Apostrophe, Animation, and Abortion," *diacritics* 16.1 (1986): 28–47; Johnson, *Persons and Things,* 189.

3. Johnson, *Persons and Things,* 195.

4. Virginia Jackson, *Dickinson's Misery: A Theory of Lyric Reading* (Princeton: Princeton University Press, 2005), 8.

5. Jackson, *Dickinson's Misery,* 114.

6. Johnson, *Persons and Things,* 207.

7. Jackson, *Dickinson's Misery,* 100.

8. See, for instance, William Blackstone, *Commentaries on the Laws of England* [1765–1769], 4 vols. (Chicago: University of Chicago Press, 1974), 1:119.

9. See, for instance, Blackstone, *Commentaries* for civil and natural death as nonidentical (1:128). *Black's Law Dictionary* defines a "person" as a "human being considered as capable of having rights and of being charged with duties," but also immediately expands the definition to exceed the human being: "Persons are divided by law into *natural* and *artificial*" (Henry Campbell Black, *A Dictionary of Law* [St. Paul, MN: West Publishing, 1891], 892).

10. Johnson, *Persons and Things,* 199; quoting *Rowland v. California Men's Colony* (91–1188), 506 U.S. 194 (1993).

11. Johnson, *Persons and Things,* 200, 204.

12. Jackson, *Dickinson's Misery,* 7–9.

13. See, for instance, Gary Lee Harrison, *Wordsworth's Vagrant Muse: Poetry Poverty, and Power* (Detroit: Wayne State University Press, 1994); Quentin Bailey, *Wordsworth's Vagrants: Police, Prisons, and Poetry in the 1790s* (Farnham: Ashgate, 2011); Toby Benis, *Romanticism on the Road: The Marginal Gains of Wordsworth's Homeless* (New York: St. Martin's, 2000); David Simpson, *Wordsworth's Historical Imagination: The Poetry of Displacement* (London: Methuen, 1987); Anne Wallace, *Walking, Literature, and English Culture: The Origins and Uses of the Peripatetic in the Nineteenth Century* (Oxford: Clarendon Press, 1993); Karen Swann, "Public Transport: Adventuring on Wordsworth's Salisbury Plain," *ELH* 55.4 (1988): 811–834; Alex J. Dick, "Poverty, Charity, Poetry: The Unproductive Labors of 'The Old Cumberland Beggar,' " *Studies in Romanticism* 39.3 (2000): 365–396.

14. Celeste Langan, *Romantic Vagrancy: Wordsworth and the Simulation of Freedom* (Cambridge: Cambridge University Press, 1995), 17.

15. Langan, *Romantic Vagrancy,* 3, 17.

16. David Simpson, *Wordsworth, Commodification, and Social Concern: The Poetics of Modernity* (Cambridge: Cambridge University Press, 2009), 3, 27.

17. Simpson, *Wordsworth, Commodification, and Social Concern,* 56.

18. Thomas Pfau, *Wordsworth's Profession: Form, Class and the Logic of Early Romantic Cultural Production* (Stanford: Stanford University Press, 1997), 228.

19. Pfau, *Wordsworth's Profession,* 15.

20. Anne Janowitz, *Lyric and Labour in the Romantic Tradition* (Cambridge: Cambridge University Press, 1998); Michael Nicholson, "The Itinerant 'I': John Clare's Lyric Defiance," *ELH* 82 (2015): 638–639.

21. See, for instance, Markus Dubber, "The Comparative History and Theory of Corporate Criminal Liability," *New Criminal Law Review* 16.2 (2013): 228, as well as my own discussion of vagrancy law in the Introduction.

22. See, in particular, Simpson, *Wordsworth's Historical Imagination*; Harrison, *Wordsworth's Vagrant Muse;* and Bailey, *Wordsworth's Vagrants.*

23. See, for instance, Alan Bewell, *Romanticism and Colonial Disease* (Baltimore: Johns Hopkins University Press, 2003), 108–126; Emily Steinlight, *Populating the Novel: Literary Form and the Politics of Surplus Life* (Ithaca: Cornell University Press, 2018), 35–37; James Chandler and Kevin Gilmartin, "Introduction: Engaging the Eidometropolis," in Chandler and Gilmartin (eds.), *Romantic Metropolis: The Urban Scene of British Culture, 1780–1840* (Cambridge: Cambridge University Press, 2005), 1–41.

24. Raymond Williams, *The Country and the City* (New York: Oxford University Press, 1973), 12, 78–79.

25. For overviews of the politics of poverty, population, and scarcity at the end of the nineteenth century, see Lynn Hollen Lees, *The Solidarities of Strangers: The English Poor Laws*

*and the People, 1700–1948* (Cambridge: Cambridge University Press, 1998), 84–107; Bailey, *Wordsworth's Vagrants,* 13–19; Lisa Foreman Cody, "The Politics of Illegitimacy in an Age of Reform: Women, Reproduction, and Political Economy in England's New Poor Law of 1834," *Journal of Women's History* 11.4 (2000): 131–150; and J. R. Poynter, *Society and Pauperism: English Ideas on Poor Relief, 1795–1834* (London: Routledge, 1969). For the place of literature in scarcity and population as central political concepts, see Steinlight, *Populating the Novel,* 35–73.

26. Adam Smith, *Lectures on Justice, Police, Revenue, and Arms,* ed. Edwin Cannan (Oxford: Clarendon Press, 1896), 3.

27. Frances Ferguson, "Malthus, Godwin, Wordsworth, and the Spirit of Solitude," in *Literature and the Body: Essays on Populations and Persons,* ed. Elaine Scarry (Baltimore: Johns Hopkins University Press, 1988), 106–124; Gallagher, *The Body Economic,* 3–8.

28. Thomas Malthus, *Essay on the Principle of Population* (London: J. Johnson, 1798).

29. Ferguson, "Malthus, Godwin, Wordsworth, and the Spirit of Solitude," 109–110; John Bohstedt, *The Politics of Provisions: Food Riots, Moral Economy, and Market Transition in England, c. 1550–1850* (Farnham: Ashgate, 2010), 167.

30. Catherine Gallagher, *The Body Economic: Life, Death, and Sensation in Political Economy and the Victorian Novel* (Princeton: Princeton University Press, 2008), 7–35; Emily Steinlight, *Populating the Novel: Literary Form and the Politics of Surplus Life* (Ithaca: Cornell University Press, 2018), 35–38. See also Aaron Fogel, "Wordsworth's 'We Are Seven' and Crabbe's 'The Parish Register': Poetry and Anti-Census," *Studies in Romanticism* 48.1 (2009): 23–65.

31. Thomas Malthus, *An Essay on the Principle of Population* (London: J. Johnson, 1803), 531.

32. Maureen McLane, *Romanticism and the Human Sciences: Poetry, Population, and the Discourse of the Species* (Cambridge: Cambridge University Press, 2009), 29.

33. All citations of "The Female Vagrant" (1798 version) are from William Wordsworth and Samuel Taylor Coleridge, *Lyrical Ballads 1798 and 1800,* ed. Michael Gamer and Dahlia Porter (Peterborough: Broadview, 2008).

34. Stephen Burt, "What Is This Thing Called Lyric?," *Modern Philology* 113.3 (2016): 439.

35. Wordsworth, "Advertisement" [1798], in Wordsworth and Coleridge, *Lyrical Ballads 1798 and 1800,* 47.

36. Anne Janowitz, *Lyric and Labour in the Romantic Tradition* (Cambridge: Cambridge University Press, 1998), 44–45; Ferguson, "Malthus, Godwin, Wordsworth, and the Spirit of Solitude," 106.

37. William Wordsworth, "The Female Vagrant," in Wordsworth and Coleridge, *Lyrical Ballads 1798 and 1800,*118–119. Celeste Langan similarly understands these lines as theorizing poetic taste as "an exquisite refinement parallel to the female vagrant's discovery of the 'pure form' of being" (78); meanwhile, Harrison and Benis both emphasize Wordsworth's mobilization of the Female Vagrant's story in service of a critique of war, inequality, and inadequate poor relief (Harrison, *Wordsworth's Vagrant Muse,* 93–94; Benis, *Romanticism on the Road,* 57–63).

38. Wordsworth, "Advertisement," 47.

39. Saree Makdisi, *Making England Western: Occidentalism, Race, and Imperial Culture* (Chicago: University of Chicago Press, 2014), 127, 129. For broader changes in the legal and cultural meaning of "Gypsy" at the turn of the nineteenth century, see Katie Trumpener, "The Time of the Gypsies: 'People Without History' in the Narratives of the West," *Critical Inquiry* 18.4 (1992): 843–884.

40. Makdisi, *Making England Western,* 100.

41. See, for instance, Stuart Curran, "Mary Robinson's *Lyrical Tales* in Context," in Carol Shiner Wilson and Joel Haefner (eds.), *Re-visioning Romanticism: British Women Writers, 1776–1837* (Philadelphia: University of Pennsylvania Press, 1994), 30.

42. Ashley Cross, "From *Lyrical Ballads* to *Lyrical Tales:* Mary Robinson's Reputation and the Problem of Literary Debt," *Studies in Romanticism* 40.4 (2001): 593.

43. Daniel Robinson, *The Poetry of Mary Robinson: Fame and Form* (New York: Palgrave, 2011), 217. For Robinson's formal experimentation, see also Curran, "Mary Robinson and the New Lyric," *Women's Writing* 9.1 (2002): 9–22.

44. All quotations from the *Lyrical Tales* are taken from Mary Robinson, *Selected Poems,* ed. Judith Pascoe (Peterborough: Broadview, 2000).

45. See James Garrett, *Wordsworth and the Writing of the Nation* (Aldershot, Hampshire: Ashgate, 2008), 13–42; and Aaron Fogel, "Wordsworth's 'We Are Seven' and Crabbe's *The Parish Register:* Poetry and Anti-Census," *Studies in Romanticism* 48.1 (2009): 23–65, for Wordsworth's engagement with enumeration, population, and the state.

46. I am indebted to Celeste Langan for this observation on the multivalence of the poem's title.

47. Thomas Laqueur, *The Work of the Dead: A Cultural History of Mortal Remains* (Princeton: Princeton University Press, 2016), 161–162.

48. See, for instance, Sophie Gee, *Making Waste: Leftovers and the Eighteenth-Century Imagination* (Princeton: Princeton University Press, 2010), 37, 121; as well as my discussion of vagrancy and the popular imagination of waste in Chapter 1.

49. Joanna Innes, "Prisons for the Poor: English Bridewells, 1555–1800," in Francis Snyder and Douglas Hay (eds.), *Labour, Law and Crime: An Historical Perspective* (London: Tavistock Publications, 1987), 42–58; Caleb Smith, "Detention Without Subjects: Prisons and the Poetics of Living Death," *Texas Studies in Literature and Language* 50.3 (2008): 244.

50. Michael Denning, "Wageless Life," *New Left Review* 66 (2010): 79–97.

51. Steinlight, *Populating the Novel,* 37.

52. Henry Fielding, *Enquiry into the Causes of the Late Increase of Robbers* (London: A. Millar, 1751), 76.

53. Fielding, *Enquiry,* 2.

54. See, for instance, Makdisi, *Making England Western,* 3–7.

55. Patrick Colquhoun, *A Treatise on the Police of the Metropolis,* 3rd ed. (London: H. Fry for C. Dilly, 1796), 410.

56. Thomas Gilbert, *A Plan of Police: Exhibiting the Causes of the Present Increase of the Poor, and Proposing a Mode for their Future More Economical and Effectual Relief and Support* (London: for G. and T. Wilkie, 1786), 17.

57. Thomas Malthus, *Essay on the Principle of Population* (London: J. Johnson, 1798), iv.

58. Charlotte Sussman, "The Emptiness at the Heart of Midlothian: Nation, Narration, and Population," *Eighteenth-Century Fiction* 15.1 (2002): 105.

59. Patrick Colquhoun, *A General View of the Depredations Committed on the West-India and Other Property in the Port of London* (London: H. Baldwin, 1799), 5.

60. Colquhoun, *General View,* 2.

61. Abigail Swingen, *Competing Visions of Empire: Labor, Slavery, and the Origins of the British Atlantic Empire* (New Haven: Yale University Press, 2015); Gwenda Morgan and Peter Rushton, "Visible Bodies: Power, Subordination and Identity in the Eighteenth-Century Atlantic World," *Journal of Social History* 39.1 (2005): 39–64; Simon Newman, *Embodied History: The Lives of the Poor in Early Philadelphia* (Philadelphia: University of Pennsylvania Press, 2003), 48–49.

62. John Torpey, *The Invention of the Passport: Surveillance, Citizenship, and the State* (Cambridge: Cambridge University Press, 2000), 1–2, 18.

63. For an overview of the politics of police reform in this period, see Andrew Harris, *Policing the City: Crime and Legal Authority in London, 1780–1840* (Columbus: Ohio State University Press, 2004).

64. See, for instance, David Philips, "'A New Engine of Power and Authority': The Institutionalisation of Law-Enforcement in England, 1780–1830," in V. A. C. Gattrel, D. Lenman, and C. Parker (eds.), *Crime and the Law: The Social History of Crime in Western Europe since 1500* (London: Europa, 1980), 155–189; and Stanley Palmer, *Police and Protest in England and Ireland, 1780–1850* (Cambridge: Cambridge University Press, 1988).

65. Elaine Reynolds, *Before the Bobbies: The Night Watch and Police Reform in Metropolitan London, 1720–1830* (Basingstoke: Palgrave Macmillan, 1998), 86.

66. Colquhoun, *Treatise,* vi.

67. Colquhoun, *Treatise,* vii–xi.

68. Michel Foucault, *Security, Territory, Population: Lectures at the Collège de France 1977–78,* trans. Graham Burchell (New York: Picador, 2009).

69. Colquhoun, *General View,* 30–31; emphasis original.

70. Colquhoun, *Treatise,* 12–13.

71. Colquhoun, *Treatise,* xi.

72. Ruth Paley, "Colquhoun, Patrick (1745–1820)," *Oxford Dictionary of National Biography Online* (January 2008); Walter M. Stern, "The First London Dock Boom and the Growth of the West India Docks," *Economica* 19.73 (1952): 62.

73. Stern, "The First London Dock Boom," 75.

74. For the place of these acts in the development of summary conviction in the eighteenth century, see Bruce P. Smith, "The Presumption of Guilt and the English Law of Theft, 1750–1850," *Law and History Review* 23.1 (2005): 154–155.

75. Colquhoun, *A General View of the Depredations Committed on West-India and Other Property in the Port of London* (London: H. Baldwin and Son, 1799), 37, 43

76. Norma Landau, "Summary Conviction and the Development of Penal Law," *Law and History Review* 23.1 (2005): 189. Another important colonial force—the militarized and

uniformed police of Dublin, first instituted in 1786—also offered a direct model for the later professionalization of police in London (Stanley Palmer, *Police and Protest in England and Ireland, 1780–1850* [Cambridge: Cambridge University Press, 1988], xvii).

77. "A Comparative View of the Old and New Systems of Discharging West-India Ships in the Port of London," *St. James's Chronicle, or, the British Evening Post,* August 11, 1798.

78. "Police Offices," *Courier and Evening Gazette,* January 25, 1799.

79. Colquhoun, *General View,* 12.

80. Mark Neocleous, "Theoretical Foundations of the 'New Police Science,' " in Markus Dubber and Mariana Valverde (eds.), *The New Police Science: The Police Power in Domestic and International Governance* (Stanford: Stanford University Press, 2006), 34.

81. For instance, the director of the West India Docks Company, George Hibbert, headed the major Jamaica firm of Hibbert, Fuhr, and Purrier, and was a well-known advocate against abolition, first as a prominent merchant and later as an MP (David Hancock, "Hibbert, George," *Oxford Dictionary of National Biography Online* (January 2008).).

82. Colquhoun was hardly alone in this; for instance, Frederick Morton Eden, now best known for his massive *State of the Poor,* also authored a tract on London docks expansion (*Porto-Bello: Or, A Plan for the Improvement of the Port and City of London* [London: B. White, 1798]), and Jonas Hanway, perhaps best known for his philanthropic efforts to house "penitent prostitutes," was also, as I discuss below, a major figure in the public response to the scandal of Asian sailors rendered destitute in London.

83. There are, of course, exceptions to this trend; Book VII of Wordsworth's *Prelude* is perhaps the most prominent.

84. Michael H. Fisher, *Counterflows to Colonialism: Indian Travellers and Settlers in Britain, 1600–1857* (Delhi: Permanent Black, 2004), 137–139. See also Rozina Visram, *Asians in Britain: 400 Years of History* (London: Pluto Press, 2002), 3–44; and Norma Myers, *Reconstructing the Black Past: Blacks in Britain, 1780–1830* (London: Frank Cass, 1996), 108.

85. Fisher, *Counterflows to Colonialism,* 149–150. For historical accounts of lascars that challenge eighteenth-century British characterizations of them as helpless objects of pity, see Devleena Ghosh, "Under the Radar of Empire: Unregulated Travel in the Indian Ocean," *Journal of Social History* 45.2 (2011): 497–514.

86. Fisher, *Counterflows to Colonialism,* 146–149; Humberto Garcia, "The Transports of Lascar Specters: Dispossessed Indian Sailors in Women's Romantic Poetry," *The Eighteenth Century: Theory and Interpretation* 55.2–3 (2014): 262–265.

87. Adela Pinch, *Strange Fits of Passion: Epistemologies of Emotion, Hume to Austen* (Stanford: Stanford University Press, 1996), 10; Miranda Burgess, "Transport: Mobility, Anxiety, and the Romantic Poetics of Feeling," *Studies in Romanticism* 49 (2010): 249.

88. Suvir Kaul, *Poems of Nation, Anthems of Empire* (Charlottesville: University of Virginia Press, 2000), 152–182; Kevis Goodman, *Georgic Modernity and British Romanticism: Poetry and the Mediation of History* (Cambridge: Cambridge University Press, 2004), 42–62.

89. Goodman, *Georgic Modernity,* 22. Of course, as Kurt Heinzelman has argued, loco-descriptive and lyric are not mutually exclusive in the Romantic period ("Roman Georgic

in the Georgian Age: A Theory of Romantic Genre," *Texas Studies in Literature and Language* 33.2 [1991]: 182–214).

90. Jordana [Jordy] Rosenberg and Chi-ming Yang, "Introduction: The Dispossessed Eighteenth Century," *The Eighteenth Century: Theory and Interpretation* 55.2–3 (2014): 137–152; see also Peter Linebaugh and Markus Rediker, *The Many-Headed Hydra: Sailors, Slaves, Commoners, and the Hidden History of the Revolutionary Atlantic* (Boston: Beacon Press, 2000).

91. "The Lascar," *The Newcastle Magazine: or, Monthly Journal* (1785): 532–533.

92. "The Lascar," 533.

93. Sara Ahmed, *Strange Encounters: Embodied Others in Postcoloniality* (New York: Routledge, 2000), 5–15.

94. "Foreign Intelligence, Domestic Occurrences, &c.," *New London Magazine* (March 1787): 163.

95. Lynn Festa has theorized the place of sympathy in the culture of empire more generally in *Sentimental Figures of Empire in Eighteenth-Century Britain and France* (Baltimore: Johns Hopkins University Press, 2006).

96. *The Late Measures of the Ship-Owners in the Coal-Trade Fully Examined, in a Letter to the Right Honourable William Pitt* (London, 1786), 41.

97. *Public Advertiser,* March 16, 1785.

98. Stephen Braidwood, *Black Poor and White Philanthropists: London's Blacks and the Foundation of the Sierra Leone Settlement, 1786–1791* (Liverpool: Liverpool University Press, 1994).

99. Braidwood, *Black Poor and White Philanthropists,* 24.

100. Ashley Cohen, "The Global Indies: Historicizing Oceanic Metageographies," *Comparative Literature* 69.1 (2017): 8.

101. Deirdre Coleman, *Romantic Colonization and British Anti-Slavery* (Cambridge: Cambridge University Press, 2005), 3.

102. *General Evening Post,* January 13, 1787.

103. *Morning Chronicle,* January 28, 1786; see also Braidwood, *Black Poor and White Philanthropists,* 72.

104. *Public Advertiser,* December 14, 1786.

105. Isaac Land, "Bread and Arsenic: Citizenship from the Bottom Up in Georgian London," *Journal of Social History* 39.1 (2005): 102.

106. Braidwood, *Black Poor and White Philanthropists,* 141.

107. Land, "Bread and Arsenic," 93–94.

108. Land, "Bread and Arsenic," 101.

109. *Report from the Committee on Lascars and other Asiatic Seamen,* House of Commons Parliamentary Papers 1814–15 (471), 6.

110. Garcia, "Transports," 261.

111. Garcia, "Transports."

112. Michael H. Fisher, "Excluding and Including 'Natives of India': Early Nineteenth-Century British-Indian Race Relations in Britain," *Comparative Studies of South Asia, Africa, and the Middle East* 27.2 (2007): 308.

113. Cross, "From *Lyrical Ballads* to *Lyrical Tales*," 593.

114. James Mulholland, *Sounding Imperial: Poetic Voice and the Politics of Empire, 1730–1820* (Baltimore: Johns Hopkins University Press, 2013), 1–3.

115. Mulholland, *Sounding Imperial,* 122.

116. Mulholland, *Sounding Imperial,* 120–134.

117. For the relation of antislavery poetic ventriloquism to the ballad tradition and its poetic afterlives, see Ivan Ortiz, "Lyric Possession in the Abolition Ballad," *Eighteenth-Century Studies* 51.2 (2018): 197–218.

118. *The King v. Inhabitants of Thames Ditton* (1785), in *Reports of Cases Argued and Determined in the Court of King's Bench,* vol. 4 (London: S. Sweet, 1831), 300.

119. For details of the case, see Carolyn Steedman, *Dust* (Manchester: Manchester University Press, 2001), 52.

120. *The King v. Inhabitants of Thames Ditton,* 302.

121. *The King v. Inhabitants of Thames Ditton,* 302.

122. Jane Humphries, "Enclosures, Common Rights, and Women: The Proletarianization of Families in the Late Eighteenth and Early Nineteenth Centuries," *The Journal of Economic History* 50.1 (1990): 37; Steven King, "'Meer Pennies for my Baskitt will be Enough': Women, Work, and Welfare, 1770–1830," in Penelope Lane, Neil Raven, and K. D. M. Snell (eds.), *Women, Work and Wages in England, 1600–1850* (Woodbridge, Suffolk: Boydell & Brewer, 2004), 140.

## Chapter 4. Settler Vagrancy

1. Caleb Foote, "Vagrancy-Type Law and Its Administration," *University of Pennsylvania Law Review* 104 (1956): 603–650; Risa Goluboff, *Vagrant Nation: Police Power, Constitutional Change, and the Making of the 1960s* (New York: Oxford University Press, 2016), 301–302.

2. Hsuan L. Hsu, "Vagrancy and Comparative Racialization in *Huckleberry Finn* and 'Three Vagabonds of Trinidad,' " *American Literature* 81.4 (2009): 687–688.

3. Michael Meranze, "Penality and the Colonial Project: Crime, Punishment, and the Regulation of Morals in Early America," in *The Cambridge History of Law in America,* vol. 1: *Early America (1580–1815),* ed. Michael Grossberg and Christopher Tomlins (Cambridge: Cambridge University Press, 2008), 178. For more on transatlantic exchange in eighteenth-century law, see Christopher Tomlins, *Freedom Bound: Law, Labor, and Civic Identity in Colonizing English America, 1580–1865* (New York: Cambridge University Press, 2010), 65–70 and 342–343; and Mary Sarah Bilder, *The Transatlantic Constitution: Colonial Legal Culture and the Empire* (Cambridge: Harvard University Press, 2004).

4. "An Act to prevent Disorders in the Night," in *Acts & Laws, passed by the Great and General Court or Assembly of Her Majesties province of the Massachussets-Bay in New-England: begun and held at Boston upon Wednesday the twenty-sixth of May 1703* (Boston: B. Green and J. Allen, 1703), 256.

5. Jen Manion, *Liberty's Prisoners: Carceral Culture in Early America* (Philadelphia: University of Pennsylvania Press, 2015), 24–25.

6. Simon P. Newman, "'In Great Slavery and Bondage': White Labor and the Development of Plantation Slavery in America," in Ignacio Gallup-Diaz, Andrew Shankman, and David J. Silverman (eds.), *Anglicizing America: Empire, Revolution, Republic* (Philadelphia: University of Pennsylvania Press), 59–82. See also my extended discussion of this history in Chapter 5.

7. Shirley Samuels, "Wieland: Alien and Infidel," *Early American Literature* 25.1 (1990): 46–66; Stephen Shapiro, *The Culture and Commerce of the Early American Novel: Reading the Atlantic World-System* (University Park: Pennsylvania State University Press, 2008), 211–242; Ed White, "Carwin the Peasant Rebel," in Philip Barnard, Mark L. Kamrath, and Stephen Shapiro (eds.), *Revising Charles Brockden Brown: Culture, Politics, and Sexuality in the Early Republic* (Knoxville: University of Tennessee Press, 2004), 41–59; Christopher Looby, *Voicing America: Language, Literary Form, and the Origins of the United States* (Chicago: University of Chicago Press, 1998), 146–186.

8. Duke of York's Laws, *Charter to William Penn, and Laws of the Province of Pennsylvania, Passed Between the Years 1682 and 1700,* ed. Staughton George, Benjamin Nead, and Thomas McCamant (Harrisburg: Lane S. Hart, 1879), 21–22.

9. *Orders made and Confirmed at the Generall Court of Assizes held in New Yorke* (1672), c.3, in George et al. (ed.), *Charter,* 72.

10. George et al. (ed.), *Charter,* 75.

11. *Laws of the Commonwealth of Pennsylvania,* 4 vols. (Philadelphia: John Bioren, 1810), 1:102.

12. Simon P. Newman and Billy G. Smith, "Incarcerated Innocents: Inmates, Conditions, and Survival Strategies in Philadelphia's Almshouse and Jail," in Michele Lise Tarter and Richard Bell (eds.), *Buried Lives: Incarcerated in Early America* (Athens: University of Georgia Press, 2012), 67–68; Michael Meranze, *Laboratories of Virtue: Punishment, Revolution and Authority in Philadelphia, 1760–1835* (Chapel Hill: University of North Carolina Press, 1996), 152–157. See also Tarter and Bell, "Introduction," *Buried Lives,* 13–15.

13. David Montgomery, *Citizen Worker: The Experience of Workers in the United States with Democracy and the Free Market During the Nineteenth Century* (Cambridge: Cambridge University Press, 1993), 27–29.

14. *Compilation of the Laws of the State of Pennsylvania Relative to the Poor* (Philadelphia: Zachariah Poulson, 1796), 55–56.

15. Philadelphia Prison System, Vagrancy Dockets (Record Group 38.44), Philadelphia City Archives; see, for example, Sarah Thompson, "Charged with being an Idle dissolute and Notorious Prostitute" (7/29/1790); Daniel Calligham, "Charged with being a deserter from the Army of the United States" (6/29/1791); Margaret Simonds, "Charged with being in Bed with a negro Man, and with being an Idle and disorderly Woman" (8/29/1791); and Joe, "A Negro," "Charged with being a Slave & Running away from his Master" (5/31/1790).

16. See, for example, William Nelson, "Charged with Misbehaving himself towards his Master and Mistress" (5/14/1791) and Abraham, "Charged with an intent to Abscond

from the service of his Master Francis Wadlington" (5/16/1791), Vagrancy Dockets, Philadelphia City Archives. For the broad scope of the enforcement of vagrancy law in Philadelphia, see Manion, *Liberty's Prisoners,* 88–92; Newman, *Embodied History,* 40–44; and Newman and Smith, "Incarcerated Innocents," 67–68.

17. For the history of these practices in England, see Norma Landau, *The Justices of the Peace, 1679–1760* (Berkeley: University of California Press, 1984), 24–26; William Blackstone, *Commentaries on the Laws of England* [1765–1769] (Chicago: University of Chicago Press, 1974), 1:342, 4:248–279; Rogers, "Policing the Poor"; and Steve Hindle, *On the Parish? The Micropolitics of Poor Relief in Rural England, c. 1550–1750* (Oxford: Oxford University Press, 2004). For specifically North American adaptations of these legal practices, see Newman and Smith, "Incarcerated Innocents" and Meranze, *Laboratories of Virtue.*

18. Sally Hadden, *Slave Patrols: Law and Violence in Virginia and the Carolinas* (Cambridge: Harvard University Press, 2001), 58–59.

19. Charles Brockden Brown, *Wieland; or the Transformation: An American Tale* [1798], in *Wieland and Memoirs of Carwin the Biloquist,* ed. Sydney J. Krause and S. W. Reid (Kent, OH: The Kent State University Press, 1978), 50. Hereafter cited parenthetically.

20. Newman, *Embodied History,* 48–49; Gwenda Morgan and Peter Rushton, "Visible Bodies: Power, Subordination and Identity in the Eighteenth-Century Atlantic World," *Journal of Social History* 39.1 (2005): 39–64.

21. Jonathan Prude, "To Look Upon the 'Lower Sort': Runaway Ads and the Appearance of Unfree Laborers in America, 1750–1800," *Journal of American History* 78.1 (1991): 124–159; David Waldstreicher, "Reading the Runaways: Self-Fashioning, Print Culture, and Confidence in Slavery in the Eighteenth-Century Mid-Atlantic," *William and Mary Quarterly* 56.2 (1999): 243–272. See also Sharon Block's discussion of runaway advertisements in "Making Meaningful Bodies: Physical Appearance in Colonial Writings," *Early American Studies* 12.3 (2014): 524–547.

22. William Godwin, *Things as They Are, or the Adventures of Caleb Williams* [1794], ed. Maurice Hindle (New York: Penguin, 1988), 246.

23. Godwin, *Caleb Williams,* 248.

24. Godwin, *Caleb Williams,* 253.

25. Godwin, *Caleb Williams,* 250.

26. Godwin, *Caleb Williams,* 253.

27. Godwin, *Caleb Williams,* 346.

28. Godwin, *Caleb Williams,* 3.

29. Pamela Clemit, *The Godwinian Novel: The Rational Fictions of Godwin, Brockden Brown, and Mary Shelley* (Oxford: Clarendon Press, 1993), 105–138.

30. Anthony Galluzzo, "Charles Brockden Brown's *Wieland* and the Aesthetics of Terror: Revolution, Reaction, and the Radical Enlightenment in Early American Letters," *Eighteenth-Century Studies* 42.2 (2009): 255–271.

31. Galluzzo, "Charles Brockden Brown's *Wieland,*" 264.

32. Galluzzo, "Charles Brockden Brown's *Wieland,*" 269.

33. Stephen Mihm, "The Alchemy of the Self: Stephen Burroughs and the Counterfeit Economy of the Early Republic," *Early American Studies* 2.1 (2004): 124. See also Myra Glenn, "Troubled Manhood in the Early Republic: The Life and Autobiography of Sailor Horace Lane," *Journal of the Early Republic* 26.1 (2006): 59–93; Steven C. Bullock, "A Mumper Among the Gentle: Tom Bell, Colonial Confidence Man," *William and Mary Quarterly* 55 (1998): 231–258. For fictionality and finance more generally, see Mary Poovey, *Genres of the Credit Economy: Mediating Value in Eighteenth- and Nineteenth-Century Britain* (Chicago: University of Chicago Press, 2008).

34. Leslie Fiedler, *Love and Death in the American Novel* (New York: Criterion Books, 1960), 26.

35. For the composition and publication history of the *Memoirs,* see Sydney J. Krause and S. W. Reid, "Introduction" to Krause and Reid (eds.), *Wieland,* x–xi.

36. David Kazanjian, "Charles Brockden Brown's Biloquial Nation: National Culture and White Settler Colonialism in *Memoirs of Carwin the Biloquist,*" *American Literature* 73.3 (2001): 460. See also Hsuan L. Hsu, "Democratic Expansionism in 'Memoirs of Carwin,' " *Early American Literature* 35.2 (2000): 137–156.

37. Charles Brockden Brown, *Edgar Huntly, or, Memoirs of a Sleep-Walker* [1799], ed. Norman S. Grabo (New York: Penguin, 1988), 3.

38. Kazanjian, "Charles Brockden Brown's Biloquial Nation," 460.

39. Katy Chiles, *Transformable Race: Surprising Metamorphoses in the Literature of Early America* (Oxford: Oxford University Press, 2014), 128. For Brown's knowledge of and extensive engagement with racial theory and natural history, see also pp. 130–136.

40. Jefferson, *Notes,* 59.

41. As Dana Nelson argues, Jefferson was not alone in this rhetorical move: "'Manliness of character,' as imagined community between manly Indians and manly Americans, could . . . restructure U.S. manhood as a dominating enterprise, under the auspices of civilization," as the "imagined 'occupation' of Indian identity could provide access to consolidating a national identity simultaneously white and manly" (Dana Nelson, *National Manhood: Capitalist Citizenship and the Imagined Fraternity of White Men* [Durham: Duke University Press, 1998], 87–88). See also Jared Gardner, *Master Plots: Race and the Founding of an American Literature, 1787–1845* (Baltimore: Johns Hopkins University Press, 1998), xi.

42. Samuel Stanhope Smith, *Essay on the Causes of the Variety of Complexion and Figure in the Human Species* [1787], in *Concepts of Race in the Eighteenth Century,* ed. Robert Bernasconi, vol. 6 (Bristol: Thoemmes, 2001), 94. For Smith's importance and influence as a theorist of race, see Chiles, *Transformable Race,* 83–84, and Bruce Dain, *Hideous Monster of the Mind: American Race Theory in the Early Republic* (Cambridge: Harvard University Press, 2002), 25.

43. Smith, *Essay,* 126.

44. Smith, *Essay,* 126.

45. Julia Stern, for example, reads Brown's gothicism as an exploration of the dark side of a liberal capitalist order that houses "liberty" in the economic actions of the (white,

male) individual and replaces trust with credit (Stern, *The Plight of Feeling: Sympathy and Dissent in the Early American Novel* [Chicago: University of Chicago Press, 1997], 184–198). Similarly, Julie Ellison characterizes disoriented wandering in Brown's novels as "the geography of masculine sensibility"—a sensibility that consolidates white male citizenship yet does not rescue the citizen from spatial and personal dislocation (Ellison, *Cato's Tears and the Making of Anglo-American Emotion* [Chicago: University of Chicago Press, 1999], 149).

46. Nelson, *National Manhood,* 28.

47. Richard MacMaster, "Philadelphia Merchants, Backcountry Shopkeepers, and Town-Making Fever," *Pennsylvania History: A Journal of Mid-Atlantic Studies* 81.3 (2014): 342–363.

48. Robert A. Williams, Jr., *The American Indian in Western Legal Thought: The Discourses of Conquest* (New York: Oxford University Press, 1990), 256.

49. Maureen Konkle, "Indigenous Ownership and the Emergence of U.S. Liberal Imperialism," *The American Indian Quarterly* 32.3 (2008): 301.

50. Allan Greer, "Dispossession in a Commercial Idiom: From Indian Deeds to Land Cession Treaties," in *Contested Spaces of Early America,* ed. Juliana Barr and Edward Countryman (Philadelphia: University of Pennsylvania Press, 2014), 90–92.

51. Konkle, "Indigenous Ownership," 302.

52. Konkle, "Indigenous Ownership," 305.

53. "The Planter, No. II," *The American Magazine and Monthly Chronicle for the British Colonies* (November 1757): 83.

54. "The Planter," 83.

55. Henry Fielding, *Enquiry into the Causes of the Late Increase of Robbers* (London: A. Millar, 1751); I discuss this argument at greater length in Chapter 2.

56. Jodi Byrd, *The Transit of Empire: Indigenous Critiques of Colonialism* (Minneapolis: University of Minnesota Press, 2011), xxiv.

57. Patrick Wolfe, "Settler Colonialism and the Elimination of the Native," *Journal of Genocide Research* 8.4 (2006): 388. See, however, Tiffany Lethabo King's critique of the centrality of land in settler-colonial studies in "New World Grammars: The 'Unthought' Black Discourses of Conquest," *Theory & Event* 19.4 (2016): n.p.

58. A. L. Beier, *Masterless Men: The Vagrancy Problem in England, 1560–1640* (London: Methuen, 1985).

59. Ted McCormick, for instance, argues that seventeenth-century commentators on population and political economy frequently identified "depopulation" as the transformation of laborers into vagrants or criminals, and formulated this in their observations as a crisis of enclosure (McCormick, "Population: Modes of Seventeenth-Century Demographic Thought," in Philip J. Stern and Carl Wennerlind [eds.], *Mercantilism Reimagined: Political Economy in Early Modern Britain and its Empire* [Oxford: Oxford University Press, 2014], 26–27).

60. See Philip J. Deloria, *Playing Indian* (New Haven: Yale University Press, 1998).

61. Nelson, *National Manhood,* 88.

62. Philip Freneau, "The Rising Glory of America," in *The Poems of Philip Freneau: Written Chiefly During the Late War* (Philadelphia: Francis Bailey, 1786), l. 26. This was a substantially revised version of the original "Rising Glory of America," which Freneau wrote collaboratively with Hugh Henry Brackenridge and which was read at the 1771 commencement at Princeton University. All following citations are from the 1786 edition.

63. Ellison, *Cato's Tears,* 147.

64. Benjamin Smith Barton, *New Views on the Origin of the Tribes and Nations of America* (Philadelphia: John Bioren, 1797), v.

65. Jefferson, *Notes,* 59.

66. See, for instance, Richard Slotkin, *Regeneration through Violence: The Mythology of the American Frontier, 1600–1860* (Middletown: Wesleyan University Press, 1973), 369–393; Jared Gardner, "Alien Nation: Edgar Huntly's Savage Awakening," *American Literature* 66.3 (1994): 429–461; Janie Hinds, "Deb's Dogs: Animals, Indians, and Postcolonial Desire in Charles Brockden Brown's *Edgar Huntly*," *Early American Literature* 39.2 (2004): 323–354; and Chiles, *Transformable Race,* 107–147.

67. Brown, *Edgar Huntly,* 166.

68. Brown, *Edgar Huntly,* 171.

69. Brown, *Edgar Huntly,* 191–192.

70. Brown, *Edgar Huntly,* 191.

71. Dean Itsuji Saranillio, "Settler Colonialism," *Native Studies Keywords,* ed. Stephanie Nohelani Teves, Andrea Smith, and Michelle Raheja (Tucson: University of Arizona Press, 2015), 284.

72. Chad Luck, "Re-Walking the Purchase: *Edgar Huntly,* David Hume, and the Origins of Ownership," *Early American Literature* 44.2 (2009): 272.

73. Wolfe, "Settler Colonialism and the Elimination of the Native," 388.

74. Andrew Newman documents the many links between Old Deb and accounts of Hannah Freeman in "'Light might possibly be requisite': *Edgar Huntly,* Regional History, and Historicist Criticism," *Early American Studies* 8.2 (2010): 331–40.

75. Dawn Marsh, *A Lenape Among the Quakers: The Life of Hannah Freeman* (Lincoln: University of Nebraska Press, 2014), 1–16.

76. Newman, "'Light might possibly be requisite,' " 335.

77. Marsh, *A Lenape Among the Quakers,* 7–14.

78. Marsh, *A Lenape Among the Quakers,* 164.

79. Marsh, *A Lenape Among the Quakers,* 16.

80. Marsh, *A Lenape Among the Quakers,* 26–30.

81. Marsh, *A Lenape Among the Quakers,* 14.

82. For more on Moses Marshall's biography and the circumstances surrounding this settlement examination, see Marshall Becker, "Notes and Documents: Hannah Freeman: An Eighteenth-Century Lenape Living and Working Among Colonial Farmers," *The Pennsylvania Magazine of History and Biography* 114.2 (1990): 249–269, and Marsh, *A Lenape Among the Quakers,* 16–18.

83. Sydney J. Krause, "Penn's Elm and *Edgar Huntly*: Dark 'Instruction to the Heart,' " *American Literature* 66.3 (1994): 463–484; Chad Luck, *The Body of Property: Antebellum American Fiction and the Phenomenology of Possession* (New York: Fordham University Press, 2014), 35–82.

84. Marshall Becker, "Legends of Indian Hannah: Squaring the Written Accounts with the Oral Tradition," *Keystone Folklore* 4.2 (1992): 1–24.

85. Newman, "'Light might possibly be requisite,' " 335; [Charles Brockden Brown], "Edgar Huntly: A Fragment," *Monthly Magazine and American Review for the Year 1799,* vol. 1 (New York: T. & J. Swords, 1800), 21. For more on Brown's introduction to this fragment and its emphasis on the local history of the Walking Purchase, see also Luck, *The Body of Property,* 35–36.

86. Moses Marshall, "Examination of Indian Hannah alias Hannah Freeman," July 28, 1797, Chester County Historical Society, West Chester, PA; reprinted in Marsh, *A Lenape Among the Quakers,* 189–190. As Marshall Becker notes, this document seems to have been composed and put into narrative order by Moses Marshall based on earlier notes from his conversation with Freeman; the earlier version of the settlement examination narrative is reproduced in full in Becker, "Legends of Indian Hannah," 12–13.

87. Lisa Brooks, *The Common Pot: The Recovery of Native Space in the Northeast* (Minneapolis: University of Minnesota Press, 2008), 13.

88. Brooks, *The Common Pot,* 35; for more on the link between land purchases and land cession treaties, see also Greer, "Dispossession in a Commercial Idiom."

89. Marshall, "Examination," in Marsh, *A Lenape Among the Quakers,* 189.

90. Marshall, "Examination," in Marsh, *A Lenape Among the Quakers,* 189.

91. Leanne Betasamosake Simpson, *As We Have Always Done: Indigenous Freedom through Radical Resistance* (Minneapolis: University of Minnesota Press, 2017), 43.

92. Jean Soderlund, *Lenape Country: Delaware Valley Society Before William Penn* (Philadelphia: University of Pennsylvania Press, 2015), 7; Marsh, *A Lenape Among the Quakers,* 112–113.

93. Marshall, "Examination," in Marsh, *A Lenape Among the Quakers,* 189. For more on the place of the Paxton Boys massacre in the political history of Pennsylvania, see Kevin Kenny, *Peaceable Kingdom Lost: The Paxton Boys and the Destruction of William Penn's Holy Experiment* (New York: Oxford University Press, 2009).

94. Richard Barnard et al., "Kindness Extended," March 1798, Chester County Historical Society; reprinted in Becker, "Legends of Indian Hannah," 13–14.

95. Marsh, *A Lenape Among the Quakers,* 163–164.

96. See, for instance, Chiles, *Transformable Race,* 128–147, and Jason Richards, *Imitation Nation: Red, White, and Blackface in Early and Antebellum US Literature* (Charlottesville: University of Virginia Press, 2017), 38–44.

97. Jacksonville Ordinance Code sec. 25–57 (1965), also quoted in *Papachristou v. City of Jacksonville,* 405 U.S. 156 (1972), 171.

98. *Papachristou,* 159.

99. Goluboff, *Vagrant Nation,* 112–146.

100. Goluboff, *Vagrant Nation,* 298–333.

101. *Papachristou,* 156.

102. *Papachristou,* 164.

103. On factors contributing to the mid-twentieth-century increase in challenges to vagrancy law, see Robin Yeamans, "Constitutional Attacks on Vagrancy Laws," *Stanford Law Review* 20 (1968): 782–793.

104. *United States v. Kilgen,* 431 F.2d 627, 628 (5th Cir. 1970). Also quoted in Risa Goluboff, "Dispatch from the Supreme Court Archives: Vagrancy, Abortion, and What the Links Between Them Reveal About the History of Fundamental Rights," *Stanford Law Review* 62.5 (2010): 1371.

105. Arthur H. Sherry, "Vagrants, Rogues, and Vagabonds—Old Concepts in Need of Revision," *California Law Review* 48.4 (1960): 557; *Papachristou,* 161.

106. William O. Douglas, "Vagrancy and Arrest on Suspicion," *Yale Law Journal* 70.1 (1960): 2–3.

107. Douglas, "Vagrancy," 7.

108. F. O. Matthiessen, *American Renaissance: Art and Expression in the Age of Emerson and Whitman* (New York: Oxford University Press, 1941), ix.

109. Leslie Fiedler, *Love and Death in the American Novel* (New York: Criterion Books, 1960), 26.

110. On the fungibility of "the vagrant" in relation to police power, see Bryan Wagner, *Disturbing the Peace: Black Culture and the Police Power After Slavery* (Cambridge: Harvard University Press, 2009), 40.

111. Henry David Thoreau, *Excursions,* 13th ed. (Boston: Houghton, Mifflin, 1868), 162; also quoted in *Papachristou,* 164–165.

112. Thoreau, *Excursions,* 177.

113. *Papachristou,* 164.

114. Thoreau, *Excursions,* 176.

115. Thoreau, *Excursions,* 178.

116. Thoreau, *Excursions,* 212. As Neill Matheson documents, Thoreau's first delivery of this essay as a lecture in 1851 began with an explicit protest against the recent enforcement of the Fugitive Slave Law in Boston (Matheson, "Thoreau's Gramática Parda: Conjugating Race and Nature," *Arizona Quarterly* 57.4 [2001]: 3).

117. Peter Coviello, *Intimacy in America: Dreams of Affiliation in Antebellum Literature* (Minneapolis: University of Minnesota Press, 2005), 2.

118. Coviello, *Intimacy in America,* 4–5.

119. Smith, *Essay,* 20.

120. Smith, *Essay,* 37.

121. Smith, *Essay,* 38, 39.

122. Smith, *Essay,* 72.

123. Ezra Tawil, *The Making of Racial Sentiment: Slavery and the Birth of the Frontier Romance* (Cambridge: Cambridge University Press, 2008); and Carolyn Sorisio, *Fleshing Out America:*

*Race, Gender, and the Politics of the Body in American Literature, 1833–1879* (Athens: University of Georgia Press, 2002), 1–46.

124. For an overview of climate theory in early America, see Chiles, *Transformable Race,* 1–30. See also Roxann Wheeler, *The Complexion of Race: Categories of Difference in Eighteenth-Century British Culture* (Philadelphia: University of Pennsylvania Press, 2000) on the circulation of climate theories of race in the eighteenth-century British Atlantic world.

125. Chiles, *Transformable Race,* 2; Tawil, *Racial Sentiment,* 11; on race, interiority, and civic belonging in the nineteenth century, see also Coviello, *Intimacy in America,* 1–49, and Christopher Castiglia, "Abolition's Racial Interiors and the Making of White Civic Depth," *American Literary History* 14.1 (2002): 32–59.

126. Tawil, *Racial Sentiment,* 49.

127. Lisa Marie Cacho, *Social Death: Racialized Rightlessness and the Criminalization of the Unprotected* (New York: NYU Press, 2012), 1. The literature on race in the ongoing legacy of vagrancy law, from "stop-and-frisk" to antigang injunctions and the "broken-windows" theory of policing, is vast; see in particular Dorothy E. Roberts, "Foreward: Race, Vagueness, and the Social Meaning of Order-Maintenance Policing," *The Journal of Criminal Law and Criminology* 89.3 (1999): 775–836; Gary Stewart, "Black Codes and Broken Windows: The Legacy of Racial Hegemony in Anti-Gang Civil Injunctions," *The Yale Law Journal* 107.7 (1998): 2249–2279; Reed Collins, "Strolling While Poor: How Broken-Windows Policing Created a New Crime in Baltimore," *Georgetown Journal on Poverty Law and Policy* 14.3 (2007): 419–439; Bernard Harcourt, *Illusion of Order: The False Promise of Broken Windows Policing* (Cambridge: Harvard University Press, 2005); and Cacho, *Social Death,* 40–46.

128. Cheryl Harris, "Whiteness as Property," *Harvard Law Review* 106.8 (1993): 1720.

## Chapter 5. Surveillance and Black Life in Equiano's Atlantic

1. Olaudah Equiano, *The Interesting Narrative of the Life of Olaudah Equiano* [1789], ed. Vincent Carretta (New York: Penguin Classics, 2003), 158. Hereafter cited parenthetically.

2. See, for instance, Saidiya Hartman on the legal recognition of the slave "as a reasoning subject who possessed intent and rationality solely in the context of criminal liability" (*Scenes of Subjection: Terror, Slavery, and Self-Making in Nineteenth-Century America* [Oxford: Oxford University Press, 1997], 82).

3. Sally Hadden, *Slave Patrols: Law and Violence in Virginia and the Carolinas* (Cambridge: Harvard University Press, 2001), 7–10.

4. F. M. Dodsworth, "The Idea of Police in Eighteenth-Century England: Discipline, Reformation, Superintendence, c. 1780–1800," *Journal of the History of Ideas* 69.4 (2008): 583–604; see also William Blackstone's elaboration on police offenses in *Commentaries on the Laws of England* [1765–1769], 4 vols. (Chicago: University of Chicago Press, 1979), 4:162.

5. Hadden, *Slave Patrols,* 58–59.

6. Hadden, *Slave Patrols,* 70.

7. Christopher Tomlins, "Transplants and Timing: Passages in the Creation of an Anglo-American Law of Slavery," *Theoretical Inquiries in Law* 10 (2009): 389–421.

8. See, for instance, Moten's discussion of Equiano in *Stolen Life* (Durham: Duke University Press, 2018), 17–95.

9. Edlie Wong, *Neither Fugitive nor Free: Atlantic Slavery, Freedom Suits, and the Legal Culture of Travel* (New York: NYU Press, 2009), 20.

10. The classic account of this emergence of the "ancient constitution" as historical narrative and political argument is J. G. A. Pocock, *The Ancient Constitution and the Feudal Law: A Study of English Historical Thought in the Seventeenth Century* [1957] (Cambridge: Cambridge University Press, 1987).

11. Simone Browne: *Dark Matters: On the Surveillance of Blackness* (Durham: Duke University Press, 2015), 21.

12. See, for instance, Charlotte Sussman, *Consuming Anxieties: Consumer Protest, Gender & British Slavery 1713–1833* (Stanford: Stanford University Press, 2000), on the rhetoric of contamination mobilized by the antislavery claim that the consumption of sugar amounted to cannibalistic consumption of the blood of the enslaved. More broadly, Srividhya Swaminathan's *Debating the Slave Trade: Rhetoric of British National Identity, 1759–1815* (Farnham, Surrey: Ashgate, 2009) reveals the embeddedness of the entire slavery debate in questions about British national identity and its stakes for the future viability of the British Empire.

13. Michelle Alexander, *The New Jim Crow: Mass Incarceration in the Age of Colorblindness* (New York: The New Press, 2010), 31. On vagrancy law and the afterlife of slavery in the United States, see also Amy Dru Stanley, *From Bondage to Contract: Wage Labor, Marriage, and the Market in the Age of Slave Emancipation* (Cambridge: Cambridge University Press, 1998), 98–137, and Saidiya Hartman, *Scenes of Subjection: Terror, Slavery, and Self-Making in Nineteenth-Century America* (Oxford: Oxford University Press, 1997), 125–132.

14. Hadden, *Slave Patrols,* 200–204.

15. Hartman, *Scenes of Subjection,* 125; Demetrius Eudell, *The Political Languages of Emancipation in the British Caribbean and the U.S. South* (Chapel Hill: University of North Carolina Press, 2002), 55–56.

16. Michal J. Rozbicki, "To Save Them from Themselves: Proposals to Enslave the English Poor, 1698–1755," *Slavery & Abolition* 22.2 (2001): 29–50.

17. Joanna Innes, "Prisons for the Poor: English Bridewells, 1555–1800," in Francis Snyder and Douglas Hay (eds.), *Labour, Law and Crime: An Historical Perspective* (London: Tavistock Publications, 1987), 42. See also J. M. Beattie, *Crime and the Courts in England 1660–1800* (Princeton: Princeton University Press, 1986),18.

18. Bradley J. Nicholson, "Legal Borrowing and the Origins of Slave Law in the British Colonies," *American Journal of Legal History* 38.1 (1994): 38.

19. Susan Dwyer Amussen, *Caribbean Exchanges: Slavery and the Transformation of English Society, 1640–1700* (Chapel Hill: University of North Carolina Press, 2007), 129; Richard S. Dunn, *Sugar and Slaves: The Rise of the Planter Class in the English West Indies, 1624–1713*

(Chapel Hill: University of North Carolina Press, 1972), 239; Tomlins, "Transplants and Timing," 397.

20. Tomlins, "Transplants and Timing," 397.

21. Amussen, *Caribbean Exchanges,* 132.

22. Amussen, *Caribbean Exchanges,* 132.

23. Dunn, *Sugar and Slaves,* 240; Barbados "Act for the Better Ordering and Governing of Negroes," Sept. 27, 1661, Barbados MSS Laws, 1645–1682 CO 30/2/16/26, UK National Archives; quoted in Dunn, *Sugar and Slaves,* 239.

24. Cedric Robinson, *Black Marxism: The Making of the Black Radical Tradition* (Chapel Hill: University of North Carolina Press, 2000), 3–4.

25. Amussen, *Caribbean Exchanges,* 111.

26. Diana Paton, *No Bond but the Law: Punishment, Race, and Gender in Jamaican State Formation, 1780–1870* (Durham: Duke University Press, 2004), 19–22.

27. Paton, *No Bond but the Law,* 27.

28. Jen Manion, *Liberty's Prisoners: Carceral Culture in Early America* (Philadelphia: University of Pennsylvania Press, 2015), 24–25; Kristin O'Brassill-Kulfan, "Vagabonds and Paupers: Race and Illicit Mobility in the Early Republic," *Pennsylvania History: A Journal of Mid-Atlantic Studies* 83.4 (2016): 444–469.

29. O'Brassill-Kulfan, "Vagabonds and Paupers."

30. William Bartram, *Travels through North & South Carolina, Georgia, East & West Florida, the Cherokee Country, the Extensive Territories of the Muscogulges, or Creek Confederacy, and the Country of the Chactaws* [1791], Documenting the American South (Chapel Hill: University of North Carolina Library, 2001), 471–472. https://docsouth.unc.edu/nc/bartram/bartram.html.

31. Hadden, *Slave Patrols,* 105–106.

32. Hadden, *Slave Patrols,* 71–102.

33. On the centrality of "free labor" and the ideal of the free market in abolitionism, see Thomas Holt, *The Problem of Freedom: Race, Labor, and Politics in Jamaica and Britain, 1832–1938* (Baltimore: Johns Hopkins University Press, 1992), 8–32.

34. Edward Long, *The History of Jamaica, or, General Survey of the Antient and Modern State of that Island,* 3 vols. (London: for T. Lowndes, 1774), 2:498–499.

35. Long, *History,* 2:493–494.

36. Long, *History,* 2:390.

37. Long specifically equates the slave trade with the transportation of European convicts when he argues that "the African states have just as good right as any European power, to banish their criminals to other parts of the world that will receive them" (2:390).

38. Long, *History,* 2:323.

39. Long, *History,* 2:504.

40. Claudius Fergus, "'Dread of Insurrection': Abolitionism, Security, and Labor in Britain's West Indian Colonies," *William and Mary Quarterly* 66.4 (2009): 757–780.

41. Abolition Act 1833 (3 & 4 Will. IV c. 73) in *A Collection of the Public General Statutes Passed in the Third and Fourth Year of the Reign of His Majesty William the Fourth* (London:

George Eyre and Andrew Spottiswoode, 1833), 729. For the many biographical links between the antislavery movement and poor-law reform, see Holt, *The Problem of Freedom.*

42. Abolition Act 1833, *Public General Statutes,* 735.

43. Srinivas Aravamudan, *Tropicopolitans: Colonialism and Agency, 1688–1804* (Durham: Duke University Press, 1999), 237.

44. David Kazanjian, *The Colonizing Trick: National Culture and Imperial Citizenship in Early America* (Minneapolis: University of Minnesota Press, 2003), 49.

45. Gretchen Holbrook Gerzina, "Mobility in Chains: Freedom of Movement in the Early Black Atlantic," *South Atlantic Quarterly* 100.1 (2001): 42.

46. Hartman, *Scenes of Subjection,* 127, 151.

47. Sarah Jane Cervenak, *Wandering: Philosophical Performances of Racial and Sexual Freedom* (Durham: Duke University Press, 2014), 4–6.

48. Cervenak, *Wandering,* 32.

49. Cervenak, *Wandering,* 10.

50. Cervenak, *Wandering,* 10; Katherine McKittrick, "On Plantations, Prisons, and a Black Sense of Place," *Social & Cultural Geography* 12.8 (2011): 947–963.

51. Cathy Davidson, "Olaudah Equiano, Written by Himself," *NOVEL: A Forum on Fiction* 40.1–2 (2006–2007): 20.

52. John Bugg, "Equiano's Trifles," *ELH* 80.4 (2013): 1054, 1048.

53. Bugg, "Equiano's Trifles," 1058.

54. See, for instance, Mary Sarah Bilder, *The Transatlantic Constitution: Colonial Legal Culture and the Empire* (Cambridge: Harvard University Press, 2008) for legal pluralism as constitutive of colonial law more broadly, and Wong, *Neither Fugitive nor Free,* 1–36, for the specific geographical complexity of laws governing slavery throughout the British Atlantic world.

55. Edward Jenks, "The Story of the Habeas Corpus," in *Select Essays in Anglo-American Legal History,* ed. Association of American Law Schools (Boston: Little, Brown, 1908), 532.

56. Paul Halliday, *Habeas Corpus: From England to Empire* (Cambridge: Harvard University Press, 2010); see also Nasser Hussain, *The Jurisprudence of Emergency: Colonialism and the Rule of Law* (Ann Arbor: University of Michigan Press, 2003), 69–72.

57. William Blackstone, *Commentaries on the Laws of England* [1765–1769], 4 vols. (Chicago: University of Chicago Press, 1979), 1:131.

58. Hussain, *The Jurisprudence of Emergency,* 70.

59. Hussain, *The Jurisprudence of Emergency,* 75–77; For a broad theorization of the racialized construction of legal subjects over and against constitutive carceral exclusions from legal personhood, see Colin [Joan] Dayan, "Legal Slaves and Civil Bodies," *Nepantla: Views From the South* 2.1 (2001): 3–39.

60. Hussain, *The Jurisprudence of Emergency,* 75–78.

61. Wong, *Neither Fugitive nor Free,* 20.

62. Granville Sharp, *A Representation of the Injustice and Dangerous Tendency of Tolerating Slavery in England* (London: for Benjamin White and Robert Horsfield, 1769), 26. The discussion of the Habeas Corpus Act begins on p. 23.

63. Sharp, *Representation,* 15.

64. Alexander Weheliye, *Habeas Viscus: Racializing Assemblages, Biopolitics, and Black Feminist Theories of the Human* (Durham: Duke University Press, 2014), 77–78.

65. *Somerset v. Stewart* (1772), 98 ER 499; for reception of the case, see Wong, *Neither Fugitive nor Free,* 20–36.

66. Wong, *Neither Fugitive nor Free,* 22.

67. Daniel Hulsebosch, "Nothing but Liberty: *Somerset's Case* and the British Empire," *Law and History Review* 24.3 (2006): 657.

68. Dana Rabin, "'In a Country of Liberty?': Slavery, Villeinage, and the Making of Whiteness in the Somerset Case (1772)," *History Workshop Journal* 72 (2011): 5.

69. Rabin, "'In a Country of Liberty?,' " 7.

70. Rabin, "'In a Country of Liberty?,' "7.

71. Wong, *Neither Fugitive nor Free,* 36.

72. [Edward Long], *Candid Reflections Upon the Judgment Lately Awarded by the Court of King's Bench* (London: for T. Lowndes, 1772), 13.

73. Bryan Wagner, *Disturbing the Peace: Black Culture and the Police Power After Slavery* (Cambridge: Harvard University Press, 2009), 4.

74. Wagner, *Disturbing the Peace,* 6–7.

75. Jeannine DeLombard, *In the Shadow of the Gallows: Race, Crime, and American Civic Identity* (Philadelphia: University of Pennsylvania Press, 2012), 1–11.

76. Nikhil Pal Singh, "The Whiteness of Police," *American Quarterly* 66.4 (2014): 1096.

77. As Vincent Carretta points out in his notes to his edition of the *Interesting Narrative,* this account of the event implies that Kirkpatrick lied to the judge when he said that he did not have Annis (288).

78. Aravamudan, *Tropicopolitans,* 270, 281.

79. Blackstone, *Commentaries,* 1:38.

80. Saidiya Hartman, "Venus in Two Acts," *small axe* 12.2 (2008): 1–14; Marisa Fuentes, *Dispossessed Lives: Enslaved Women, Violence, and the Archive* (Philadelphia: University of Pennsylvania Press, 2016); Christina Sharpe, *In the Wake: On Blackness and Being* (Durham: Duke University Press, 2016); Katherine McKittrick, "Mathematics Black Life," *The Black Scholar* 44.2 (2014): 16–28.

81. Browne, *Dark Matters,* 6.

82. Browne, *Dark Matters,* 21.

83. See Browne, *Dark Matters,* 67, for a discussion of lighting as a technology of racialized surveillance.

84. Hadden, *Slave Patrols,* 114.

85. Cervenak, *Wandering,* 10.

86. Sharpe, *In the Wake,* 17.

87. McKittrick, "Mathematics Black Life," 22.

88. Bugg, "Equiano's Trifles," 1058.

89. Such theorizations of personhood, the human, and the racial foreclosures that constitute these forms are extensively theorized in both classic and contemporary work in black studies, particularly building on the tradition of Sylvia Wynter; see, for instance, Wynter, "Unsettling the Coloniality of Being/Power/Truth/Freedom: Towards the Human, After Man, Its Overrepresentation—An Argument," *CR: The New Centennial Review* 3.3 (2003): 257–337; Weheliye, *Habeas Viscus;* Denise Ferreira da Silva, *Toward a Global Idea of Race* (Minneapolis: University of Minnesota Press, 2007).

## Coda

1. For more on this tendency and its analytical limits, see Micol Seigel, *Violence Work: State Power and the Limits of Police* (Durham: Duke University Press, 2018), 6.

2. Stephen Best and Sharon Marcus, "Surface Reading: An Introduction," *Representations* 108.1 (2009): 1–21; Rita Felski, "Context Stinks!," *New Literary History* 42.1 (2011): 573–591; Heather Love, "Close but Not Deep: Literary Ethics and the Descriptive Turn," *New Literary History* 41.2 (2010): 371–391.

3. Felski, "Context Stinks!," 574.

4. Felski, "Context Stinks!," 589.

5. V21 Collective, "Manifesto of the V21 Collective" (2015), http://v21collective.org/manifesto-of-the-v21-collective-ten-theses/.

6. V21 Collective, "Manifesto."

7. Patricia J. Williams, *The Alchemy of Race and Rights* (Cambridge: Harvard University Press, 1991), 3–51.

8. See, for instance, Nathan K. Hensley, "Curatorial Reading and Endless War," *Victorian Studies* 56.1 (2014): 59–83; Emily Hodgson Anderson, "Why We Do (or Don't) Argue About the Way We Read," *The Eighteenth Century: Theory and Interpretation* 54.1 (2013): 125–128; and Crystal Bartolovich, "Humanities of Scale: Marxism, Surface Reading—and Milton," *PMLA* 127.1 (2012): 115–121.

9. See, for instance, Carla Freccero, *Queer/Early/Modern* (Durham: Duke University Press, 2005); Valerie Traub, "The New Unhistoricism in Queer Studies," *PMLA* 128.1 (2013): 21–39; Ari Friedlander, "Introduction: Desiring History and Historicizing Desire," *Journal for Early Modern Cultural Studies* 16.2 (2016): 1–20.

10. Elizabeth Freeman, *Time Binds: Queer Temporalities, Queer Histories* (Durham: Duke University Press, 2010), 62.

11. Freeman, *Time Binds,* 63.

12. *Graham v. Connor,* 490 U.S. 386 (1989), 386.

13. *Graham v. Connor,* 490 U.S. 386 (1989), 386–387.

14. George L. Kelling and James Q. Wilson, "Broken Windows: The Police and Neighborhood Safety," *The Atlantic* (March 1982): 29–38.

15. See, for instance, Bernard Harcourt, *Illusion of Order: The False Promise of Broken-Windows Policing* (Cambridge: Harvard University Press, 2001), 25–47; Dorothy E. Roberts, "Forward: Race, Vagueness, and the Social Meaning of Order-Maintenance Policing," *Journal of Criminal Law and Criminology* 89.3 (1999): 775–836; Reed Collins, "Strolling While Poor: How Broken-Windows Policing Created a New Crime in Baltimore," *Georgetown Journal on Poverty Law & Policy* 14.3 (2007): 419–439; Jerry Fagan and Garth Davies, "Street Stops and Broken Windows: *Terry*, Race, and Disorder in New York City," *Fordham Urban Law Journal* 28 (2000–2001): 457–504; Gary Stewart, "Black Codes and Broken Windows: The Legacy of Racial Hegemony in Anti-Gang Civil Injunctions," *The Yale Law Journal* 107.7 (1998): 2249–2279.

16. Dorothy Roberts and Bernard Harcourt both critique this presumption (that "law-abiding" and "criminal" people are such essentially different and knowably distinct populations that they will react to disorder in entirely opposite ways) as a foundational logical fallacy of the essay (Roberts, "Forward," 803; Harcourt, *Illusion of Order*, 132–133).

17. Kelling and Wilson, "Broken Windows," 30.

18. Kelling and Wilson, "Broken Windows," 32.

19. Bernard Harcourt, *The Illusion of Free Markets: Punishment and the Myth of Natural Order* (Cambridge: Harvard University Press, 2012), 207.

20. Kelling and Wilson, "Broken Windows," 35; for histories of race and criminality, see Khalil Gibran Muhammad, *The Condemnation of Blackness: Race, Crime, and the Making of Modern Urban America* (Cambridge: Harvard University Press, 2011); Elizabeth Hinton, *From the War on Poverty to the War on Crime: The Making of Mass Incarceration in America* (Cambridge: Harvard University Press, 2017); Lisa Marie Cacho, *Social Death: Racialized Rightlessness and the Criminalization of the Unprotected* (New York: NYU Press, 2012).

21. Craig Willse, *The Value of Homelessness: Managing Surplus Life in the United States* (Minneapolis: University of Minnesota Press, 2015), 90.

22. See, for instance, Kim Phillips-Fein, *Fear City: New York's Fiscal Crisis and the Rise of Austerity Politics* (New York: Metropolitan Books, 2017); Thomas Sugrue, *The Origins of the Urban Crisis: Race and Inequality in Postwar Detroit*, rev. ed. (Princeton: Princeton University Press, 2014); Ruth Wilson Gilmore, *Golden Gulag: Prisons, Surplus, Crisis, and Opposition in Globalizing California* (Berkeley: University of California Press, 2007).

23. Heather Ann Thompson, "Why Mass Incarceration Matters: Rethinking Crisis, Decline, and Transformation in Postwar American History," *The Journal of American History* 97.3 (2010): 703–734. See also Jeremy Kaplan-Lyman, "A Punitive Bind: Policing, Poverty, and Neoliberalism in New York City," *Yale Human Rights and Development Law Journal* 15 (2012): 177–222.

24. Anderson, "Why We Do (or Don't) Argue About the Way We Read," 127.

25. See, for instance, Angela Davis, *Are Prisons Obsolete?* (New York: Penguin, 2003); Dan Berger, *Captive Nation: Black Prison Organizing in the Civil Rights Era* (Chapel Hill: University of North Carolina Press, 2014); Jordan T. Camp and Christina Heatherton (eds.), *Policing the Planet: Why the Policing Crisis Led to Black Lives Matter* (New York: Verso, 2016); and

Keeanga-Yamahtta Taylor, *From #BlackLivesMatter to Black Liberation* (Chicago: Haymarket Books, 2016).

26. Carrie Hyde, "Novelistic Evidence: The Denmark Vesey Conspiracy and Possibilistic History," *American Literary History* 27.1 (2015): 31.

27. Kelling and Wilson, "Broken Windows," 33.

28. Kelling and Wilson, "Broken Windows," 34, 30.

29. Kelling and Wilson, "Broken Windows," 35.

30. Risa Goluboff, *Vagrant Nation: Police Power, Constitutional Change, and the Making of the 1960s* (New York: Oxford University Press, 2016), 59–60, 186–187.

31. Hinton, *War on Poverty;* Thompson, "Why Mass Incarceration Matters."

32. This is one of the central theoretical claims of Bryan Wagner's analysis of the police power in *Disturbing the Peace;* it is also empirically observed, on a smaller scale, in the legal proceedings that were the direct result of Giuliani's embrace of "broken-windows" policing in New York City; as Issa Kohler-Haussman argues, misdemeanor arrests in New York City in the early 2000s reveal a model of "managerial justice" that is concerned less with adjudicating criminal responsibility and more with "managing potentially risky populations with record-keeping and sorting" (Issa Kohler-Haussman, "Managerial Justice and Mass Misdemeanors," *Stanford Law Review* 66.3 [2014]: 617).

33. Ravit Reichman, "Law's Affective Thickets," in Elizabeth Anker and Bernadette Meyler (eds.), *New Directions in Law and Literature* (New York: Oxford University Press, 2017), 117–118.

34. Bartolovich, "Humanities of Scale," 116.

35. Bartolovich, "Humanities of Scale," 116.

36. Bartolovich, "Humanities of Scale," 116.

37. Saidiya Hartman, "The Anarchy of Colored Girls Assembled in a Riotous Manner," *The South Atlantic Quarterly* 117.3 (2018): 470.

38. Hartman, "Anarchy," 475.

39. Carolyn Dinshaw, *Getting Medieval: Sexualities and Communities, Pre- and Postmodern* (Durham: Duke University Press, 1999), 1.

40. Philadelphia Prison System, Vagrancy Dockets (Record Group 38.44), Philadelphia City Archives.

41. See also Julie Stone Peters, "Law, Literature, and the Vanishing Real: On the Future of an Interdisciplinary Illusion," *PMLA* 120.2 (2005): 442–453, for a broader methodological critique of tendencies to posit literature as the ethical redemption of the law.

42. Robert Cover, "Violence and the Word," *Yale Law Journal* 95 (1986): 1601–1629.

43. Hyde, "Novelistic Evidence," 31.

# *INDEX*

Page numbers in *italics* indicate illustrations.